THE PLAY IN THE SYSTEM

THE PLAY IN THE SYSTEM

THE ART OF PARASITICAL RESISTANCE

ANNA WATKINS FISHER

DUKE UNIVERSITY PRESS Durham and London 2020

Designed by Aimee C. Harrison
Typeset in Minion Pro and Vectora by Copperline Book Services

Library of Congress Cataloging-in-Publication Data
Names: Fisher, Anna Watkins, author.
Title: The play in the system : the art of parasitical resistance / Anna Watkins Fisher.
Description: Durham : Duke University Press, 2020. | Includes bibliographical references and index.
Identifiers: LCCN 2019054723 (print) | LCCN 2019054724 (ebook)
ISBN 9781478008842 (hardcover)
ISBN 9781478009702 (paperback)
ISBN 9781478012320 (ebook)
Subjects: LCSH: Arts—Political aspects—History—21st century. | Arts and society—History—21st century. | Artists—Political activity. | Feminism and the arts. | Feminism in art. | Artists and community. | Politics and culture. | Arts, Modern—21st century.
Classification: LCC NX180.P64 F57 2020 (print) |
LCC NX180.P64 (ebook) | DDC 700.1/03—dc23
LC record available at https://lccn.loc.gov/2019054723
LC ebook record available at https://lccn.loc.gov/2019054724

ISBN 9781478091660 (ebook/other)

Duke University Press gratefully acknowledges the support of the Office for Research (UMOR) and the College of Literature, Science and the Arts (LSA) at the University of Michigan, which provided funds toward the publication of this book.

This book is freely available in an open access edition thanks to TOME (Toward an Open Monograph Ecosystem)—a collaboration of the Association of American Universities, the Association of University Presses, and the Association of Research Libraries. Learn more at the TOME website, available at: openmonographs.org.

For Antoine

CONTENTS

ILLUSTRATIONS

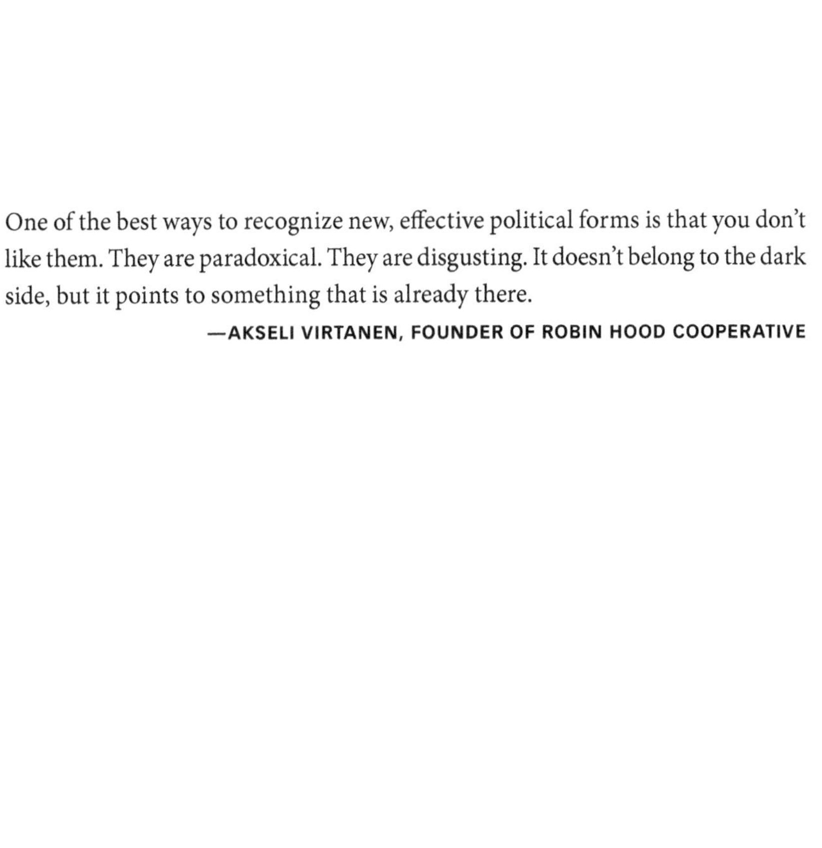

One of the best ways to recognize new, effective political forms is that you don't like them. They are paradoxical. They are disgusting. It doesn't belong to the dark side, but it points to something that is already there.

—**AKSELI VIRTANEN, FOUNDER OF ROBIN HOOD COOPERATIVE**

INTRODUCTION TOWARD A THEORY OF PARASITICAL RESISTANCE

The tactics of appropriation have been co-opted. Illegal action has become advertisement. Protest has become cliché. Revolt has become passé. . . . Having accepted these failures to some degree, we can now attempt to define a parasitic tactical response. We need to invent a practice that allows invisible subversion. We need to feed and grow inside existing communication systems while contributing nothing to their survival; we need to become parasites.—**NATHAN M. MARTIN FOR THE CARBON DEFENSE LEAGUE, "PARASITIC MEDIA" (2002)**

In 2006 the tactical media collective Ubermorgen gained access to Amazon's digital library, capturing more than three thousand copyright-protected books sold on the site by manipulating its "Search Inside the Book" feature.[1] Unleashing a series of software applications known as "bots," Ubermorgen sent five thousand to ten thousand requests per book and reassembled them into PDFs that were then distributed for free via peer-to-peer (p2p) networks. The bots tricked Amazon's preview mechanism (designed to limit user previews in accordance with copyright protections) into furnishing complete volumes of the books. Rather than hacking Amazon's digital library, Ubermorgen acquired the files through what they described as a mode of "frontdoor access."[2] The group merely accepted Amazon's invitation to preview the books, albeit at a much higher rate than Amazon intended. The project, *Amazon Noir: The Big Book Crime* (figures I.1 and I.2), is one installment of what the self-described "big media hackers," in collaboration with Alessandro Ludovico and Paolo Cirio, call their *Hacking Monopolism Trilogy*. The trilogy is a series of "conceptual hacks" with which they claim

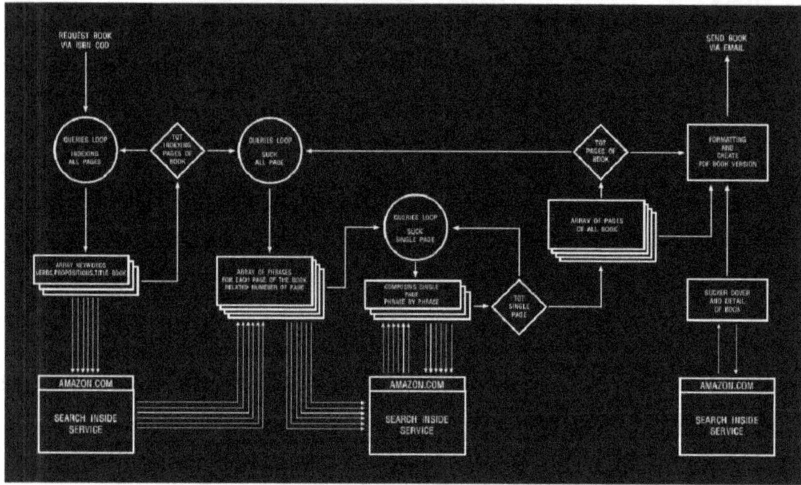

FIGURES I.1 AND I.2 Ubermorgen (with Alessandro Ludovico and Paolo Cirio), *Amazon Noir* logo and diagram, 2006. Source: Ubermorgen.

to have exploited "unexpected holes in [the] well-oiled marketing and economic system" of "three of the biggest online corporations (Amazon, Facebook, and Google)."[3] After Amazon threatened Ubermorgen with legal action, the case was settled out of court with Amazon buying the *Amazon Noir* software for an undisclosed sum on the condition that Ubermorgen sign a nondisclosure agreement, effectively containing the disruption and restoring the former system. What had been previously a fairly straightforwardly subversive artwork thus became financially implicated in Amazon's blackboxing practices.

But even by giving in, Ubermorgen tells us something in their shift to complicity. Crucially, Ubermorgen had not only located a loophole in Amazon's marketing strategy; by obliging Amazon to settle in secrecy to ensure that the software stayed out of the public domain, the tactical media group exposed the corporation's investment in *an appearance of openness*. In the mid-2000s Amazon had begun pushing publishers to let them digitize their lists, a move that eventually helped the company secure a monopoly on the industry by making publishers dependent on Amazon for sales. *Amazon Noir*, and its co-option by Amazon, points to the hypocrisy by which big corporations like Amazon benefit from restricting the free circulation of information (strongarming publishers into exclusive agreements, dodging government regulation, criminalizing content sharing beyond their own site, forcing Ubermorgen into a nondisclosure agreement) while capitalizing on the ideal of shared access (its "Search Inside the Book" feature).[4] "Search Inside the Book" is a marketing tool that enables users to search through books while preventing access to the whole book. With *Amazon Noir*, as Nicholas Thoburn observes, Ubermorgen discloses "the inequity of the privatization of the nonscarce resource digital text, while taking advantage of the means by which the technological affordances of digital text are mobilized to excite consumer desire."[5] But not only does Amazon employ digital technology to privatize access; Amazon does not redistribute the profits it makes to the writers and contributors whose work it digitizes and samples via the tool.[6] The artwork—and resulting settlement—thus highlights the false pretenses by which Amazon profits from imposing a strong legal and moral distinction between the "good openness" represented by the company's free preview and the "bad openness" represented by Ubermorgen's pirated open access.[7] By insisting on its role as the good guy, Amazon disavows responsibility for how its dominant market position—the result of predatory business practices such as aggressive customer data mining and deep discounts intended to drive out small businesses and secure the cooperation of publishers—intimidates potential challengers. This shields the company from having to face up to its own compromised status: its potential liability for copyright infringement and antitrust violations.[8] Amazon's ability to claim the uncontested legal and moral high ground, to position itself as a champion of openness, is a function of its status as a monopoly—a position ironically secured by monopolizing and privatizing openness. As part of the settlement, Ubermorgen agreed not to discuss *Amazon Noir* publicly, and all media coverage of the artwork ceased.

The critical issue at hand is not whether Ubermorgen's actions are right in the conventional legal or moral sense but why the same scrutiny is so rarely leveled at major players like Amazon. While a culture of nondisclosure agreements portends an era of posttransparency, wherein corporate and state interests feel little compunction to hide their nontransparent governance, *Amazon Noir* shows that powerful corporations like Amazon are nevertheless still invested in concealing their opacity and structural nonaccountability.[9] They selectively engage the law so as to keep their coercive practices in a proverbial black box—in this case, by avoiding going to court, black-boxing Ubermorgen's algorithm, and prohibiting any further press about the artwork.[10] It is not that they no longer hide their protocols, but they no longer hide that they are hiding them. The rise of big tech platforms like Amazon has been closely linked to the fulfillment of a postwelfare logic of capitalism that many have called neoliberalism. Digital technology both accelerates and emblematizes this reorganization of contemporary life and its turn toward privatization and deregulation, as a handful of leviathan-like corporations increasingly monopolize all aspects of industry, leaving democratic principles and institutions crippled in their wake.[11] Corporate monopolies' nontransparency and nonreciprocity (e.g., obstructionist strategies such as mandatory closed-door arbitration and settlements out of court) have become an open secret, even an expectation. As a result Amazon's commodification of a highly calculated form of open access cannot be remedied by an act of simple unmasking. Precisely because the hypocrisy of the system is already exposed, undermining it must necessarily take other forms.[12]

Ubermorgen's intervention effectively held Amazon hostage to the company's own purported openness (and legality) even as it performed a fundamental concession to the nontransparency of the system by agreeing to settle out of court. Put simply, the collective both called Amazon's bluff and folded at the same time. In the act of settling, Ubermorgen managed to make Amazon the patron of the anticorporate artwork. But by making Amazon the patron of their work, the group also sold out. What are we to make of the dual effect of this action? Does *Amazon Noir* ultimately reject or reinforce Amazon's monopolization of information? Is the artwork *resistant* or is it *complicit*? And more to the point, are these designations mutually exclusive? Does Ubermorgen's settling with Amazon nullify the critical potential of the work?

Like *Amazon Noir*, the performance-based artworks explored in this book manifest a logic of aesthetic resistance whose meaning and effects are far more indeterminate, far harder to pin down, than those which animated much of avant-garde and oppositional art in the late twentieth century. These artworks take seriously the ambiguity that is already implied by the word *resistance*, as an act that necessarily presupposes the structural conditions against which it struggles, precisely because it cannot destroy or escape them outright. By turns irreverent, irksome, and disturbingly amoral, the artworks I discuss are not virtuous. They are not good or reassuring in the way we may typically think of political art. But these works nevertheless raise necessary and difficult questions about the meaning and value of resistance, and the very possibility of critique, in a moment of ubiquitous appropriation and financialization characterized by extreme consolidations of capital and ever more enmeshed and dependent relationships to power. Can something still be considered resistant if it is complicit with the structural conditions it challenges? Is resistance thinkable from a position that is not autonomous but embedded?

This book responds to calls for politico-aesthetic strategies adequate to the waning sense of agency in a moment when the political tools on hand appear co-opted in advance. It begins from the premise that conventional notions of radical art and politics, gestures of transgression and refusal inherited from twentieth-century avant-garde aesthetics and revolutionary politics, traffic an idealism that does not fully account for the deep structural enmeshment of the contemporary subject. As corporate and state entities have become more efficient at recuperating disruption back into the workings of capital—and as digital technologies have intensified surveillance and accelerated appropriation—control and resistance have become nearly indistinguishable. Projects of artistic subversion and activist resistance not only appear to be impotent gestures or anachronisms of a bygone era, but, even more perniciously, seem to throw gas on the fire of systems of extraction and exploitation.[13] What are the meaning and value of a politics of disruption when artworks that are critical of corporations and government institutions can be said to help them—however inadvertently—close their loopholes? When hackers actually help states and corporations improve the security of their information systems?[14] When anti-establishment art and modes of critique are adopted as profitable marketing strategies?[15] What, we might ask, is the efficacy of resistance when it performs an immunitary function that renders the mechanisms it seeks to challenge all the more impervious to it? Today, when disruption and critique are not what threaten the stability of the system but are essential to its functioning, would-be radical artists and critics find themselves implicated in, even feeding, the very power structures they seek to oppose.[16]

The Play in the System is not a book about specific digital platforms, practices, or technologies; neither is it a book that focuses on contemporary artists and interventionists either working in a particular media or visual genre or representing a specific ethnicity or gender. It is a book about an idea, a system, the emergence of a new aesthetic and critical formation in response to the blunted force of frontal resistance in the face of ever more accommodating and entrenched systems of power. The digital is not necessarily the medium or site of exhibition of these artworks; it is the informing condition of their emergence. The digital constitutes a favorable milieu for the consolidation of power structures that predate it, for technologies, sold as empowering, draw us ever more tightly into their ideological mechanisms through apparatuses of capture and economies of dependency. This study reconceives resistance under what Gilles Deleuze famously termed the regime of control, where power has moved outside disciplinary spaces of enclosure and made openness its constitutive promise.[17] Control, as compared to discipline, describes a formation of power that is more indirect, unbounded, and "flexible."

The book introduces and theorizes this tactic of complicit resistance as *parasitism*. Parasitical works use art as a means to wedge open—to redirect or subtly re-incline—the mechanisms used to justify and legitimize the privatization of resources and access. Parasitism responds to a contemporary political economy in which less powerful players are increasingly constrained and made dependent by the terms of their relationships to more powerful players. A new landscape of mass precarity has emerged in the wake of the 2008 global financial crisis and the rise of the digital platform economy, as wealth and influence have consolidated ever more narrowly in the hands of a powerful few. Neoliberal conditions in the Global North (this book focuses specifically on the United States and Europe) present a seeming impasse for the once more reliable strategies of opposition and refusal associated with 1960s-, 1970s-, and 1980s-era anti-institutional, Marxist, and feminist art and critique as hegemonic power has immunized itself against these strategies by absorbing and monetizing once radical projects. As second- and third-wave feminism, cultural studies, and institutional critique have been integrated into and canonized by prestigious higher education and art institutions, the sites of analysis from which structural power has been most effectively critiqued have themselves threatened to become hegemonic. At the same time, the economic precarity of a new generation of radical artists and activists has been made more and more dependent on corporate and institutional resources for their financial survival, weighing down their political commitments with a sense of ambiguity. This techno-cultural and economic shift has transformed contemporary interventionist and feminist aesthetics, and it is the parasitical works of artistic resistance that emerge from this climate change that this book explores.

To understand how some have forged resistance within these conditions, the book convenes an original archive of (mostly) lesser-known and emerging artists and interventionists working on the margins of the mainstream art world and the traditional scholarly canon, who have been compelled to operate within this inhospitable—or rather, all too hospitable—order. I argue that the uptake (and rejection) of parasitism within particular strands of art and activism signals a tactical repositioning, a means by which certain artists and interventionists have sought to highlight and operationalize their contingent and derivative status with respect to established radical critical and aesthetic traditions. The artworks in this book at once inherit from and sit in uneasy relation to aesthetic strategies and practices associated with the twentieth-century feminist avant-garde insofar as they contest power structures while also highlighting their own complicity with such structures. The conditions that constitute these artists' host milieus vary from chapter to chapter. For interventionist artists working in the vein of institutional critique, it is the inexorability of digital and legal apparatuses of corporate and state power; for experimental women artists and writers, it is the dominating presence of an already established male avant-garde; and for a younger cohort of performance artists struggling to survive in the postcrisis economy, it is the outsized institutional shadow cast by an earlier feminist art canon. Many of these artists have found themselves precariously employed, increasingly reliant on the creative and academic gig economies of the neoliberal university and art market. Stringing together experimental festival appearances and adjunct teaching, performances in alternative art spaces, and exhibitions on social media while living off credit cards, most of the artists represented in this book reflect the burdens of a landscape of mounting debt, failing public infrastructure, and diminishing professional horizons. Here generation is thus understood less as a question of age than of sensibility and situation, for it is now defined by one's perceived contingency within the new economy of precarity.

The book is organized around the escalation and distortion of this tactic of resistance. It examines artworks across a number of genres and sites of practice that increasingly problematize the parasite-host binary over the arc of the book; as the political stakes of these works get messier, they increasingly display the critical and ethical limits, some might argue the reductio ad absurdum, of parasitism as a minoritarian tactic as it slides into autocritique. The book focuses on art because art has always been parasitical—always already compromised by virtue of being caught up in the economy of its consumption and patronage. This introduction lays out an affirmative theory of parasitical resistance, while the chapters that follow are case studies and readings of how it works in practice. The first part of the book explores parasitism in the context of interventionist works of systemic and institutional critique, and the second part looks at works in the arena of feminist art and aesthetics. The difference in scale between the examples in the first and second parts and the power differentials they represent are necessary to the book's investigation of the various faces and strategies of dominant power and the nature of its investment in appearing open and accessible, for these power differentials shape the forms of resistance it affords. The feel-good conceptualism of *Amazon Noir* looks a bit like a Robin Hood story, with hackers robbing the powerful and redistributing the spoils to the people. But when later artworks examined here use the same parasitical tactics against individuals, without the same altruistic effects, it can be harder to see them as resistance to power.

In 2009 a London-based Irish conceptual artist, Roisin Byrne, performed a very similar operation of parasitical resistance to Ubermorgen's. Instead of a megacorporation, though, Byrne targeted the German conceptual artist Jochem Hendricks, ripping off one of his most famous works. Byrne, then an MFA student at Goldsmiths, enticed Hendricks into an extended email correspondence after being, as she put it, "moved by an admiration for his work."[18] Posing as a fan, she turned Hendricks's reputation as a gadfly back on him, imitating and raising the stakes of his own methods at his expense. Whereas Byrne is a relative unknown (despite appearing on the BBC4 doc series *Goldsmiths: But Is It Art?* the same year), Hendricks is known for controversial works that challenge legal and moral boundaries. He has displayed the taxidermied corpses of fighting dogs (*Pack*, 2003–6) and paid undocumented workers to count millions of grains of sand (*Grains of Sand*, 1999–2007), even going so far as to describe the latter work as a magnanimous move on his part.[19] Hendricks characterizes his practice as a game without limits: "I start the game but whatever happens is fine, as long as people aren't bored."[20] He explores what he can get away with in the name of art.[21] Hendricks's work tests avant-garde art's capacity to function as a site of critical reflexivity and thus to be used as an alibi for actions that would otherwise be considered illegal or immoral. By staging art's potential complicity with exploitative economies of animal abuse and vulnerable labor, his work provides a platform for reflection on practices of exploitation, while at the same time Hendricks himself profits from circulating these practices as art.

When Hendricks came to Goldsmiths as a visiting lecturer, Byrne intervened as the university was processing his payment, replacing the bank information on his invoice with her own, rerouting his payment to her account. (Byrne exhibits a copy of the invoice but provides few details about how she accomplished this.) She then used the funds to create a replica of Hendricks's best-known work, *Tax* (2000). For *Tax*, Hendricks had purchased gold bars in the exact amount that he owed to the government and claimed them as "artist's materials" on his tax return. She called the piece *Look What You Made Me Do.* Arguably Byrne only played Hendricks's own script back to him. But when she told him what she'd done, he insisted on differentiating her practice from his. In an email responding to Byrne, he wrote, "If you are able to convince me with a profound concept and content, we can talk." Hendricks's response suggests that he did not take Byrne's work seriously, for he characterized the piece as a joke ("Of course I was laughing when I read your confession") and asked Byrne to further justify the merits of the piece ("Meaning, content are the major points," he pontificated).

Just as Ubermorgen demonstrated that Amazon's dominant market position enabled them to set the terms of access—to distinguish between their free preview (good openness) and Ubermorgen's pirated open access (bad openness)—Byrne's *Look What You Made Me Do* puts on display Hendricks's dominant position, his investment in his ability to act as gatekeeper, to determine what constitutes a legitimate artwork and what is merely a bad feminist prank or a lazy student imitation. In her artwork Byrne cleverly uses the copy (a symbol for what is considered secondary, degraded, feminized) to highlight how differently the same conceptual art script signifies when the artist is female.[22] The title of Byrne's piece, *Look What You Made Me Do*, uses the language of a (usually male) abuser, suggesting provoked aggression and the inevitability of retaliation while inverting the gender dynamic; in so naming her replica of *Tax* (a piece that symbolizes Hendricks's financial and social capital as a white European male), Byrne invokes systematic sexism as her alibi, in the same way that Hendricks himself uses power and exploitative social and economic structures as alibis. By parasiting the parasite, she discloses the masculine privilege that underwrites his claim to legitimate subversion. In creating a replica of his most famous work, Byrne literalizes and hyperbolizes long-held notions of femininity as a bad copy of or vampiristic threat to masculinity. As an act of feminist revenge,

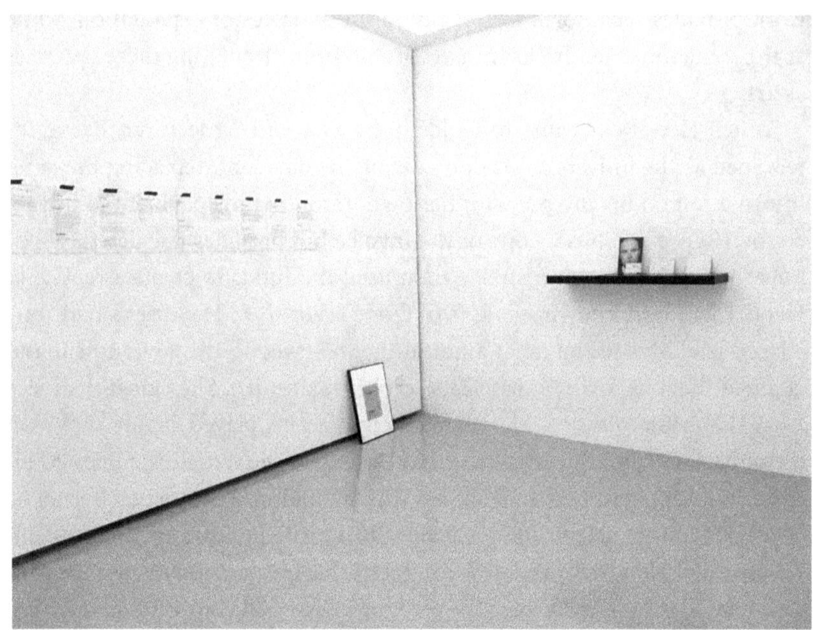

FIGURE I.3 Installation view of Roisin Byrne, *Look What You Made Me Do*, The Goma, Madrid, 2009. Photo by Borja Díaz Mengotti.

however, Byrne's replica "enacts the literalism that would enable its own dismissal," as Sara Ahmed has argued of Valerie Solanas.[23]

But the project's act of replication is only one facet of *Look What You Made Me Do*, which, though also comprising sculpture, photography, conceptual art, and installation, is best understood as a work of performance art, insofar as Hendricks's response to Byrne's provocation is the centerpiece of the work. (Similarly, Ubermorgen touted *Amazon Noir* as a "performative media event," and the project encompassed the reactions of the corporate entity, mainstream media, and legal system to their provocation.)[24] The critical gesture of Ubermorgen's and Byrne's artworks is not the copies themselves but the unauthorized acts of appropriation they represent and the responses they elicit. When Byrne shows the piece in a gallery setting (as she did in 2009 at The Goma in Madrid), she also exhibits Hendricks's artist monograph and headshot, a photograph of *Tax*, and redacted copies of the invoice and their email correspondence—"trophies" of her intervention (figure I.3).[25] Like Ubermorgen, whose logo and diagram for *Amazon Noir* resembles nothing less than the black box of Amazon's business practices, the work on display at The Goma is what Byrne is *able to get away with taking*.

Hendricks's *Tax* purports to be a critical reflection on what it means to take capital out of circulation (gold bars being the reserve for those who do not participate in the exchange of virtualized capital), yet Hendricks himself remains possessive of his own cultural currency. Both *Tax* and *Grains of Sand* are artworks precisely about how the meaning and value ascribed to actions depend on the bodies that perform them or contexts in which they are performed, yet when Hendricks finds himself the target—when he is given an opportunity to yield some of his capital (both literal and symbolic) to Byrne—he is unwilling to acknowledge the legitimacy of her conceptual project. He reserves for himself the role of authority, which is precisely the role that his work takes pride in subverting—a remarkably unreflexive response. By retreating into the discourses of originality, Hendricks betrays the limits of his willingness to play the game, whose limits he once boasted were boundless. In his exchange with Byrne, Hendricks manifests his authority as an established white male artist, both as a function of individual identity and as a structural position; he has a monopoly on the position of the subversive artist in the context of their relation, and so he has the power to set the terms of their encounter.[26] Whereas Ubermorgen's incursion into Amazon's marketing tool fits within a recognizable anticapitalist narrative, Byrne's targeting of Hendricks provokes a more complicated response. While few are likely to identify with Amazon (which is faceless, impersonal, and dominant), more are likely to identify with Hendricks or at least find him sympathetic, thus complicating the effect of Byrne's critique. Because her act of appropriation is so imitative and so off-putting, Byrne's intervention simultaneously calls out and recalcifies Hendricks's positionality—an outcome she likely did not intend.

What critical and political value do such artistic projects have in our current moment? Do they ultimately achieve anything? Certainly their implications as anticapitalist and feminist interventions are debatable. Their gains appear mostly symbolic. Their effects, typically kept off the official record, are largely unverifiable. By probing and testing the oppressive conditions they inhabit, these works risk inadvertently legitimizing and expanding such conditions by reinforcing what they set out to critique. Yet for all of their limitations, works like *Amazon Noir* and *Look What You Made Me Do* also tell us something important about the systems of power in which they operate, for they manifest the ambivalence that necessarily contaminates any artistic or critical project of resistance today. They demonstrate a sense of being out of options. But more hopefully, they outline ways it may still be possible to express a kind of resistance from *within* this problematic.

This book explores the following questions: What subversive possibilities might the complicit subject still hold? Can complicity be refashioned into a tool of resistance and redistribution? Both Ubermorgen and Byrne model ways of animating complicity as a tactic of furtive resistance. The fear of being complicit has helped maintain the idea that proximity to dominant power means allegiance to the social order. But the projects described here explore whether certain subjects can leverage their complicity (structural or circumstantial) with more powerful entities in order to open up unanticipated lines of intervention, redistribution, and potentially solidarity with more marginalized subjects—subjects whose identities do not always allow complicity as an option.[27] The artworks sketched in this introduction, like those that are analyzed in the rest of the book, exemplify the compromised performance of resistance that this book advances as *parasitism*. The term calls to mind insects, bacteria, viral agents. But this book is about something else: here parasitism captures the inescapability of dominance and the problem of structural dependency—perennial feminist concerns made newly urgent by an inexorable and hypernetworked neoliberal present wherein the experience of subjectivity has assumed the general form of parasitism. The problem of the parasitical guest, made complicit by its dependent circumstances, reanimates classic preoccupations of feminist theory, namely the secondary, supplementary, precarious status of women and of sexual and racial minorities under patriarchy.[28] To be a parasite is to be a guest in one's own home.

The theory of parasitical resistance advanced in this book draws on a range of critical and aesthetic experiments with the parasite as an ambivalent and nonemancipatory figure of institutional and systemic critique and intervention, ranging from the writings of the French philosopher Michel Serres to embedded art and design practice, from the digital incursions of tactical media to the tactics of free riding and "weapons of the weak."[29] While these previous engagements with and invocations of parasitism are not the book's focus, this body of work grounds and informs my conceptualization of parasitism as a blueprint for a compromised ethics of feminist, queer, and/or subaltern appropriation, wherein the parasite undermines its host system only to the degree that it can get away with it.

In its ideal form, the parasite advanced here is a figure neither of false consciousness nor of romanticized complicity but one imbued with the capacity for subliminal dissent: a form of alterity able to swim in hostile waters, if only temporarily. The parasite is an agent that can successfully install itself within the host system and can survive the host's attempts to inoculate itself against the parasite. As the parasitologist Claude Combes explains, parasite-host systems work differently from prey-predator systems. In prey-predator systems, after a mouse is eaten by a cat, its body and genetic information soon disappear. In parasite-host systems, the parasite enters into a persistent state of intimate cohabitation in its host, and its genetic information is conserved side by side with that of the host; the parasite's genetic material is not metabolized into the host but remains discrete within it (figure I.4).[30] The parasite-host system thus offers a temporal (*enduring*), spatial (*immanent*), and relational (*dependent*) model in which embeddedness and relative contingency do not mean total subsumption or eventual assimilation; instead they signal the possibility of incrementally redirecting the host's resources from inside. In an all-pervasive contemporary social, political, and economic system, parasites demonstrate that enmeshment need not be antithetical to disruptive action. The parasite's incremental undermining offers a sorely needed alternative to the overdetermining binary of radical versus reformist action. Parasitism inverts the dynamic at work in what Rob Nixon has called "slow violence" and Lauren Berlant "slow death" (the gradual and often invisible toll of environmental crisis and neoliberal attrition of social welfare on the poor), operating instead a kind of *slow resistance*, which goes along with the falsely innocuous and inviting front of hegemonic entities in order to allow something else just as imperceptibly to emerge.[31]

I am not suggesting that radical politics are obsolete, nor am I suggesting that frontal action is ineffective. Parasitical resistance on its own is necessarily inadequate. Rather, in a moment when modes of direct opposition are subject to violent elimination and rapid co-option, this book explores how we might account for nonfrontal or oblique (nonconfrontational) expressions of resistance that might otherwise go overlooked, whose mechanisms and implications are easily read and dismissed as mere capitulation. Parasitism is foremost a politics of disidentification. My understanding of the parasite's antagonistic yet unavoidable relationship to its host system (its status as both different from and part of the host), and thus the critical potential of its performance of complicity, is fundamentally informed by José Esteban Muñoz's theory of disidentification. For Muñoz, the disidentificatory subject of queer of color performance operates neither a straightforward identification nor a counteridentification with majoritarian culture but instead a "working on, with, and against . . . at a simultaneous moment."[32] Muñoz writes, "Instead of buckling under the pressures of dominant ideology (identification, assimilation) or attempting to break free of its inescapable sphere (counteridentification, utopianism), this 'working on and against' is a strategy that

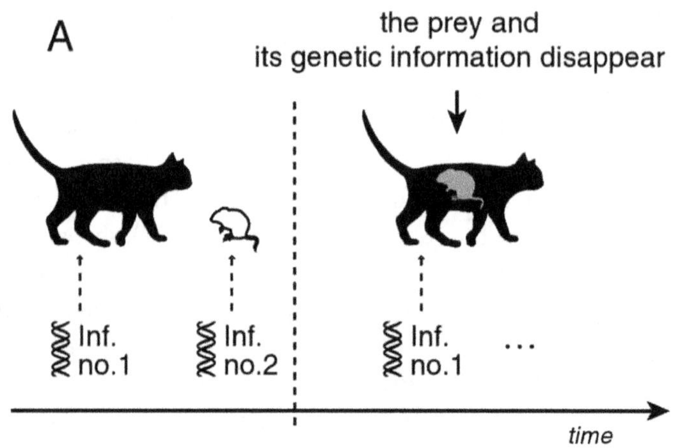

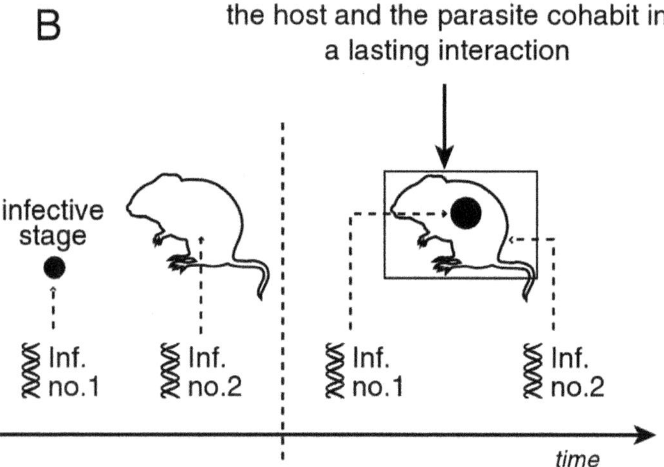

FIGURE I.4 Illustration from Claude Combes's *The Art of Being a Parasite*, 2005.

tries to transform a cultural logic from within, always laboring to enact permanent structural change while at the same time valuing the importance of local or everyday struggles of resistance."[33] Whereas queer performance theorists like Muñoz and Judith Butler have focused on how subjects outside the racial and sexual mainstream negotiate, appropriate, and rework dominant culture as a strategy of survival, this study explores how minoritarian subjects with the racial or cultural capital to pass within and access protections within majority culture can manipulate the appearance that they acquiesce to power so as to undermine its functioning.[34] In these accounts of disidentification *performance* is not simply a concealment but a mode by which processes of subjectivation are negotiated and contested in ways that are not immediately recognizable as such. Where the more radical subject of Fred Moten and Stefano Harney's undercommons, that "unassimilated underground" of institutional life, is said "to be in but not of" the hegemonic space it occupies, the more ambivalent parasitical subject can be said to be *both in and of* the space of the host—or, more precisely, it is both *of* and *not of*.[35] In this sense the parasite always walks the line between disidentification and overidentification, a hyperbolic form of mimicry by which privileged actors can parody authority.[36] These accounts offer a means of foiling the systematic work of interpellation and leave open the possibility for resistance from within.

As corporate practices and digital technologies have consolidated the project of privatization, they have incorporated and commodified difference and dissent, transforming the social field into a system, a closed circuit, a rigged game. *The Play in the System* advances an account of resistance in the face of increasingly totalizing analyses of power in critical and media theory in recent decades. The book brings the critical paradigm of performance to bear on the contemporary co-option of resistance. It is a work of cultural studies that stages a rare encounter among the fields of digital studies, performance studies, feminist and queer studies, political theory, and contemporary art history and criticism. Curating an archive of little-studied and emerging artists and interventionists not previously discussed in relation to one another, this study develops a logic of artistic resistance for a neoliberal networked era in which it is not a question of getting out but, following Foucault, it is instead "a question of how to work the trap that one is inevitably in."[37] The book discloses acts of parasitical resistance across sites of extreme consolidation and nonreciprocity: corporate monopolization, state power, toxic masculinity, and millennial precarity. Employing methods of discourse analysis and textual and visual close reading, it builds an analytical framework for understanding the adoption of this new critical and aesthetic paradigm of resistance in the spheres of digital art activism, institutional critique, and feminist art and performance.

But before we can imagine or access such forms of resistance, we need to ensure we fully understand the problem itself: the host milieu in which the parasite must operate. When I theorize a particular instantiation of parasitism as a minoritarian performance, I am thus also theorizing a particular mode of hospitality as a majoritarian performance. This dyadic structure is captured in the coerciveness of the host's *nongenerous giving* and the resistant effect of the parasite's *nonproprietary taking.* I argue (1) that powerful entities, from corporate monopolies to privileged individuals, perform hospitality, promoting and instrumentalizing precarity while masquerading as generous; and (2) that this performance of what I call *coercive hospitality,* while oppressive, contains within it a possible kernel of resistance.

THE NEOLIBERAL HOST AND COERCIVE HOSPITALITY

Who or what precisely is a host? I reserve the term *host* for an entity whose ability to claim a universal status endows it with the power to authorize or withhold resources and access. Corporations and digital platforms are some of the most easily recognizable hosts given the seemingly inescapable nature of their power. Indeed parasitism's new visibility as a critical and aesthetic formation is inseparable from the sense of inexorability wrought by our technopolitical juncture, from the totalizing logics of the internet to the unprecedented scalar complexity of life in the Anthropocene. Today neoliberal citizens find themselves reliant on a system whose conditions they have little or no ability to negotiate. In this system hospitality is the new dominant as experiences of uncertainty and dispossession, once consigned to the downtrodden few, move up the socioeconomic ranks.[38] To live in and with neoliberalism over the past decades is to have witnessed: 1) *the rise of a host economy,* as the privatization of social life has given way to an extreme consolidation of power in the hands of a few; and 2) *the recasting of the citizen as a parasite,* as citizenship has undergone a violent redefinition as a condition of precarity. Precarity describes the state of being dependent on the generosity of another: the Latin *precarius* refers to that which is "given as a favour" or "the idea of being given something—the right to occupy land, or to hold a particular position—'at the pleasure of' another person, who might simply choose to take it back at any time."[39] The generalizability of the parasite as a model of neoliberal subjectivity is thus indexical of the extent to which a certain form of power has increasingly represented itself as hospitable. (This neoliberalized soft power of coercive hospitality, however, has not replaced but rather is coextensive with the hard power of militarized policing and neofascism.)[40] Conceiving of neoliberalism as a host system through the classical paradigm of hospitality enables us to see it as a paternalistic logic that operates through the promise and withholding of protection and care to citizens, addressed as dependents.

By now the narrative of neoliberalism's entrenchment in social and political life is well rehearsed: in the drive to maximize profitability, risk and economic burden are placed on the very individuals and institutions that prop the system up.[41] Workers' benefits are repackaged as entitlements for the undeserving, and charity is instrumentalized in the guise of corporate responsibility. Voters are no longer shareholders of the state, which now unapologetically seeks to please its private investors. Public administration gives way to corporate governance, and citizenship is recast as a debt to be paid. Commonwealth resources such as water and scientific knowledge, in which in principle all citizens hold an equal interest, are taken out from under them and privatized. As private interests have held tighter sway over public life, the possibilities for occupying public space have been constricted as the expanded dominion of private property has made the commons ever more inhospitable to citizens.

These developments have not been experienced in the same way by all; a nuisance for some, they have meant a constant challenge to survival for others.[42] Laws have criminalized basic human activities such as eating and sleeping precisely at the moment when the number of homeless people outstrips the shelter beds available, making it effectively impossible for people to survive outside of the capitalist economy.[43] The assault on the homeless exemplifies the constriction and criminalization of public life under neoliberalism: LA restaurants and markets have erected elaborate enclosures to "protect" their garbage from growing homeless populations; France has only recently outlawed practices requiring that employees throw bleach on discarded food, ostensibly discouraging dumpster divers "to avoid being implicated in case someone gets sick"; and "anti-homeless spikes" and benches with armrests proliferate in urban centers from Montreal to Tokyo, making it difficult to sleep in public spaces.[44] These "hostile architectures" evidence the narrowing of acceptable scripts for occupying public and commercial space.[45] This has had the effect of inscribing contemporary social life within a logic of imposition: rent and taxation, credit and debt. It has reframed the terms of neoliberal citizenship as those of a patronage system. Expropriated from the commons, citizens are then offered the commons back *for rent*—an illusory choice within a system of coercive hospitality.

As many have shown, the reprivatization of what already belongs to the people is the defining feature of the twenty-first-century economy. This shift makes visible the logic at the heart of the digital platform economy, wherein users must go through gatekeepers to retrieve their own data, pay a third party to interact with one another, and submit to ever-changing terms and conditions to access their own content. As one IBM executive summed it up in an internal memo titled "The Digital Disruption Has Already Happened," the "World's largest taxi company owns no taxis (Uber)," the world's "largest accommodation provider owns no real estate (Airbnb)," the world's "largest phone companies own no [telecommunications infrastructure] (Skype, We-Chat)," and the "most popular media owner creates no content (Facebook)."[46] The new economy is a host economy. What we find today is a multiplication of intermediaries, a growing economy of hosts that create no original content and offer no services in the traditional sense; instead they sell access to territory and infrastructure while capitalizing on the work of those who build and use it.[47] By strategically positioning themselves as "platforms," Tarleton Gillespie has argued, such companies monetize the content produced by others while minimizing liability.[48] They wear the mantle of generosity while capitalizing on spectacles of their own magnanimity; they pose as free and open while concealing the rent or tax they take.

Hospitality becomes coercive when the host alone is able to set the terms of its relationship with the guest and when those terms disavow the unequal and nonconsensual nature of the relationship.[49] Coercive hospitality thus speaks to the capacity of certain entities and actors to exempt themselves from or buy themselves out of the very ethics of care and structures of accountability that they profess to embody and to which they subject others. Crucially, however, coercive hospitality describes a specific disposition of power or mode of structural entitlement that exists both at the level of institutional and bureaucratic protocols and at the more mundane interpersonal level. The host is always at home, always entitled to space, always dictating the terms of access and belonging to others. The host's "rightful place" is never up for discussion; his papers are never demanded.[50] But like the parasite, the host is a *structural position* rather than a specific identity or subject position (though certain identities or subjects occupy this position more readily than others).[51] Who occupies the positions of host and parasite is ultimately less a matter of fact than of perspective and power; the normative language of social parasitism is, as Serres has shown, a deictic maneuver by which certain subjects get called out and others don't.[52] The host and parasite are, moreover, neither ontological entities nor fixed identities. As this book will show, the same entity can occupy the position of host and parasite at different times—sometimes even at the same time. The performance of the host need not be cynical nor even fully conscious; performance is not mask play but a complex staging of power. Indeed, more often than not, the host does not recognize its structural position and the violence of its capacity to include and exclude. When called out by the parasite, it is often quite sincere in its surprise. Just as Hendricks feels miscast in the story Byrne tells about him and his work, Amazon executives are unlikely to characterize the corporation's monetization of openness as a dispossessive strategy. If anything, the host's power rests precisely on this capacity not to recognize its structural authority over others.

Given the position's scalar relativity, it follows that not all hosts are created equal. The hosts I discuss range from powerful multinational corporations and states to individuals. Each chapter examines how *privatization* and *privacy* work hand in hand as immunitary strategies by which host entities and actors cultivate unanswerability in different ways. Each examines a different mode or valence by which majoritarian actors have privatized the commons or commandeered their privilege, in turn opening up different modes or valences of parasitical resistance. The respective hosts in these chapters prevent their own exposure to scrutiny, closing gaps and possible breaches, using technical, legal, moral, and intimate protocols to distance themselves from their parasites: the black box of big corporations' exploitative business practices (Ubermorgen's *Google Will Eat Itself* and Robin Hood Cooperative, discussed in chapter 1); the red tape of bureaucratic inefficiency and the liberal-democratic state's obfuscatory investment in its ethical righteousness (Núria Güell's *Stateless by Choice* and Kenneth Pietrobono's *Void [The Opposite of Property]*; chapter 2); the cease-and-desist letter and accusation of invasion of privacy that suggest the male cultural critic sees himself as outside of the cultural critique he offers (Chris Kraus's *I Love Dick*; chapter 3); and the use of intellectual property to refuse to cede a place for younger performance artists at work in Marina Abramović's protectiveness over her legacy (Anya Liftig's *Anxiety of Influence* and Ann Liv Young's *Sherry Is Present*; chapter 4).

If part I, "Redistribution: Institutional Interventions," is tonally different from part II, "Imposition: Intimate Interventions," in its affective charge and level of intimate proximity, this is a function of the scale and nature of their hosts. Each chapter examines how a different hegemonic figure or functionary—the "open" corporate platform, the "welcoming" security state, the "progressive" male cultural critic, the "receptive" iconic woman artist—projects itself as a moral authority, a figure of conscience; while they prefer to regard themselves as outside of the power structures in which they operate, these figures and functionaries employ postures of benevolence and receptivity as alibis to cover the strategies that maintain their grip on power—hoarding their access to resources (wealth, private property, social capital, dynastic privilege) and restricting the access of others. When we name such entities *hosts* (without suggesting their equivalence or ascribing an ontology to them), what dynamics become visible?

In part I the host targets are leviathan-like structures, labyrinthine corporate and state institutions that exploit their massive scale through protocols of unanswerability. Chapters 1 and 2 investigate the strategies by which the multinational corporation and neoliberal state ensure and normalize their structural nonaccountability. Chapter 1 examines how corporate platforms enlist technological protocol as an alibi for their nonaccountability to their users and employees, and chapter 2 explores how the state tautologically invokes the law to justify itself. In part II the structural targets (or hosts) are individuals, public figures chosen as metonyms for forms of structural power. In chapter 3 I examine Chris Kraus's *I Love Dick*, in which the real-life cultural critic Dick Hebdige is made to stand trial as a symbol of heteropatriarchy (the ultimate Dick); similarly, in chapter 4, I examine how a younger generation of white female performance artists (including Ann Liv Young, Anya Liftig, and Lauren Barri Holstein) reckons with the recent institutionalization of feminist performance art by targeting the equally celebrated and loathed performance artist Marina Abramović as the personification of a winner-take-all postcrisis art market. Part I thus explores the quandary of individual action and political refusal under present conditions; it is primarily diagnostic, more interested in making the limits of radical intervention visible than in transgressing them. In contrast, part II examines parasitical works that aggressively and queasily insist on intimacy with their hosts. When there would otherwise be no one to be held accountable, the artists nominate a single individual as representative of the hostile system in question in order to force a response, making it impossible for their hosts to ignore them or to remain indifferent. All these artworks thus address structural power, but the latter works stake their critiques in the personal rather than the institutional realm.

THE LOGIC OF THE PARASITE

Let us now examine the other side of this codependent dyad. Parasitism describes a relation whereby an organism depends on a host for its continued survival. There is no outside to the parasite's relationship with the host: if the parasite kills its host, it goes down with it. Because the parasite is not separable from the host systems it attacks, it represents an ethically and politically complex model of nonoppositional resistance. The double-dealing parasite maintains itself by flattering and aggrandizing the host to its face while undermining it behind its back. The affordances of the parasite, which cannot dictate but can only respond to the terms of its environment, are well suited to the inescapability of the contemporary condition.

Despite common perceptions, parasitism was originally a social rather than a biological paradigm; scientists in the seventeenth century borrowed the term to describe forms of life that depend on others for survival, draining nutrients or gaining shelter at the expense of others.[53] Long before it came to be associated with biology, parasitism referred to a performance of complicity with subversive potential in ancient religious practice. In its little-known earliest form, parasitism described a mode of social passing at the table of the host, whereby a figure of lower birth is welcomed as a special guest of those in power in return for simulating affection and deference. A priest or temple assistant, the parasite earned his name (meaning "next to" the "food" [*para sitos*]) because he was permitted to dine with superior officers and enjoy meals at the host's expense as a reward for his specialized knowledge and religious consultation.[54] (This derivation is echoed in the biological concept of *commensalism*, which denotes an association between organisms in which one benefits while the other is not harmed; it is from the Medieval Latin *commensalis*, meaning *com-* "sharing" + *mensa* "a table.") The parasitical guest, aware of its precarious status at the table, its not-belonging, finds an opening for itself (and protection from reprisal) in the ritual form of obligation that lies at the heart of the ancient concept of hospitality as *xenia* (guest-friendship). These rituals of sharing forge an alliance of reciprocity between individuals from different social strata and yield benefits to both, such as shelter or favors.[55] By accepting the host's gifts, companions may be folded in as accomplices to (and occasional beneficiaries of) the host's power, by virtue of their social proximity and performance of friendship.

The parasite's means for responding to its situation, while not fully determined, are heavily constrained by its dependency on the host. The parasite is individuated, yet it is inconceivable—literally impossible—outside the ecosystem it inhabits. Parasitism, then, is best understood as a performance of social acquiescence under coercion rather than as a mode of action predicated on individual subjectivity. What is so provocative and so difficult about parasitism as a paradigm of resistance is that it threatens to upend conventional critical rubrics for assessing political and ethical agency—notions of individual will and intentionality that presume an autonomous and rational subject. Lacking the full range of choice implied by such frameworks, the parasite is imbued with the quasi-subjectivity of the performer who must sing for their supper.

Its early association with social mobility was retained in the parasite's later use as a stock character in ancient Greek and Roman comedy—literally, a persona non grata, a position that could be occupied by donning its character mask.[56] The figure of the parasite was for much of its ancient history a neutral figure, coming into circulation as a derogatory term when it left the stage to threaten the wider economies of the world. At stake in the hatred of the parasite (a decidedly patriarchal fear of a kind of simulation that is unmistakably feminized) is its ability to trade in performance: it can use imitation as a tool to bend the protocols of the dominant order without being detected.[57] For Plato, mimesis, or the ability to "play" by manipulating appearances—in the parasite's case, to reflect back the desired image of the host—represents a troubling loophole by which one can interfere with the natural hierarchy of things.[58] Mimesis represents for him a counterfeit economy, an aesthetic loophole or dark art by which the artist can, through the trickery of artifice, upend the accepted truth of the social order and make it possible for slaves to be confused with kings.

It is this provocative (if not fully subversive) potential that informs Serres's characterization of the parasite as a *duplicitous guest*.[59] In what is the best-known philosophical account of the parasite, Serres offers a master theory of the parasite as an interdisciplinary, transhistorical actor with the potential to short-circuit normative hierarchies and economies of exchange.[60] In his most salient description, he uses the framework of immunology to describe the reaction the parasite elicits from its milieu, characterizing the parasite as a "thermal exciter" of its ecosystem. The parasite does not radically or obviously change the nature of the system; rather it introduces into the system a "minimal" and "differential" form of interference. The parasite smuggles in alterity under the guise of similarity. As Serres explains, by secreting a tissue identical to the host, the biological parasite neutralizes the host system's standard mechanisms for rejecting the potential threats posed by foreign bodies. By making the host think that it is cut from the same cloth, then incrementally revealing itself, the parasite stuns the host's usual defenses. By the time the host realizes that it has been hijacked, it is too late: "The parasited, abused, cheated body no longer reacts; it accepts it; it acts as if the visitor were its own organ. It consents to maintain it; it bends to its demands." The interloping parasite *plays* its environment; it "plays a game of mimicry"; it "plays at being the same."[61]

But this parasitical mimicry is not a straightforward aping. The parasite does not so much *copy* the host as *adopt the script* of its host system. It does not imitate the host but simulates assent to it, dissolving its own singularity in the process. It disappears, as Serres puts it, "into the milieu that is the other."[62] The figure of the parasite, then, is abhorred not for its claimed inability or refusal to contribute to its host economy but for the threat it represents: its ability to pass as (or give the appearance of being) nonthreatening to the host and thus its potential to undermine the host-guest hierarchy. The parasite represents a breach that threatens to expose the contradictions of the "hospitable" values of its host economy.

As a mode of artistic intervention, parasitism is thus productive on two levels: *pragmatically* and *heuristically*. Pragmatically, it offers ways to envision a different form of politics when direct activist modes are foreclosed. While it can seem that the house always wins, parasitism demonstrates that systems too can be made to adapt. If neoliberal power works by dressing up market strategy as generosity through the masquerade of public image, then the parasite accepts its given role in order to remain in the game. The crucial dynamic is not opposition but (the appearance of) radical acceptance. Unlike their radical counterparts, parasitical works do not visibly challenge or openly contradict their host systems but adapt to operate on their terms. When leaving the system is not an option, playing along with one's constraints becomes, paradoxically, a means of owning one's lack of agency. Parasites affirm their hosts with manic intensity, jarring the hosts' routine operations by following their hegemonic scripts to the letter. The parasite locates a point of contradiction in its host (such as Amazon's and Hendricks's wish to appear to be moral authorities and thus legitimate arbiters of access) and moderately recalibrates the host's protocols of access, if only for a moment. Even as the host jostles to deflect this appearance of hypocrisy, the parasite often also provokes a response from the host akin to an immunological reaction, a bodily defense that attempts to neutralize the foreign agent. We see this kind of immunological reaction in Amazon's offer to settle and Hendricks's patronizing rationale, both attempts to discredit and neutralize their parasites. I argue that where bigger actors answer their parasites by trying to delay or avoid having to respond, black-boxing in order to protect a semblance of openness, smaller actors answer by acting offended or by invoking the discourses of privacy and private property. But these reactions only draw more attention to the original contradiction of the host's investment in appearing generous.

As a heuristic, parasitical works thus make several things explicit. First, they display the discursive mechanisms and administrative protocols by which the host tries to differentiate its own actions from those of its so-called parasites in order to rationalize its exceptional status—and that the host need not justify itself beyond a certain point. Second, they foreground the fact that what the host promotes as gratuitous acts of generosity are actually functional necessities, as hosts that claim to be autonomous and self-sufficient need their parasites. Third, they make visible the invisible stratification that pervades the system of institutional access, despite its claims that everyone is equal on the level of human capital. Consequently the parasite makes clear that the host's protocols, which purport to be fair and universal, are in fact conditional and mutable—if more for some than others.

Like hosts, those who can be said to hold parasitical subject positions do not all occupy the same relationship to dominant power; as such, they are not equally accommodated. The discourse of parasitism is often invoked to describe the struggle for survival of the most vulnerable subjects for whom, under especially hostile conditions, as Muñoz observes, resistance cannot be too frank or too conspicuous for fear of retaliation.[63] But parasitism is not only a function of the struggle to survive. The sense of parasitism foregrounded in this book emphasizes a more implicated, entangled, and ambiguous relationship to dominant power. This less cut-and-dried sense of parasitism comprises those subjects who serve as dominant power's chosen companions, its trophies of inclusion; these parasites are others or duplicitous hangers-on who can pass as belonging within spaces coded as white, as gender-conforming, as straight, as middle-class. They occupy social positions that afford them special access to those with power, yet they are denied autonomy by this arrangement; they remain precarious, for their inclusion is granted (or revoked) at the whim of the host.

Rather than seeking to expose this hypocrisy, to show the real face of power (as if such a thing were possible), the parasite enacts a second-order exposure. It exposes not the thing itself but the exploitability of its performance. Parasitical artists play this fiction of hospitality, which is an unguarded point of access to the host. The contemporary artists and interventionists explored in this book engage parasitism as a counterstrategy for using more powerful entities' pretense of benevolence—their desire to see themselves as inclusive of difference and dissent, however symbolic and perfunctory—as an opening by which certain minoritarian subjects can gain access. The phrase *the play in the system* invoked by my title refers to the working tolerance that exists within a system (required for its operation), which might be manipulated to alter the system's functions and to open up spaces of redistribution and critique that wouldn't otherwise be possible. It speaks to the possibility of accepting (and exploiting) the invitation that protocols of coercive hospitality make available to different ends from those intended by the host. The defining feature of parasitical works is their ability to make the very entities and institutions they confront into the reluctant hosts and patrons of their disruptions. The parasitical artist does this through exaggerated performances of dependency that compel the host either to accommodate them or to reveal the terms by which its hospitality is conditional. What I identify as resistance may not be fully conscious or even realized in the artworks I discuss. As we will see throughout the book, the parasite, almost as a matter of course, loses ground or gets co-opted in the process of launching an attack. What I call resistance is the differential between *what the host is willing to give* and *what the parasite is able to get away with taking.* It is the parasite's ability to calibrate its actions to this interval of accommodation, this limited room for maneuver, that is the play in the system.

THE THRESHOLD OF ACCOMMODATION

"How does the parasite usually take hold? He tries to become invisible. We must speak of invisibility again," Serres observes.[64] Let us map more precisely *how* the parasite becomes invisible: how it evades reprisal in spaces of domination, how it makes its opposition seem negligible or even useful to the host. The parasite's survival on the territory of the host is calibrated to what we might call the *threshold of accommodation* at which the host will allow it to endure without taking decisive action against it. Much as drivers who go only five to ten miles per hour over the speed limit (the threshold of accommodation within which they are unlikely to be ticketed), the parasite takes advantage of the margin of subjective enforcement, knowing that (for reasons of limited resources or potential equipment error) small-scale transgressions are unlikely to draw scrutiny from authorities. (This analogy, however, falsely presumes that all drivers bear the same relation to the police state and to detectability, when African American drivers are the most likely to be stopped and, like Hispanics, are ticketed, searched, and arrested at higher rates than white drivers. As antiblack police brutality has shown, non-white subjects are not met with the same leniency.)[65] This margin of tolerance afforded to some also serves the state, which gives only as much accommodation as it needs to in order to maintain the allegiance of those it governs. In the interlude that follows this introduction, I examine more systematically the thresholds of accommodation by which the host differentially enforces the access it grants to parasitical subjects.

The parasite's ability to inhabit and exploit the interval opened by the degree of leniency granted by the system is most of all a function of the potential loss posed to the host by what the parasite takes and the resources available to the host to surveil and discipline the parasite.[66] The parasite's performance of submission is on a continuum with that of the enslaved subject, the colonized subject, or the peasant—figures that, as Saidiya V. Hartman, Homi Bhabha, and James C. Scott have shown, respectively, feign acquiescence, even pleasure in submission, in order to survive.[67] These scholars elucidate the selective historical deployments of hospitality as a strategy of white supremacist, colonial, and imperial domination. However, in its Western, bourgeois manifestations, parasitism's performance of submission might be closer to Joan Riviere's 1929 psychoanalytic account of "womanliness as masquerade," in which she observed that highly intellectual women wear "the mask of femininity," flattering and wooing men by feigning delicacy and confusion.[68] The rather more privileged and duplicitous parasite examined in this book can still presume a degree of safety if it is detected; unlike the enslaved subject, the colonized subject, and the peasant, it is not faced with the consequences of bodily harm or death.

In such accounts of resistance and survival, the greater the risk posed by the performance, the more tightly the mask is worn. Hartman has observed that demonstrations requiring slaves to feign compliance and contentment for the slaveholder's pleasure ("puttin' on ole massa") were difficult to unmask as performances; how does one tell the difference, Hartman asks, between "the simulation of compliance for covert aims" and plain compliance?

> At the level of appearance, these contending performances often differed little. At the level of effect, however, they diverged radically. One performance aimed to reproduce and secure the relations of domination and the other to manipulate appearances in order to challenge these relations and create a space for action not generally available. However, since acts of resistance exist within the context of relations of domination and are not external to them, they acquire their character from these relations,

and vice versa. At a dance, holiday fete, or corn shucking, the line between dominant and insurgent orchestrations of blackness could be effaced or fortified in the course of an evening, either because the enslaved utilized instrumental amusements for contrary purposes or because surveillance necessitated cautious forms of interaction and modes of expression.[69]

Similarly it is difficult to think through the parasite's resistance as it plays its host because its performed acquiescence has ambiguous effects. In this description of the master-slave relation, Hartman affirms the indeterminacy opened up by power's desire to be affirmed (what I have described as neoliberal authority's wish to be perceived as open and accessible). This account of resistance applies also to the broader host-parasite relation, in which the conspicuousness of the enactment of submission is bound to its conditions of subjection and enforcement. The parasite's potential as a figure of furtive resistance also relies on the undecidability of its intentions. The parasite finds momentary refuge in the flash of indeterminacy, the blind spot created by its ambiguous relationship to the host (*Is it or isn't it sincere?*).

Consider an example of how the parasite leverages a form of temporary illegibility or local know-how to negotiate the threshold of its host's hospitality. For his series *paraSITE* (1998–ongoing), the Iraqi American artist Michael Rakowitz attaches plastic inflatable shelters to the heating and cooling vents outside buildings in Boston and New York City. Using the air leaving the buildings to inflate and heat the structures, he appropriates the spare energy they emit to provide shelter for the homeless (figure I.5). Likewise, for *Parásitos Urbanos* (2005–7), the Mexican artist Gilberto Esparza creates robotic sculptures inspired by the surplus economy of Mexico City street vendors, who redirect stray electricity from nearby electric poles to power their stands.[70] Temporarily diverting the city's spare resources, these works model the parasite as a figure that locates and siphons off untapped pockets of energy in its host system. They showcase the fact that the parasite's reconfiguration of access points to resources is often situational, illicit, and makeshift.

Rakowitz has said that *paraSITE* was never intended as a replacement for social services but rather was "a symbolic strategy" designed to raise awareness about homelessness.[71] In the same way, the parasite can make its host system adapt (redirecting the wasted energy generated by industry into a rough and ready stopgap for the problem of homelessness) without questioning its foundations (making activist demands about the need for social services). The parasite can make the system adapt precisely because it does not call into question its fundamental principles. In Rakowitz's case, the parasite

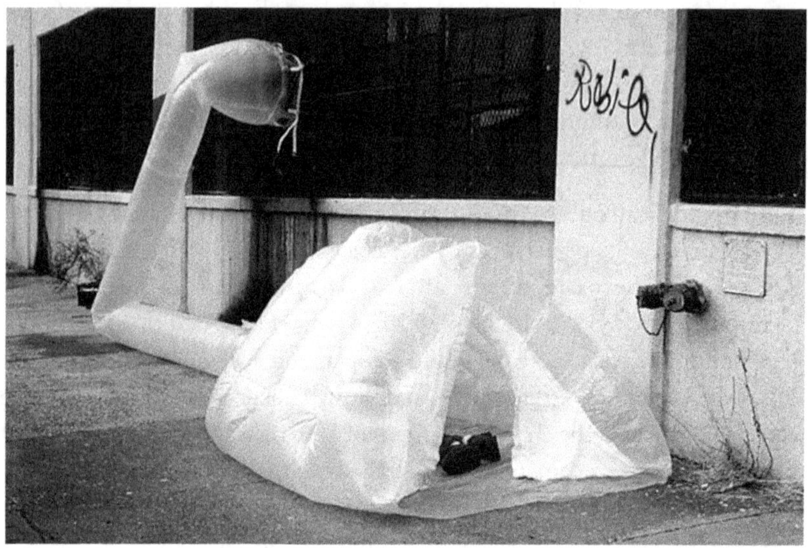

FIGURE I.5 Michael Rakowitz, *paraSITE*, 2000. Source: Michael Rakowitz.

does this practically by showing that this excess *can* be redistributed at no cost to the system and conceptually by calling out the greed and wastefulness of a postwelfare system of private ownership, while appearing relatively harmless. Rakowitz's and Esparza's parasites demonstrate the capacity to lay low or the social capital to pass without setting off too many alarms. The artists rely on the deniability provided by the projects' status as artworks (rather than activism) to ensure that their installations are not destroyed and that they are not arrested.

PLAYING ALONG: RETHINKING COMPLICITY FOR AN AGE OF EMBEDDEDNESS

The compromised position in which the artists and interventionists explored in this book find themselves recalls the feminist predicament famously captured by Audre Lorde as trying to dismantle the "master's house" using the "master's tools." How can one fight the man while being paid by him, drinking his Starbucks, and using his Apple products? As Lorde's argument goes, those who stand "inside the circle" of social acceptability can never get rid of structures of domination so long as they need and benefit from them. Meanwhile, for those subjects from whose survival and well-being the system has continually divested—predominantly poor women, lesbians, and women of color, Lorde argues—radical oppositionality is not a privilege but the only imaginable recourse.[72] How are we to understand the master's house today, when complicity with exploitation is an increasingly pervasive and automated structural condition, when those on the bottom need what those on top control and provide? In the contemporary digital economy, the master's house more closely resembles a platform; the liberal dream of every citizen owning their own home has been replaced by the neoliberal affordances of the rental economy represented by Airbnb. This transformation captures the neoliberal conversion of the welfare state into a *host*—a provider and facilitator of access that retains the rhetoric of care (but only the rhetoric). There is a hollow paternalism at the heart of neoliberal policy and discourse, which replaces the social safety net with individual responsibility, demonstrating care by enjoining individuals to take care of themselves.[73] The designation *host* attests to the difficulty of challenging forms of consolidated power that disavow their threat of physical violence (unlike the overt *master, oppressor, despot*) but whose capacity for violence nevertheless remains implicit in the formal and legal structures of ownership that still underwrite their authority.

As neoliberalism's automation of domination suggests, there is an unreconciled tension in how scholars have approached resistance as a small-scale tactic. Sometimes such tactics, which are premised on acting within the space of power, are characterized as the tools of weak or less-resourced actors (such as in certain media theory representations of the exploited citizen-user under digital capitalism); at other times they are characterized as the tools of privileged or more resourced actors (such as in certain critiques by queer and feminist of color scholars, for whom resistance is too reactive and too accepting of the status quo and for whom only the politics of radical refusal and practices of collective care are adequate to the intolerable conditions of life under racial capitalism).[74] Rather than resolving this tension, parasitism offers a third term. It is neither the selective interventionism of those who can afford to intervene, to play the game and then retreat, nor is it the absolute refusal of the most marginalized. Parasitism is not—in its appearance, methods, or effects—a liberationist politics; it does not directly fight, destroy, or refuse the conditions of capitalist, imperialist, white supremacist oppression. But when it redistributes what it takes from these host systems, the parasite can find common cause with more radical projects. My argument thus runs not counter to Lorde's but underneath it. It traces the contours of a submerged possibility whereby those inside the circle might simulate or exaggerate their complicity with the master as a tactic for undermining the master's house. Whereas Lorde emphasizes the impossibility of using the master's tools to completely dismantle the master's house, *The Play in the System* explores the room within structures of domination for something less than total dismantling but still capable of wearing away at them.

By passing as nonthreatening or even sympathetic, the artists I examine act as double agents or Trojan horses; they introduce forms of immanent and lateral interference, transforming their complicity with hegemonic structures into a counterintuitive resource for undermining them in plain sight. They get away with this by leveraging the ambiguous status of art and performance, which are perceived as relatively harmless, merely symbolic. The parasite's covert rebellion thus represents a tactical possibility afforded to those with the racial, sexual, and cultural capital to pass within spaces of white heterosexist masculine privilege. In all of the artworks I examine, the artists' complicity with the host economies they attempt to subvert bleed over, making the viewers or readers of the work also complicit and demonstrating that, while some are more compromised than others, no one is immune from this entanglement.

The chapters proceed from the more palatable and recognizable examples of this tactic to the more challenging. As the chapters progress, the artists' complicities with the structures they try to subvert reverberate more strongly. The political coordinates of the book shift, becoming both more pointedly self-critical and more feminist in orientation, as the parasite's fire begins to ricochet back on it. This intensification reflects the escalating levels of investment and thresholds of accommodation of the parasites explored here and the increasingly personal targets of the parasites' weaponization of complicity: complicity with the market in chapter 1, with state belonging in chapter 2, with heteropatriarchy in chapter 3, and with the legacy of white liberal feminism in chapter 4. Part I theorizes how the logic of coercive hospitality subtends institutional protocols. Chapter 1, "User Be Used: Leveraging the Coercive Hospitality of Corporate Platforms," examines how platform cooperativist projects play the scripts of coercive hospitality back on corporate platforms. Chapter 2, "An Opening in the Structure: Núria Güell and Kenneth Pietrobono's Legal Loopholes," examines legal incursions into state sovereignty and private property by the Spanish artist Núria Güell and the Chilean American artist Kenneth Pietrobono. These works investigate, at something of a remove, the system and the institutional structures that make up its economic, legal, and social operations; they read the fine print and work within the confines of the "9 to 5"; they ask big questions about how the system works and test its mechanisms—but mostly from a safe distance. These incursions into corporate and state protocols have a certain conceptual cleanness to them: they settle out of court, they close the box, they do it all with an air of professional discretion. The relative sterility and formality of the opening chapters' parasitical interventions are a function of the institutional nature of their corporate and state hosts and the kind of bureaucratic tactics they make allowable.

In contrast, the artworks in part II deploy more visceral, relentless, and cringe-inducing tactics of parasitical resistance. Embracing parasitism as an emblematic site of feminist aesthetic practice, these works enact a far more aggressive confrontation with the host. They are messier, riskier, more audacious: fewer containment measures are taken, and as a result, they at times suggest an enactment of the parasite that poses real risks to its survival. It is not that the structural problematic or artistic methods are different than those in the first part, but that the targets have moved closer to home—to include the parasite's own romantic attachments and means of financial subsistence. Chapter 3, "Hangers-On: Chris Kraus's Parasitical Feminism," reads the literary motif of correspondence onto the host-parasite dyad by examining epistolary art projects by Chris Kraus (*I Love Dick*, 1997) and Sophie Calle (*Take Care of Yourself*, 2007). These projects engage in practices of viral accumulation, producing hundreds of love letters that stalk, and eventually overwhelm, the male hosts of their projects. Chapter 4, "A Seat at the Table: Feminist Performance Art's Institutional Absorption and Parasitical Legacies," complicates the apparent oppositionality of this sexual warfare by examining an antagonism within feminist aesthetic practice itself. The chapter foregrounds disidentificatory performances by a younger, precarious generation of would-be feminist performance artists, including Ann Liv Young, Anya Liftig, Amber Hawk Swanson, and Lauren Barri Holstein. These artists disidentify with an earlier generation of white liberal feminism, the generation that spawned these artists themselves, by employing a tactics of alienated self-parody and aggressive homage. Finally, in the coda, "It's Not You, It's Me: Roisin Byrne and the Parasite's Shifting Ethics and Politics," I examine the mutual dependence of art and criticism, following a chain of events whereby Roisin Byrne, previously known for stealing and forging the works of well-established male artists, began to steal and forge my scholarship on her art practice. These latter chapters refuse the discretion and propriety that characterized those earlier chapters, a refusal that is markedly feminist and that demands to know: Who gets to remain clean or to keep things hidden behind a screen? Who has the ability to stop the game? These chapters revisit the problem of the corporations' black-boxing of responsibility to show that propriety is also an alibi for privatization and that privacy is a feminist problematic.

The charge of complicity is often a disqualifying accusation marking the end, rather than the beginning, of a conversation about radical action (the inevitable rejoinder "You say you're anticapitalist, but . . ."). When many argue it is precisely at this moment that complicity must be called out and eradicated and that opposition must be at its most pure because to work within the system is to grant it legitimacy, these artists embrace complicity as a strategic opportunity for resistance. To be made complicit, as the word's etymology attests, is to be embraced, welcomed, folded in.[75] Our relentlessly accommodating neoliberal moment, which leverages individuals' structural dependence on large-scale informational and institutional powers, demands not a simple binary understanding of complicity (complicit/not complicit = bad/good) but a complex understanding, able to take the measure of a vastly asymmetrical and relational field of responsibility.[76] The autonomous individual (implicitly raced and gendered as white and cis male), imbued with the capacity for consent or refusal on which traditional conceptions of radical action are based, has progressively been replaced by a fragmented quasi-subject embedded in a system of hegemonic power and exploitation.[77] The purity and idealism implied by the political and ethical frameworks of intention and agency based on the notion of the liberal subject (a category from which so many have been excluded) no longer align with the ever more diffuse and improvisational expressions of neoliberal power. The rise of the network as a dominant cultural form, Patrick Jagoda has argued, can lead to a sense of despair, since it posits that everything is interconnected and "makes scarcely imaginable the possibility of an alternative or an outside uninflected by networks."[78] Users and citizens are interpellated as subjects who have the ability to be ethical and moral—and are financially, legally, and juridically held accountable for being so—while at the same time we are profiled and managed algorithmically within big data regimes that are indifferent to our subjective will.[79] For example, systems of data collection, as Finn Brunton and Helen Nissenbaum observe, are "still theoretically voluntary" but

> the costs of refusal are high and getting higher: a life lived in ramifying social isolation . . . [with] only very particular forms of employment, living far from centers of business and commerce, without access to many forms of credit, insurance, or other significant financial instruments, not to mention the minor inconveniences and disadvantages—long waits at

road toll cash lines, higher prices at grocery stores, inferior seating on airline flights—for which disclosure is the unspecified price. It isn't possible for everyone to live on principle; as a practical matter, many of us must make compromises in asymmetrical relationships, without the control or consent for which we might wish.[80]

But even as this book explores the possibilities opened up by short-circuiting the idea that complicity is the opposite of resistance—that in order to challenge domination, minor actors must be unimplicated—it should not be misunderstood as a celebration of complicity. To the contrary, the book traces how hegemonic entities routinely excuse themselves by accusing others of complicity, by presenting the compromised actions of individuals as commensurate with their own, much more impactful and damaging actions. Discussions of the catastrophic implications of climate change, for instance, routinely interpellate all actors, regardless of their actual habits of consumption, as equally responsible for the overdeveloped capitalist world's dependence on fossil fuels.[81] The tactical complicity of the parasite thus follows work by Anna Lowenhaupt Tsing, Alexis Shotwell, Donna Haraway, and Jagoda, who have called for a new ethical ground of implication that relinquishes purity, an ethics of "justice without progress," a politics of "staying with the trouble" and "learning to inhabit a compromised environment."[82] "To be against purity," Shotwell writes, "is to start from an understanding of our implication in this compromised world."[83] Rather than console ourselves with the redemptive narrative offered by an imagined outside, this book examines what it could mean to inhabit embeddedness as the ground for a nonproprietary ethics.

These artworks offer no definitive answers, and likewise, my own study does not propose anything such as a solution—a deus ex machina, an escape from the inescapable condition with which it tries to reckon.[84] Rather, it advances parasitism as a necessary critical category for understanding the latent or unspoken political stakes of artistic projects of resistance not otherwise recognizable as such. The book's aim is neither to promote nor to denounce parasitism—to deliver judgment on whether it is good or bad—but to critically assess its new visibility as a compromised praxis of resistance in the field of contemporary art and interventionism. The book both develops a theory of parasitical resistance and weighs the risks of this gambit. It reads the ethical purchase of these works within the frame of feminist and queer studies scholarship that theorizes agency under nonemancipatory and nonteleological conditions. As the promise of freedom or an emancipatory outside has been shown to be an effective instrument of control, parasitical artworks eschew historical leftist benchmarks based on autonomy and oppositionality. If this form of interventionism holds subversive potential, it is a subversive potential that is necessarily compromised from the start.

PARASITICAL RESISTANCE AND ITS CHALLENGES TO CRITIQUE

Even as it poses new possibilities for our moment, parasitical intervention blurs the line of what constitutes resistance. How can one evaluate—let alone hold accountable—a form of resistance possible only for those subjects already afforded leverage within the system? If everyone is now complicit by virtue of the scale of neoliberal capitalism's coercive hospitality, is there any way to differentiate between degrees and forms of complicity? At times parasitism opens up clear forms of resistance; at other times it serves less as a strategy of subversion and solidarity than as a screen or alibi for active forms of bad faith and further exploitation. But the parasite is always a compromised figure. What criteria, then, can be used to assess not only parasitism's effectiveness as a mode of resistance but also its ethical implications?

Parasitism represents an intensification of the turn to immanent critique in 1990s and 2000s tactical art, media, and activism as it has given rise to ever more ethically and politically ambiguous styles of resistance; in their embeddedness and enduringness, parasitical interventions differ from tactical art and media's more punctual incursions.[85] Rather than causing a momentary disruption, the parasite nests within the host. Parasitism has no clear limits, no absolutely discernible beginning or end. Its constitutive ambivalence and complicity with the host cannot easily be resolved or wished away. This enduringness is the unique temporality of the parasite: its inevitable subsumption provides the ground for future planning.

But, because of its abiding temporality and ambiguous character, conventional critical methods and principles can initially appear to falter on their encounter with the parasite. The parasite's embeddedness and enduringness pose clear challenges to criticism's customary investment in externality and stability—objectivity, critical distance, and detachment—and its reliance on binaries (the word *criticism* deriving from the Greek *krinein*, meaning "to decide," "to cut"). For traditional critical methods to activate the parasite's potential, they must be able to ascertain its political intentions and effects. Therein lies the rub: in order to realize its political potential, as I have argued, the parasite can never appear to the host to be a fully coherent agent. Parasitism traffics in indeterminacy and is a paradigm that is necessarily immanent and nonbinary. The parasite's political potential thus lies in and depends on precisely what makes it so evasive to criticism.

But the parasite need not pose an insurmountable impasse for criticism. Rather it offers an opportunity to reassess criticism's historical attachment to the autonomous subject—to clearly recognizable and stable political positions and to legal and moral value systems based on propriety and private property that code payment and protocols of authorization as inherently moral—as grounds for making ethical and political judgments. These traditional critical attachments do not account for how the ethics and politics of the parasite are necessarily conditioned by the host. While we may not easily be able to draw boundaries around the parasitical agent or work or determine with certainty the ethical and political intentions of the parasitical act, this does not mean that we cannot make claims about the ethical and political valences of a parasitical work of art. Parasitical resistance emerges in response to the pervasive sense that the epistemology of exposure is no longer an efficient engine of political change in a neoliberal information economy in which it has become painfully obvious that knowledge does not equal power. While the act of critical exposure is not the solution, it nonetheless remains an important political tool; however, it is one tool among others. As a work of criticism, this book remains invested in the act of critical exposure, if not in the belief that knowing will necessarily facilitate concrete change, then as a tool for glimpsing the subversive charge of artworks that will not or cannot themselves avow their political efficacy or potential. Parasitism calls for methods for reading a performance of hegemonic power that cannot be unmasked by a discourse of truth. It demands political tools that are not absolute or predictable but relative and improvisational, pragmatic and situated, that are responsive to a dynamic ecology of relations in which there is no "once and for all" answer but highly contingent and conditional thresholds, loopholes, and openings that might yield more transparent, redistributive, and equitable relations among people, institutions, and systems.

While the parasite must be careful not to show its hand, the critic can (and where possible, must) still read for its political and ethical intentions without falling back on a model of criticism based upon discerning a fully coherent intentional subject. (Some parasites have tells. Certain parasites, for instance, signal their criticality by employing irony; a wry or camp sensibility permeates many of these works.) In my analysis, intention—how did the artist *feel* toward their chosen target?—remains a significant factor in how I understand the politics of the work. It *matters* that Ubermorgen at least articulated a critical stance toward Amazon rather than admiring Amazon and wanting to be bought out by it; it *matters* that Byrne signaled her work as a critical statement about gendered authorship and legitimacy, as opposed to being hostile toward Hendricks for other reasons.

But because the parasite's intention is always at least partially effaced, and thereby cannot be ascertained with absolute certainty, the task of the critic is to adjudicate the parasite's political and ethical efficacy primarily by other means. This means adopting a mode of reading that prioritizes effect over intention. Much as Eve Kosofsky Sedgwick called for the recognition of the limits of the epistemology of exposure, introducing the reparative complement she calls "weak theory," I propose two provisional criteria for assessing the ethics and politics of parasitical works whose intentions cannot be fully known.[86] These criteria map onto the two halves of the book: the work's *redistributive effects* and its *disruptive charge*. The redistributive effects of parasitical works refer to their ability to recirculate what they take from the host beyond the parasite's own interest and in solidarity with similarly or more precarious others—to work against privatization, to open hosts' black boxes and disseminate the material, symbolic, or conceptual resources stashed therein. The disruptive charge is the work's ability to impose on and make visceral the host's hypocritical instrumentalization of openness so as to compel it to host the parasitical work, effectively turning the host's words and actions against it. Whether the parasite is resistant ultimately depends on whether the effects of its redistribution or disruption positively outweighs the cost of its original act of complicity.

While these criteria can be complementary with each other, they can also be directly opposed. In order to have a disruptive charge, a parasitical intervention has to call attention to itself in some way; conversely (as we see in the cases of Ubermorgen's *Amazon Noir* and Rakowitz's *paraSITE*), evading attention and remaining invisible for as long as possible can be necessary for the artwork's redistributive effects to be maximized. Moreover because the artists seek to support themselves through their art, they have a material interest in their works being recognized that can impede the more furtive dimensions of parasitism. Insofar as these works facilitate their own exposure via protocols of exhibition and promotion, their visibility raises questions about how much more effective the project would have been (for others, not necessarily the artists themselves) had they kept it quiet for longer and enabled more people to benefit from them. And yet by not being visible enough, by not explicitly appealing to their host-patron's public images, they might have been shut down earlier and even more decisively.

Whether particular deployments of complicity will be put to redistributive or self-serving ends cannot be known in advance. The works examined in this book are not didactic, and they are rarely exemplary; they largely avoid being consigned to any single aesthetic category or critical or political position. My investment in these works, moreover, is neither one of fan nor apologist. It is not a matter of *liking* these works, many of which have been described by critics as unlikeable or unsavory, for they are largely uninterested in formal concerns or aesthetic pleasure; rather it is a matter of contending with their critical force. These works invest in art as, rather than a formal medium, a blunt tool for accomplishing a particular objective. While the book's methods are feminist, the works themselves are not necessarily feminist or even progressive. While the parasite can be critically and politically useful, it is only a temporary vector, a moment of possibility: when it finishes its work, it is no longer a parasite.

Moreover the parasite's and critic's investments are not necessarily aligned. During the course of writing the book, it became clear that my own investment in a feminist and anticapitalist mode of criticism was undermined by certain parasites' self-serving opportunism or self-destructive drive. As the chapters develop, there are progressively more moments when the parasite's personal interests and risky tactics exceed my critical containment measures and escape my grasp. As I was writing the book, several of the artists began to respond to, contest, and even plagiarize previously published chapters' characterizations of their practices as parasitical. Kraus challenged the charge in an earlier published version of chapter 3 that she was dependent on her then-husband's press, Semiotext(e). Byrne, by adopting the terms of my analysis of her work, would compel me to reassess my initial optimism about her deployment of parasitism, as I explore in the coda. These works initiated a certain call and response between scholarly work and experimental practice, with the artists' responses effectively breaking the fourth wall of the project's conceptualization of parasitism. Their responses crystallized in artistic practice my efforts to theorize the parasitical relation from which there is no safe retreat. These moments forced me to recognize my implication in my attempts to immunize myself against the parasite's work—to manage, to suppress, or to redirect certain parasites' manifestly unethical or volatile charge. This is where the act of criticism shows its hand. The book thus explores the tension between the progressive critical possibilities of the parasite and its artistic applications. In its metaconceptual framing, this book interrogates the dissolving boundaries between criticism and practice in a digital era of instantaneous circulation and appropriation, in which critics are never only purely reactive but also participate in constituting the meaning of the work.

These works are not radical but parasitical. The parasite's appearance of acquiescence is the condition of possibility for trafficking in something different when it wouldn't otherwise be possible, perhaps even something radical. But the parasite remains a dangerous figure on which to base a politics. There are no guarantees against its mechanisms. Just as these artworks can subvert and siphon the power of their hosts, they can also fortify them. Far from a replacement for direct action, the parasite is a politics of last resort. And precisely because it flatters and mirrors the system, it cannot easily be identified, unlike oppositional art practices where the mask is eventually taken off. There is no revelatory epiphany, no happy ending—yet the parasite is neither a nihilistic nor merely cynical actor. It demands a different metrics: a wider lens, a determination to account for the coercive and asymmetrical structures that attend contemporary conceptions of choice and agency, a form of critique attentive to dynamics of scale and economy. But for all its limitations, the parasite cannot be judged in isolation because it always carries with it the system that conditions its existence in the first place.

INTERLUDE
THRESHOLDS OF ACCOMMODATION

Not all parasites are equally equipped for survival, just as not all subjects are charged with the same potential for resistance. Before proceeding further, it is necessary to address more systematically the privilege or capital that is presupposed by parasitical resistance in this book. Which parasitical subjects can play the system or afford to resist in spaces of domination? Why are some minoritarian subjects granted the accommodation necessary for acts of resistance and others are not? To answer these questions, we must first define more clearly the conditions of the host's hospitality.

Hospitality, as I advance it in this book, is a paternalistic logic of administration that distributes and controls access under the guise of care. The host presides over an economy of dependency—*economia* deriving from the Greek οικονομία, designating the rules by which a household is managed. The host carves up and allocates resources at its pleasure within the symbolic economy of the home, setting the terms of belonging for all who enter. The host's regulation of access has the effect of making less powerful subjects reliant on it for their survival. Digital platforms are key to understanding the consolidation of this logic under neoliberal networked capitalism (what I call *coercive hospitality*), as there have become ever sharper distinctions between those with capital and those shut out from it with the rise of leviathan-like monopolies and the concentration of individual capital in the winner-take-all postcrisis economy. In this contemporary political economy, the inviting rhetoric of openness, access, and sharing has been used as a strategy of domination, harnessed to secure and further the dominion of already powerful entities, while such entities efface the authority that confers power upon them. This book starts from the example of digital corporate platforms' wide-scale privatization of access and proceeds to trace how this infrastructural logic of privatization works across a range of other relationships and milieus also founded on the principles of ownership (private capital, private property, personal privacy, patronage, and legacy). It explores how the *host-parasite* relation plays out in the dependent relations of the *digital platform–user* (chapter 1), *state-immigrant* (chapter 2), *man-woman* (chapter 3), and *institution–contingent laborer* (chapter 4). As these various iterations of dependent relations attest, there is a substantial gradient within the category of the parasite: the category includes those relatively privileged minoritarian subjects who can afford to test the host's generosity and those who, by doing so, risk their very survival.

It is crucial, then, to examine more closely the thresholds of accommodation that determine the differential risk faced by minoritarian subjects who are not all equally equipped to gain access to and resist the host system. In this interlude I differentiate three logics that demarcate the provisional limits of the host system: the *threshold of detection, threshold of tolerance,* and *threshold of care* (table Interlude.1). Minoritarian subjects are not all precarious in the same way, either in degree or kind; these thresholds help elaborate the differential tactics and frequency of risk by which the conditions of dependency are enforced, survived, and negotiated. The threshold of accommodation is not a strict line of demarcation but a margin below which something is not perceived. Like a line, a threshold has a discriminating function, but by virtue of its spatial logic it has slightly more allowance—it is something that can be played. It is by working these thresholds, by staying below the limen of detection (or, if detected, by dissimulating their presence or appealing to the host's interests or sense of its own magnanimity), that parasites are accommodated by a system that claims neither to want nor need them.

UNACCOMMODATED PARASITES: THE THRESHOLD OF DETECTION

The threshold of detection speaks to the disruptive or dissident possibilities of the parasite that has not yet been detected by the host. We find an illustration of this in Ralph Ellison's 1952 novel, *Invisible Man*, in which the unnamed black protagonist describes finding ways of leveraging "the advantages of being invisible," such as stealing electricity and living rent-free in the forgotten basement of a building rented only to whites.[1] Within the threshold of detection, the parasite temporarily harnesses a mode of social invisibility

TABLEINTERLUDE1 THREE THRESHOLDS OF ACCOMMODATION

THRESHOLD OF DETECTION

Not yet detected as a parasite; either alterity passes as similarity or has effect of social invisibility.

*High-risk tactic

REPRESENTATIVE FIGURE
The so-called stranger or foreigner unknown to the host.

LIMEN OF DETECTION

*If detected and perceived as an *outside threat,* the parasite is subject to violent expulsion from host system.

THRESHOLD OF TOLERANCE

Parasite detected but perceived as so minor a threat as not to warrant the expenditure it would take for the host to expel it.

Parasite is barely accommodated. Calculus of accommodation is predominantly (but not exclusively) economic, and parasite is subject to regular scrutiny; parasite construed as *outsider-guest.*

REPRESENTATIVE FIGURES
Those nonintimate dependents deemed necessary to host: servants, foreigners known to the host (those of a lower social order).

THRESHOLD OF CARE

Parasite detected; difference is perceptible, and even potentially harmful, but parasite performs function of propping the host's self-image as compassionate and caring.

Calculus of accommodation is predominantly social, one of keeping up appearances; parasite construed as *insider-guest.*

REPRESENTATIVE FIGURES
Intimates, dependents on the host: women, children, friends (those of the same social order).

(in this case, a mode that is a paradoxical consequence of the black body's hypervisibility) as a tactical advantage. Ellison's novel, Hortense J. Spillers argues, transfigures blackness from "a condition of physiognomy" into a symbolic strategy ("Under the 'laws' of this novel, the game of 'blackness' . . . came home, as it were, right between the ears, as the glittering weapon of an 'invisible' field of choice").[2] "I am one of the most irresponsible beings that ever lived," claims the Invisible Man. "Irresponsibility is part of my invisibility. . . . But to whom can I be responsible and why should I be, when you refuse to see me? Responsibility rests upon recognition, and recognition is a form of agreement."[3] With the undercommons, Fred Moten and Stefano Harney update this black aesthetic practice of invisibility to theorize the hidden underground, "the downlow low-down maroon community," of minoritarian collectivity and resource sharing through which marginalized subjects defy the systemic violence of institutional life.[4] Ellison's articulation further resonates with Simone Browne's account of how the ineluctable glare of mass surveillance and biometric technologies operates on and through black bodies.[5] It also speaks to minoritarian, black, queer, and/or trans politico-aesthetic projects of invisibility, undetectability, and countersurveillance, such as Finn Brunton and Helen Nissenbaum have described as "obfuscation," Shaka McGlotten as "black data," Zach Blas as "informatic opacity," and Toby Beauchamp as "going stealth."[6]

Playing the threshold of detection is a particularly risky operation for black, brown, trans, queer, indigenous, and/or migrant subjects for whom the system's sanctions are disproportionately higher: for those perceived as outside threats and who if detected are vulnerable to violent expulsion from the host system, for the threshold of detection presents that subject as a *stranger*.[7] This representation of the parasite is deeply racialized and ethnicized.[8] Typically such a parasite is perceived as having infiltrated the host system by crossing a border. For parasites that are called "terrorist" or "illegal alien," this border is a national one, while the Invisible Man's "intrusion" into a building rented only to whites conjures instead the crossing of a racial border. The parasite represented as a stranger is construed as a threat to the "purity" and coherence of the body politic, "a hostile invader of the host nation or group." As a structure of speech, the epithet *parasite*, which connotes an excess or supplement, attempts to establish a strict partition demarcating inside from outside.[9] This immunological trope is taken up in racist and xenophobic discourses to call for the securing of borders (the borders of the body, the family, the community, or the nation) by vanquishing what is supposedly other to it. A trope of nationalist propaganda, the language of parasitism exacerbates lines of fracture (job insecurity, anti-immigrant sentiment) to stoke social antagonisms for political gain. In its extreme expression in totalitarian propaganda, the discourse of parasitism represents certain groups as less than human ("vermin," "pests") and thus as susceptible to extermination—a rhetoric that, as Roberto Esposito has argued, was part of the Nazis' "epidemiological repertoire," which referred to Jews as "bacteria," "viruses," and "microbes" that must be eradicated for the health of the nation.[10]

The ability to be perceivable as socially unmarked within the host system is thus less accessible to visible minoritarian subjects: dark-skinned racial and ethnic minorities, non-gender-conforming and visible religious minorities, among others, who necessarily operate at a different threshold of visibility and identification in relation to power. But even those minoritarian subjects who hold "the dubious honor of being largely invisible or unreadable" (light-skinned racial and ethnic minorities, gender-conforming homosexuals, certain religious minorities, etc.) are rarely at home in spaces of passing.[11] Indeed, for many racial, ethnic, and sexual minorities, the strategy of performing complicity, even when it is possible, holds little appeal. "With their commitments to conflict and antagonism as consciousness-raising and revolutionary ideals," Rachel C. Lee has shown, "postcolonial and race studies often regard as suspect an ethics that endorses hospitality (alternately, caretaking) across conditions where parties refuse to or cannot recognize their reciprocity and interdependence."[12]

ACCOMMODATED PARASITES: THE THRESHOLD OF TOLERANCE AND THE THRESHOLD OF CARE

Unlike the threshold of detection, which construes the parasite as a stranger, the threshold of tolerance and the threshold of care construe the parasite as a *guest*. Both of these thresholds speak to the conditions under which the host will knowingly accommodate certain parasites. These accounts explicitly highlight how the terms of accommodation are shaped by those of paternalistic domination. In her feminist account of hospitality, Tracy McNulty explains:

> *Potis* names the master of the home, the one who makes the law in the house—the *casa*. As master of the house, he is also master of all of the subordinates who make up the household (servants, slaves, and dependent women), as well as the livestock or chattel that form his personal

property. The Greek *despótes* (lord, despot) and its Latin equivalent, *dominus*, represent the extension of domestic authority into the field of social and symbolic power; both terms designate the "head of the clan," as well as the "lord" or "possessor"—the one who has power over and is able to dispose of his subjects.[13]

In this schema (one that is based on a heteropatriarchal slave economy), servants, slaves, and dependent women (not to mention cattle) are lumped together into a generalized minoritarian class of "dependents." Compared to those subjects without freedom ("marked" with a ring around the neck), the wife, children, friends, and other loved ones of the head of the household enjoy a form of protection in ownership as "unmarked" subjects. But even their limited or provisional agency can at any moment be taken away at the behest of the master. They are both inside and out, equal and not. "As a model of social order, the patriarchal family depended upon duty, status, and protection rather than consent, equality, and civil freedom," Saidiya Hartman affirms. "Subjection was not only naturalized but also consonant with the sentimental equality of reciprocity, inasmuch as the power of affection licensed the strength of weakness. Essentially, 'the strength of weakness' prevailed due to the goodness of the father, 'The armor of affection and benevolence.'"[14] Within this plantation logic, dependents' access to resources for survival varies greatly according to the logic of their possession by the master of the house. The two categories of dependents—*protected* and *unprotected*—signal a divergence in the paternalistic logics of hospitality. Some dependents (nonintimates or foreigners) are barely accommodated or accommodated according to a calculus based on economic or other strategic factors (*threshold of tolerance*), while others—intimates such as dependent women, children, friends—are accommodated to the extent that they prop up the host's need to be regarded as generous (*threshold of care*).

Whereas Ellison's Invisible Man attests to the cost of detection for some racialized subjects, the films *Six Degrees of Separation* (1993) and *Get Out* (2017) explore how some hosts occasionally accommodate racial difference (and the perceived dangers represented to both parties by such an alliance of strategic inclusion). In both of these films, a young black male protagonist gets in the door by fulfilling a white liberal fantasy of assimilated blackness. By incorporating the figure of the young black male into the white traditional family home, the white liberal host is able to rationalize their self-image as inclusive and progressive. Riding the line of the thresholds of tolerance and care, these examples speak to the selective, tokenistic inclusion of certain racial and ethnic minorities—for example, the so-called model minority, endowed with a preferred status, and other exceptional subjects who are allotted a seat at the table while others are left outside the room.[15]

A POINT OF VULNERABILITY: THE THRESHOLD OF CARE

As these thresholds show, there are a number of stories that can be told about the parasite-host relation; I am telling only one of these. The parasitical performances I explore in this book fall under the threshold of care. The artists I examine, almost all of whom have been threatened with legal action that was ultimately not pursued, dodge culpability by tapping into the plausible deniability that is afforded by the ambiguous legal, ethical, and moral status of digital technology, art, and performance.[16]

But more crucially, parasites locate a point of vulnerability in the host's (disavowed) need of its parasites: the host's need to believe it is magnanimous, or to be perceived as magnanimous by those dependents it cares or professes to care about. Given the contingency of the host's authority, the parasite can play on the host's need to be reassured that it has the affection and approval of those it dominates: the master who wants to be a "good guy," the boss who wants his jokes to be laughed at, the patron who expects his beneficiaries to kiss the proverbial ring. Following Michel Feher, who traces neoliberalism's paternalistic and patriarchal logic back to chivalry and the gift economy built into the feudal relation, I argue that the parasite takes advantage of the host's investment in maintaining *the public appearance* of equal footing; this is particularly true in an era when state and corporate largesse (strategic diversity, corporate responsibility, state diplomacy) are calibrated according to the optics of risk and brand reputation management.[17] The parasite effectively traps the host in the contradiction between the host's public values and private actions. The parasite compels the host to accommodate it by harnessing the host's desire not to appear hypocritical.

Some artists in the book play the threshold of care by seizing the advantage afforded by their technical expertise or know-how (Ubermorgen, Robin Hood Cooperative) and others by leveraging the intimate access to power provided by citizenship (Güell) or social standing within the affluent queer community (Pietrobono). Still others (Kraus, Calle) weaponize the dubious privilege and chivalrous protection afforded to femininity, as Byrne does with Hendricks. By performing heterosexual white femininity as a means of lateral access, a kind of Trojan horse, these artists reanimate fierce historical debates about complicity in feminist and antiracist criticism. The complicit status of white femininity, long an integral and complex site for propping up the project of white supremacist patriarchy, is raised in particular by these works.[18] White women's "assumed delicacy and helplessness" has been a favorite alibi of white supremacy, serving as the historical justification for centuries of antiblack violence.[19] Femininity benefits from the economic and social protection of patriarchal structures, much as, Frank B. Wilderson has shown, whiteness necessarily feeds on the spoils of white supremacy. "Whiteness is parasitic," Wilderson writes, "because it monumentalizes its subjective capacity, its lush cartography, in direct proportion to the wasteland of Black incapacity."[20]

However, these artists wield whiteness and/or femininity, positioned at the nexus of straightness and middle-class-ness, not as identities but as performative tools and tactics of complicity that afford them access to and protections within the inner sanctums of power. Roisin Byrne, Núria Güell, Chris Kraus, and Sophie Calle embrace feminine archetypes of the clingy female admirer, the plus one, the vampiristic hanger-on. Under the threshold of care, these parasitical intimates of the host operate a kind of counterpassing. While passing is typically understood as moving from stranger to guest, they invert that dynamic, shifting from guest to stranger. In this move, those subjects who are most perceived as docile and nonthreatening, and who are most likely to be welcomed as guests, are instead (slowly) revealed to be strangers—parasites. This tactic of parasitism hinges in part on the gradual character of this estrangement and the strategic possibilities opened up by its delayed recognition.

As a tactic of the more privileged, parasitism can represent a means of owning and subverting one's complicity; it can represent an alternative to what can often amount to the platitudes and false innocence of allyship. By mobilizing whiteness and femininity not as fixed identities but as complicit modalities, these artists hold out the possibility for a strategic disidentification with their own privilege—one that might be used to forge a kind of solidarity with those who, by virtue of their positions in relation to the host, must mobilize their parasitism differently.

While my discussions of the artworks depart from the thresholds of accommodation I set up here, this framework remains an essential analytic for conceptualizing the social politics of interventionism that in discussions of tactical art and media too often relies on the notion of a universal subject of capitalism, ignoring or leaving undeveloped the gendered, raced, sexualized dimensions of the subject and the system under discussion. One of the book's organizing questions—What does one's position allow one to get away with and what forms of resistance can that latitude facilitate?—examines how the parasite's accommodation is conditioned by the racial, gender, and class privilege that subtends the very possibility of parasitical resistance, for these axes of visibility and identification determine the amount of play that is possible in systems of white heteropatriarchal neoliberal control.

PART I

REDISTRIBUTION INSTITUTIONAL INTERVENTIONS

ONE USER BE USED

LEVERAGING THE COERCIVE HOSPITALITY OF CORPORATE PLATFORMS

Let us begin with what is for many today the most recognizable—if also the most invisible—example of the privatization of openness: the big tech platform. The platform economy is paradigmatic of the logic of consolidated power and one-way accountability that this book examines. Big tech platforms capture the underlying architecture of coercive hospitality, wherein corporate technologies sold as enabling access and sharing contain hidden costs borne by the user. Such technologies have helped an ever-narrowing number of monopolies accrue power and influence by concealing their authority. Megacorporations like Google and Amazon have presented themselves as hospitable services—as mere hosts and intermediaries, mere "platforms"—to gain sway over the market, extracting user data and amassing capital, even as they are increasingly unanswerable to users, workers, and governments. The term *platform* suggests a progressive and fair arrangement that promises to support those who rely on it. Mobilizing the rhetoric of democracy in order to privatize public goods and services, these monopolies use the appearance of openness to facilitate closedness—fueling inequality, killing off competition, and limiting opportunities for workers and local communities.

This chapter examines how global corporations have also gotten in on the act, as companies like Walmart and McDonald's have borrowed this playbook. More specifically, the chapter investigates how these companies have sought to adopt for themselves the image of digital technology as neutral and egalitarian in order to obscure their ever more predatorial business practices, as they have invented new methods for making the poor pay (literally) for their own immiseration. By embracing the rhetoric and affect of the digital, by presenting themselves as virtual (rather than a physical presence) and their actions as automated (rather than strategic calculations), these corporations have made it harder for workers and consumers to challenge them or to build a lasting grassroots response to their impacts.[1] When threatened with exposure for manipulating the appearance of hospitality to exploitative ends, these corporations adopt the appearance of network protocol (the neutral authority of the faceless administrator) to sidestep accountability for their actions.

Corporate monopolies' wish to appear caring, charitable, and accessible need not be a subjective desire but may be an economic calculation; the question is not the cause of their performance of hospitality but its effects and the ends to which it is used. Can this pretense of openness be turned against them? To answer this question, I look to a series of artistic and social collectivist experiments that test the possibility of using the market's supposed openness to bend the arc of privatization instead toward recommunalization and redistribution. These experiments include Robin Hood Cooperative's "Parasite" algorithm (which mirrors the investment patterns of the most successful traders on Wall Street) and Ubermorgen's *Google Will Eat Itself* (2005–8), made in collaboration with Alessandro Ludovico and Paolo Cirio. Whether they aim at divesting from finance or platform capitalism using the stock market or attempting to take down Google using its own advertising revenue (or, in another, similar effort, to buy Kickstarter using Kickstarter), these parasitical works model how performances of exaggerated complicity might open up new political scripts. Ubermorgen and Robin Hood Cooperative employ imitative tactics in order to siphon resources from the data economy and redirect them toward social groups or causes that seek to "rebuild the commons." By literally investing in the very structures that they seek to dismantle, these works model the parasite as a political actor with the potential to harness platform capitalism to different ends, if with largely ambiguous results and symbolic returns.

AN OPEN PLATFORM

The platform is but a recent variant of digital capitalism's long-standing investment in the rhetoric of openness. The digital's much-touted virtue of openness—its collapse of hierarchy, explosion of secrecy, democratization of knowledge—is central to how the medium has been defined from its inception. Sold as "the great equalizer" enabling circulation and free access to information for all, the early internet—the network—heralded a brave new world of viral circulation, even as it was used to overstate both the equalizing effects of circulation and the reciprocity of exchange, as if speed alone could lubricate democracy or level socioeconomic disparity. With the privatization of the internet in the mid-1990s (placing the once public project in the hands of corporations), the rhetoric of openness and access, as Wendy Hui Kyong Chun has shown, served to grease the wheels of capital in the name of democracy.[2] This rhetoric advanced a false equivalency between individual users and corporate actors, addressing all "users"—states, corporations, and individuals alike—as commensurate nodes within the network.

Yet, as Andrew L. Russell argues, the digital's constitutive "openness" is in fact deeply ideological, for it redefines access for commercial ends: "For individuals, 'open' is shorthand for transparent, welcoming, participatory, and entrepreneurial; for society at large, 'open' signifies a vast increase in the flow of goods and information through a global, market-oriented system of exchange. In the most general sense, it conveys independence from the threats of arbitrary power and centralized control."[3] And yet this form of power and control is precisely what this rhetoric is used to install. "When a new app is said to be democratizing something—whether robotic personal assistants or sepia-toned selfies," argues Nathan Schneider, "it means allowing more people to access that something. Just access, along with a big, fat terms of service. Gone are those old associations of town meetings and voting booths; gone are co-ownership, co-governance, and accountability."[4] The celebrated openness of the digital, Astra Taylor points out, rather than serving as a leveling force, amplifies already existing disparities. "Online, just as off-line, attention and influence largely accrue to those who already have plenty of both," she writes. Big media have thus given way "not [to] a revolution but a rearrangement" in which "giants like Amazon, Apple, Google, and Facebook remain the gatekeepers" and "the new order looks suspiciously like the old one."[5] What is perhaps new is the mask of egalitarianism. Taylor observes that this rhetorical ploy is often wielded in ways that sidestep "discussions of ownership and equity": "While openness has many virtues, it is also undeniably ambiguous. Is open a means or an end? What is open and to whom? Mark Zuckerberg said he designed Facebook because he wanted to make the world more 'open and connected,' but his company does everything it can to keep users within its confines and exclusively retains the data they emit."[6]

More recently big media corporations' adoption of the strategic position of the platform has demonstrated their use of openness as a tool of skillful misdirection. As Tarleton Gillespie has shown, the term is a "discursive resting point" employed by corporations to subtly but meaningfully recalibrate their responsibility to others. According to Gillespie, these entities selectively perform their agency: they present themselves as a valuable service in some moments and as a mere platform in others. When companies position themselves as platforms—as simply accommodating the activity of others—they are able to monetize content without having to be liable for it.[7] Nick Srnicek elaborates: "While often presenting themselves as empty spaces for others to interact on, they in fact embody a politics. The rules of the product and service development, as well as marketplace interactions, are set by the platform owner. Uber, despite presenting itself as an empty vessel for market forces, shapes the appearance of the market. . . . In their position as an intermediary, platforms gain not only access to more data but also control and governance over the rules of the game."[8] We can see this active positioning when Google and Facebook executives speak, for example, about their role in policy and legislative matters as being those of mere hosts, conduits, or carriers of content, as opposed to publishers. They present themselves as neither promoting nor championing the content they disseminate, and therefore as not liable for offensive, dangerous, or hateful material that might appear on their platform.[9]

What distinguishes the platform model from the traditional, transactional business model is the posture by which, despite the visible presence of site-based advertising (not to mention other invisible forms of marketing), these corporations insist on their role as hosts rather than users in their own right. (While companies like Facebook, Google, Airbnb, and Uber are the most commonly cited examples of platforms, Walmart and others increasingly also position themselves as platforms, pioneering supply-chain management practices that do not buy products but effectively contract with suppliers to rent shelf space, paying their contractors only for the items that sell.)[10] Such platforms position themselves as hosts, providing infrastructure and facilitating interaction, while at the same time nontransparently monetizing the data they acquire through these services.

One might call the platform economy a parasitical outgrowth of the postcrisis era. It has been suggested that the 2008 global financial crisis was "a key enabling condition" for the rise of the platform economy.[11] The neoliberal advancement of deregulation, privatization, the unraveling of the public sector, a low interest rate climate for venture capital, and high levels of unemployment (leaving behind a precarious class of workers with few protections), as Srnicek and Gary Hall have shown, helped companies like

Airbnb and Uber become unavoidable almost overnight.[12] Operating on a postwelfare model of capitalism, these companies repackage hospitality as rent. They turn acts of generosity like ridesharing and couch-surfing into commodities. Writes Hall:

> In the case of Uber and Airbnb . . . these assets take the form of seats in vehicles and rooms in properties that are otherwise occupied on an infrequent and temporary basis. In other words, they are idle resources it has up to now been difficult for capital to commodify and whose value from an entrepreneurial point of view has therefore been wasted. . . . Even if this form of economy is presented as a revival of community spirit, it actually has very little to do with *sharing* this access to goods, activities, and services and everything to do with *selling* this access. (Many people insist on referring to it not as the sharing economy but as the *renting economy* for just this reason.)[13]

While Airbnb and Uber sell hospitality as rent, Facebook and Google purport to provide it for free. They overstate the individual user's agency by downplaying the platform's authority to set the terms and conditions of use: the companies sell themselves as free services and insist that online subjects are their equals, counterparts able *to use and be used equally*, all while quietly transforming the content and information produced by such usage into data sold for enormous profit. Facebook boasts, "It's free and always will be"; Google, as Siva Vaidhyanathan points out, accepts no money for the algorithmic labor it performs to give the appearance of simplicity to the messy work of sorting and ranking search results.[14] The pervasive rhetoric of the online "user" does similar work for the seductive fiction that digital technologies are hospitable by quietly flattening and neutralizing ethical and political distinctions and placing practices of consumption and participation alongside those of exploitation. The narrative of user empowerment is at best incomplete. These rhetorical sleights of hand intentionally muddy the question of *who is in control*—of who is a *host* and who is a *guest*—and the precarity of the latter position (the terms of use serve not the user but the corporation).

Yet increasingly, digital corporate platforms are an invitation that cannot be refused. More and more our relationships with corporate and state entities are predetermined by contracts that shift legal and ethical responsibility onto individual users, consumers, and citizens. To participate online is to find oneself tacitly or automatically conscripted into a larger matrix of control.[15] As Vaidhyanathan argues of Google's "choice architecture," the choice to "opt out" can mean very little when, simply "by accepting the invitation to participate, the user finds him or herself implicitly engaged in a contract that is subject to ongoing modification without warning and whose terms can only ever be accepted or declined."[16] There is, to borrow a phrase from Theodor Adorno and Max Horkheimer, "no mechanism of reply"—at least not if the answer is no.[17] Without the capacity to respond, to negotiate, users find themselves subject to the will of a system of social control and power. Even those users in the Global North for whom internet access is a given are all too aware, Vaidhyanathan notes, that it is not a privilege that can be forgone, for it would mean being shut out from a valued, even indispensable service.

Such is the coercive hospitality of platform capitalism, whereby the very terms of participation (as use) are premised on accepting an invitation that can be declined only at significant cost, if at all. The rhetoric of the user, wherein to be a digital citizen is to participate as a user in a community of users, compels a reappraisal of the ideological work of use. The nomination *user* (unlike *guest*) suggests active agency; it overstates the individual's volition within online space and understates the dominance of platforms. "In order to operate . . . the Internet turns every spectator into a spectacle," argues Chun. "Users are used as they use."[18]

PERFORMING PROTOCOL

The language of the RFC was warm and welcoming.—KATE HAFNER AND MATTHEW LYON, *WHERE WIZARDS STAY UP LATE*

Even before corporate platforms like Amazon and Google existed, hospitality was the founding logic of the networking protocol on which the internet is built. The idiom of *host domains, servers, clients,* and *feeds* is not arbitrary; it lifts into view the ideological armature of new media. In 1967 a small group of Advanced Research Projects Agency (ARPA) researchers gathered in Ann Arbor to discuss plans for a system of resource-sharing that would not rely on a centralized computer and thus be less vulnerable to attack. It was at this meeting that Larry Roberts put forward the idea of a national network of "host computers" connected to each other over dial-up telephone lines.[19] Networking functions, Roberts proposed, could be handled by "hosts" that would act as both research computers and communications routers. Later, Wes Clark would suggest an ingenious modification: insert smaller computers between the host computers to map a subnetwork of interconnected nodes. These separate computers, dubbed "Interface Message Processors"

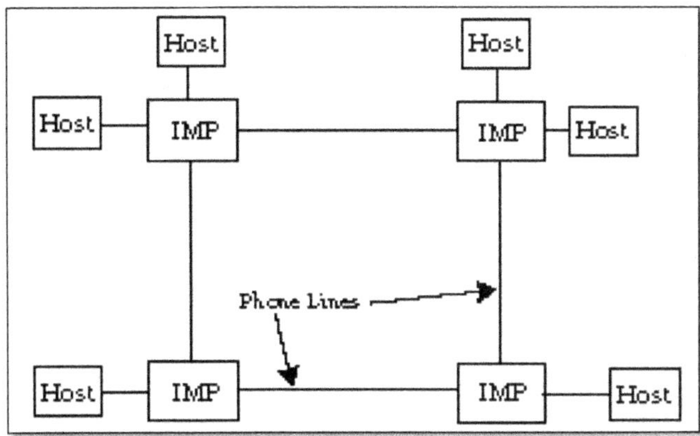

FIGURE 1.1 Early ARPAnet sketch, "The Subnet and Hosts." Source: James Pelkey.

or IMPS, would act as packet-switching nodes (what we call routers today), serving as messengers between the host computers.[20] This "Host-IMP" topology would serve as an early blueprint for the infrastructure of Advanced Research Projects Agency Network (ARPAnet) protocols (figure 1.1).[21] As the semantic and logistical bedrock of early network protocol, then, hospitality is the implicit structure that makes the very idea of the internet thinkable.[22] As such, it constitutes the proto-language of protocol and the paradigm of political economy in which the system insistently and unreflexively traffics. The language *host* appears self-evident, attributed by default, ideologically null. And yet how deeply strange, and ultimately symptomatic, it is that a medium premised *on exchange*—on the sending and receiving of messages—would be imagined as a network made up *only of hosts*.

Protocol, writes Alexander Galloway, is the "set of recommendations and rules that outlines the computational standards or procedures by which technologies function." Protocol's ambition is to be a good host: "It must accept everything, no matter what source, sender, or destination."[23] In his book *Ethical Programs: Hospitality and the Rhetorics of Software*, James J. Brown Jr. notes the ethical dilemma of networks' invitation to open yourself up to a form of one-way access, when you never "really [get] to decide in any thoroughgoing way who or what enters your 'home' (your apartment, your laptop, your iPhone, your thermostat)."[24] A term associated with performances of social etiquette, *protocol* is "a method of correct behavior under a given chain of command."[25] Like protocols that govern social or political practices, networking protocols establish the common rules of ceremony or formality that enable systems to function effectively.[26] Galloway explains this, but also insists on the limits of the analogy, for "instead of governing social or political practices as did their diplomatic predecessors, computer protocols govern how specific *technologies* are agreed to, adopted, implemented, and ultimately used by people around the world. What was once a question of consideration and sense is now a question of logic and physics."[27]

While the protocols of hospitality built into the ARPAnet may have little to do with the kind of hospitality performed by today's corporate platforms, the relationship between hospitality and digital protocol is nevertheless instructive. Here we might probe Galloway's sharp distinction between the sociopolitical and the technological for what it can tell us about the performance of protocol. When Galloway argues that protocols "encapsulate information inside a technically defined wrapper, while remaining relatively indifferent to the content of information contained within," he appears to leave the fiction of hospitality intact; he does not address the way that technological protocols create and inform social protocols.[28] So why does this matter? Representing protocol as nonideological and ideal receptivity obfuscates the system's interestedness. When protocol is posed as logical, it enables hosts to dodge acknowledging the rules or agreed-upon conventions that most benefit those who make them. In other words, protocol is what systems use to *perform logicality* as a means of disavowing their agency. We must be wary of the façade of hospitality that alibis networks' adherence to protocols, which instrumentally impose and regulate a distinction between the so-called hosts and guests of the system.

Informatic protocol pervades the texture of daily life, even in offline interactions; everyday interactions with corporations more and more assume the air of navigating a website. The rare exchange with a human employee follows a predetermined script, taking on a protocological affectation. Agency—even for the corporation's appointed representatives—only ever seems to exist elsewhere. This kind of technological standardization, online and offline, is a widely accepted mode of corporate performance within a digital service economy that, Noam Chomsky asserts, works to "transfer costs to the people":

> So, for example, suppose you find a mistake in your checking account and you call the bank to try and fix it. Well, you know what happens. You call them up, and you get a recorded message saying "We love you, here's a menu." Maybe the menu has what you're looking for, maybe it doesn't. If you happen to find the right option, you listen to some music, and ev-

ery once and a while a voice comes in and says "Please stand by, we really appreciate your business," and so on. Finally, after some period of time, you may get a human being, who you can ask a short question to. That's what economists call "efficiency." By economic measures, that system reduces labor costs to the bank; of course, it *imposes costs on you*, and those costs are multiplied by the number of users, which can be enormous—but that's not counted as a cost in economic calculation. And if you look over the way the society works, you find this everywhere.[29]

But technological standardization is not merely a source of frustration for those living under hypernetworked late capitalism; it is how network protocol (both a vehicle of dissemination and a mode of address) expands the field of exploitation under neoliberalism.

THE CORPORATE RUSE OF HOSPITALITY

Megacorporations mimic the supposed neutrality of administrative protocol by posing as mere platforms, and it is through this mimicry that they have reframed their own practices of exploitation as expressions of generosity. Consider the following example. In November 2013 a news story broke about a Walmart in northeastern Ohio that had decided to hold a holiday canned-food drive for its underpaid employees. "Please Donate Food Items Here, So Associates in Need Can Enjoy Thanksgiving Dinner," read the sign accompanying plastic bins at the Canton-area superstore.[30] ("Associate," the name that Walmart gives employees who don't receive benefits, is used in place of "employee," much as retail employees are now trained to refer to customers as "guests"; these are terms that enable the corporation to keep its hierarchy intact while simultaneously disavowing it.) Rather than Walmart itself engaging in one-off bonus holiday giving (already a vastly inadequate, short-term panacea), the company asked its low-wage employees to provide bonuses for its other low-wage employees.

Defended by a company spokesperson as "evidence that employees care about each other," the request was nonetheless made in the name of Walmart—a move that positions the company as a surrogate supplicant for its employees.[31] Walmart both asks its employees to take responsibility for themselves (and for each other) and, perversely, takes credit for the generosity of care that those in need are asked to give themselves. The event capitalized on American cultural traditions of gift giving and charitable donations around the holidays ("Secret Santa" and Salvation Army gift drives) to project an aura of generosity and good tidings. But what Walmart's performance of benevolence masked was an extraordinary act of *taking*—first, in the withholding of wages and benefits that made the supplication necessary at all; second, in the good public relations the company gained by hosting the event; and third, in the additional profits to be made in the likely event employees shopped at Walmart for the goods they gave each other. Thus its performance of generosity was an all-out profit-making scheme to increase sales by co-opting the gift exchanges that it prompted in the first place. Rather than a unique case, this example follows a wider trend in corporate responsibility toward charitable giving that is hosted by the corporation but entirely paid for by the customer, such as "Donate your change" programs and apps promoted by various banks, grocery stores, and food delivery platforms.

From Walmart's actions we can discern three identifiable moments in this ruse of hospitality. First, the corporation commits an initial act of exploitation (e.g., Walmart's low wages). Second, the corporation invokes protocol as an alibi for displacing and disavowing ownership of that act of exploitation (e.g., Walmart poses as a mere intermediary of hospitality rather than a causal agent and interested party). This has the effect of cleaning the corporation's hands, of keeping the dirty laundry in-house. Third, the corporation, now sufficiently removed from the original exploitation, attempts to turn its initial act of exploitation into a new source of revenue by presenting itself anew as the solution to this exploitation (e.g., Walmart attempts to siphon off good PR by asking its employees to provide for each other).

While the first and second of these moves are familiar, the third—in which an entity attempts to profit from the misfortune they themselves have created—carries a certain neoliberal novelty. The seeming generosity of the corporation is revealed as a ruse; the corporation channels the neutral or technological character of protocol to present itself as a hospitable platform, disavowing the nonreciprocity that it coercively establishes as its very terms of use—terms to which you must agree or be denied access.

Around the same time Walmart kicked off the canned-food drive for its underpaid employees, McDonald's updated its McResource Line, a website that provided the company's 1.8 million employees with financial and health-related advice. In one article on the site, titled "Digging Out of Holiday Debt," the world's largest fast-food chain suggested that workers, who make on average $7.75 an hour, sell "unwanted possessions on eBay or Craigslist" to "bring in some quick cash." The company also encouraged employees to break food apart when they ate, explaining that "breaking food into pieces often results in eating less and still feeling full." Elsewhere the website offered workers (or, as McDonald's refers to them, "team members") assistance in applying for food stamps.[32] Still another page advised, "Quit complaining: Stress hormone levels rise by 15% after ten minutes of complaining."

The McResource campaign is not McDonald's only venture of this kind: that same year, the company launched two related initiatives in partnership with Visa. First, the company created a website to teach its minimum-wage employees how to create a budget. The sample monthly budget was roundly criticized: it presumed that the worker had two jobs (based on the national minimum wage figure of $7.25 per hour); it budgeted only $20 per month for health insurance (*Forbes* puts the national average for an individual at $215 per month); and it excluded many necessary expenses, including child care, groceries, clothing, and gas.[33] The budget, ostensibly intended to help underpaid employees manage their finances, inadvertently bolstered the fair wage movement's cause by demonstrating the practical impossibility of living on a minimum wage.[34]

The budget web page was hosted by Visa's corporate responsibility platform Practical Money Skills (practicalmoneyskills.com). Visa describes this program as the product of the company's belief "that greater financial knowledge can empower people to better manage their money and improve their quality of life."[35] The sentiment disavows Visa's profit model, which is based on interest paid; in other words, its business model depends on individuals who are unable to pay their bills outright each month and must instead rely on credit to cover the shortfall. With motivational platitudes like "Every day and every dollar make a difference" and a downloadable "budget journal" that directs employees to track their spending for a month and contemplate their goals ("Knowing where your money goes and how to budget it is the key to your financial freedom"), the site offers up a spectacular show of bad faith.[36] Employees are addressed as empowered financial agents by resources telling them that the only things between them and financial freedom are discipline, introspection, and planning—individual action, coded as a moral duty. David Graeber points out that in theory the debt relation presupposes reciprocity, but Visa's financial model is invested in maintaining nonreciprocity.[37]

McDonald's used the Practical Money Skills website to introduce Visa-branded payroll cards to pay its employees. "Who needs a paper paycheck? Paper paychecks are becoming outdated and for good reason," the website stated. It cited the inconveniences of check cashing (with no mention of direct deposit, an option said to be reserved for managers and assistant managers) and positioned pay cards as "a faster and safer alternative."[38] The partnership between the two companies was met with mounting concern, as critics observed that the PayChekPLUS! Elite Visa Payroll Card, issued by Comerica Bank, charged minimum-wage workers fees to access their own wages.[39]

These campaigns received significant backlash after the publication of news stories on the progressive news sites *Slate* and *Think Progress* and in the business news outlets *Forbes* and *Bloomberg.* These stories were widely circulated on Facebook and Twitter and were further ridiculed when they were picked up by *The Daily Show* and *The Colbert Report.* (What work remains for the satirist, we might ask, when faced with something so unsubtle? Moreover, as neoliberal corporate practices have taken on the guise of their former parodies—e.g., the satirical shenanigans of the Yes Men's impersonations of ExxonMobil and Dow Chemical—it is hard to imagine a satirical response that would be adequate.) One could argue these instances of public ridicule narrate coercive hospitality's failure. But for every such program that attracts public criticism, there are others that are less often noticed and much more successful. Though I would be more inclined to argue that these moments of public criticism (episodes of corporate misbehavior often treated by these shows like a string of anomalies) demonstrate not coercive hospitality's occasional failure but a "he said–she said" discourse and counterdiscourse that is the relentless circularity and binaristic nature of political critique today. Ultimately it is not because people are necessarily fooled by the flagrant duplicity of corporate-speak that these corporate techniques are not still effective in raking in ever higher profits (though many may either believe the sincerity of the corporation's claims to care or give them little thought).

After the negative attention, the budget and Practical Money Skills sites were taken down, and both pages now redirect to the same error page.[40] In October 2013 the labor advocacy group Low Pay Is Not OK released a taped phone call from a longtime Chicago-based McDonald's employee to the McResource Line. She asked for assistance meeting her financial obligations, only to be referred to federal and state agencies (i.e., food stamps, food banks, Medicaid).[41] The recording prompted further public outcry, which led McDonald's to finally shutter the McResource website as well.[42] The company issued the following statement explaining the decision: "We have offered the McResource program to help our valued McDonald's employees with work and life guidance created by independent third party experts. A combination of factors has led us to re-evaluate, and we've directed the vendor to take down the website. Between links to irrelevant or outdated information, along with outside groups taking elements out of context, this created unwarranted scrutiny and inappropriate commentary. None of this helps our McDonald's team members. We'll continue to provide service to them through an internal telephone help line, which is how the majority of employees access the McResource services."[43]

Just as online content providers self-identify as platforms in order to sidestep their own culpability, McDonald's uses its statement to shift responsibility for its ill-conceived campaign onto "independent third party experts" and "outside groups." In renouncing its ownership of the site, the company positions independent PR consultants, activists, and critics as the problem, admonishing the "unwarranted scrutiny and inappropriate commentary" of critics who point out the incongruity between the company's advice and the choices that it makes. It portrays itself as furnishing a responsible solution to the problem ("we've directed the vendor to take down the website").[44] All the while McDonald's maintains business practices that keep their employees in a cycle of poverty, ignoring widespread employee protests to raise the minimum wage and to gain the right to unionize.

Food drives and advice websites are textbook cases of corporate paternalism, with Walmart, McDonald's, and Visa in the position of the responsible patriarch and the employee as the child-dependent (a position that has many of the same racial and gender valences attending the discourse of the "welfare queen"). This is how to be responsible, to save your allowance, to eat right. The programs curtail the freedoms and imaginable futures of low-wage employees while claiming to act in their best interests. The implication is clear: If you are in debt, it is your fault. They infantilize and patronize employees for their inability to thrive under the conditions that the companies themselves create—indeed they charge the employees a fee for failing to do so.

What might the digital afterlives of these PR fails tell us about the selective accountability of the corporation? How does the manipulability of the digital archive—or what David Weinberger has called the "weird" historical status of web documents—keep companies from having to face accountability?[45] How do corporations masquerade as neutral or purely logical by hiding behind the public's limited understanding of how networking protocol works? After the "Digging Out from Holiday Debt" page was taken down, the web page initially redirected to a company-branded error message that read, "Hmmm. We couldn't locate the content you were looking for. It's possible that it doesn't exist anymore, or has simply been moved to another location" (figure 1.2). The page now redirects to a standard "Not Found" Error

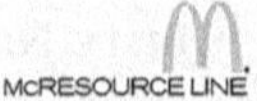

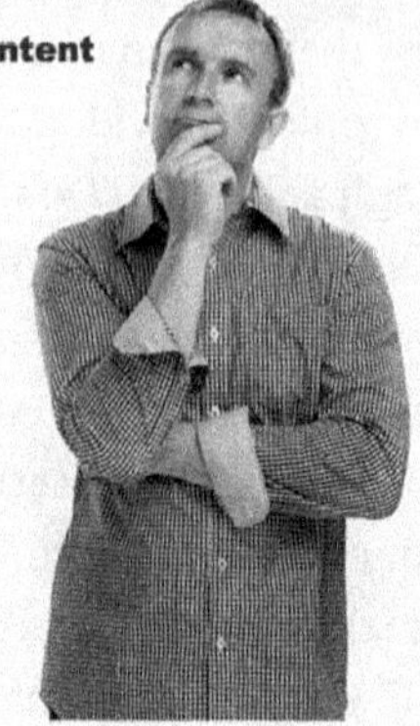

FIGURE 1.2 McDonald's McResource Line "Digging Out from Holiday Debt" error message.

404 message and is not recoverable via the Internet Archive Wayback Machine.[46] The Wayback Machine software was developed by the Internet Archive to "crawl and download all publicly viewable websites and take 'snapshots' of them, in order to record the websites at different intervals over their life spans."[47] In fact, in light of the relative unreliability of the Wayback Machine, these webpages would not be recoverable at all if not for hyperlinks to their original URLs in online progressive and business news stories about the campaigns, tenuous and crucial public archives documenting corporate actions that would otherwise be erased.[48] Lisa Gitelman observes that the transfer status code "Error 404" typically occurs when "a user selects an outdated hyperlink or mistypes a URL, indicating the address of a Web server but not a viable page." In this case it seems that the formerly functional McResource web page has been made unavailable not because of a lack of server support or an incorrect URL; instead it is a web page that McDonald's intentionally refaced to resemble an error page. The company attempts to capitalize on the ambiguous causality, the nonaccountability associated with Error 404, which is employed to invoke the sheer incomprehensibility of the technological sublime. "Error 404 does not specify who committed or what caused the error to occur," writes Gitelman. "It implies a dizzying potential for mistakes—more than four hundred different kinds—but stops short of laying any blame." Gitelman continues:

> It answers a particular request with a denial that affirms the constancy and ubiquity of the Web administration, which is at once authoritative and impersonal—a system of protocols, really, that is seldom acknowledged but always present. Corresponding error messages, like the prefatory announcements on early phonograph records, hail users individually but are not by or from anyone in particular. Even when a Web master or systems operator replaces the generic error message with a server-specific version, she does so as a ventriloquist, speaking with the impersonal, authoritative voice of Web administration itself—a voice that reventriloquizes the impersonal authority that has so long hailed and conscripted its subjects to the mediated public: "post no bills"; "all circuits are busy"; "stay tuned for more."[49]

With the "Digging Out of Holiday Debt" error message, McDonald's seizes upon the alibi of a technological protocol, which is performed here as a cute irregularity (not unlike Facebook's own error message of a thumb with a bandage on it [figure 1.3] or a series of Amazon error messages with images of a "company dog," launched as part of an internal PR effort to promote Amazon as "an awesome place to work" [figure 1.4]).[50] McDonald's personifies this irregularity in the image of white, white-collar masculinity, a goofy, confused sitcom dad, here summoned to represent the "impersonal authority" of the web master—a choice that discloses the racial, class, and gender politics of digital memory, social forgiveness, and corporate accountability. Cuteness, Sianne Ngai argues, is "an aesthetic of powerlessness," which is linked to the juvenile, feminine, and nonthreatening.[51] In these error messages the cute is marshaled to present the nontransparent operations of the corporation as inoffensive, even pleasurable. The harmless dopiness of McDonald's white dad, the charming woundedness of Facebook's boo boo, and the sweet helplessness of Waffles the Amazon puppy are leveraged to elicit a sentimental attitude toward the corporation, which momentarily poses as vulnerable. "Digging Out of Holiday Debt" thus lays bare who is exposed to risk and who isn't. The host's and the parasite's asymmetrical relationships to risk reveal a hypocrisy at work in the nonaccountability of the host; insulated from actual risk, the host withdraws from the social relation, disappearing back into the machine when asked to settle its accounts.

FIGURE 1.3 Facebook error message.

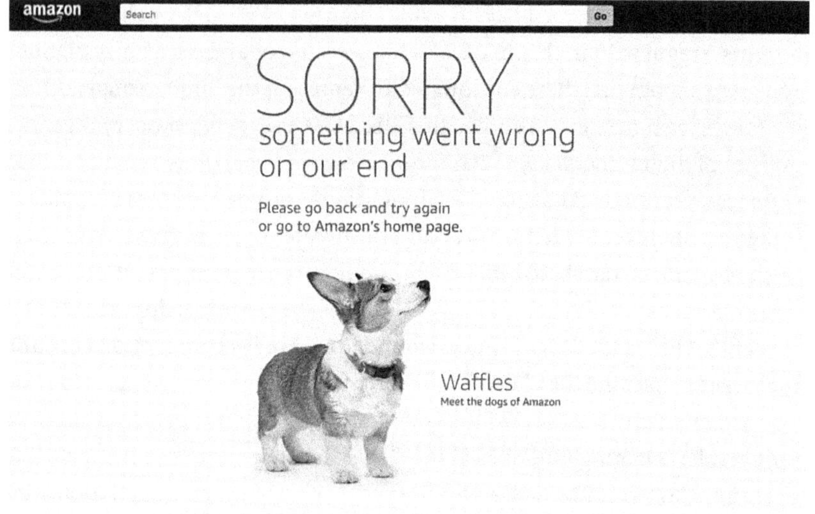

FIGURE 1.4 “Dogs of Amazon” error message.

Corporate social responsibility is a strategy for attracting investors and raising a brand's value by selling civic engagement as part of a company's business model. The rise of the narrative of corporations as "good guys" is, as Laurie Ouellette has shown, a consequence of the transformation of contemporary governance under neoliberalism: "an assemblage of reforms encompassing public sector downsizing, the encouragement of public-private partnerships, the outsourcing of many government services to commercial firms, and the dismantling of welfare programs." Corporate responsibility uses the interstices that are left open by such reforms as strategic opportunities for profitable marketing campaigns and public-private partnerships.[52] The architects of neoliberalism such as Milton Friedman believed that "the social responsibility of business is to increase profits," a form of unabashed capitalism that makes little show of caring about the greater good; however, the performance of ethical capitalism represented by new notions of corporate social responsibility suggests an important shift in the public discourse of neoliberalism.[53] While corporations still seek to maximize profits, they recognize that in order to achieve maximum profitability "they must now *act virtuously*."[54] The modern corporation borrows the discourse of the welfare state at precisely the moment in which the state and the corporation are engaging in mutual surrogation: the state increasingly takes on the model of the firm, while the corporation increasingly professes responsibility for caring for the public. The corporation thus dismantles the very civic interests that it purports to maintain, and the continuity of civil society is now a farce in which the state is also complicit.[55] But as these campaigns show, corporations are not taking the place of the welfare state. Walmart and McDonald's offer no material assistance to those who need it. They simply cloak themselves in the moral authority of the welfare state while obscuring their own reliance on government aid in various, far less visible forms. It is the megacorporations that are the real "welfare queens." With their low-wage employees receiving billions annually in assistance from U.S. taxpayers (and their fabulously wealthy CEOs and founders receiving billions in tax breaks from the same citizens), Walmart and McDonald's are in fact subsidized by their tax-paying employees, whom they refuse to pay a living wage.[56]

These scenarios demonstrate the tightening of a previously more protracted feedback loop of corporate responsibility. They manifest the accelerated speed of appropriation today—the collapsed duration between Walmart and McDonald's refusal to remunerate their employees and their appropria-

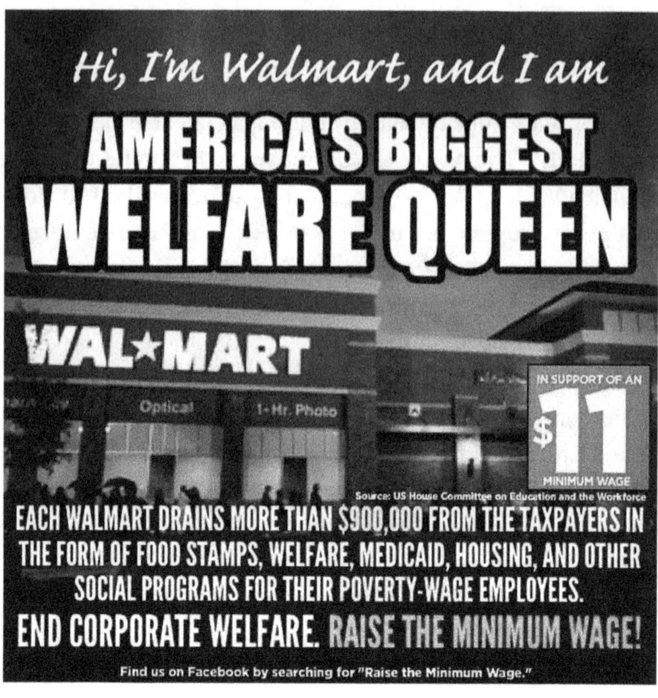

FIGURE 1.5 Walmart "welfare queen" meme.

tion of their poverty as empty spectacles of charity. Corporate responsibility is a strategy for attracting investors; by making it into mere theater, these companies perform generosity as a marketing tool that, rather than ameliorating poverty, instrumentally sustains and reproduces it. Not only do they not pay their employees a living wage but they also repackage and sell this denial of care *as care* in the secondary economy of public image–branding campaigns, where the denial of care masquerades as corporate responsibility. They sow poverty and disempowerment and harvest them as new financial markets, while they perversely take credit for the generosity of the care that those most in need must in fact give themselves.

One of the most visible leftist strategies of the past decade for fighting such corporate aggressions has been to reverse the neoconservative rhetoric of parasitism. Activist retorts ask the public to look more closely at which individuals and organizations truly feed off the work of others while contributing little or nothing in exchange. The Occupy movement and other anti-austerity organizers, for example, have mobilized the language of parasitism to mirror back the parasitical character of the system itself. By imposing themselves on city centers—spaces emblematic of the collusion of corporate and state interests—protestors denounce the absurdity of a world system that exploits its workers while calling them parasites. With the battle cry "We are the 99%!" Occupy captured a certain standoff at the heart of the discourse of parasitism, with each side of the barricade decrying the other as the real user in the system. This back and forth exposes a curious reversibility that lies at the heart of the host-parasite relation; the interchangeability of the two positions (*hostis* etymologically refers to both the guest and host)[57] has been highlighted in a number of popular memes (figures 1.5 and 1.6), which depend upon the classic Marxist reversal that positions capital, not labor, as the "true parasite" of the system.[58]

Much as I argued of satirical shows like *The Daily Show* and *The Colbert Report* in their responses to the actions of McDonald's and Visa, these memes earnestly invest in the epistemology of exposure at the very moment when the social media platforms by which they travel have been shown to function as echo chambers;[59] memes therefore do not circulate between ideological camps but instead preach to the converted. And such viral memes' circulation as critique depends upon and reinforces the power of social media platforms, which monetize circulation while being indifferent to content, making the meme authors complicit with the very systems they attack.

Dependency—which has long been "pathologized, feminized, and racialized" by the U.S. welfare state—is framed as "the condition of an individual, rather than a social position."[60] However, such memes seek to expose the hypocrisy of a system in which precarious subjects are reviled for their dependence by the very entities that create their poverty. The working poor have been defined in terms of this dependence on a rigged system;

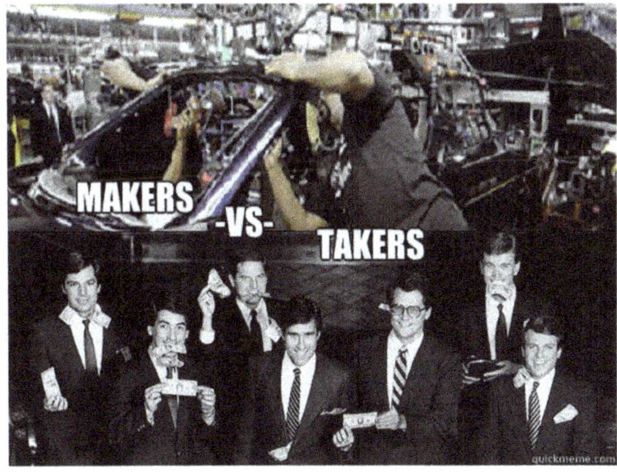

FIGURE 1.6 "Makers vs. Takers" meme.

they are seen as *social parasites*, a term revived by neoconservatives in post–financial crisis popular and political discourse, as state and corporate responsibility and risk are systematically offloaded onto individuals. From representations of "welfare queens" to the language of "Takers vs. Makers" and the "dependent 47%," the discourse of social parasitism disproportionately targets women and minorities whose contributions to society—including domestic work and dependent care—are kept off the official record.[61] For example, the notion of the so-called welfare queen has historically been circulated as a "coded reference to black indolence and criminality designed to appeal to working-class whites."[62] This rhetoric is part of a long history of discrediting women and minorities in order to block their attempts at downward redistribution and punishing vulnerable populations for their efforts to survive.[63]

Within this framework vulnerable subjects are twice condemned: Walmart's and McDonald's campaigns deploy technological automation as a screen to allow them to refuse accountability for the violence they perpetrate or enable, instead making their victims accountable for the harm done to them.[64] There are many examples of this. The city of Cleveland attempted to sue Tamir Rice's family for the $500 EMS ride after the unarmed twelve-year-old was shot by police; Columbia University sought to bill protesting students who carried mattresses around campus in support of Emma Sulkowicz after the university failed to expel her alleged rapist; and Flint, Michigan attempted to make its citizens pay for toxic drinking water.[65] In these scenarios the powerful entity asks its victims to pay for their own exploitation, as when repressive governments charge "bullet fees" to the families of those they execute. In its most obvious form, prisons and jails charge incarcerated individuals for their room and board; if they are too poor to pay the fees upon their release, they are now required to sign contracts promising to pay them in installments or return to jail. Through the criminalization of poverty, under neoliberalism, state and private institutions have turned their nonaccountability to the most vulnerable into a stream for revenue generation. Jackie Wang writes:

> For me, these methods of extraction mark a turning point in what some have called the neoliberal era. . . . Nearly half a century of economic policies that have eroded the power of labor and enabled a high degree of capital mobility has not only resulted in a fiscal race to the bottom that has gutted the tax base in this country, but has also transformed the nature of governance itself. If—to borrow Wolfgang Streeck's taxonomy—the

> *tax state* (i.e., the postwar Keynesian welfare state) has evolved into the *debt state* (which authorizes austerity) then what we are witnessing now is the emergence of the *predatory state*, which functions to modulate the dysfunctional aspects of neoliberalism and in particular the realization problem in the financial sector. . . . In short the outcome of neoliberal policies and federal fiscal retrenchment has been not only privatization and austerity, but predatory and parasitical governance on the state and local levels and indebtedness as a generalized social condition.[66]

"Over the past few decades," Lester Spence affirms, "cities have turned to policing to fulfill two functions: to surveil and discipline black populations hardest hit by economic shifts and to collect revenue in the form of fines."[67] In this logic, argues Jasbir Puar, subjects are precarious because they are precarious—an intentional tautology: "Surveillance and securitization economies work through a sort of monetization of ontology—certain bodies are intrinsically risky investments via a circular logic of precarity whereby these bodies are set up as unable to take on risk in the very system that produces them as risky."[68] Puar notes that this can be seen in the fact that it was overwhelmingly African American and Latino populations who were subject to foreclosure when the financial bubble burst.

These techniques of nonaccountability, under which the poorest and most vulnerable to systemic racism pay for their own oppression, shroud exploitation in the supposedly apolitical protocols of low-level administration: opaque bureaucratic protocol and employees "just doing their jobs." Powerful corporations take advantage of the perception of a hard line between the sociopolitical and the technological (a perception that protocol functions to maintain) in an attempt to hide the fact that these systems are neither neutral nor consistent but rather dynamic and improvisational. The double exploitation that I have described in this section is the logic by which companies such as Facebook, Google, Walmart, and McDonald's present themselves as mere hosts, while also acting as voracious parasites.

USER UNFRIENDLY

So how can artists and users intervene in such a conjuncture?[69] In the remainder of the chapter I highlight a series of art and political experiments, largely conceptual in nature, that model how we might exploit the coercive hospitality of the system, to use the user. These projects follow what Trebor Scholz has called "platform cooperativism"; they introduce the possibility of leveraging digital tools and platforms in the service of enhancing and growing not capitalism but new channels for sharing or redistributing resources.[70] Insofar as they use megacorporations' own techniques in their attempts to wrest ownership back from private corporations and put it into the hands of users, they undermine the corporations in such a way as to force them to eat themselves, recalling the image of the ouroboros (the ancient symbol of the serpent eating its own tail).

The first of these is an ongoing project by the Robin Hood Cooperative.[71] Founded in 2012, the Finnish group characterizes itself as an alternative hedge fund that "bends powers of finance to the production and protection of the commons."[72] Sometimes they frame their work as art (as "economic performance art"); at other times they describe their work as a business, and still others as activism. Robin Hood Asset Management Cooperative (RHAMC) invests in the New York Stock Exchange, guided by an algorithm called "The Parasite." Akseli Virtanen, one of the group's founders and a self-described radical political economist and finance theorist, calls the algorithm a "cooperative, counterinvestment of the precariat." Rather than stealing or hacking the corporation's black box (like Ubermorgen's *Amazon Noir*), or indeed fixing it, the algorithm mimics it.[73] The algorithm works by tracking and mimicking the investment patterns of "the best players on the market" (investors with more than $100 million in the U.S. market). "When we see that a swarm starts to emerge . . . like they all start to buy Nokia, we just follow the crowd," Virtanen explains. "We buy too. We let them do all the work and just follow. And last year buying Nokia was a very good move for us. This is, to put it very simply, what we do: We just imitate. It's a space of pure mimesis." He continues, "Robin Hood looks like a perfectly normal financial operation. But we turn it around, tinker with it and so it is a bit strange. . . . In a sense we reengineer finance, cash and risk flows, flows of dependencies and potentialities, we work with its materiality, with the divergent capacities lying latent but definitely built into its matter. And we have the power and imagination to do this. Financial technologies are very moldable, plastic, synthetic—just waiting for an artist's touch to start producing something else than debt relationships."[74]

The group claims to redistribute a portion of the total profits earned to causes that "expand the commons and the public domain," but it does not explain on their current website (which is in the process of being relaunched: "2.0 coming soon!") how they do this redistribution, precisely what channels they use, and what projects or actors receive it.[75] According to an account by someone close to the group, however, members pay a $60 minimum fee to join and can invest as much as they like into the fund.[76] They can determine how much to keep and how much to return into the common pool, which is rechanneled toward projects that group members elect based on their promise "to produce and protect the common." It tests the possibilities of reversing the dynamic that puts to work democratic principles of openness and sharing for proprietary models by putting to work proprietary models for democratic principles of openness and sharing.

The project's claim is that financial markets that capitalize on structural exploitation and the precarity it creates can be leveraged by appropriating some of this capital and reinvesting it in projects that support redistribution. Tiziana Terranova observes that this strategy—of playing the stock market in order to reinvest in the commons—is subject to the Marxist and leftist critique that it is "ultimately reinforcing the logic of financialization rather than supporting an alternative."[77] (This critique, she notes, is likely only to intensify with the group's relaunched version, which will use blockchain technologies and includes plans to grow its capital investment.) Pekko Koskinen, a member of the Robin Hood Cooperative, echoes this sentiment: "People often want clear boundaries between good and evil, professional and amateur, Right and Left, but Robin Hood breaks those binaries. We're creating a Trojan horse to warp the rules of the market."[78] Regardless, RHAMC suggests an ingenuous weaponization of the tools of private capital (digital automation, financialization) for redistributive ends (to support precarious groups or progressive projects). It proposes a mechanism for appropriating the information and tools of the rich (what the group calls the wealthy's "most important means of production—their knowledge, their relations, their position") to distribute proceeds to underresourced groups. Still, while the funds may generate excitement over the creation of an "alternative economy" that is self-generating, it is impossible to dissociate the funds from the original "host economy" from which they are first appropriated. RHAMC's scheme depends on committing an initial act of complicity, an original sin, to gain financial capital that can then be redirected in a second, virtuous act of redistribution. But it remains to be seen if the project only serves to install a new class of patrons. The parasitical tactics of the Robin Hood Cooperative stand in stark contrast to grassroots cooperatives like the Detroit Community Technology Project and Cooperation Jackson, which have sought to rebuild the commons from the ground up by insisting on communities' right to self-determination over the technological infrastructures that shape their lives.[79]

We can think of Robin Hood Cooperative's work alongside another work by Ubermorgen, the self-styled "big media hackers" with whom I opened the book. In 2005 the Swiss Austrian American artistic duo and real-life couple Hans Bernhard and Lizvlx, working with the Italian net artists Alessandro Ludovico and Paolo Cirio, began a web-based collaboration called *Google Will Eat Itself.* In this project the group tries to take down Google using the mechanisms built into its own advertising scheme. Calling the project an "auto-cannibalistic system," the collaborators ran approximately fifty hidden websites packed with Google ads that regularly generate clicks using an army of online bots. "This isn't that hard to do if you have the technical skills," Bernhard explains. "Google's system is not perfect." The trick, he adds, is to keep each bot below Google's click fraud threshold. At the end of each month, Google pays the group for these clicks, which they then move to a Swiss bank account. Having accrued 819 shares of Google stock valued at over $405,000 by the conclusion of the project, they estimate that, at that rate, they would fully own Google in roughly 202 million years. A 2005 press release titled "Hack the Google Self-Referentialism" explains the project: "The greatest enemy of such a giant is not another giant. It's the parasite. If enough parasites would suck small amount[s] of money in this self-referentialism embodiment, they will empty this artificial mountain of data and its inner risk of digital totalitarianism."[80] (In an intriguing parallel, McDonald's offered its employees the chance to invest in company stock as part of their Practical Money Skills campaign, their responsible financial planning website. McDonald's characterized the opportunity to "build ownership in McDonald's" by purchasing McDirect Shares as a "benefit" for employees, heralded by the website as "just more ways that McDonald's is showing its commitment to your future."[81] Employees are thus called upon to invest, literally, in their own demise.)

Google Will Eat Itself (2005–8) uses on Google itself the methods by which it has made an estimated $36.5 billion in advertising revenue in one year alone: by using algorithms to analyze and sell what users search and send over Gmail and then using the data to sell targeted ad space.[82] Yet Google has hardly eaten itself. Over the course of the project, the amount of time until the artists would own Google didn't decrease but rather *increased* by 345,117 years. With Alphabet Inc.'s stock price valued at $1,082.80 a share at the time of this writing in 2019, the project, rather than exposing the effectiveness of a tactical micropolitics, calculates the limitations of its own parasitical response. In its leveraging of small-scale use of capitalist platforms on the massive scale of financial and data economies, *Google Will Eat Itself* anticipates two comparable artworks: Nikolas Bentel's *Data Arbitrage* (2015), a bot that purports to sell users' social media data to brokers and then use the funds

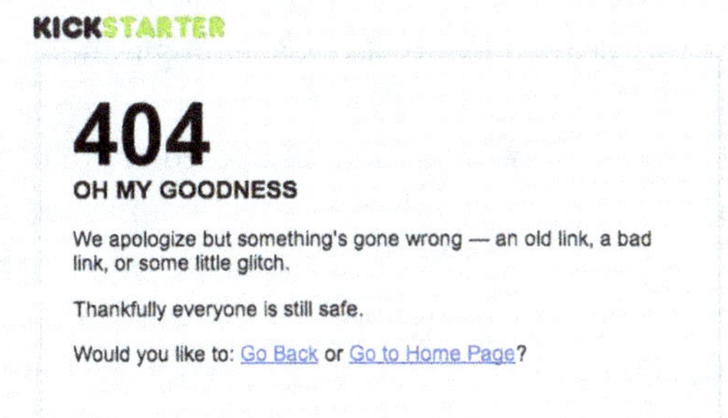

FIGURE 1.7 Kickstarter error message.

to buy fake accounts, which it in turn sells; and Irena Haiduk's *Frauenbank* (2017), an art installation that enables museum visitors who identify as women to acquire membership to a woman-only financial cooperative.

In March 2012 a project similar to Robin Hood Asset Management Cooperative and *Google Will Eat Itself* appeared on Kickstarter, a website that facilitates capital investments in various projects and collects a small fee (5 percent) on the money pledged, whether or not the project is fully funded. Kickstarter is often used to crowdsource the funding of art projects, an answer to the privatization of arts funding in a largely postnational funding era. The Los Angeles–based comedian Eric Moneypenny advertised his plan to buy Kickstarter by raising money on Kickstarter, which at the time was valued at $18.6 million. The ad was soon removed with an "Error 404" message appearing instead: "Oh my goodness. We apologize but something's gone wrong—an old link, a bad link, or some little glitch" (figure 1.7).

This response was much like eBay's response to Keith Obadike's 2001 digital performance *Blackness for Sale*, in which the artist attempted to sell his "blackness" on the site (promising the buyer a "certificate of authenticity")—a sale that was deemed "inappropriate" by the site. Similarly Moneypenny's prank compelled the system, which is ostensibly transparent, open, without limitation, to expose its limits. Although these artists and media activists follow the same protocols that media corporations (Google, Amazon, Kickstarter) use, they are nevertheless treated as parasites. Their projects compel the network to address them as such, treating as exceptions—as "bad links" or "little glitches"—the protocols that the corporation itself has imposed. As forms of systemic mimicry, these interventions are part of the ouroboros; they participate in a ceaseless feedback loop of appropriation; they leverage the parasitical substrate of digital media in order to take advantage of the host system's infrastructural vulnerabilities. But more significantly, they compel conglomerates, which are purportedly designed to be user friendly, to expose that they cannot easily be used in return; they highlight the asymmetry of the relationship.

As targets of parasitical resistance, the monopolies explored in this chapter are relatively obvious hosts compared to other systems I examine in this book. The scale of global corporations' dominance and influence makes them relatively easy to identify and criticize as hosts. How, then, can we understand the outsized status of hosts like McDonald's and Walmart in relation to the examples I discuss in the following chapters, which make hosts of the liberal-democratic state and of private individuals? Are these all on a continuum (some more extreme and readily identifiable than others), or does the logic of the host itself operate differently?

TWO AN OPENING IN THE STRUCTURE

NÚRIA GÜELL AND KENNETH PIETROBONO'S LEGAL LOOPHOLES

Chapter 1 examined the extent to which the coercive openness of platform capitalism, as a mechanism by which monopolies consolidate their hegemony, might instead be siphoned as a tool of redistribution. In this chapter I focus on artworks that explore how the rights granted by private property and citizenship might be leveraged toward economies of recirculation, rather than accumulation. I turn to imaginative attempts by two artists to subvert the coercive hospitality of the Western neoliberal-democratic state. Known for art practices that highlight the hypocrisies of state ideology, the anticapitalist activist-artists Núria Güell and Kenneth Pietrobono pursue interventions that attempt to resist the nation-state and its juridical powers by divesting from paradigms of legal sovereignty that they find unjust. In *Stateless by Choice: On the Prison of the Possible (Apátrida por voluntad propia)* (2015–16), Güell struggles to identify the proper bureaucratic channels to renounce her Spanish nationality and become stateless; in the proposed but unrealized work *Void (The Opposite of Property)*, Pietrobono tries to classify a piece of private property as unowned. Güell defiantly seeks a way out of the complicity with state violence implied by citizenship by birth, grappling with nationality inherited by descent or "right of blood" (*jus sanguinis*); Pietrobono, a U.S. citizen who grew up in a family with mixed legal status and who is a product of an assimilationist immigrant narrative, delves deeper into the myth of American uplift via private property—nationality as earned by "right of the soil" (*jus soli*).

These artworks thus explore a parasitical relationship not to corporate structures but to the larger structure of the state, which in its alignment with corporate power under neoliberalism has adopted the strategic performance of coercive hospitality. Hiring lawyers, drafting legal documents, and navigating government bureaucracy, Güell and Pietrobono earnestly attempt to locate within the purview of the law a way of subverting its coercive structure. When their attempts at frontal opposition fail, they instead undertake to document the rhetorical and bureaucratic protocols of nontransparency by which the state curtails the freedoms that it purports to guarantee. When they find that a way out is not possible, Güell and Pietrobono seek to repudiate this coercive framework by sneaking through the loopholes created by their relative privilege and inclusion in order to undermine the state from the inside. Like Robin Hood Cooperative, these artist-activists invest in alternative economies of power, represented by the commons. Rather than imagining that because the parasite is attached to the host it necessarily reproduces the logic of the host, Güell and Pietrobono perform the parasite as an unpredictable agent with the potential to incite transformation, even redistribution, in ways the host cannot anticipate.

THE RIGHTEOUS HOSPITALITY OF THE NEOLIBERAL SECURITY STATE

The undocumented immigrant is a structuring absence in the work of both Güell and Pietrobono. Before examining more deeply their practices and the place of the undocumented immigrant in their respective oeuvres, I want to briefly sketch how the U.S. state's construction of the undocumented immigrant as a hostile invader of and dependent threat to the nation-state has been used to increase corporate and state profit in practices of border securitization. The nativist rhetoric that portrays the immigrant as a parasite on the host body of the nation-state is especially pervasive, as Jonathan Xavier Inda has argued of the Mexican immigrant in particular.[1] The racist and xenophobic slur *illegal alien* is meant to invoke the image of Hispanic criminality, just as the epithet *welfare queen* is a "coded reference to black indolence and criminality designed to appeal to working-class whites."[2] This slur, however, ignores the fact that the U.S. national economy depends on undocumented labor. How does the state's performance of border securitization hide itself under the aegis of protecting citizens from those entities deemed "outside threats"?[3] How does it perform protocol so as to present its operations as fair and rational, to project an idealization of the liberal-democratic state as ethically righteous in ways that elide its financial interestedness? Consider two examples of the emerging neoliberal economies of U.S. border security, as seen from both sides of the border.

Take the promotional video *Welcome: Portraits of America*, which is shown in the arrivals hall at international airports in the United States and at U.S. embassies and consulates. The video, which plays on a loop while international travelers wait to be questioned, fingerprinted, and searched, has been described by the Department of State as part of an effort to provide "a warm welcome" in the aftermath of the Patriot Act; it was commissioned under the Bush administration as part of the Rice-Chernoff Initiative, a government partnership with Walt Disney Parks and Resorts, which reportedly gifted the seven-minute video to the U.S. Department of Homeland Security and the Department of State in order to aid with post-9/11 public diplomacy.[4] The video offers highly scripted depictions of racial, ethnic, religious, and regional diversity and tolerance (figure 2.1). Its montage of cowboys and Muslims, interracial couples, a farmer driving a tractor, and a girl celebrating a quinceañera makes for an ironic welcome mat in an era of securitization that has in the wake of 9/11 disproportionately targeted racial, ethnic, and religious minorities for scrutiny. The video uses American visual rhetoric of rugged individualism, racial uplift, and the self-made man as a kind of background music that is played while biometric technologies like digital fingerprinting, iris scanning, and facial recognition—"sold as necessary to protect us from a dangerous world"—are employed to "spin the bodies of prisoners, welfare recipients, and [in this case] travelers into valuable data."[5] In this moment when, as Wendy Hui Kyong Chun has asserted, "freedom is conflated with security," the idealization of democracy and the realization of state control are shown to be isomorphic with one another.[6] In Disney's representation of "America the free," democratic tolerance and free-market capitalism are shown to be coextensive.

The monetization of the U.S. War on Terror and the project of "securing the homeland" is also reflected in entrepreneurial ventures of the Transportation Security Administration (TSA), an agency of the Department of Homeland Security. These ventures include the regular selling or auctioning of confiscated and lost TSA items (e.g., knives, snow globes, jewelry) on websites like eBay and GovDeals.com.[7] The TSA also runs multimillion-dollar marketing campaigns seeking to popularize its expedited security screening program, PreCheck, which exchanges faster security lines for an $85 subscription fee for five years.[8] There is also the biometric security program CLEAR (a technology specially certified by the Department of Homeland

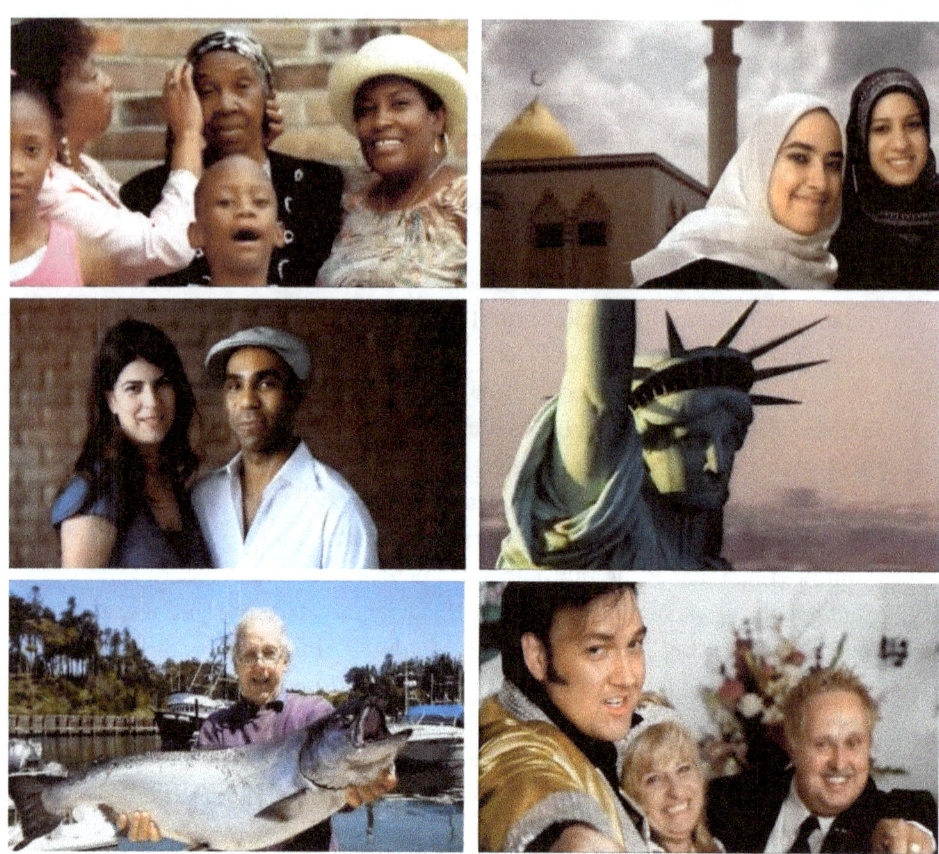

FIGURE 2.1 *Welcome: Portraits of America* promotional video stills.

Security) that allows travelers to bypass security checkpoints by using fingerprint and/or iris identification for a subscription fee of $179 per year. And the TSA has approved a pilot program with the Florida-based firm SecurityPoint Media to sell corporate advertising space at the bottom of its security bins (for companies like Microsoft, Zappos, and Charles Schwab that are eager to target business travelers).[9] TSA thus offloads federal costs to private companies, which upgrade the airport checkpoint equipment at no cost to the federal government.[10] The U.S. government's supposedly neutral stake in antiterrorism border security is in fact webbed with hidden private interests.

The shift to antiterrorism protocols as new economies for private capital extends beyond the U.S. border. Every year thousands of Mexican immigrants are deported from the United States for minor infractions, such as running a red light or getting a speeding ticket; they are sent across the bor-

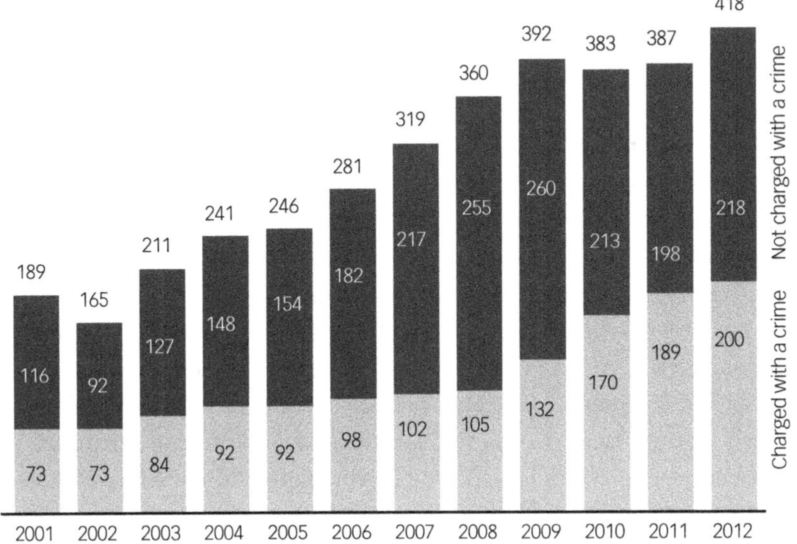

FIGURE 2.2 Deportations by U.S. Department of Homeland Security, 2001–12. Figures represent 1,000s

der and then handed pamphlets recruiting them for one of the many globally outsourced call centers based in Tijuana and other border cities.[11] These call centers are almost entirely staffed by deportees, who are employed to converse with customers of U.S. companies such as FedEx and DirecTV—typically with a starting salary of around $150 per week.[12] Call centers have increasingly been outsourced to Mexico; the sharp rise in deportations under the Obama administration (figure 2.2)—which corresponded to a dramatic increase in the funding allocated to U.S. border patrol during this same period—helped ensure a steady flow of native Mexicans who speak English fluently with an American accent.[13] This example further shows how the project of U.S. border security and control works in tandem with the project of multinational capital. Border securitization is used to supply a low-wage surplus labor economy. Violations of immigration law are used to isolate and capture new pools of skilled, highly vulnerable labor. Much as Walmart and McDonald's deploy social responsibility as mere theater (see chapter 1), the U.S. Department of Homeland Security repackages the neocolonial outposts opened up by immigration law for companies like FedEx as "auspicious employment opportunities" for recent deportees.

These scenes of border capitalism evidence how the "two faces" of state sovereignty—*hospitality* and *hostility*—work in tandem. The system's hostility is inextricable from its performance of hospitality; as the etymology of *hostis* (meaning both "guest" and "host") suggests, hospitality conceals within it its opposite. These scenes demonstrate just how easily the state that presents itself as hospitable is capable of hostility. The two faces of sovereign power are captured in the Department of Homeland Security's stated mission: "to secure America's borders while welcoming legitimate visitors to the United States."[14] The *Welcome: Portraits of America* video's seemingly benign spectacle of hospitality might be likened to what the Swedish anthropologist Magnus Fiskesjö has shown in his analysis of the U.S. presidential turkey pardon to be a ritual enactment of sovereign power; it masquerades as lighthearted but is in fact a public performance of clemency that shores up the state's power to command matters of life and death.[15] Similarly, the video's staging of a warm welcome functions as a tool of sovereign power, for it welcomes as guests those visitors it deems legitimate and excludes those it deems illegitimate.

Undocumented immigration, as these examples demonstrate, is thus not outside but central to the workings of a capitalist sovereign power, for it presents as rational and natural the protocols by which it distinguishes between guests and strangers, between those who are met with the welcoming face of the state and those who are met with its repressive face. Looking to the work of Núria Güell and Kenneth Pietrobono as models, how might individuals divest from the coercive hospitality of a neoliberal security state that belies a networked economy of exploitation and exclusion?

ATTEMPTED ESCAPES

I now turn to two artworks that represent earnest and frontal attempts by Güell and Pietrobono to address their complicity with state ideology—for Güell, an ideology that is represented by citizenship by birth, and for Pietrobono, by the immigrants' myth of the American dream (the notion that, with enough hard work and determination, every citizen has an equal chance of achieving prosperity and private property). Born in Girona, Spain, in 1981, Güell spent several years in Cuba, where she says she was "born as an artist," eventually training with the performance artist Tania Bruguera at her Behavior Art School (Cátedra Arte de Conducta).[16] Güell's work explores what she calls "hegemonic morality" (*morales hegemonica*), by which she means the narrative that the state perpetuates about itself as morally justified. Her work is interested in the social contract by which citizens must abide despite never having signed it. In 2015 the artist began *Stateless by Choice*, in which she petitioned the Spanish government to allow her to renounce her nationality and assume the status of a stateless person, in solidarity with stateless migrants. In her official declaration of her desire to renounce her citizenship (which initially reads like a breakup letter), Güell enumerates her reasons for making the request. "I do not feel identified within the structure of the nation-state, with the nationalist processes or concept of fatherhood," she begins. The letter, addressed to the government subdelegate of Girona, lays out Güell's critique of the idea of the nation-state: It is an arbitrary invention. It is historically outmoded. It is a xenophobic and racist colonial construct. "I have never signed a contract accepting the State as my legal sphere and the fatherland as a superior value to pay homage to," she writes, articulating the problem that has long preoccupied philosophers of the social contract. "And it aggrieves me when political leaders take on the office of spokesperson for a supposed collective will in which they include me through my national identity."

Stateless by Choice explores the disjuncture between Güell's anarchist political identification (that of an outsider) and her structural privilege as a Spanish citizen (that of an insider). Güell tries in her art practice to use her citizenship to undermine the idea of citizenship itself—an objective that, if achieved, would by her logic "redistribute" (extend to people who are involuntarily stateless) the affordances enabled by her European citizenship. (Though abdicating can mean something quite different from redistributing, as gestures of solidarity, such as heterosexual couples who boycotted marriage "until everyone could do it"—a symbolic act met with fairly diverse responses within the LGBTQ community—have demonstrated. Unless Güell is able to pass on her unused citizenship to someone else, this is not strictly speaking redistribution.) Nevertheless, troubled by how her Spanish citizenship foists upon her colonial and imperialist ideologies she rejects, the artist attempts to use the operations of the law to challenge Spanish law. "Nationality is conceived as the quality that infuses in a person the fact of belonging to a national community organized as a state," she explains of her motivation. "This project is born from my dis-identification with the nation-state structure and my rejection of nationality as an imposed identity construction." The work circulates via Güell's personal website and its exhibition in the form of performance documentation: annotated legal documents, provided in both Spanish and English, and testimonial photography and video of the artist's efforts to process her renunciation application at various government institutions (figures 2.3 and 2.4). For the work's 2016 exhibition at Barcelona's ADN Galeria, the artist displayed an enlarged photograph of

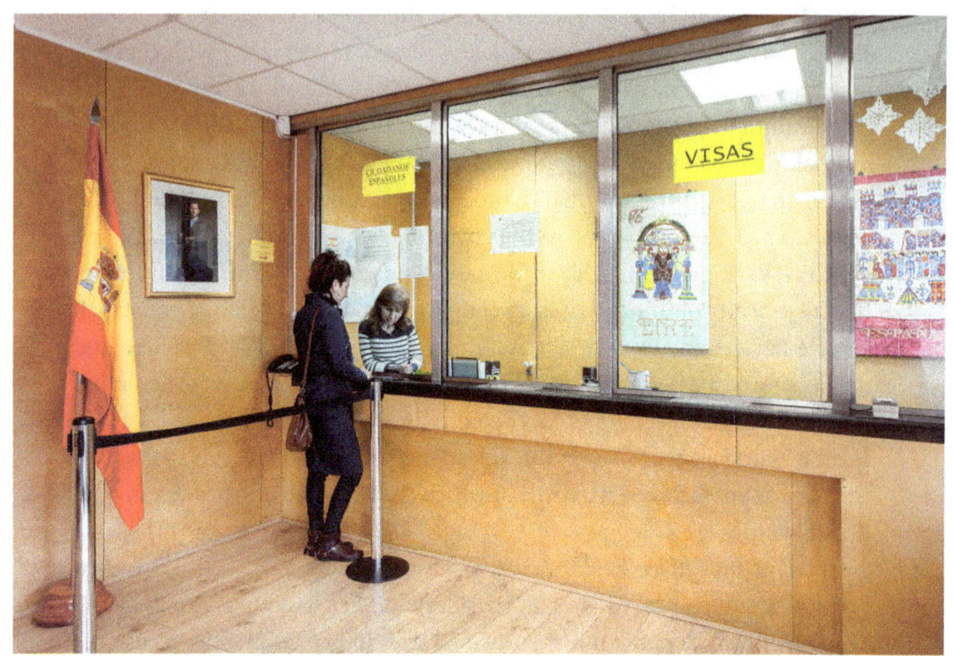

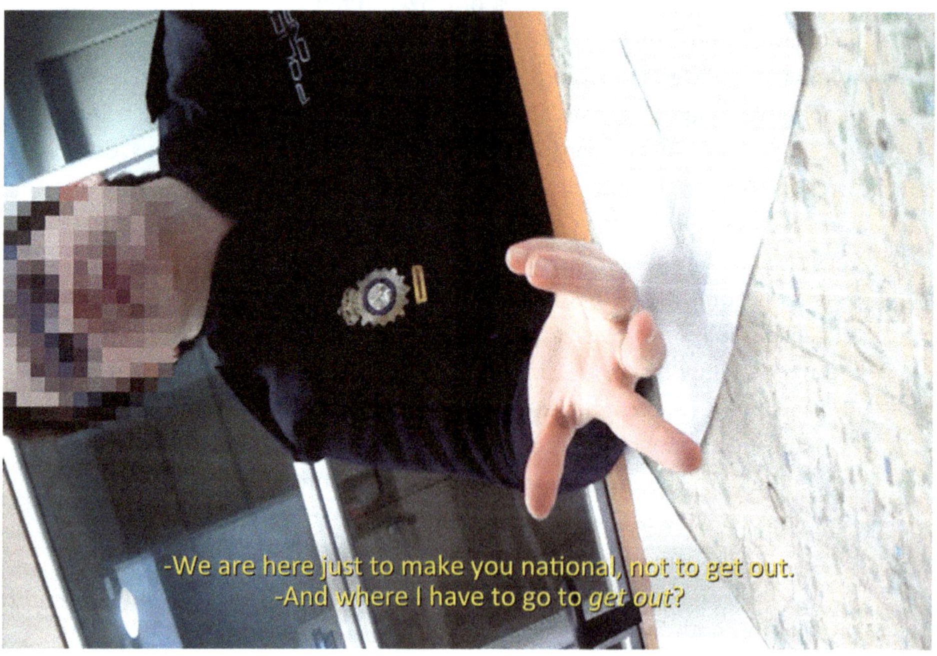

FIGURES 2.3 AND 2.4 Núria Güell, *Stateless by Choice: On the Prison of the Possible*, 2015–16. Source: Núria Güell.

her at the Spanish embassy alongside her framed legal correspondence with the state and played the video documenting her attempts on a continuous loop on a small television in the corner of the gallery.[17] The images are not aestheticized; they are rather humdrum scenes of state bureaucracy—an exterior shot of the artist entering the Spanish embassy in Dublin, a glass building reflecting the Spanish flag flying amid blue skies, an interior shot of an embassy clerk behind what appears to be bulletproof glass, offset by a flag and a portrait of the head of state. "We are here just to make you national, not to get out," a confused government clerk explains in an English-subtitled video still.

When her request is denied without "meaningful explanation," Güell hires an attorney to help her investigate the legal parameters of abdicating Spanish citizenship.[18] She learns that citizenship can only be taken away, not renounced: it is possible to lose Spanish citizenship only as a penalty from the state. In effect, the state can decide not to host you, but you cannot decide not to be hosted. "I don't want to lose it [citizenship] as a punishment," she specifies in a note to her attorney; "it is an issue of respecting the will of the person in [their] rejection of nationality."[19] Güell later commissions a second report to find out if she can divest herself of her nationality on the grounds of exercising her legal right of self-determination. This right is based on Article 1 of the United Nations' Universal Declaration of Human Rights, which holds that "all human beings are born free." In the eyes of the law, Güell wonders, is she free to be free?[20] Does her right of nationality give her the ability to reject her nationality? The legal report finds that the right to self-determination is conceived only as a collective right to create another state or nation. Güell eventually receives an official answer to her petition: "A year and a half later, the Ministry of Justice has notified me that my petition is unviable. The current Spanish legal framework does not contemplate the existence of people without a nationality of their own free will. That is, every human being *must compulsorily belong to a state*. To sum up, although the state does not allow human beings to give it up, it reserves the right to expulsion."[21]

By establishing the impossibility of renouncing this legal entitlement on moral grounds, exposing the illegitimacy of citizens' implied consent and the uses to which it is put by the nation-state, Güell highlights the nation-state's coercive hospitality. ("Where is the will of the subject???" she writes in the margins of the legal report she commissions.) She concludes that the right of nationality is essentially a nonright because it "only allows you to reproduce the same structure." Nationality, Güell concludes in her writings for

Stateless by Choice, is a way of containing certain subjects within the order of the liberal-democratic state while denying others admittance. A citizen's inability to withdraw individually from the structures by which the nation-state perpetuates itself is encapsulated by the subtitle that Güell ultimately gives the project, *On the Prison of the Possible. Stateless by Choice* challenges the Spanish government's moral and legal right to claim its state power as lawful; because the individual citizens over which that power is exercised are permitted neither to reject nor to decline their nationality, they cannot withdraw the consent by which state power claims to be justified. The state seems, in this case, to turn the people, in aggregate, against the people, in their individuation. Moreover the state's claim that it has the support of the people, as an abstraction, is curiously nonverifiable and tautological. Nationality is a form of imposed belonging into which natives are conscripted at birth (by dint of what the Spanish Civil Code terms "autonomic acquisition")—belonging that others are systematically denied.[22] Eventually Güell is notified that her petition is unviable, the issue settled in advance by a law to which she never consented.

In 2015 the Queens-based artist Kenneth Pietrobono responded to a call for proposals for a public artwork commemorating those affected by HIV/AIDS, to be placed in front of city hall in Provincetown, Massachusetts. Pietrobono's proposal, which was submitted with the working title *Void (The Opposite of Property)*, aspired to create an artwork that could elude the category of private property: he proposed to mark off a plot of land as unowned. In his proposal he asked what might constitute "the opposite of property"—not lost property, disowned property, or property that is unowned, but unproperty. He proposed to section off a segment of the property, set up a blind trust, and have the city de-succession the land to the blind trust, much like the siphon represented by Robin Hood Cooperative's Parasite algorithm. In contrast to the platform cooperativist experiments of chapter 1 that explore the possibility of forging a path to self-ownership, Pietrobono is more interested in leveraging the logic of private property toward a nonproprietary model. While the legal framework behind the idea appears never to have been fully substantiated, his concept was for the city to pay a lease every year on the land, with funds going to HIV/AIDS research. Pietrobono's interest was in hacking property—as Güell sought to hack nationality—as a tool for redistributing the power inscribed in legal access. The artist explains his intention: "Because the law can't see outside of itself, the interest in the unowned . . . was always a deeper interest in some practice that would show an 'outside' to something that is all encompassing."[23] Like *Stateless by Choice*, Pietrobono's proposed work was an experiment to see if the law can be undermined on an individual level, using its own terms against it: "I was really just trying to think, what if I could make a crack in actual legal frameworks?" Pietrobono said of the piece. "How can I really intervene?"

Pietrobono would later learn from a lawyer that the project was not viable within the current U.S. legal framework, in which ownership is compulsory.[24] "The truth is it is an impossibility and you have to set up some kind of sovereign to keep the land unowned [because] it has to be owned. It has to have a steward." The HIV/AIDS memorial that the city ultimately chose, which was inaugurated in 2018, is the antithesis of Pietrobono's proposal: a traditional sculptural form symbolizing collective ownership and marking closure. Designed by the sculptor Lauren Ewing, the memorial is a seventeen-ton Brazilian quartzite square monument shaped like a cross-section of an ocean floor, in the style of a traditional gravestone, inscribed with the word *remembering*. In choosing the ocean as her inspiration, Ewing explained, she wanted to design "something that belongs to everyone"—precisely the opposite of Pietrobono's attempt to design something that belongs to no one. Ewing's sculpture is a monument to community proprietorship and consolidation instead of a gesture of collective dispossession and redistribution.

It is in these works' failure to move outside of the structures of the nation-state and private property that they succeed in becoming effective heuristics. They demonstrate, most basically, what most surmise but few know for sure: that one *cannot not be a citizen* and *something cannot be unowned*. They open up spaces for examining what state ideologies make *thinkable* and *not thinkable* by creating spaces for imagining the unimaginable, for not wanting what citizens, to invoke Gayatri Spivak, "cannot not want": citizenship and private property.[25] Everywhere is the possibility of wanting and not having; nowhere is the possibility of not wanting or not having. These works further demonstrate that, like corporations (Amazon's nondisclosure agreement with Ubermorgen and McDonald's Error 404 message), states have the power to defer their responses or avoid accountability; instead they operate their power through administrators, who function as intermediaries. The black box of the powerful multinational corporation finds its analog in the red tape of state and local governmental bureaucracy, for red tape manifests a government's unwillingness to open its own black box, to avow its own inner workings and legal limits.[26] In public management and organization studies, there are long-standing debates about whether red tape is a sign of the "malevolence or incompetence" of bureaucracy.[27] Whatever its intention, the red tape is piling up exponentially; as Frank Pasquale argues, institutional secrecy and complexity are increasing, and this in turn increases the asymmetry in power between institutions and individuals: "Even our political and legal systems, the spaces of our common life that are supposed to be the most open and transparent, are becoming colonized by the logic of secrecy. . . . But while powerful businesses, financial institutions, and government agencies hide their actions behind nondisclosure agreements, 'proprietary methods,' and gag rules, our own lives are increasingly open books [subject to] surveillance cameras, data brokers, sensor networks, and 'supercookies.'"[28]

Centralizing the medium and performance of the contract, these artworks follow a certain contractual logic to its furthest conclusions. What is presented as a contract (an agreement to which both parties consent) is increasingly an agreement to which there is no affirmative assent, and therefore no possibility of dissent. And yet this asymmetrical contract between parasite and host does encode some odd form of mutual agreement, or at least mutual dependence, for the host needs and depends on its parasites while at the same time it seeks to control them. These artworks insist on getting in writing things that the state presumably will not articulate; they cut through its red tape, which delays or defers definite answers in order to not say no, preserving the illusion of agency in citizenship; they pressure state institutions to back up their claims to ethical legitimacy (claims that are based on principles of consent, freedom, and equality) and document the state's unwillingness to do so. Nationality and property do not have opposites, for liberal constitutional regimes do not recognize uncitizenship (native statelessness) or unproperty. In the eyes of the law, there must be a positive or affirmative value; the structures of the law do not allow for negation but only accretion, and sovereignty will not retract but only expand.

LAWFUL PARASITES

In other works Güell and Pietrobono turn to parasitical methods that seek to use their complicity with the state against its mechanisms. If, as I've argued in this book, institutional authority's investment in an appearance of openness represents a condition of possibility for resistance in the neoliberal present, how might the state's minimal and highly choreographed appearance of receptivity be operationalized against its exclusionary and repressive functions? In order to theorize the narrow window of possibility that inheres in the structural logic of sovereignty, I turn to the etymology of *loophole*. The term is commonly used to describe a certain room for maneuver in a given rulebook—a little play in the system. It typically refers to a gap, opening, or out created in the way a law, code, or contract is written. *Black's Law Dictionary* defines a loophole as an "ambiguity, omission, or exception . . . that provides *a way to avoid a rule without violating its literal requirements*."[29] It is an oversight, whether through error or inexactitude, on the part of the enforcer that enables those subject to it to evade their obligations. How this evasion is read depends on who is viewed as the sympathetic party. In some cases it is perceived as a miscarriage of justice, as when wealthy corporations exploit available loopholes to avoid paying their taxes. In others it is celebrated as a rare moment of escape from domination without reprisal, when the little guy catches a break.

Güell's and Pietrobono's parasitism rests heavily on their creative manipulations of the law to renegotiate the terms of their hosts. Making spectacles of the law's affordances, the artists foreground and play with the symbolic meaning of the hole (in loophole). So as not to appear to be obviously or explicitly defiant, they rely on making the terms by which the system's power operates as literal as possible—by asking to get the letter of the law in writing—so that they can sidestep the law's intention without violating its literal interpretation. My interest is not in actual or available legal loopholes but in the idea of the loophole—the potential elasticity, the play within the structure of sovereignty, enabled by the liberal-democratic state's purported investment in free circulation. To what extent can the liberal-democratic state's supposed openness to forms of alterity deemed legitimate be used to disrupt state ideology within its own terms? Here I follow Judith Butler, who argues that hope for negotiations with power can emerge from an improvisational engagement within dominance's very terms. "If subversion is possible," she writes, "it will be a subversion that emerges from within the terms of the law, through the possibilities that emerge when the law turns against itself and spawns unexpected permutations of itself."[30] In its contemporary usage, the term *loophole* refers to *a narrow window of escape* or *point of vulnerability*, a meaning that can be traced to the late sixteenth century, when the word referred to a feature of medieval castle architecture. *Loophole* derives from a now-obsolete sense of *loop*, meaning "window" or "small opening." A medieval loophole, or "arrowslit," was a narrow slit in the castle wall, not unlike a keyhole in appearance, through which small arms (bow and arrow and, later, crossbow and musket) could be fired. The loophole's thin vertical aperture was cut at an angle so as to enable the archer to have a wide field of fire. (The French for arrowslit, *meurtrière*, means literally "murdering window.") In the sixteenth and seventeenth centuries, the decorative feature was often built in the shape of a cross, making the loophole the weaponization of a pious form (figure 2.5). The architectural form of the loophole captures the extreme asymmetry of access and thus the overwhelming advantage of the entity behind the castle wall over the outsider who must be extremely precise with his shot. As narrow windows of escape from accountability, loopholes are things that the powerful structure in themselves to give themselves an out, but I am interested in how these same loopholes can also be used to give an outside attacker an in.

The loophole is an immunological technology. Its function is to preserve the difference between inside and outside. Conceptually and literally it describes a narrow space in the edifice of sovereignty that allows it to secure its interests and protect itself from the outside world. The sovereign state's architectural form was designed to *appear closed*, and the liberal state's architectural form was designed to *appear open*, but both are immunological models insofar as they function only in relation to the outside. They must therefore allow the minimum amount of openness necessary for exchange to be possible while regulating what comes in. This sense of *loophole* speaks to the reversibility of the play in the system that I describe in this book. While the loophole gives a significant advantage to those inside, its aperture nevertheless still represents a site of vulnerability to external forces.

Like the previous works by Güell and Pietrobono, the works examined in the next section attempt to locate loopholes—spaces of tolerance integral to the law—in the rights of citizenship and private property by lodging themselves in the law's gray areas.[31] The artists exploit their positions as relative insiders to the legal and ideological structures they work against in order to locate loopholes that allow them to siphon off resources from within. The following works explore whether the state's investment in appearing open and tolerant to those deemed legitimate by its threshold of accommodation might open up new and unexpected channels for critical reflection and social redistribution. Can those guests provided with the rights and protections afforded by legal citizenship and private property turn the law against itself in order to channel these rights and protections toward others? Or does attempting to do so only draw more scrutiny to vulnerable individuals, placing them in further peril, and only serve to fortify structures already in place?

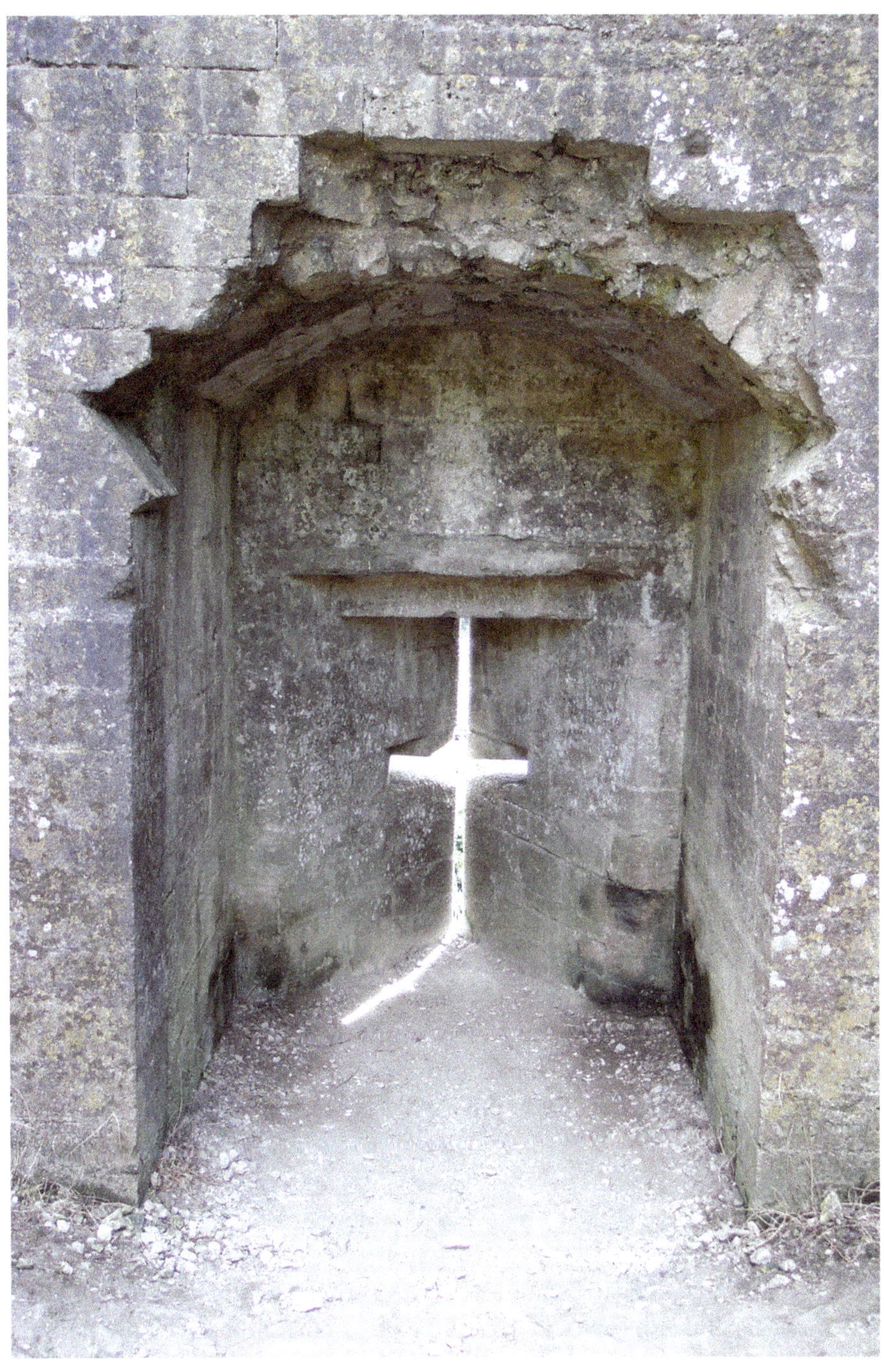

FIGURE 2.5 Interior perspective of loophole at Corfe Castle, Dorset, England. Source: John Bointon, under Creative Commons License Attribution 2.0 Generic (CC BY 2.0).

HUMANITARIAN AID (AYUDA HUMANITARIA)

In 2008 Güell held a contest to find a husband. She distributed a flyer in the streets of Havana announcing her intention to marry a Cuban who wished to emigrate to Spain. She invited interested men to compete by writing "the world's most beautiful love letter" (*Chica espanola se ofrece como esposa al cubano que le escriba la carta de amor mas bonita del mundo*). She offered to pay for all expenses associated with the wedding, the couple's travel to Spain, and her husband's application for Spanish citizenship. Once he achieved the status of citizen, they would divorce, and any proceeds related to the sale of the artwork would be split down the middle. In exchange, she asked two things: that he keep a diary of his experiences in Spain until they divorced and that he attend art openings with the artist. The artist hired a jury of local sex workers to judge the entries. The winning submission, entitled "The Letter for My Rose," is written from the point of view of a yearning gardener to his rose (figure 2.6). Its English translation reads:

> Your gardener is writing to you having worked all his life plucking roses, all beautiful and of different types, but there is a great mystery in them that I don't know but would like to discover. Because every time I get near to one of my roses it greets me with angry thorns, pricking my fingers, and then you notice how ungrateful some of these roses are with you. You are in charge of making these beautiful flowers look ravishing and shining as they should always do. But this time I am tired of my garden and the beauty of my flowers and have decided to explore other flowers that do not grow in my country, but in a beautiful place everybody knows by the name of: Barcelona. I do not know the flower yet and do not know "if it bears thorns." Perhaps this is the flower that will let me walk around her places and let me take care of her petals? Which flower will it be . . . the one I have dreamed of having some day with no spots or thorns. Because, if you are my flower, allow me to be your gardener for THE REST OF MY LIFE.
>
> Your gardener
> 20/10/08[32]

Among other documentation of the artwork is a wedding video (posted to YouTube) that includes footage the artist and her husband produced as "proof of love" for Spanish authorities (figures 2.7, 2.8, and 2.9).[33] Opening on a stock image of champagne glasses and red roses and set to Louis Arm-

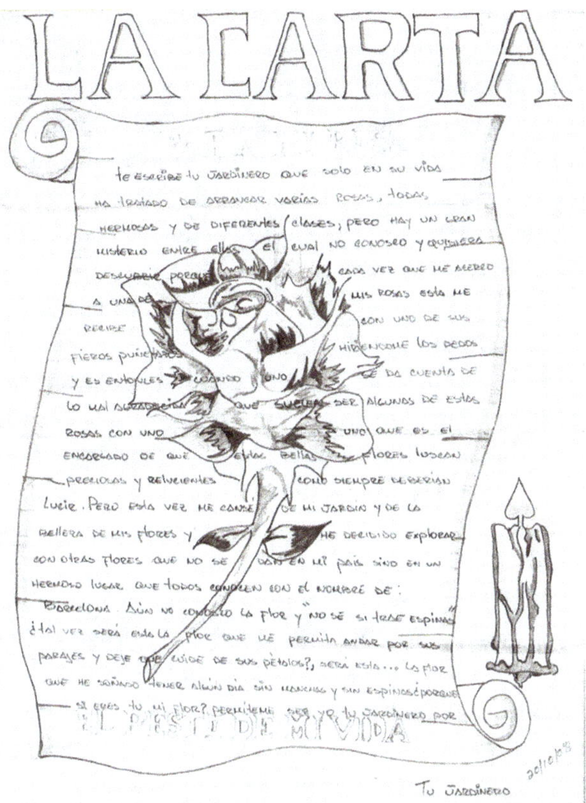

LA CARTA

te escribe tu jardinero que solo en su vida
ha tratado de arrancar varias rosas, todas
hermosas y de diferentes clases, pero hay un gran
misterio entre ellas el cual no conosco y quisiera
descubrir porque cada vez que me acerco
a una de mis rosas esta me
recibe con uno de sus
fieros puñetasos hiriendome los dedos
y es entonces cuando uno se da cuenta de
lo mal agradecida que suelen ser algunos de estas
rosas con uno uno que es el
encargado de que estas bellas flores luscan
preciosas y relucientes como siempre deberian
lucir. Pero esta vez me cansé de mi jardin y de la
belleza de mis flores y he decidido explorar
con otras flores que no se dan en mi país sino en un
hermoso lugar que todos conocen con el nombre de:
Barcelona. Aún no conozco la flor y "no sé si trae espinas"
¿tal vez será esta la flor que me permita andar por sus
parajes y deje que cuide de sus pétalos?, será esta... la flor
que he soñado tener algún dia sin manchas y sin espinos ¿porque
si eres tu mi flor? permiteme ser yo tu jardinero por
EL RESTO DE MI VIDA

20/10/08

Tu Jardinero

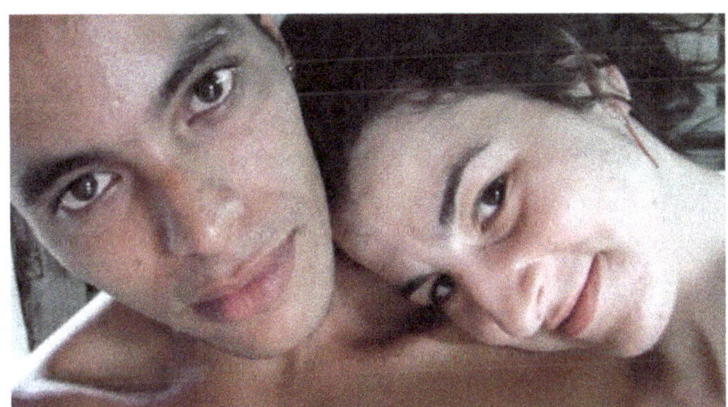

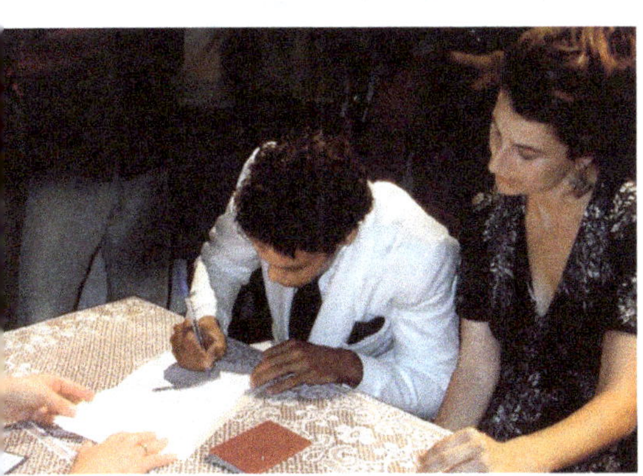

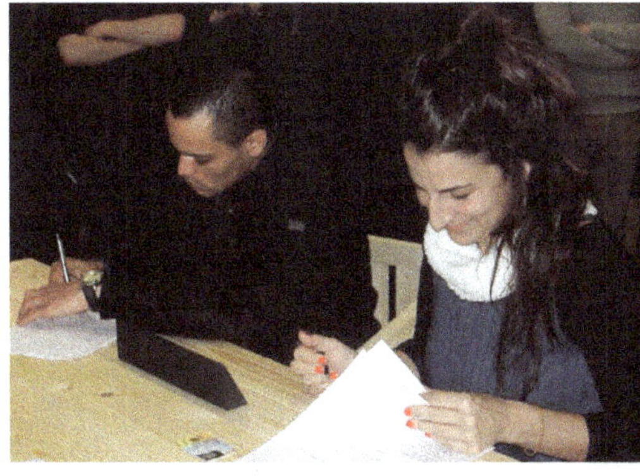

FIGURES 2.6, 2.7, 2.8, AND 2.9 Núria Güell, *Ayuda Humanitaria* (*Humanitarian Aid*), 2008–13. Source: Núria Güell.

strong's "What a Wonderful World," the video features the cliché trappings of romantic love. It includes candid photographs of the couple—her kissing his back, them goofing off on the beach, them intimately embracing. She sits while waiting to have her makeup done. During the 2009 ceremony, both Güell and her groom look nervous, she in a dress and he in a white tuxedo jacket, cameras flashing around them. "It is my consideration to attest that they have the legal capacity for this act," the justice of the peace says before reciting the Cuban civil marriage code.

In this work, Güell seems to say to the Spanish state that had denied her the right to renounce her citizenship, "Oh, you want to add, not subtract? I'll show you adding." Unable to escape her complicity with the state, she weaponizes it. The artist appropriates love as an authorized means (authorized by the state's conferral of citizenship after marriage) through which to traffic in difference. Love is a siphon, a "plus one" that is a minus, subtracting (in the act of addition) the negative value of the unwelcome guest in the eyes of the xenophobic state. For Güell, marriage—an institution intended to add wealth to the nation—is a loophole, an activist tool that can also be used against the state's exclusionary apparatuses. By simply doing what is within her rights as a citizen, she redistributes her privilege. Her artist's statement plainly avows her parasitical methods. "The main resources that she uses in her work are to flirt with the established powers, complicity with different allies and the uses of privileges that artistic institutions she works with have, as well as those socially granted to her for being Spanish and European," reads the English translation on her website.[34]

Güell demonstrates the completeness of what she describes as her disidentification with the state by marrying without love, betraying the tacit agreement that relationships recognized by the state with citizenship be sincerely based on love. In her staging of the letters she solicits from men, she makes their ability to feign sincere attachment her only requirement for marriage; the men must be able to *simulate* love, which she knows to be false but which the state cannot disprove. And who better to judge this performance of simulated affection than a sex worker? The sex worker emblematizes Güell's weapon of choice: a woman's terrifying ability to simulate affection. Indeed the act of simulating emotion is always a threat to the state; historically the prostitute and the actor are equally reviled because they use their bodies and their simulated emotions in exchange for money. As Jonas A. Barish notes in his classic book on the hatred of theatricality, under Roman law, actors, like prostitutes, were forbidden to vote, to hold public office, to occupy the very seats of the theater in which they themselves performed, and even to leave the profession, to cross the threshold into civil respectability.[35]

We might ask about the extent to which Güell's gesture in *Humanitarian Aid* is truly redistributive. Her very performance of it as art, her documentation and exhibition of the process, put her spouse (the parasite's parasite, as it were) at risk, while posing substantially less risk to her. Güell's project *has* to put a person more precarious than herself at risk in order to make and benefit artistically from her project—a fact that is not acknowledged in what is presented as a magnanimous performance of generosity on her part—at least until later in the work. The ethical stakes of the work grow much knottier after the couple settles in Spain. In 2012, three years into their marriage, an audio testimonial (in Spanish) about *Ayuda Humanitaria* by Güell's husband, Yordanis, was uploaded to Soundcloud.[36] (The same recording was also posted to the Immigrant Movement International project, a website run by Güell's mentor Tania Bruguera, strongly supporting its authenticity—and Güell's active participation in its dissemination.) In the recording he explains that he has lived in Spain for almost a year and still cannot find work:

> I cannot find a job so I rely on my dearest wife. This situation forces me to do several things with no right to claim like taking care of the cleaning of the house, cooking, doing the laundry, washing the dishes, ironing, walking the dogs, feeding them, shopping in Mercadona. But I don't think this is so bad, because she is in her right because she works and brings the money. I cannot be against her or against what she asks me to do because otherwise, where would I go? I don't have a job and now it is really hard to find one. I don't have anyone or anywhere to go here in Spain.

The marriage, intended to be a means of reallocating privilege, is shown to depend on a larger economic structure for Güell's husband to have the autonomy necessary to enjoy its benefits. The testimonial concludes oddly, with a change of register akin to an "ask the audience" reality TV segment. He closes by asking if he has become a hostage to the socially engaged artwork:

> I have to do what she asks me: People might say that I am laying at her feet and eating from her hand. Am I right in what I'm saying? Am I correct? Or am I wrong? Do you think she is abusing me? Yes or no? I hope your answer is correct, please help me with this. I send warm greetings to the person who is listening to me. Once more I say goodbye and thanks for listening.

One problem with Güell's project is that its very status as an artistic project undermines its stated intentions, which, it would seem, would be best served by keeping the constructed nature of the venture a secret. Pietrobono, by contrast (in a project with considerably lower stakes than Güell's), enlists outside participants who have (it appears) *more* power and security than he; it is Pietrobono, not his hosts, who assumes the risks of the performance. Although he, as an artist, may benefit from the performance, these potential benefits do not contradict the point of his project in the way that Güell's might be said to do.

EASEMENT (VERMONT 1)

After learning that his proposed project *Void (The Opposite of Property)* was not viable, Pietrobono began work on what would become *Easement (Vermont 1)*, a piece that represents a compromised version of his original aim: to upend ownership by transforming it into rent paid to charity. In 2016 Pietrobono approached a couple in rural West Townsend, Vermont, about making a work on their property. The artist asked property owners Christopher Keefe and Mike McGrath to grant him an easement, the legal term for the right to use another's property for a specific purpose. Easements are typically granted to utility companies to run power lines or broadband cables or to private individuals whose access to their land requires passing through a neighbor's yard; they are maintained in property law for the purposes of supporting private property rights and commercial enterprise. Broadly, what interests Pietrobono about private property is its ability to confer security and agency to the owner. Easements confound this, for they confer a nonpossessory right of use. With the easement, Pietrobono sought to locate what he calls "fissures in the structure" of ownership by redirecting the benefits of ownership from within the legal structure of private property itself. "I wanted to exert at least one challenge on that idea that ownership is absolute," the artist explains.[37] At first he toyed with concepts that included using the easement to calculate a percentage of a private property or to use the overall property tax to extract a kind of livelihood from the property, but the fine print soon showed these concepts to be unworkable under Vermont property law.[38]

When Pietrobono initially made a similar proposition to Keefe and McGrath as he had to the city of Provincetown, "to create some kind of financial siphon that would attach to the property value," the owners demurred. "It became very clear from conversations that an easement was as far as they were willing to go," he said. "They were happy to have me work on the land . . .

but legally, they did not want to fuck with their deed." While Pietrobono envisioned *Easement* as contributing to alternative imaginings of social relationships to those configurations represented by capitalist property and wealth structures, the owners and the legal frameworks within which he had to work were less radical. The landowners appeared to find a benefit, the artist speculated, in "expressing a kind of 'solidarity' without having to do much to what they hold in the first place." "My main sense," he says, reflecting back on the process, "is that for them 'going further' with *Easement* was simply a door to too many uncertainties . . . and beyond what they were willing to expose themselves to directly."[39]

The original concept for *Void* and *Easement* of using private property to create a legal or financial siphon was influenced by the work of the American conceptual artist Cameron Rowland. Rowland's work investigates the persistence of the U.S. slave economy and its institutional legacies in contemporary neoliberal capitalism, from exploitative prison labor to the system of asset forfeiture. Pietrobono's interest in identifying a "laundering mechanism" recalls a project Rowland undertook in 2016 called *Disgorgement*. For that work, which also takes the form of a contractual agreement, having established that the insurance company Aetna held slave insurance policies for slave owners, Rowland set up what he calls the Reparations Purpose Trust after purchasing approximately $10,000 worth of Aetna shares, in partnership with the work's exhibiting gallery, Artists Space. The gallery and artist hold the shares in trust until the U.S. government makes financial reparations for slavery, at which time the shares will be liquidated toward the payment of reparations. The artwork both pressures debates around reparations and, given the possibility that the shares will accrue value during this indefinite period, underscores its own potential complicity with the economic afterlife of chattel slavery.

The landowners agree to an easement providing Pietrobono with official access to a designated section of the property, if "only after a personal relationship was established."[40] Once the legal paperwork was in place, drafted with the help of a local attorney, Pietrobono began a two-day durational performance on the land. He selected a small corner of the property and, with the couple's blessing, set about digging a three-by-eight-foot hole in the July heat (figure 2.10). The artist wore a T-shirt printed with the words "On the Backs of Others." When he finished, he returned the soil to the hole and placed a neat border of rocks around the exhumed land. Pietrobono thus *voids* the product of his own labor, closing it off as symbolic. The effect is that of a freshly dug grave (figure 2.11).

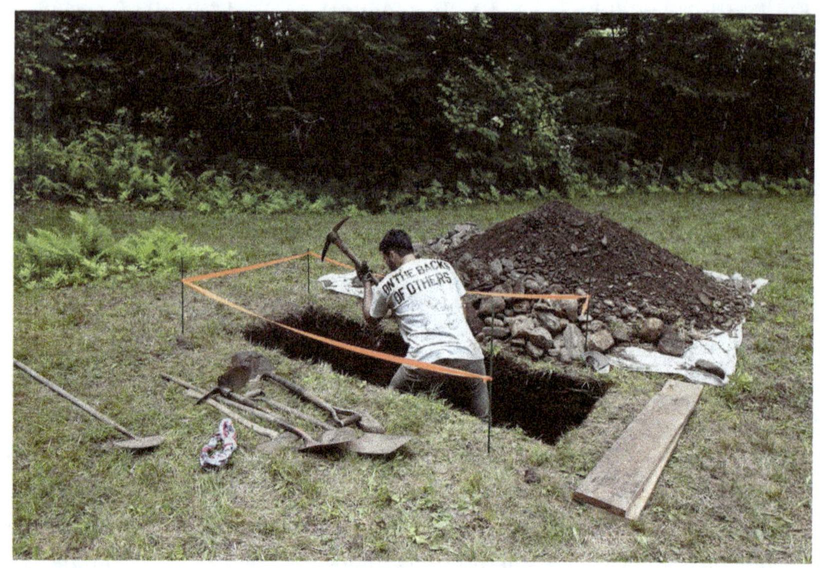

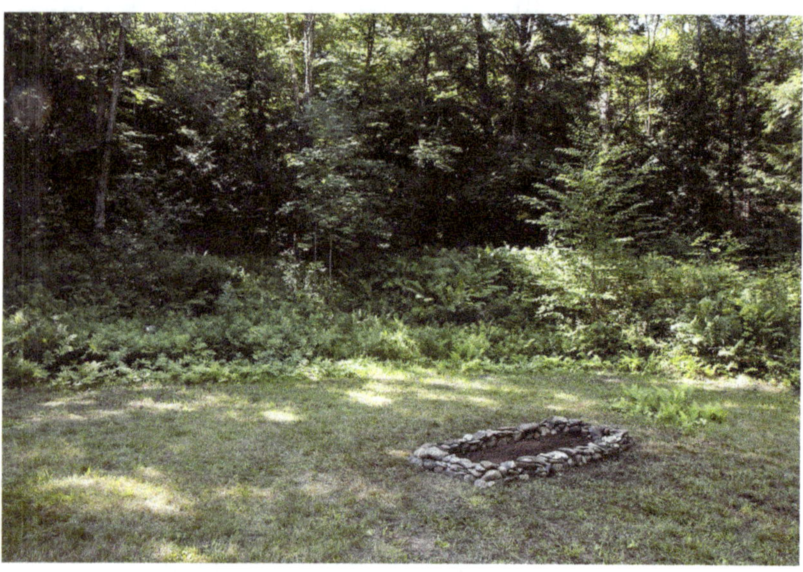

FIGURES 2.10 AND 2.11 Kenneth Pietrobono, *Easement (Vermont 1)*, 2016. Source: Kenneth Pietrobono.

Easement assumes multiple forms across multiple media, and each differently inflects the dimensions of the labor and the materiality of the work. First, there is Pietrobono's physically demanding durational performance, the live event of the work's materialization. Second, there is the resulting land installation, which serves as material index and remainder of the live performance. Third, there is the work's secondary (likely more enduring) exhibition on the artist's website via digital photographs, documentation, and written marginalia. (These materials include curated photographs of the artist bending and sweating with a raised pickaxe, copies of the legal contract, and an in-progress critical statement about the work.) Finally, there is the easement itself: the abstract legal manifestation of the social relationship brokered between the artist and the property owners. It is this final form that is privileged by the work's title.

Easement's ability to subvert the power structure inherent in private property both depends on and problematizes the essential contradiction of ownership (what Derrida terms the "aporia of hospitality"): to remain a host, one must not be too welcoming.[41] To be a host, one has to give, but if one gives too much, one can no longer be a host. "The terms of ownership create a contradiction, an impossibility of hospitality," Irina Aristarkhova glosses Derrida's insight.[42] The work effectively puts on display the terms and limits of the hospitality offered by Pietrobono's hosts. So while Pietrobono does not manage to convert the owners' property value into a siphon, he does temporarily neutralize the terms of ownership via *Easement*'s status as art. "Their ownership of my artwork is contingent on them giving up one of the aspects of the ownership of their land," Pietrobono points out. Significantly the work makes the owners patrons of an artwork that is critical of their structural positions as hosts *on their own turf*. Ultimately, Pietrobono reasons, more than the easement itself, from his perspective, the true medium of the work became his relationship with the property owners, "because it was the one material that actually is available to be voided, erased, allowed to end, allowed to dissolve and not be enclosed by one party or the other."[43] The condition for the owners' possession of the artwork, in other words, is in their nonpossession of it.

Pietrobono's other performances of social and institutional critique have also begun to garner wider attention.[44] His body of work, the performance theorist Josh Takano Chambers-Letson observes, "can be understood as a mediation of the contradictory nature of state power as it is represented, spatialized, and landscaped within the US."[45] The "On the Backs of Others" T-shirt he wore during the *Easement* performance (the front of the shirt

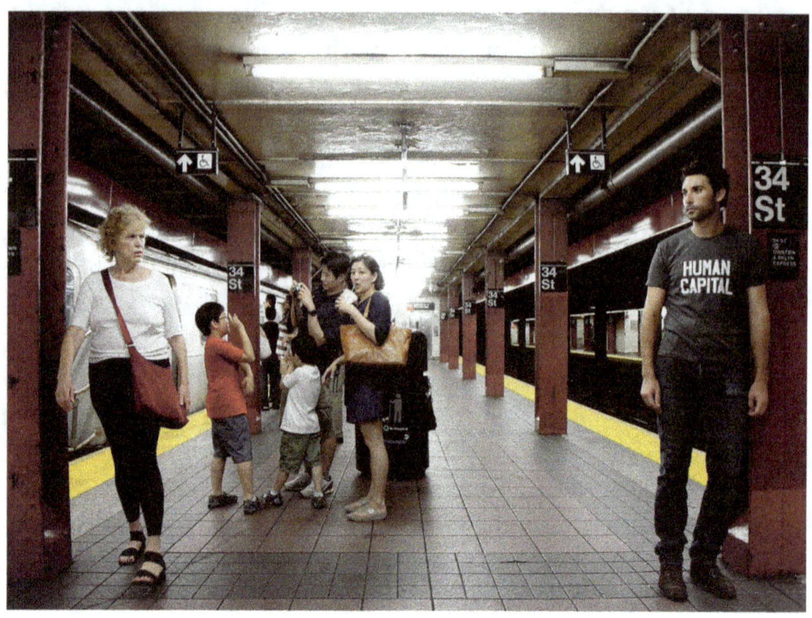

FIGURE 2.12 Kenneth Pietrobono, *Terms and Conditions*, 2012–ongoing. Source: Kenneth Pietrobono.

reads "From Utility to Commodity and Back") references another of the artist's ongoing works, *Terms and Conditions*, begun in 2012. For *Terms and Conditions*, Pietrobono initially committed to wearing thirty T-shirts printed with phrases such as "Human Capital," "Privilege," and "Games We Can't All Win" over a period of thirty days (figure 2.12). The project appropriates the customizable T-shirt, a ubiquitous symbol for the hypercommodification and branding of certain bodies, to expose the capitalist unconscious that underwrites everyday exchanges. The shirts are a vehicle for exploring how the queer Chilean American artist's body functions in public space, and the unwritten rules, the "terms and conditions," that underwrite the social economies in which he circulates. Pietrobono says, "For me personally, the shirts are an attempt to stand back and assess an illogical system, my place in it, the ways it works against me, and the ways it directs me beyond my control." He explains, "In a way, its [*sic*] a big game of Marco Polo, calling out to these dynamics which are mostly unseen."[46] Photos taken for the project show Pietrobono wearing the T-shirts while shopping at Macy's in Herald Square ("Disposable Income"), buying a hotdog from a New York City street cart ("Coincidence of wants"), contemplating views of Ellis Island and the

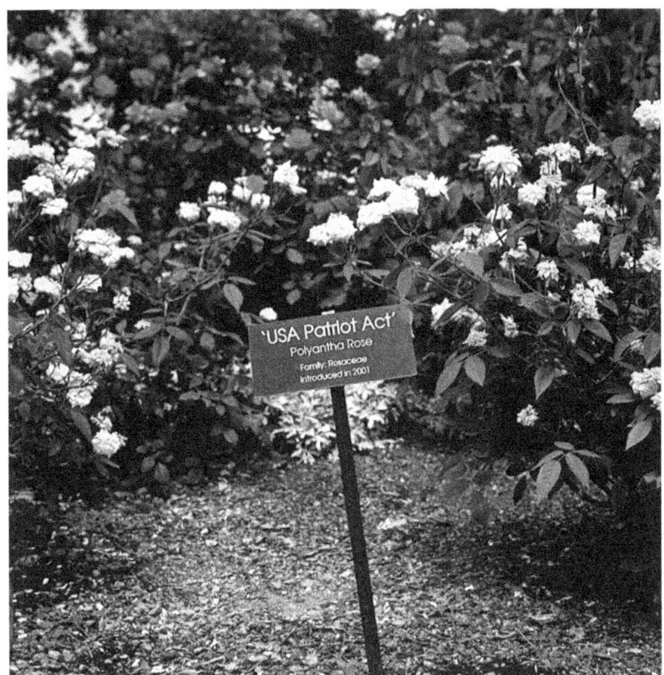

FIGURE 2.13 Kenneth Pietrobono, *National Rose Garden*, 2009–ongoing. Source: Kenneth Pietrobono.

Statue of Liberty ("Legitimate expectations"), and loitering in Zuccotti Park, home of Occupy Wall Street, after it was cleared ("Protect me from disappointment"). With the artist's trademark bookish deadpan, the shirts sloganize the rigged game of racialized capital.[47]

A similar deadpan address marks Pietrobono's *National Rose Garden* project (2009–ongoing), which in much the same way exposes the disjuncture between how U.S. imperialism represents itself and how it is experienced by those subject to it. The project includes a series of digital photographs of roses with names such as "Don't Ask Don't Tell" and "USA Patriot Act" (figure 2.13). It also encompasses a series of hand-numbered *National Rose Garden* special commemorative plates, made of porcelain and featuring phrases like "Super PACs," which he made available for purchase. *National Rose Garden* offers a send-up of the false sentimentality of U.S. empire. Both projects' ironic sensibilities are not so much the artist's as those of the system itself—the open secret that it is founded on unequal access to resources.

Like *Terms and Conditions* and the *National Rose Garden* series, which inscribe in real or symbolic space the forms of systemic exclusion and imperialism that remain implicit, *Easement* makes apparent the hidden and expropriated labor that underwrites private property. The piece's labor is given an additional valence by Pietrobono's T-shirt, "On the Backs of Others," and by the performance's location and social context. The artist worked closely with the curator Cindy Smith to devise the piece in response to an invitation to participate in the Stream Festival, a community-funded summer art festival hosted on the creek that runs along Keefe and McGrath's property.[48] Inaugurated in 2014, the annual festival is a nod to Allan Kaprow's 1975 performance piece *Echo-logy*, which took place in a New Jersey stream. When Pietrobono received the invitation to participate, he was struck by the peculiarity of an art festival being hosted on private property. He decided to use the festival as an opportunity to explore the historical relationship between private property and citizenship in the United States.

Although Pietrobono did not choose the festival's location in the rural valley of Vermont's southern hill towns, *Easement* is better for its fortuitous local symbolism. This is an area in which the land has itself proven resistant to appropriation. A promising agricultural economy in the early nineteenth century, the area later fell into economic decline because the dense, craggy terrain made the land difficult to develop. In the project Pietrobono strains to chip away at the rocky, difficult soil, provoking reflection on how dispossessed laborers must struggle to create an opening onto the rights of ownership. The shirt's inscription, "On the Backs of Others," references the history of US slavery. It also disrupts the historical forgetting that underpins the notion that hard labor is necessarily an expression of agency or a path to self-determination, reminding viewers that such labor is still routinely outsourced to undocumented immigrants, migrant laborers, and the working poor—subjects who have historically been denied not only citizenship but also humanity. The phrase recalls those laborers for whom an extreme physical toll did not, and does not, yield the dignities of state-recognized personhood and the freedoms of self-possession. Reenacting this disavowed labor, the artist puts forward his body as a surrogate, standing in for those for whom labor has represented not the key to self-possession but an instrument of dispossession. With *Easement*, Pietrobono asks what justifies continuing to treat property as patrimony today. The artist set out to challenge received ideas about the supposedly natural correspondence between property and labor, formalized in John Locke's labor theory of property. Locke's theory was used to justify the Homestead Principle, which holds that one may gain ownership of an "unowned" natural resource by exerting labor, which is an act of "original appropriation." "In my mind I was thinking about all of this security that property gives you and all of this stability and agency. Even the root of property is the Latin word *proprius*, which means the deepest sense of oneself. The closest legal expression of personhood is ownership. Even your possession of yourself . . . owning property as the highest form or expression of independence. *'I am an independent agent. I own this land. This land is mine!'* . . . [But] labor isn't isolated. There is rarely one agent."

With *Easement*, Pietrobono attempts to reverse-engineer the ideological mechanism of private property. Where Locke asks "How do I own something that is unowned?," Pietrobono asks "How do I try to unown something that is already owned?" The answer to both questions is "labor." The work seeks to show the falsity of the promise of self-determination through ownership, which has historically been used to determine citizenship in the Americas. (This is the Lockean logic behind the expropriation of land from Native Americans, who were seen as not cultivating private ownership or self-determination through labor.)

Why dig a grave for no one, with no purpose? What is the grave, with all of its significatory excess, meant to represent? Is it meant to enact Pietrobono's own (familial) claim to the rights of citizenship? To mark those (real and social) deaths that have been the consequence of principles of landownership? Pietrobono affirms that the answers to these questions, and his preoccupation with themes of citizenship, labor, and access, are rooted in his own family history and in the history of oppressed groups in the United States. He describes *Easement* as an investigation into the possibility of finding an opening or backdoor onto the rights and privileges bequeathed by private property. He himself comes from a family who spent roughly twenty years as noncitizens: he was born in Florida in 1982, not long after his family emigrated from Chile to the United States, but his family did not acquire documented status until 1996. "I recall the import of this being the arbitrary condition that the mere location of my birth gave *me* a completely different position within the law than my family," Pietrobono explains. The artist confesses his preoccupation with what it means to claim citizenship as a second-generation immigrant with "no blood in the land" ("because so much has been justified by that logic: so-and-so has blood here"): "[When I was thinking about what to do for the festival] I was thinking, how does someone like me, a child of immigrants, not a lot of money to speak of, hack into that? How do I get some level of protection and stability and growth that landowners get? Which then [led] to the whole thinking about the racialized history of land ownership and who had place under the law to lay claim on land." *Easement*, Pietrobono explains, was motivated by the question of how the rights of landownership are conditioned by and complicit with structures of violence and exclusion ("over native populations, on extracted labor, on displaced labor, on women"). "I was thinking a lot about the violence required to create property—to protect it, to regulate it, to safeguard it."[49]

Freedom, ownership, and subjection are intertwined in the liberal context. As Saidiya V. Hartman has noted, freedom contains within itself a paradoxical double bind, grimly described by Marx as the "double freedom" wrought by primitive accumulation: the freedom to exchange one's labor, while being free of material resources. For Marx, this double bind is encapsulated in the moment when the subject is free to circulate as a worker and sell his labor but is not free to own himself, to reap the benefits of his labor. For Marx, primitive accumulation refers to "the expropriation of the immediate producers, i.e., the dissolution of private property based on the labour of its owner." Here Marx describes the alienation of the worker not only from his labor but also from the land. Uprooted, the worker must now circulate to find work. Marx writes, "Private property . . . is . . . personally earned, . . . based, as it were, on the fusing together of the isolated, independent working individual with the conditions of his labour"; under capitalism, private property (the fruits of one's labor) "is supplanted by capitalist private property, which rests on the exploitation of alien[ated], but formally free labour."[50] Hartman sees this irony as resonating most cruelly in the "freeing" of the former slave's labor, which she argues is the freedom to have one's labor power exploited: "Within the liberal 'Eden of the innate rights of man,' owning easily gave way to being owned, sovereignty to fungibility, and abstract equality to subordination and exploitation." Hartman continues, "If sovereignty served 'to efface the domination intrinsic to power' and rights 'enabled and facilitated relations of domination,' as Michel Foucault argues, then what we are left to consider is the subjugation that rights instigate and the domination they efface."[51] What Hartman wants to show is what Pietrobono wants to show: that what is legally owned conceals the untold expropriation and violence that the discourse of legality obfuscates.

The relation of violence to the policing of property rights is explored in a critical text written by Pietrobono, "The Opposite of Property," that accompanies his documentation of *Easement* on his website. He situates *Easement*'s investigation into the role played by private property in the high-profile deaths at the heart of the Black Lives Matter movement. He points to the way that private property's "management and enforcement set the stage" for the use of lethal force against black bodies: Florida's Stand-Your-Ground law that alibied George Zimmerman, who murdered Trayvon Martin on the basis of a claim that some people have the right to be in particular places and others do not; the charge of "illegal vending" used by the police to justify their initial reason for approaching Eric Garner, who was allegedly selling loose cigarettes and taking "rightful" profits out of the pockets of store owners; and the fatal denial of Philando Castile's legal right to possession of (i.e., recognized right to ownership of) a gun, a right that in practice seems reserved only for white people.[52] In all of these cases, the right to protect private property trumped the right to life. Pietrobono says that his aim with *Easement* was "to mark the land so that the property owners couldn't have it without considering this kind of negative space, the socialized aspect that actually allows this property to exist." The grave he digs is the grave for all those black and brown bodies denied the right to self-possession and protection. Rather than stating outright that he intended to dig a grave, the artist let the work's political intentions remain implicit in his exchanges with the owners: "It was always, 'I will exert an intervention in the land in the shape of a 8 foot by 3 foot rectangle.'" Pietrobono left the very raw symbolic stakes of the project implicit in these conversations, presumably so as not to offend his hosts, whose goodwill he needed to complete the work. Although they were initially perplexed by the formality (and legality) of his request to use their land, the owners eventually complied: "It took a while for them to even understand why I would want [the easement] because in their mind [they were like] we know you now so you can just come here whenever you want. You don't need an easement to come here. I had a hard time articulating why, for me, it was important it was a legal relationship." By insisting on a legal agreement, Pietrobono created not just an informal guest relation but a formal, legal relation. The legal easement gives the queer sociality that makes his intervention possible the official status necessary for it to circulate as a formal art object.

A year after making *Easement*, Pietrobono visited Maria Eichhorn's *Building as Unowned Property* (2017) at Documenta 14 in Athens. In this work Eichhorn, like Pietrobono, attempted to identify a legal path to designate a property as unowned. The artist bought Stavropoulou 15, a two-story building that had fallen into disrepair, for €140,000, using funds from Zurich's Migros Museum. The dilapidated neoclassical-revival is located near Amerikis Square, a culturally diverse, working-class neighborhood. Eichhorn claims to have bought the building to protect it from gentrification and real estate speculation. For now it remains a shuttered building with a lock on the door and a peeling façade. "It was painful to see the piece but interesting," Pietrobono said of Eichhorn's house. "I think that is the difficulty of this kind of art. You are trying to produce a commons while participating in this highly 'winner take all' individuated authorial world and it is one of the inherent contradictions of being an artist and wanting to produce socially in any way." In other words, how does the artist use the tools available but to different ends?

Building as Unowned Property raises the irony of contemporary art tourism: Is it better than the real estate tourism it replaces? Is Eichhorn better than other prospectors? The ethical questions raised by Eichhorn's act of repropriety recalls a project by Güell, another wry critique of humanitarianism called *Good Intentions* (2016) that she developed with her frequent collaborator Levi Orta; it is a proposal for public donations to save looted Syrian antiquities by purchasing them from the black market. Much as Robin Hood Cooperative's Parasite algorithm leaves open the question of whether producing a commons is a matter of being *a better patron*, Eichhorn's work poses the question of whether it is a matter of being *a better owner*, a good host? Does setting a property apart in order to protect it from more rapacious owners make it a commons? As Pietrobono sees it, Eichhorn claims that by taking something out of circulation, she circumvents the logic of ownership—but she then capitalizes on her good intentions by circulating the piece as an art commodity, an emblem of her cultural capital. Here we find an instance of where the work of redistribution and of symbolic disruption butt up against each other—when the potentially redistributive act is recaptured and absorbed back in the art economy. For him, the solution to the problem of private property is not repossessing or owning with good intentions (as a symbolic gesture that remains mostly within the art world); it is redistributing and communalizing that property.

THE PARASITE DELINQUENT

Both Pietrobono (a founding member of New York City's Occupy Museums) and Güell see their work as responding to the relationship between contemporary art and capital (both social and economic) after the 2008 global financial crisis.[53] Güell sees banks as paradigmatic of hegemonic power's nonreciprocity. With her piece *Displaced Legal Application #1: Fractional Reserve* (*Aplicación Legal Desplazada #1: Reserva Fraccionaria*) (2010–11), she organized a series of events to teach the public how to turn the law against the banks, as (she argues) the banks have used the law against the people. She named the work after the fractional-reserve banking system, "the mechanism through which banks create money out of nothing." Under this system the bank does not own the money it lends; it loans out other investors' and depositors' money. They effectively create money by "monetizing" the IOUs of businesses and individuals.[54] (When the reverse happens, however, Güell observes, it is considered a crime, such as when writing a check without having the funds to back it up.) Güell's artwork—a performance-based, socially engaged experience in the vein of participatory art—comprised a conference and a manual, downloadable for free on her website, called "How to Expropriate Money from the Banks." The manual featured strategies, legal information, and commentary from her collaborators, who included the anarchist activists Lucio Urtubia and Enric Duran.[55] While Güell situates her actions as artworks, neither Urtubia nor Duran do so. Called modern-day Robin Hoods, Urtubia and Duran are well known in anarchist circles for successfully expropriating ("robbing") funds from big banks and redirecting the money to revolutionary and social justice causes. Both Urtubia and Duran model a redistributive ethics of parasitism, and their work exemplifies how complicity can function as a tool of power: it can force individuals to internalize the moralism of the state or it can give the powerless a loophole, the access needed to gum up the inner workings of the system.

LUCIO URTUBIA

Urtubia was the original hacker. A lifelong bricklayer born in autonomous northern Spain in the 1930s, in 1977 he famously forged $20 million worth of Citibank traveler's checks—an act that is considered his masterwork. At the time, Citibank (then known as National City Bank) was the largest bank in the world. The famous anarchist used the money to aid guerrilla movements such as the Tupamaros in Latin America, the Black Panthers in the United States, and the antifascist struggle in Spain. The forgery cost the bank much more than the $20 million in counterfeit checks, for it prompted a crisis in confidence in the checks themselves, which were spread across Europe. The bank had no choice but to suspend the use of traveler's checks, putting thousands of tourists in limbo and causing its stock to fall. Urtubia was finally arrested in 1980, when he was stopped with a suitcase full of the falsified checks. Despite the large scale of the forgery, however, he served only six months in jail after he struck an extrajudicial agreement with Citibank. The bank, which had continued to receive and pay out false traveler's checks, agreed to drop the charges in exchange for Urtubia's supplying the printing plates he used to make them. Citibank thus neutralized Urtubia's disruption by becoming the patron of his act of forgery, much as Amazon became the patron of *Amazon Noir* by buying Ubermorgen's code. However, unlike Ubermorgen's, Urtubia's action has a clear redistributive function that goes well beyond its heuristic dimension. Urtubia sums it up this way: "As the revolutionaries say, robbing and expropriation is a revolutionary act as long as one doesn't benefit from it."[56]

ENRIC DURAN

In 2008 Enric Duran, a Catalan anticapitalist activist, announced that over the course of two years he had "robbed" thirty-nine Spanish banks of nearly 500,000 euros, taking out sixty-eight commercial and personal loans: "I have 'robbed' . . . from those who rob us the most," he said in an online statement and video, characterizing his actions as "financial civil disobedience."[57] He used the funds to finance projects aimed at building alternatives to capitalism. Like Urtubia's, Duran's methods made the banks complicit with his action. It can be argued that Duran stole from the banks only insofar as he accepted the banks' invitations to borrow money he could not afford to pay back, again and again. He exploited a loophole in the banking system by which an individual can pass himself or herself off as a company, avoiding the scrutiny of a credit check, in order to get the same loan from multiple banks for a single item (e.g., a video camera). Duran writes:

> After some research and attempts, in the spring of 2006, I started going ahead definitely with this idea; I was making various banks, savings banks and financial credit establishments think that I wanted to refurbish my flat or buy a new car. In some cases, I was doing that by using a company I created with the aim of justifying certain investments as the purchase of audiovisual materials for a production company. *The advantages of asking for a loan by a company are that debts as a company, even when it is a sole shareholder company, do not get registered in your personal credit history, so you can always increase your debts indefinitely without being detected by* CIRBE *(information system about debts from the Bank of Spain).* . . . These loans were applied without any guarantee neither from another person nor from any properties, just by my signature and an invented occupation with a great false payroll that was making them believe I was earning enough money to cover the financing by far.[58]

As Duran explains it, banks promote indebtedness without meaningful regard for the risks; the fact that the banks have no functional structure for confirming whether the lendee can repay the amount or for confirming collateral (such as payroll records, which may be falsified) means that they are irresponsible in their lending practices (a claim that seems to have been confirmed by the 2008 global financial crisis). Rather than purely relying on the bank's mechanisms, Duran misrepresents his intentions to the banks so as to shape their decision to loan to him—introducing, on his part, a degree of moral ambiguity into the act.

Since that time Duran has shifted his efforts to radical cooperativist organizing of the kind discussed in chapter 1; he initially used the funds he got from the banks to set up Catalan Integral Cooperative, a network of cooperatives operating in the separatist region of Catalonia. But his latest project is FairCo-op, what has been described as "no less than a whole new kind of global financial system" wherein "cooperatives around the world would be able to trade, fund one another's growth, redistribute wealth, and make collective decisions."[59]

Duran's actions can be seen as a response to the Belgian philosopher Michel Feher's call to undermine neoliberal capitalism by engaging it on its own terms, by *embracing the status of the investee.* Feher suggests that while leftists—reformist and radical alike—have insisted on approaching the problem of neoliberalism from the outside, they would do better "to accept and inhabit a certain mode of subjection in order to redirect it or turn it against its instigators."[60] He calls for "the possibility of defying neoliberalism from *within*—that is, by embracing the very condition that its discourses and practices delineate," an approach he locates in early feminist and labor movement tactics.[61] (What Feher is calling for here is what I term "parasitism.") Duran argues that citizens' participation in the economy of debt demonstrates their complicity with the wider forms of oppression and exploitation that attend a capitalist system; the banks need to extend credit to justify their own existence, and complicity maintains individual investment in a system that relies on their sense of indebtedness to keep them paying. But Duran's project, much as the Strike Debt movement has, calls the bluff of a predatory debt system: "Banks need to grant loans because that is the main way for them to get benefits and . . . because the financial system needs to sign out more and more bank credits to create more and more money each time. By keeping loans, credit cards and checking accounts, we are an accessory to the banks which represent the heart of the capitalist system that is spreading our planet's destruction, poverty and our life's slavery all around."[62]

Duran did not internalize responsibility for the loans. Instead he embraced the position of the defaulter. His indifference to legal authority recalls a scene in Foucault's *Discipline and Publish:* the thirteen-year-old delinquent

Béasse, charged with vagabondage, models a kind of freedom in his refusal of legal rationality (a refusal to internalize legal authority and social responsibility for his crime) in the face of the court. In this encounter between the unaffected delinquent and the judge reading out his punishment, Foucault sees a model of what he calls indiscipline: "Hearing his sentence of two years in a reformatory, Béasse 'pulled an ugly face, then, recovering his good humour, remarked: "Two years, that's never more than twenty-four months. Let's be off, then."'" Foucault writes that this scene anticipates anarchist resistance to come. In the late nineteenth century, "taking the penal apparatus as their point of attack," anarchists recognized in delinquency a militant rejection of the law: a means "to disentangle delinquency from the bourgeois legality and illegality that had colonized it; when they wished to re-establish or constitute the political unity of popular illegalities."[63]

The disentanglement from legality *and* illegality that characterizes delinquency is also the position of the parasite. However, the parasite maintains the fiction that it is in fact still beholden to "bourgeois legality"; the parasite manipulates the host's false perception that proximity indicates investment in and faithfulness to the social order—that the parasite's structural position in relation to the host means that they share the same goals. This perception is maintained by the fear of complicity, but the sense that proximity equals similarity can also be weaponized by the parasite. In Güell's and Pietrobono's performances of parasitism, they use their complicity as a tool of solidarity with others who have less access to the host. These works gesture toward the redistributions that are enabled by parasitical performances of complicity that refuse to internalize belief in the intrinsic ethics of the law. In a neoliberal system increasingly invested in generating responsible moral subjects in order to exonerate itself, the parasite models what it could mean to refuse (or to perform its refusal) to internalize a position of indebtedness (both literal financial indebtedness and the debt of gratitude that the guest is thought to owe to the host). In the process, these performances also challenge the overdetermined narrative of interpellation. In other words, the parasite embedded in its host is not an ontological condition but a structural one. At the same time, where the figure of the reformist or the cynic presupposes externality, the parasite cannot be extricated from the system in which it operates. Detaching their identification from the larger structures they inhabit, these works attempt to forge a redistributive ethics of the parasite.

PART II

IMPOSITION

INTIMATE INTERVENTIONS

THREE HANGERS-ON

CHRIS KRAUS'S PARASITICAL FEMINISM

In many cases, the man can commit acts with woman's complicity that degrade her without tarnishing his lofty image. . . . Officially the man renounces her, those are the rules of the game. . . . When one speaks to these women of dignity, honor, loyalty, and all the lofty virile virtues, one should not be surprised if they refuse to "go along." They particularly snigger when virtuous males reproach them for being calculating, actresses, liars: they know well that no other way is open to them. . . . The woman has been assigned the role of parasite.—**SIMONE DE BEAUVOIR, *THE SECOND SEX***

The title of Chris Kraus's 1997 cult novel, *I Love Dick*, rings out as an admission of shame and a badge of defiance: I am attached to and titillated by a patriarchy that oppresses me. It is a performative study of the female abasement and complicity that attends heterosexual desire—a problematic that radical feminist thought has long explored in terms of the maligned "female parasite." Panned by early critics, the book has since become a full-blown cultural juggernaut, embraced by a new generation of internet-savvy feminists and reappraised by critics as a feminist classic that arrived "20 years early."[1] "Critics don't seem to like Chris Kraus' 'novels' much," observed Joan Hawkins in her afterword to the book's 2006 reissue. "I say 'novels' (in quotes) because I'm not entirely sure Kraus' works belong in the generic category of 'novel.' Rather . . . Kraus' prose works constitute 'some new kind of literary form,' a new genre, 'something in between cultural criticism and fiction.'"[2] In a 1998 review for *Bookforum*, David Rimanelli memorably described it as "a book not so much written as secreted," a frank characterization of a work that viscerally enacts the very abjection that it sets out to critique.[3] In *I Love Dick*, Kraus chronicles the romantic obsession of her protagonist, "Chris Kraus," with "Dick," a character later identified as the British cultural theorist Dick Hebdige.[4] Dick is an academic colleague of Chris's husband, "Sylvère," an influential French theorist and downtown cult figure presumably based on Kraus's then-real-life husband, Sylvère Lotringer. (The conflation of real and fictional and the ambiguities it produces is encapsulated in this confusion over names; to minimize this confusion, I use first names to refer to the characters—as the book does—and last names to refer to the writers and public figures.) After only a single meeting, which Dick describes as "genial but not particularly intimate or remarkable," Chris makes Dick into an idol, an object of worship, a figure to whom she confesses both her intellectual rapacity and her feminist shame at being Sylvère's frequent "plus-one," his perceived "hanger-on."[5] In over two hundred letters written to Dick, she rewrites him, transforming him from a real, unique person into a faceless, patriarchal screen (as in "every Tom, Dick, and Harry") onto which she projects her sexual fantasies, personal anxieties, and critical interventions.

Where the first half of this book examines the redistributive potential of the parasite, this chapter initiates the second half's exploration of parasitism as an emblematic site of feminist politics. The chapter reads *I Love Dick* and its critical reception to theorize a particular type of parasitism as a manic mode of feminist performativity. It pursues a comparative analysis of the compromised utility of a parasitical feminism by reading the novel alongside the French conceptual artist Sophie Calle's epistolary art project *Take Care of Yourself* (2007). Both works mobilize the genre of epistolary exchange, and both model practices of feverish accumulation, producing hundreds of love letters that feed on and ultimately destabilize the male lovers—the ostensible hosts of these works—who have jilted them, making these men unwitting symbols of heteropatriarchy. Calle and Kraus are not the first writers or artists to marshal epistolary and diaristic practices, often seen as feminized literary forms (at least in the European tradition), to challenge the role played by heterosexual love and romance in the abjection of women.[6] Their works draw on conventions within feminist art practice established by works such as Carolee Schneemann's *Interior Scroll* (1975), Adrian Piper's *Calling Cards* (1986), and Tracey Emin's *Love Poem* (1996), which use an autobiographical epistolary address to raise questions of sexual and racial abjection.[7] In Calle's and Kraus's projects, correspondence represents a kind of ludic back and forth in which gendered opponents feed on each other in a dynamically unstable game (though this play remains unidirectional in these works, as the overtures are unreciprocated). These correspondences recall a question posed by Judith Butler: "Can the exchange of speech or writing be the occasion for a disruption of the social ontology of positionality?"[8] In these works, women's desire (both real and performed) to "literalize," to put into letters their social revenge takes on a decidedly literary character; reading and writing become conditions of possibility for turning the "law of the father" against itself, letter by letter.

What is particularly ingenious about *I Love Dick* is that it is underwritten by the very poststructural stakes by which Hebdige, as a Birmingham school cultural critic, made his name: an openness to experimentation and radical transgression that is articulated through his work on symbolic resistance and punk subcultural style.[9] In a dynamic that echoes that between Byrne and Hendricks, Kraus calls Dick's intellectual bluff, showing that this self-proclaimed "subcultural transgressor" and theorist of power is himself unable or unwilling to play along when he is the one being transgressed. In his refusals to respond to Kraus's letters and his rumored attempts to block the book's publication, it seems that Dick would prefer to see his position as outside of the structures of power that his scholarship theorizes. Elizabeth Gumport writes of Hebdige's response to the release of *I Love Dick*:

> Shortly after *I Love Dick* was released, *New York* magazine reported that Hebdige had attempted to block publication of the book on grounds that it invaded his privacy. "I don't like reading bad reviews," he said, "and this book reads like a bad review of my presence in the world . . . If someone's writing gets read because it exploits a recognizable figure, then it really is a despicable exercise." Kraus defended her project on the grounds it "explod[ed] the 'right of privacy' that serves patriarchy so well." Hebdige scoffed: "A feminist issue? Tell her to take it up with Princess Diana."[10]

Hebdige thus responds to Kraus's transgression by dismissing the value of her contribution in terms strikingly similar to those Hendricks uses to dismiss Byrne. He refuses to countenance Kraus's work as a critical intervention on its own merits, characterizing it as an unoriginal "review" of him. As Kraus counters, Hebdige invokes privacy as an alibi against women's right to a public discourse about misogyny's specific interpersonal guises and manifestations. Hebdige's attempt to legally block the book's publication for invasion of privacy operates similarly to Amazon's nondisclosure agreement with Ubermorgen, as both are attempts by hosts to use their power to prevent their exposure.

Dick was a ready-made allegory for British cultural studies' early exclusion of women. Hebdige was criticized by feminist Birmingham school scholars like Angela McRobbie for framing subcultural style as a predominantly male phenomenon, ignoring its gender ambiguities and the extent to which it is informed by "patriarchal meanings."[11] Kraus's parasitism of Hebdige can in turn be read as allegorizing what Stuart Hall called the "ruptural" intervention of feminism on male-dominated British cultural studies in the early 1970s.[12] Hall recalls the intrusion of feminism into Birmingham's Centre for Contemporary Cultural Studies having witnessed male cultural studies pioneers struggle to account for the blind spots of their own internalized sexism. Pioneering feminist cultural studies scholars have also published important reflections on this moment, but Hall's recollection is worth quoting at length:[13]

> As the thief in the night, [feminism] broke in; interrupted, made an unseemly noise, seized the time, crapped on the table of cultural studies. . . . Because of the growing importance of feminist work and the early beginnings of the feminist movement outside in the very early 1970s, many of us in the Centre—mainly, of course, men—thought it was time there was good feminist work in cultural studies. And we indeed tried to buy it in, to import it, to attract good feminist scholars. As you might expect, many of the women in cultural studies weren't terribly interested in this benign project. We were opening the door to feminist studies, being good, transformed men. And yet, when it broke in through the window, every single unsuspected resistance rose to the surface—fully installed patriarchal power, which believed it had disavowed itself. There are no leaders here, we used to say; we are all graduate students and members of staff together, learning how to practice cultural studies. You can decide whatever you want to decide, etc. And yet, when it came to the question of the reading list . . . Now that's where I really discovered about the gendered nature of power. Long, long after I was able to pronounce the words, I encountered the reality of Foucault's profound insight into the individual reciprocity of knowledge and power. Talking about giving up power is a radically different experience from being silenced.[14]

Hall captures firsthand the men's rush to immunize themselves against claims of sexism. The men's "good-natured" self-justifications in response to challenges to their positions demonstrate how power is disavowed not on a systemic or institutional level but on a personal level and, further, how propriety is employed as a shield for this disavowal.

The symbolic place Hebdige is made to occupy is as if fated by the misfortune of the punning endowment afforded by his first name. But while Hebdige's real-world persona is essential to the success of Kraus's conceptual gesture, *I Love Dick* is ultimately not about Dick Hebdige, any more than it is about any other specific man of his social standing; rather it is about the patriarchal symbolic capital he both represents and benefits from. Kraus's decision to violate the condition of privacy presumed by interpersonal intimacy or familiarity in order to make a feminist statement about the routine sexual humiliation of young women prefigures similar post-digital-era accounts such as those associated with the Me Too movement and call-out culture, which have brought into the mainstream this kind of public exposure and real-name truth-telling about power dynamics under patriarchy and white supremacy. Many have debated the ethics of these tactics of public exposure, while others have pointed out how normative ethical approaches to this question continually position the targeted individual's comfort and privacy as the paramount considerations.

In the case of the Me Too movement, such acts of public exposure buck intense pressure to continue doing what women have been doing forever: internalizing and dissociating their shame by not talking about a sexual culture that is, as the blogger Katie Anthony has put it, "fucking awful and ordinary."[15] Rather than silently accepting her abjection, Kraus hyperbolizes and publicizes it. By manically embracing and performing her social role as a "romantically dependent" woman, the protagonist of *I Love Dick* reappropriates as a tactical model the figure of the parasitical woman, long reviled in nineteenth- and twentieth-century radical Western feminist history and criticism. In this way Kraus follows Simone de Beauvoir's call in *The Second Sex* to take up, to intensify the role of the parasite to which woman has been consigned. For Beauvoir, woman (who is, for her, French, white, bourgeois, and heterosexual) is locked into a degraded role by a patriarchal order that makes her dependent upon it and then punishes her for it. She can either fight this structural role and lose, or she can accept it and play it to her advantage: "those are the rules of the game." In Beauvoir's framing, woman's parasitical social position constitutes a kind of loophole; woman's lack of self-determination can allow her to evade culpability. "There is, however, an advantage that woman can gain from her very inferiority," she writes. "Since she is from the start less favored by fortune than man, she does not feel that she is to blame a priori for what befalls him; it is not her duty to make amends for social injustice, and she is not asked to do so."[16] These works explore how women's secondary status might allow them to sidestep their supposed ethical and moral responsibility to a patriarchal system on which they depend but in which they hold no stake of ownership (akin to the woman who may run the house but whose name does not appear on the deed)—an alibi that feminists might turn to tactical or reparative ends.

Exemplifying the deep historical interlocking of femininity and complicity, the female parasite consolidates feminist anxieties about the romantically and financially dependent woman whose identity performance as heterosexual and/or bourgeois makes her complicit with patriarchal structures and relations (such as marriage and domestic life). Rather than fleeing charges of overattachment, Kraus embraces the compulsiveness and overintimacy with which the so-called dependent woman has already been charged. (In this way *I Love Dick* can be read as part of a longer history of feminist guerrilla tactics that might include the Irish suffragette Mary Maloney, the original femme troll, who followed Winston Churchill around for a week ringing a dinner bell whenever he tried to speak publicly.)[17] Kraus's performance of her real identity traffics a parasitical representational politics that is at once subversive and reactionary. As Amber Jamilla Musser has argued of female masochism, femininity functions here as a screen for the problem of complicity as "a product of [woman's] relative powerlessness in a patriarchally ordered world."[18] This chapter likewise attempts to theorize complicity as a tool for fashioning modes of feminist agency in patriarchal spaces where women cannot set the terms of engagement.

DEAR DICK

I first began writing about *I Love Dick* in 2004, when it was an unlikely object of academic inquiry. When Kraus's book was first published, it horrified many readers, including many feminists who read it as a confessional memoir and found troubling its gleeful self-abasement and reckless exhibitionism.[19] In two articles, published in 2011 and 2012, I argued that this reading of the novel as a straightforward autobiography failed to register the feminist value of its ambivalent address, which I contended should instead be read as a performance.[20] Around that time the book appeared at last to find its core readership in millennial feminists (generally middle class and urban-dwelling). In the intervening years there have been public acknowledgments of its influence by the writers Sheila Heti, Heidi Julavits, and Ariana Reines and celebrities like Lena Dunham, and discussions of it have circulated virally via feminist fanzines, Instagram, and Tumblr. The book has become a rallying cry for young feminists, who seem to read it as empowering—not as a story of reveling in abjection but as a story of refusing to play the silent counterpart in a coercive script.[21] Loosely adapted as an Amazon original series in 2016, the book has now been absorbed into the cultural zeitgeist (if for only a niche population).[22] In the wake of its television debut, the novel *I Love Dick* was widely revisited and positively reviewed in venues such as the *New Yorker* and the *London Review of Books*.

This dramatic shift in critics' appraisal of the book since it was reissued in 2006 is largely thanks to a new willingness to acknowledge it as having innovated a hybrid genre combining memoir with fiction. The performance studies scholar Barbara Browning sums it up well: "*I Love Dick* is only interesting . . . if one recognizes it as a work of fiction. That is, if you read it simply as a compulsive, stalkerish, neurotic confessional narrative, it's 'interesting' in a kind of vulgar way, but it really gets theoretically interesting when Kraus is pushing you to contemplate the performance of academic rock stardom, and the fictional construction of erotic and intellectual cathexis."[23] Within this double frame *I Love Dick* becomes recognizable not as mere autobiography but as a performance of autobiography. The scandal of the novel remains its insistence on itself as real. "But Dick, I know that as you read this, you'll know these things are true," Chris writes in one letter. "You understand the game is real, or even better than, reality, and better than is what it's all about. . . . Better than means stepping out into complete intensity."[24] The performative excess of her insistence places the narrative's content in tension with its form (i.e., its generic packaging as fiction). Kraus rides the line between fiction and nonfiction, unflinchingly (some say heedlessly) using real names and real historical circumstances.

While Hawkins calls this genre "theoretical fiction" and others call it "autofiction," I argue it is best read as performance art, a medium defined by its capacity to hold as one the ambiguous imbrication of life and art, real and performed bodies. Indeed Kraus writes admiringly about performance art in *I Love Dick*, calling the performance artist Hannah Wilke "a model for everything I hope to do."[25] Applying critical reading methods in performance studies to Kraus's text, Browning elsewhere observes this about Kraus's mode of address: "If one of the goals of performance art is to make audiences aware of their own complicity in the event, this confessional mode of performative fiction, often incorporating direct address, similarly puts a demand on a reader to contemplate his or her own performative force in the encounter on the page. But another part of the implicit contract with the reader/listener is his or her acceptance of the possible unreliability of the narrator."[26] Browning follows the performance theorist Richard Schechner in her insistence that the character Chris Kraus is not Chris Kraus and yet not not Chris Kraus.[27] *I Love Dick*'s claim to be real (which cannot be ignored even if it cannot be taken as fact) is explicitly lodged as doing feminist work because it aspires to say something about actual bodies, events, consequences: "Why does everybody think that women are debasing themselves when we expose the conditions of our own debasement?" Chris writes in another letter. "Why do women always have to come off clean?"[28]

Ultimately the conceptual payoff of the project depends on Kraus's reader allowing for both frames of her narrative, reading it as both real and fictional. The constitutive undecidability of performance lends the author-character amalgam Kraus-Chris a double cover against the pitfalls to which feminists are particularly vulnerable, including narrative overdetermination and theoretical delegitimation. The narrative technique by which Chris insists on the material trace of her body pushes against the generic limits of the novel form, enacting in writing what Rebecca Schneider has called the "explosive literality" of the work of feminist body artists like Wilke, Karen Finley, and Annie Sprinkle.[29] Browning suggests that Kraus's "confessional mode of performative fiction" was likely informed by her close proximity to and occasional participation in precisely this burgeoning scene of 1980s downtown performance art.[30]

Kraus and her character Chris use the genre of correspondence rather than her body as the medium for her performance. In *I Love Dick*, Chris turns to the letter form to avenge her sense of personal and sexual abjection. With the force of Chris's pen, the proper name Dick becomes dick, the phallus; he is thrust into the Symbolic. Now an abstraction, he is made to stand for the very idea of men, occupying the structural position of Man in Chris's litany of disappointments in the spheres of love, sex, and art. Chris graphically recounts her humiliations, from Dick's refusal to get romantically involved with her to the "insults, slights, and condescension" that she endured as the self-described "failed filmmaker" wife of a successful, tenured academic and public figure. He gets top billing; she is his perpetual "plus one." Sylvère (like Lotringer, a longtime Columbia University French professor) is an avant-garde philosopher. Known for his kinky sexual and critical appetite, he plays dominant-submissive to her submissive-dominant, academic host to her abject professional parasitical supplementarity. She has a place in the worlds of art and academia only insofar as he provides it. "Sylvère's fans were mostly young white men drawn to the more 'transgressive' elements of modernism, the heroic sciences of human sacrifice and torture as legitimized by Georges Bataille," writes Chris. She notes that they were often rude to her, and she responded by "milking money from Sylvère's growing reputation, setting ever-higher fees [for his professional appearances on his behalf]." Chris's claimed outsiderness is complicated by her status as a very well connected (if still parasitical) "hanger-on." A self-described financial and emotional drain on her husband's resources, she is emotive excess, spilling over the boundaries of institutional permissiveness granted to Sylvère with his subversive Ivy League deconstructive critical cachet. This emotional excess seems deliberately performed, as when Chris writes to Dick, "And I wonder if there'll ever be a possibility of reconciling youth and age, or the anorexic open wound I used to be with the money-hustling hag I've become." She swears her love for Dick, concluding her daily letters to him with affirmations of his sexual power, critical majesty, and patriarchal omnipotence. Her shrill performance of sincerity hits some hilariously deadpan notes. She signs off in one entry, "I keep you in my heart, it keeps me going," and in another, "Knowing you's like knowing Jesus. There are billions of us and only one of you so I don't expect much from you personally. . . . I'm touched by you and fulfilled just by believing."[31]

Chris's "love letters" to Dick constitute an act of public exhibitionism. In this sense the project recalls Derrida's reflections on the postcard as an open letter, a mode of intimate exchange that remains unsealed and can thus be read at any moment.[32] The letters taunt Dick, mocking him for being forced to watch from the sidelines ("You, poor Dick, do not deserve to be exposed to such a masturbatory passion") while inviting him to participate in his own spectacularization by writing the introduction for the letters' publication. "It [the introduction] could read something like this," Sylvère (who has agreed to play the role of co-conspirator) suggests in one letter. "I believe these letters will interest the reader as a cultural document. Obviously they manifest the alienation of the postmodern intellectual in its most diseased form. I really feel sorry for such a parasitic growth, that feeds upon itself." The letters, both personal and impersonal, are received as irritants, like spam or junk mail. In their address to Dick, they insist on being read because they are personal rather than anonymous, even as they make him anonymous, make him stand in for any man. The letters make him into the parasitical appendage—make him, ultimately, an appendix to her book. *I Love Dick* concludes with the letter that Dick eventually sends to Sylvère, in which he misspells Chris's first name: "I found the situation initially perplexing, then disturbing, and my major regret now is that I didn't find the courage at the time to communicate to you and Kris [*sic*] how uncomfortable I felt being the unwitting object of what you described to me over the phone before Christmas as some kind of bizarre game."[33] Dick's missive, directed to Sylvère and intended to remain between the two men, recalls Gayle Rubin's account of the transacting of women in homosocial kinship networks.[34] By excluding her from this conversation about her work, Dick attempts to write Chris out of her own story.

In the larger economy of the book's publication and publicity, Kraus's correspondence continues to stalk Dick, assigning him in the public record of her "open book" the role of reluctant art object. Dick is given no choice but to hold the position Kraus has given him. Her subterfuge turns Dick's own logic (the logic of the dick, of patriarchy) against him. She insists on the excess produced by the system's supposedly supplementary parts—namely, feminine affect—that cannot be taken into the court record; she uses the "nonserious" mediums of love letters and diary entries because they are unlikely weapons, inadmissible evidence. Kraus's work perverts the normative meaning of the letter, which is typically a private exchange between two entities, for the letters in *I Love Dick* are one-way projections, serialized and bound. They render Dick impotent, not only through the manic intensity of their proliferation but also, finally, through their legitimacy once circulated as a published book.

Despite the lengths to which Chris goes to perform the wretchedness of her own unflattering female self-portrait, the joke always appears to be on Dick, and as the letters mount, the project's conceptual chorus sings louder and louder: "Dick, you're so vain. I bet you think this book is about you." On his own, though, Dick is mostly a token of exchange, first between Chris and Sylvère and then between Kraus and her reader, for the book guarantees that the letters written "to his address" are intercepted by the reader. As "Dear Dick" replaces "Dear Diary," the form of the letter becomes a means of transforming Dick from subject to object, writer to text, critic to critique.

FEMINIST VIRALITY

Love can be the becoming which appropriates the other for itself by consuming it, introjecting it into itself, to the point where the other disappears.—LUCE IRIGARAY, *ELEMENTAL PASSIONS*

Throughout the pages of *I Love Dick*, Kraus acknowledges her debt to Sophie Calle, the French artist widely credited with having set the gold standard in the genre of "breakup art" with works such as *No Sex Last Night* (1996) and *Exquisite Pain* (2004).[35] Many of Calle's works begin from flirtatious collaborations with various boyish artists, intellectual studs, and theoretical father figures: *Suite vénitienne* (1980) with Jean Baudrillard; *Appointment with Sigmund Freud* (1998), a project about the archetypal father figure; *Psychological Assessment* (2003), a collaboration with Damien Hirst, which originated in Calle's request that Hirst send her a love letter; and her creative entanglement with the U.S. writer Paul Auster, out of which grew a whole series of performance-based projects, including *Gotham Handbook* (1994), *The Chromatic Diet* (1997), and *Days under the Sign of B, C, & W* (1998). Calle thus made her career on explorations of the conceptual politics of romantic art practices and on one-way investigatory performances.

In 2007 Calle upped the ante on these methods with her much-praised Venice Biennale exhibition and subsequent book project, *Take Care of Yourself (Prenez soin de vous)*. Both exhibition and book showcase the abundance of the return on Calle's missive to 107 women professionals: she requested that these women read and analyze, according to their particular occupational skill sets, a breakup email that she claims to have received. Calle writes, "I received an email telling me it was over. I didn't know how to respond. It was almost as if it hadn't been meant for me. It ended with the words, 'Take care of yourself.' And so I did."[36] And so they did—over a hundred women, chosen for their professional skills and distinctions. The lexicometrist produces an extended literary and linguistic analysis of the email, noting the overwhelming dissymmetry in sentence structures with *I* to *you* pronouns (a ratio of 4 to 1). The proofreader rips the email apart, citing "clumsy sentence openings" and "long, ill-constructed sentences." The cartoonist literally makes him into a caricature of himself. The press agent turns him into "yesterday's news."

Take care of yourself. In jilting her, her ex-lover leaves her with a polite imperative to do as he asks one final time. Yet in appropriating his parting words, it is Calle herself who has the last word. *Take Care of Yourself* highlights the arrogance of that parting line, announces itself as a critique of the Western patriarchal tradition that paradoxically offers the door to freedom as a trap. How can one exercise one's freedom if to do so means obeying an imperative? Calle, like Kraus, attempts to negotiate what appears to be the coercive hospitality of a patriarchal injunction to be independent. In both Dick's and the letter-writing ex's desires to rid themselves of Chris's and Calle's attachments, the men disavow that they are the ones who set the terms.

Grand in size and ambition, *Take Care of Yourself* is a massive effort that matches the frantic multiplication of *I Love Dick*. Barbara Cassin notes Calle's use of seriality as a formal technique: "To create a series oneself via oth-

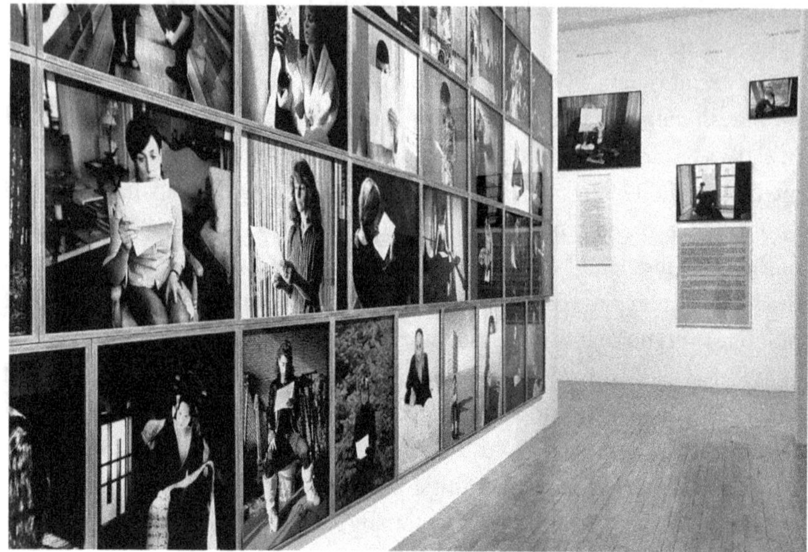

FIGURE 3.1 Installation view, "Sophie Calle." Whitechapel Art Gallery, London, 2009–10. Source: Sophie Calle and Paula Cooper Gallery.

ers, the others making up a series themselves to the extent that they have an identity trait—you'll all be women reacting to his way of leaving me . . . you're all laid out in this notebook. . . . In the case of me barbara, it's in the role of a philologist to fill in the sophie series. You want to be used up this way, you want that? Yes I want."[37]

The viewer's encounter with Calle's ex is signified by the very sign of multiplication: in the place of its absent referent (the ex) is the signature *X*.[38] Calle outsources to these women a task of interpretative labor that they mass-produce, alchemizing the host text (the original breakup email) into an intermedial army of feminist re-representations (figure 3.1): photographic portraits of Calle's sister-readers, each holding the email, their accompanying textual analyses personalized in a diverse lexicon of styles (handwritten, digitized, animated), as well as filmed performances of some of them singing or citing the text. Calle welds together a network of diverse media—film, performance, painting, sculpture, text, and photography—into a sophisticated conceptual weapon that she turns on X's crude and informal original text. The massive art book that archives the exhibition, exceptional for its sheer size (424 pages), is the product of skilled and networked creative mass production.

Calle thus masterminds in *Take Care of Yourself* a viral and networked feminist aesthetic, which is uncannily mirrored in the way that *I Love Dick* emerged as a viral meme on the social media platforms Instagram and Tumblr. The Tumblr account "Selfies with *I Love Dick* by Chris Kraus," maintained by the writer and blogger Emily Gould, features hundreds of selfies of young feminists holding up the book, including a photoshopped image of Lisa Simpson with her head in the book (figures 3.2 and 3.3). Feminist social media's embrace of *I Love Dick* cannot be overstated; the logics of the internet are central to its legibility as a feminist act. Today it's a cliché to observe that the digital has exploded the public-private distinction, bringing information that was formerly confined to the private sphere into the public forum. Digital-savvy, twenty-something feminists have sought to appropriate social media to feminist ends (with debatable results), anticipating practices now associated with the Me Too movement and call-out culture. Some have posted dating interactions they've had with real men on Tumblr accounts; others, like Marie Calloway, have (like Kraus) published intimate descriptions of private interactions with noted public figures; and many feminists of color have leveraged the public nature of social media to denounce individuals whose actions would otherwise go unchecked.[39]

While the male figures Dick and X are ostensibly at the core of these projects, they begin to look insignificant as they become buried under Kraus's proliferating sentiments and Calle's multiplicity of interpersonal mediations. Calle writes, "I asked 107 women . . . to analyze it, comment on it, dance it, sing it. Dissect it. Exhaust it. . . . Answer it for me."[40] And just as Calle's triangulated dissections undo X, Kraus's words ultimately pick Dick apart. Both men become details that recede into the background of the vast expanses of the projects' more striking conceptual and aesthetic fields; with so much else to take in, they are soon forgotten.[41] These works of viral proliferation have the effect of burying the men alive. As Joan Hawkins observes of Chris's early collaboration with Sylvère in the book, "At first they just share the letters with each other, but as the pile grows to 50 then 80 then 180 pages, they begin discussing some kind of Sophie Calle–like art piece, in which they would present the manuscript to Dick. . . . 'Dear Dick,' she writes at one point, 'I guess in a sense I've killed you. You've become Dear Diary.'"[42] Similarly Calle admits in an interview, "After one month I felt better. . . . The project had replaced the man."[43] Dick and X are thus perfect hosts, supplying the very structures that threaten them, feeding the artists' discursive attacks against them, growing these women's projects until the hosts are emptied of substance and the artists are lauded as never more original. Kraus and Calle

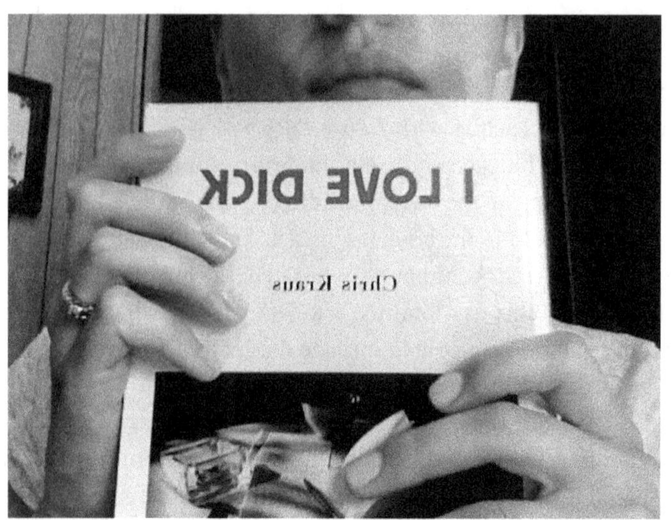

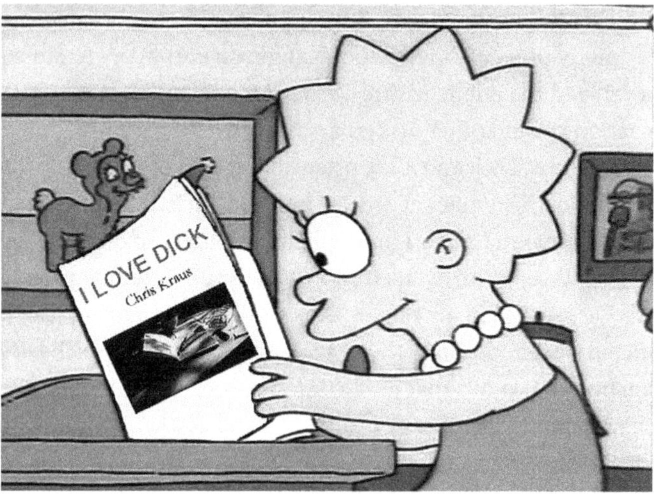

FIGURES 3.2 AND 3.3 "Selfies with *I Love Dick* by Chris Kraus" Tumblr account. Source: ildselfies.tumblr.com.

exploit the strategic supplementarity of the parasite in relation to her host to operate a feminist remapping of the structural dynamics of gendered territoriality: the parasite comes to overwhelm the terrain of its host.

Of all of Calle's work, *I Love Dick* most closely resembles not *Take Care of Yourself* but *The Address Book* (1983), an early work that experimented with invading the privacy of a real man—a project with which Kraus and Lotringer would have been familiar. Having found an address book on the street, Calle photocopies its contents before anonymously returning it to its owner, whom she dubs "Pierre D."[44] Calle then interviews all of the people whose addresses appeared in the book, constructing an exhaustively researched, speculative portrait of its owner.[45] Yve-Alain Bois writes, "Each morning the newspaper published an interview along with a related photograph, not necessarily taken by Calle (that of an artwork Pierre D. was said to like, for example). The fact that the piece kept building for a whole month, day after day, added to the mystery. . . . Three weeks after the final entry appeared, *Libération* published, in the same half-page format, the furious response of Pierre D. (who signed his real name, Pierre Baudry)."[46]

Baudry, a documentary filmmaker, had been in Norway the whole time, and it was only upon his return that he discovered the exposure of "so many facts of his life and traits of his character—including his repugnance toward any form of publicity."[47] In discussing the work, Calle notes how the deniability afforded by her status as an artist served as an effective cover until it was revealed that her target was a real person:

> There was a huge discussion because the journalists wanted to know why, as an artist, I was allowed to do something in the newspaper that they were not allowed to do: intrude into someone's life. Many people liked it because they thought it was a fiction, but when the guy answered and gave his name, proving that he really existed, it became evident that it was not a fiction, and the same people started to really dislike it because of the outrage. Then others, who didn't like it initially because they thought it wasn't risky enough, started to like it. It was a complete mess![48]

According to Calle, Baudry retaliated by publishing a headless nude photograph of her, but this attempt at what would today be called revenge porn was defanged by the fact that she had already published *The Striptease*, a project that featured a topless photograph of her working as a stripper in Pigalle.[49] Calle said later, "He is still resentful. He has let me know."[50] But despite the one-sidedness of her feelings, Calle professed in later interviews to have fallen in love with Pierre D: "I lost control. . . . I completely fell in love with that man, I changed my life for him. . . . I went to live in his neighborhood, only saw his friends, went to eat in the places he liked to go. . . . When he came back he hated me and I really felt rejected, but at the same time it's better than real love, because all this was completely fake."[51] Calle's and Kraus's projects' claim to being about love is reflected in this process of narcissistic deterritorialization, which Roland Barthes equates with love: "It is my desire I desire, and the loved being is no more than its tool. I rejoice at the thought of such a great cause, which leaves far behind it the person whom I have made into its pretext."[52]

The Address Book is an uncanny precursor to *I Love Dick*, both in life and art. It was reported that Baudry threatened to sue for invasion of privacy (Calle said in 2011 that she had nearly been sued twice), much as Hebdige is said to have tried to block the publication of *I Love Dick* and reportedly threatened to sue Kraus on similar grounds.[53] Some argue that this attempt to keep private life out of the public eye is a patriarchal gesture, one aimed at protecting men by delegitimizing women's experiences and concerns (certainly, privacy is deployed to serve whiteness in much the same way). Elizabeth Gumport writes of *I Love Dick*:

> What the pretense of privacy often does is protect us from reality. It is called on to conceal the fact that there are two realities: the world as it is lived in by men, and the world of women, which has historically been exiled from political and philosophical consideration. It has been regarded as beneath such consideration, its truths narrowly and inescapably personal—rather than universal—and therefore inevitably trivial. Hence Hebdige's invocation of Princess Diana. . . . Placing domestic and intimate relationships outside the boundaries of legitimate public interest in this way condemns them permanently to the status of intractable nature, or "frivolous gossip," discouraging intervention and thereby preserving invisible practices of domination.[54]

Just as Hendricks questioned and dismissed Byrne's work, relegating it to a student project or a bad imitation, Hebdige refused to acknowledge the critical and artistic legitimacy of Kraus's work. He implied that the book's only interest lay in its trafficking of his celebrity, in its attempt to cash in on a personal relationship, rather than as a legitimate exploration of the dynamics of that relationship (and the relationship between men and women, between patriarchy and feminism). Like Hendricks, Hebdige refuses to regard Kraus as an artist. Instead he insists on treating her as a mere documentarian, classifying her work not as fiction or literature but as autobiography.

This is a misogynist framing that disavows the intellectual labor that its creation required. "People acted when I wrote the book," Kraus has said, "as if it had just appeared on my pillow because I slept with Dick—like I didn't have to do anything at all."[55]

In all of these projects, the male hosts minimize the roles of the parasitical female creators that target them: Hendricks dismisses Byrne's work as imitation, as a student project that she must justify to him; Baudry attempts to punish Calle by transforming her into a disembodied sexual image; and Hebdige classifies Kraus's task as simply recording information rather than creating art. Hebdige's rejection of her piece as art, a study worthy of critical examination, is an attempt to eject the parasite, to expunge it from its host's body. Shortly after its publication in 1997, Hebdige made his only known public comments about the book in an interview with *New York* magazine: he said that the book was "beneath contempt," a sentiment the interviewer would characterize as "a surprisingly earnest complaint coming from a semiotician of popular culture."[56] Dick's attempts to exclude her from the artistic conversation is equally clear at the end of the book in his response to the project, which he addresses to Sylvère, merely sending Chris (whose name he misspells) a photocopy of the letter.

While the hosts attempt to minimize or exclude their female parasites, the artists make their male hosts into oversized projections. We find in Deleuze and Guattari's reading of Kafka's letters to his "father figure" the basis for such a parasitical tactic of feminist viral or manic proliferation in response to the overwhelming presence of the male figure. In *Kafka: Toward a Minor Literature*, Deleuze and Guattari describe "the interest of the letter" as lying in "a particular sliding effect" by which Kafka moves from a classic Oedipal conflict, "where the beloved father is hated, accused, and declared to be guilty, to a much more perverse Oedipus." "The letters are a rhizome, a network, a spider's web," they write. "There is a vampirism in the letters, a vampirism that is specifically epistolary."[57] Like Calle's multiple crowdsourced replies to X and Kraus's unfettered stream of letters to Dick, which hyperbolize and reduce them from complex individuals to mere symbols, to occupiers of particular structural positions, Kafka's letters dramatize and allegorize the father to the point of rendering him unrecognizable as an individual entity.[58] Deleuze and Guattari describe Kafka's reproach to his father as "a reproach that is so strong that it becomes unattributable to any particular persons and unlimited . . . and passes through a series of paranoid interpretations." They propose that Kafka's hyperbolic inflation of the overpowering image of the father figure paradoxically creates a "way out":

> The goal is to obtain a blowup of the "photo," an exaggeration of it to the point of absurdity. The photo of the father, expanded beyond all bounds, will be projected onto the geographic, historical, and political map of the world in order to reach vast regions of it . . . an Oedipalization of the universe. . . . Beyond that, to the degree that one enlarges Oedipus, this sort of microscopic enlargement shows up the father for what he is; it gives him a molecular agitation in which an entirely different sort of combat is being played out. One might say that in projecting the photo of the father onto the map of the world, Kafka unblocks the impasse that is specific to the photo and invents a way out of this impasse.[59]

By re-presenting the father of the classic Oedipal narrative in these outsized terms, Kafka produces the father as an outsized caricature of patriarchy, whose exaggerated pores are distended into pixelated openings primed for infestation. In *I Love Dick*, this infestation gains entry by means of love letters that operate like spam—fired off in rapid succession, hitting random targets. As Deleuze and Guattari note, the epistolary genre itself has a vampiristic—or, in my terms, parasitical—quality. By obsessing over Dick and X, by making them the unwilling muses and patrons of their artworks, Kraus and Calle shield themselves behind Kafkaesque blown-up images of their hosts, which serve as cover, allowing the parasites to grow unnoticed until it is too late for their hosts.

FEMINIZED PARASITES

Complicity is like a girl's name.—CHRIS KRAUS, *I LOVE DICK*

In the history of Western art and literature, femininity is often figured as an alien threat to an otherwise healthy patriarch, one that gradually weakens him through her dependence. In the 1969 novel *The Estate*, Isaac Bashevis Singer's narrator observes, "He had seen women ruin men. They wove a net about a man, entangled him with duties, ensnared him with parasitic children, and finally destroyed him."[60] Parasitism is a misogynist trope that portrays femininity as smothering and overly reliant: the "clingy" mistress, the idle "trophy wife," the "kept woman," the "plus one," the "hanger-on" who "makes it [her] profession to dine at another's table."[61] (Though the parasitical feminine is typically deployed as a descriptor of bourgeois womanhood, it need not be biologically female.) Such pejoratives denigrate and disavow the labor of the feminine (femme or feminized) companion—usually labor that is invisible, reproductive, affective. Typically the feminized parasite is figured (as it is in botany) as a form of suffocating dependency that femininity poses to masculinity.[62] The gendering of the parasite is described by J. Hillis Miller in his influential essay "The Critic as Host," his retort to attacks casting deconstruction as a parasitical mode of criticism. Miller writes that the parasite "suggests the image of 'the obvious or univocal reading' as the mighty, masculine oak or ash rooted in the solid ground, endangered by the insidious twining around it of ivy. English or maybe poison, somehow feminine, secondary, defective, or dependent, a clinging vine, able to live in no other way but by drawing the life sap of its host."[63] It is the femininity attached to this image of clinging that interests me; in his epigraph to this essay, Miller further highlights the feminine nature of clinging, citing the French proverb "Je meurs où je m'attache," which translates literally as "I die where I cling/I am attached"—effectively "'Til death do us part." A poetic symbol of feminine devotion and fidelity, this image can be traced back to Ovid's *Metamorphoses* and the Book of Psalms, and it also appears as an Elizabethan homily on marriage in Shakespeare's *The Comedy of Errors*:

> Thou art an elm, my husband; I a vine,
> whose weakness married to thy stronger state
> makes me with thy strength to communicate.
> If aught possess thee from me, it is dross,
> usurping ivy, brier, or idle moss,
> who, all for want of pruning, with intrusion
> infect thy sap, and live on thy confusion.[64]

The feminine, then, is historically framed, even defined as that which is parasitical, which can survive only at the pleasure of another. But this image has been put not just to misogynist ends. Feminists have also long employed the language of *female parasites* to critique certain women's investment in maintaining the patriarchal, bourgeois, and white supremacist status quo for its material benefits. Parasitism became shorthand for the problem complicity with patriarchal structures poses for radical feminists, from Victorian suffragettes to lesbian separatists. As early as 1792 Mary Wollstonecraft employed the imagery of the ivy and the tree, writing, "It might be proper, in order to make a man and his wife one, that she should rely entirely on his understanding . . . the graceful ivy, clasping the oak that supported it."[65] (Wollstonecraft's use of the image was not negative but used to symbolize the complementarity of the masculine and feminine.) But by the early twentieth century, the parasite is consistently invoked as a negative dependency on a patriarchal capitalism. In 1911 the suffragist Olive Schreiner compared women's dependence on men to "the most deadly microbe."[66] In 1912 Rosa Luxemburg warned that bourgeois women, complicit consumers of what their husbands extort from the proletariat, are "parasites of the parasites of the social body."[67] In 1949 Simone de Beauvoir called women "clinging," "dead weight," "parasite[s] sucking out the living strength of another organism."[68] In 1970 Germaine Greer famously urged "feminine parasites" to stop "cajoling and manipulating" and instead to claim "the masculine virtues of magnanimity and generosity and courage," and Gloria Steinem called them "dependent creatures."[69]

Parasitism, as it was eventually absorbed into the U.S. and European feminist mainstream, captures an early strand of radical feminist thought arguing for a kind of feminist separatism. These feminists saw certain women as capitulating to the patriarchal norms of heterosexual domestic life, marriage, and child rearing in exchange for the protection and rewards of bourgeois privilege, a dynamic encapsulated by the figure of the housewife.[70] "For the master's tools will never dismantle the master's house," Audre Lorde famously argued, concluding, "This fact is only threatening to those women who still define the master's house as their only source of support."[71] In her landmark 1970 manifesto, "The Dialectic of Sex," Shulamith Firestone writes, "Unless revolution uproots the basic social organization, the biological family—the vinculum through which the psychology of power can always be smuggled—the tapeworm of exploitation will never be annihilated."[72] The militant lesbian feminist Valerie Solanas equated married women with men "and other degenerates."[73] In various radical feminist critiques, wage labor, the annihilation of the nuclear family, and sexual autonomy have been seen as liberating women from the tyranny of dependence.

These texts differ in the degree of individual agency they ascribe to women's complicit status.[74] Schreiner advanced in her 1911 *Women and Labour* an excoriation of "feminine economic parasitism," the characteristic feminist belief of the period that "women were responsible for their own freedom," even if they were not necessarily materially able to realize it, and that their continued subordination was therefore attributable to them.[75] Beauvoir at times used rhetoric similar to Schreiner's, but in *The Second Sex* she described dependency as a structural role: "The woman has been assigned the role of parasite: all parasites are necessarily exploiters; she needs the male to acquire human dignity, to eat, to feel pleasure, to procreate; she uses the service of sex to ensure her benefits; and since she is trapped in this function, she is entirely an instrument of exploitation."[76] Generally, though, parasitism has been viewed in certain strands of feminist history and criticism as a contaminating lack of self-sufficiency, and the abiding concern with it speaks to how the liberal discourse of the rational, autonomous subject (woman as free agent) has underwritten twentieth-century feminist conceptions of power and agency. Such liberal feminist mandates of freedom, autonomy, and self-determination have been critiqued by scholars such as Gayatri Spivak, Saba Mahmood, and Linda Zerilli.[77]

Parasitism thus encapsulates a fundamental problem for twentieth- and twenty-first-century feminism and feminist theory: that women—and feminism—are constituted in relation to and in reaction to patriarchal structures. In her 2009 book *One-Dimensional Woman*, a treatise on the state of contemporary feminism, philosopher Nina Power observed, "Many of the tactics of feminism thus far—rewriting cultural histories, reclaiming the body, occupying 'male' positions—have had significant effects, but have not been able to touch the basis of the problem at hand."[78] When asked "What's 'wrong' with feminism today?" during a 1991 interview, Avital Ronell answered, "Feminism today has a parasitical, secondary territoriality. . . . If you respond to present conditions, you're subject to reactive, mimetic, and regressive posturings. So the problem is: how can you free yourself? How can you not be reactive to what already exists as powerful and dominating? How can you avoid a resentimental politics?"[79] Here Ronell seems to mean a "reactive" politics, but her choice of word also evokes the Nietzschean concept of ressentiment, which denotes a psychological state arising from feelings that cannot be acted upon and results in a symptomatic form of self-abasement. In *On the Genealogy of Morals*, Nietzsche describes the moment of ressentiment as the one in which suffering crystallizes around a site of external blame, a figure upon which one can avenge, and thus displace, one's hurt. In *States of Injury*, Wendy Brown revisits Nietzsche's account to argue that ressentiment has effected a contemporary political identity that understands itself as mediated through notions of injury and redress rather than freedom, producing versions of "resistance" that are prefigured and conditioned by the very structures they purport to oppose. Brown contemporizes Nietzsche's notion by making it speak to the liberal subject of U.S. leftist politics of that time. She argues that liberalism contains from its very inception a generalized incitement to ressentiment as "the moralizing revenge of the powerless," or for Nietzsche, "the triumph of the weak as weak." "Ressentiment in this context is a triple achievement: it produces an affect (rage, righteousness) that overwhelms the hurt, it produces a culprit responsible for its hurt, and produces a site of revenge to displace the hurt (a place to inflict hurt as the sufferer has been hurt)," writes Brown. "Together these operations both ameliorate (in Nietzsche's terms, 'anesthetize') and externalize what is otherwise 'unendurable.'"[80] While both Nietzsche and Brown articulate ressentiment as a problem—Brown describes it as liberalism's "wounded attachment" to the trauma associated with systems of inequality—ressentiment finds a useful inflection in the metaphor of the parasite. Ressentiment mimics parasitical logic in that it facilitates a productive if counterintuitive move away from closure, suture, and healing. In her outline of a feminist tactics of a Nietzschean ressentiment, Beauvoir observes, "The tyranny wielded by the woman only manifests her dependence: she knows the success of the couple, its future, its happiness, and its justification, resides in the hands of the other; if she bitterly seeks to subjugate him to her will, it is because she is alienated to him. She makes a weapon of her weakness; but the fact is she is weak."[81] In *Sensational Flesh*, Amber Jamilla Musser ties Beauvoir's employment of the language of parasitism (which Musser characterizes as that of ressentiment) to Beauvoir's engagement with masochism, seeing both as a means of reflecting on women's internalization of their own complicity with "the paucity of choices" available to them ("as parasites who dwell on their own victimization"). Musser writes, "Masochism is born from female objectification under the male gaze and women's compliance with the dictates of patriarch." In her reading of female masochism in Pauline Réage's *The Story of O*, Musser locates potential "pockets of agency" in an aesthetics of complicity in precarious spaces prescripted by domination: "When O is framed as complicit with her objectification, complicity emerges as a mode of self-fashioning in which agency and aesthetics collide."[82]

Advising feminists as one would a friend trapped in a bad relationship, Ronell and Beauvoir ask how women might free themselves (Beauvoir: find "living strength of their own" and "the means to attack the world and wrest from it their own subsistence"), how they might move forward and beyond their structural dependence on patriarchy. They ask how wounded and attached women can recover, once and for all, and achieve a sense of wholeness and independence—a question that posits the space of feminism as outside of the patriarchal order. But to "treat" feminism's ressentiment as a malady that women must heal themselves from—to posit that women should take care of themselves—is, following Lauren Berlant, an engagement in a neoliberal feminist politics of cruel optimism. "Cruel optimism is the condition of maintaining an attachment to a significantly problematic object," she writes.[83]

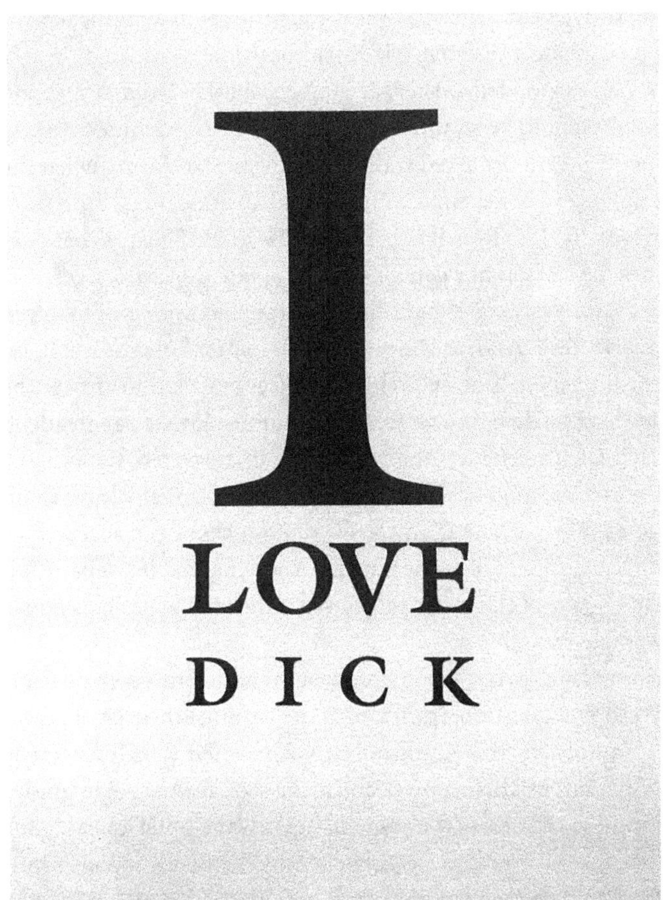

FIGURE 3.4 Title page of *I Love Dick*, Semiotext(e), 1997.

Calle and Kraus, if with different intensities and to different ends, reframe ressentiment not as a reaction, a form of weakness, but as a mode of feminist performativity. As Dick and X are erased, the women's engagements with them shift: "It's all about you" slowly turns into "It's all about me." This shift is visually represented on the title page of the 1997 Semiotext(e) edition of *I Love Dick*, which features a large, bold *I* that dominates the *Love Dick* below it, in smaller print (figure 3.4). In Calle's project, the designation X comes to represent the absent center, the male figures that haunt these projects, caught in significatory limbo. X represents Calle's conceptual ex, whose email to the artist invites the extended reading that he unwittingly agrees to host. When Dick invites Kraus and her husband to dine with him, he steps into the role of host, naïvely inviting in the parasite.

Is it possible for Dick and X to answer these projects in an ethical fashion? Would it have made a difference if X had not signed his email in this way, or if Dick had responded earlier? It may be that Dick didn't respond because he doesn't want to be swallowed up by the Kraus machine—the instinct that helped Paul Auster avoid Calle's trap for him, refusing when she asks him to script a year of her time. What would an ethical response from Dick or X even look like? As Ronell asks in *The Telephone Book*, "What does it mean . . . to make oneself answerable to it in a situation whose gestural syntax already means yes, even if the affirmation should find itself followed by a question mark: Yes?" And, as she writes, "No matter how you cut it, on either side of the line, there is no such thing as a free call."[84] If to answer the call is to rise to meet its demand, to accept the imposition or pay the debt, we might say that Dick at first lets the phone ring unanswered, then finally takes it off the hook. We might ask whether these projects really leave room for Dick or X to answer—whether any answer might have been accepted or acceptable. Can the host welcome the parasite knowing that it is a parasite? Perhaps the inadequacy of the men's responses is inevitable; perhaps no response is answerable enough.

How to be answerable, to be personally accountable to one's own power is a difficult and resonant question, from which the feminist theorist of power herself is not immune. In 2018 Kraus publicly supported Ronell when she was accused of having used her power abusively by a former male graduate student, who filed charges of harassment against the philosopher.[85] She framed the student's "accusations [as] couched in the disingenuous sentiments of #MeToo" and characterized him as "an empowered and privileged actor . . . [who] feigned helplessness after the fact."[86] Kraus's defense of Ronell disparaged the movement that she helped inspire and engaged in victim-blaming that protected alleged toxic behavior of the very kind that *I Love Dick* empowered a generation of feminists to stand against. The episode exemplifies how compromised Kraus and Ronell (as well as other prominent figures I cite and rely on for my argument in this chapter) have become as they have grown ever more deeply embedded in academia and the art market. Other feminist and queer luminaries who signed the letter of support for Ronell (including Judith Butler) are also radical theorists who have made their careers spotlighting, contesting, and analyzing structural power but who in the process have accrued plenty of their own.[87] For many, Kraus's cultural prominence now exceeds that of Hebdige; she is far from the self-described "failed filmmaker" she claimed to be when she wrote *I Love Dick*. This development does not nullify the critical and feminist potency of the book, but it does demonstrate the historical and contextual contingency of radical authorship. While no one wants to admit their own implication in these systems, it is a reminder that no one is outside of this structural ecology; who inhabits the positions of the parasite and host is not a given.

FEMINIST ENDGAMES

While *I Love Dick* and *Take Care of Yourself* mirror and reinforce one other, their performances of parasitism also diverge in important ways. There would seem to be something altogether more unhinged about Kraus's "parasitical growth" than Calle's, which remains carefully calibrated to the conceptual boundaries of her coolly played representational game. Whereas for Calle parasitism represents a mask that can be taken off and put away, for Kraus it is not so easy to rid yourself of your attachments. Calle's relationship with X is indulged more in the realm of the symbolic, remaining an ongoing hypothetical in her collaborator's interpretations, but Kraus's relationships to Dick and Sylvère are more exposed, as shown by her willingness to name names of real men, both public figures. Kraus recounts telling Dick, "'Cause don't you see?' I said, 'It's more a project than a game. I meant every word I wrote you in those letters. . . . Don't you think it's possible to do something and simultaneously study it? If the project had a name it'd be *I Love Dick: A Case Study*.'"[88] Kraus's relationships with Dick and Sylvère make her a parasite in double measure. Lotringer's professional success feeds, clothes, houses, and affords Kraus's creative work and also helps ensure the book's publication by Semiotext(e), the press that he founded.

Meanwhile, Calle's previous work notwithstanding, one can never be sure that X is real. Calle plays the parasite, but one has the sense that it is just that: a piece of theater or a game with a finite duration.[89] One can visit the exhibition and grab dinner after. Perhaps Calle "takes care of herself" after all by modeling a parasitism that is not self-destructive. She puts far less of herself on the line in her project, instead enlisting others to speak on her behalf. Kraus's game, on the other hand, has no foreseeable end and no visible boundaries. For Kraus, there is little buffer between fact and fiction; deeper drives seem to be at work for her. Names are not changed to protect the innocent, leaving everyone who is naïve enough to let Kraus near looking somewhat guilty.

Calle and Kraus perform parasitical feminism to different ends. Kraus's performance manifests a certain resistance to resolution—a desire to have it continue on beyond the boundedness of the encounter, the page, the book—and, at the same time, a reckless disregard for survival. For Calle, the performance of the parasite is worn as a mask that leaves viewers wondering "Was she or wasn't she playing herself?" Calle's parasitism is a carefully elaborated game that endures to play again, whereas Kraus's performance takes on the inflection of an opening night that is mere minutes from a very real breakdown. Her parasitical performance would appear to signal a performance whose emotions (even as they are being rehearsed) the performer is still really experiencing. At the halfway mark of *I Love Dick*, Chris and Sylvère decide to separate. Her husband, who was once game, is no longer sure if the structure of their marriage can withstand the hacking blows dealt it by each letter to Dick. (Kraus and Lotringer have since divorced.) In the midst of this, Chris claims to have shown up unannounced to Dick's home and had sex with him, a claim Kraus has reiterated in interviews.[90] While unverified, if true these actions would have transgressed (at least within the diegetic frame of the novel) the rules of her epistolary game.

"You have to pay for indulgence," Lotringer later said of the project in an interview, "it was a risky operation."[91] As if surgically to remove herself-as-appendage from her husband's overpowering career, Kraus's conceptual project hacks away at the relentlessly accommodating structure of patriarchy without considering what would happen to her if it collapsed. If the parasite is rejected by its hosts (Dick and Sylvère), who will bestow the intellectual nod of approval on which the project at times appears to depend—who will publish her manuscript, if not Semiotext(e), the press Lotringer founded in 1974? In other words, can the parasite survive without its host? What will happen when the bond is severed? Kraus's dedication to the project bespeaks the intensity of an artist willing to cut deeper and further than anyone expects her to go. Unlike Calle, who feeds at the surface of the skin, operating in the sphere of the conceptual, Kraus burrows ever deeper into the real until the accommodating structure finally gives way. Kraus writes in *I Love Dick*, "But Dick, I know that as you read this, you'll know these things are true. You understand the game is real, or even better than, reality, and better than is what it's all about. . . . It's not about giving a fuck, or seeing all the consequences looming and doing something anyway." She closes the letter, "Sylvère thinks he's that kind of anarchist. But he's not. I love you Dick."[92]

THE BRACKETED FEMININE

In May 2011, I received my own correspondence from Chris Kraus. An article I had published about *I Love Dick* had come to her attention.[93] "The concept you develop of parasitical feminism is provocative and fascinating," she wrote. "I respect your right to discuss the book on your own terms but would like to bring a factual error to your attention." Kraus was uncomfortable with my claim that *I Love Dick* was framed by an infrastructural dependence on Lotringer for its publication by Semiotext(e). She objected to my suggestion that she was supplemental to and parasitical on, not Lotringer himself, but his press, where she was a coeditor. "*I Love Dick* was published by Semiotexte in 1997," she wrote. "I became a co-editor of Semiotexte in 1989 when I launched the Native Agents imprint. . . . Therefore, *I Love Dick* was self-published (abjection maybe of another kind) but not dependent on Sylvère's editorial decision."[94] She added in a subsequent email:

> I had already published books by Ann Rower, Cookie Mueller, Kathy Acker, Lynne Tillman and Barbara Barg in the Native Agents series. Sylvère and I saw the fiction books as an American analog to French theories of subjectivity (Deleuze Guattari Foucault) published in the Foreign Agents series—which, by the 90s, had already in our minds run its course—by that time, these theorists were being published by university presses in the US; Semiotexte had already done its job by introducing them. Our goal has always been to intervene intellectually at certain cultural moments. Semiotexte remains an amateur enterprise: our list is highly curated—we never do a book that we don't feel is vitally important. So when [*I Love Dick*] shaped up as a book, with the upstate NY essays, it seemed like a perfect fit for the series.[95]

Kraus's description of her role in the founding of the Native Agents series, and more generally her influence in the operations of Semiotext(e), was reiterated in an essay published by Elizabeth Gumport in the February 2012 issue of *n+1*. Gumport notes that Kraus established the Native Agents series as a feminist corrective to Lotringer's Foreign Agents series:

> Kraus—who had met Lotringer earlier that decade . . . suggested Semiotext(e) turn to face America directly and recover the original, unpardonably forgotten contribution the United States had made to intellectual life in the years after 1968, namely, feminism. This recovery took the form of the Native Agents series. . . .
>
> When the imprint was launched in 1990, with Kraus as editor, Foreign Agents had never published a book by someone who wasn't a white man. Semiotext(e) had "missed out" on the feminist movement entirely. "It happened," Lotringer told an interviewer, "and I wasn't aware of it." He hadn't published women, Kraus explained, "because the only women he

knew writing theory were doing psychoanalytic theory, which he wasn't so interested in."[96]

Kraus insists that Semiotext(e)'s publication of *I Love Dick* was not a result of her being Sylvère's plus one but an independent action that she took on her own account ("self-published"). Yet Semiotext(e) made its name by supporting and sustaining a "boys only" theoretical network, and it is difficult to argue that the Native Agents series was not a compensatory measure for the publishing house's long-standing "bracketing of the feminine," formalized in the "silent e," in French the grammatical marker of the feminine (*e muet*).[97] This is a bracketing that Kraus nevertheless persisted in trying to unbracket in her exchange with me, in each of her emails writing the title of the press as "Semiotexte" rather than "Semiotext(e)." By pointing out in its title what I see to be a structural secondariness of the feminine, Semiotext(e) is performing a kind of institutional hospitality for Kraus, who holds a position much like that of the Native Agents series itself: a kind of integrated outsider, a feminist parasite on the masculinist Foreign Agent series. I do not mean to diminish Kraus's merits in any way; quite the contrary, the story of the Native Agents series further illustrates the persistently disavowed feminine supplementarity that *I Love Dick* so unflinchingly calls out.[98] But her initial defensiveness at being labeled a parasite off the page betrays a residual attachment to seeing herself as autonomous rather than dependent.

How exactly are we to understand Kraus and Lotringer's contract? Who is the contractual host and who is the parasite? In other words, where is the power in this host-parasite relation located? In 1989 (the year Kraus became a coeditor at Semiotext(e) and launched the Native Agents series) Kraus and Lotringer cowrote the foreword to their reprint of Leopold von Sacher-Masoch's *Venus in Furs*. "Sacher-Masoch was an early feminist," they write playfully. "He supported 'women's studies' and celebrated them throughout the ages. . . . Masoch unconditionally supported women, urging them to be strong the way he wanted them to be."[99] Here Lotringer and Kraus point to the irony of Sacher-Masoch's contract (the s/m contract between the master and the slave, whom we might reframe in terms of the host and the parasite) as one that ultimately serves the masochist.

In her work on male masochism, Suzanne R. Stewart further elaborates this critique, writing of *Venus in Furs*, "It is here, before the signing and the writing [of the masochistic contract], where the question 'Am I a man or a slave?' is posed, that Severin finds his identity. . . . It will depend on the possibility or the promise that Severin can see himself being seen, on the condition that the passive phrase 'I am tortured by Wanda' means 'I can direct my own torture at the hand of Wanda.' Thus, the passive or masochistic subject-position must be just that: a subject-position in charge of its own destiny." Stewart reads in *Venus in Furs*' sadomasochistic contract, which passively constructs male masochism, a feminist problematic. Male masochism is always framed by the contract, "the letter of the law," which is always underwritten by patriarchal dominance. In effect, male masochism is a topping from the bottom; even when it is submissive, patriarchy still covertly exercises control by scripting the terms of its submission. In the novella it is Severin who determines his own submissive position—a prescripted vulnerability that, as Stewart notes, is subject to interruption and redirection. Although Wanda appears to take control of Severin, she still does not dominate him, for it is he who scripts their encounter.[100] The story of Wanda's dominance of Severin is just one narrative within the novella's larger narrative framework, where it serves as a story within a story, a scripted dialectics of power playing out within the larger metanarrative of gender relations in patriarchal society.

In much the same way, *I Love Dick* represents a contract between Kraus and Lotringer wherein she plays (emphasis on *plays*) the sadist to his masochist, as triangulated through Dick. But these dynamics do not appear to be fully transferable to their professional relationship. The limits of Chris's dominance, like the limits of Wanda's, become abruptly clear when one considers the legal contract that binds the two: although both their signatures appear under the foreword, Lotringer alone is credited on the copyright page of *Venus in Furs*, which reads only "Foreword © Sylvère Lotringer." (In getting the first word, Sylvère has the last word.) As such, it appears that it is only within the bounds of that which is labeled fiction—under the cover of "just playing," acting, performing—that woman is able to assume the role of self-determination, for the terms can be set by male editorial discretion.

Kraus has said that the art she likes most "doesn't try to make itself loveable."[101] Still, Chris's love for Dick always appears to be a performance that is intended primarily for Sylvère. Her anarchic parasitism, with its willful destructiveness (and unflinching rawness), allows Kraus to show up Lotringer's investment in the kinds of transgression that are valorized by the French theory published by Semiotext(e). By deconstructing Dick, Kraus pushes poststructural premises to their furthest conclusions. Kraus positions herself as the Thelma and Louise of deconstruction, as willing to drive feminism right off a cliff. By piercing and feeding on Dick and X, both Kraus and Calle swell with critical significance, bloated parasites who slowly dwarf their hosts. These projects reverse the idea that women's emotionality is a point of weakness by remapping affective and sexual attachments as para-sites—sites of the *para*, a prefix indicating "beside or alongside, wrongfully, harmfully, unfavorably, among," which, Miller notes, has come to mean "the boundary line, threshold, or margin, and at the same time beyond it . . . at once a permeable membrane connecting inside and outside [and] confusing them."[102] In the parasite, femininity's claimed dependency is transfigured, becoming something that pierces that boundary, creating a loophole, a backdoor, a tunnel to a possible outside. There is a space in performance for feminized subjects undetectably to change the game. But the opening offered by a parasitical feminism does not guarantee survival or even successful escape. Casualties are inevitable.

FOUR A SEAT AT THE TABLE

FEMINIST PERFORMANCE ART'S INSTITUTIONAL ABSORPTION AND PARASITICAL LEGACIES

If I was trying to do something that nobody else has done, I would, like, shoot myself on stage. I'm not trying to break some boundary. . . . I'm aware that people have done things before me.—**ANN LIV YOUNG, INTERVIEW**

The parasitical feminist practices examined in chapter 3 took the heterosexual couple as its site of intervention. This chapter displaces that gender conflict onto a generational divide. At a January 2011 show for the American Realness Festival of contemporary dance and performance at New York City's Delancey Lounge, the choreographer-turned-performance artist Ann Liv Young taunted the pioneering gay rights activist Jim Fouratt (an audience member she didn't recognize) about his age, only to have the emcee Penny Arcade confront the younger performance artist for disrespecting her elders.[1] According to a tabloid write-up of the show in the *New York Daily News* declaring "intergenerational hipster warfare," Arcade, a fixture on the downtown performance art scene since the late 1960s, who has worked with the likes of Jack Smith and John Vaccaro, yelled, "Pull off her head!" Young responded by throwing things at the stage, hitting another attendee in the head with a large ceramic necklace.[2] As Young proceeded to remove her top, Arcade boomed, "Being topless in the East Village [in 2011] is not radical!"

This intense onstage confrontation condenses a dramatic shift in the relationship between younger female performance artists like Young and the artists who blazed the trail for this new generation. The aptly named Young has claimed that she is not interested in "studying performance history or what other people have done."[3] Indeed, when she gave one interviewer an example of an "original idea," she volunteered that she would shoot herself on stage—not, in fact, an original idea, but a restaging of Chris Burden's *Shoot* (1971), one of the most iconic and widely discussed works of the performance art canon. When asked about the Delancey Lounge incident, Young stated that she did not know who Fouratt was, adding, "I still don't," and mused that Penny Arcade was "probably [just being] defensive about her own age."[4] She said that her only "real regret" about the performance was losing her necklace.

What is to be made of this unhinged spectacle of willful historical ignorance on one side and territorial defensiveness on the other? This chapter explores a curious development: an emerging cohort of younger female performance artists who, while recognizably working within the vein of 1960s, 1970s, and 1980s U.S. feminist performance art, refuse to revere, or at times even acknowledge, the feminist artists and traditions from which they nevertheless pilfer and whose work they appropriate and ironize.[5] At a moment when established female performance artists such as Marina Abramović, Carolee Schneemann, Hannah Wilke, Adrian Piper, Yayoi Kusama, Karen Finley, and Ana Mendieta (to name a few) were receiving mainstream recognition and art historical canonization, this younger cohort was facing a generational resource gap and negotiating the period of austerity caused by the 2008 global financial crisis.[6] Young's performed refusal to acknowledge her forebears is not a simple display of cluelessness or disrespect, as some have framed it; it signals a growing mistrust, both real and performed, among younger performance artists toward the generation of pioneering artists that preceded them. While feminist performance art has always been a vocation that garners little recognition and even less pay, this mistrust evidences a recent transformation in how both *liberal feminism* and *performance art* are perceived within this small niche as it has shifted from a site of struggle and marginalization to one of (relative) exclusivity and increasing institutionalization. The monumentalization of 1960s, 1970s, and 1980s feminist performance art—once a fringe genre, seen as anathema to commodification—is eroding the genre's original "claims for resistance to commodity capitalism," grounded in "the idea that performance does not offer an object for sale."[7] As high art institutions like the MoMA, the Whitney, the Guggenheim, and the Getty have spent the past decade acquiring performances for their permanent collections and hiring curators to preserve and exhibit them, these foundational ideas no longer bear the same transgressive signature. The genre's new institutional status is reflective of the younger generation's changing relationship to feminism, both as an aesthetic practice and as a mode of identification.

Early feminist performance artists worked to reclaim their images and bodies, using them to draw attention to patriarchal systems and social norms, to fight the systemic sexism that excluded them from institutions, and to represent their social experience. These women's defiant and transgressive work thematized questions of agency and self-representation by exploring powerful, taboo subjects like pornography, explicit sexuality, and trauma, both sexual and social.[8] What happens when a formation that has historically been understood as radical and minoritarian comes to be perceived as hegemonic by its would-be beneficiaries? What changes when those who have long identified as parasites become institutional stakeholders with cultural and financial capital—in other words, when they are able to occupy the position of host?

This chapter examines how the institutionalization of feminist performance art creates a growing disjuncture between how two generations of artists view the works (and artists) that founded their genre. Certain pioneering feminists of the earlier generation see themselves as embattled and disenfranchised, while a precarious younger generation instead sees them as occupying structurally powerful and privileged positions. The younger artists, facing mounting student debt and narrowing professional prospects in an ever more proprietary landscape for performance-based art, appear increasingly to view the legacy left by the previous generation of artists not as a gift but as an imposition, a debt to be paid. This dynamic was crystallized by Abramović's 2010 Museum of Modern Art blockbuster retrospective *Marina Abramović: The Artist Is Present*. The decade-defining exhibition, a galling instance of the performance of coercive hospitality that I theorize in this book, spotlighted "reperformance," a generational patronage model (as it was devised for the Abramović exhibition) by which an established artist hires less-established performers (generally working artists in their own right) to reenact their work.

The work of the contemporary artists examined here suggests that in order to be a feminist artist today, one cannot be a feminist artist; the syntagm *feminist artist* now registers as something of a contradiction in terms. The avant-garde art market demands originality, enjoining the artist to break with her predecessors, but at the same time a certain invocation of second-wave feminist politics demands deference to those predecessors. The issue at hand is not necessarily with feminist politics itself but with the particular demand of fidelity made on the contemporary generation of feminist artists, many of whom are struggling to survive in a neoliberal climate of austerity, precarity, and the gig economy. This is a double bind: feminist identification can be neither fully refused nor fully accepted. In the face of this dilemma, younger white performance artists have taken up parasitism as an artistic strategy for *disidentifying* with—adopting, exaggerating, and critically reworking—the structural privilege that comes with being a white middle-class feminist, which is made visible in this inheritance. I argue that younger performance artists—Ann Liv Young, Anya Liftig, Amber Hawk Swanson, Kate Gilmore, and Lauren Barri Holstein—have sought to resolve this tension of feminist inheritance by articulating their relationship to feminism ironically or through layers of mediation; they have done this, moreover, by channeling the performed indifference of the adolescent figure, by enacting a kind of teenage rebellion. By characterizing this mode as parasitical, I mark how these artists have appropriated and played their derivative and contingent status vis-à-vis their feminist art forebears as an ambivalent mode of feminist identification. These artists wield the strategic short-sightedness of the parasite—its presentism, its short-term memory, its claimed indifference to history, its intentionlessness—as a disidentificatory register for contending with what it means to make feminist performance art in the present moment on their own terms.

The younger performance artists discussed in this chapter pointedly stage the problem of feminist legacy as a mother-daughter conflict. This conflict seems like a straight recapitulation of tired generational models and heteronormative family metaphors, and it troublingly posits feminism as consisting of two distinct waves or generations, both primarily white.[9] But these younger artists' engagements do not straightforwardly identify with whiteness or femininity or even generational transmission; rather these works enact a mode of critique, an ironic "putting on" of white feminist complicity and privilege that is signaled by these younger artists' hyperbolic and irreverent identification with the stereotypical signifiers of hypercommodified femininity (often depicted white): high heels, hair ribbons, tattered prom dresses, candy-colored teen girl clothes, synthetic blond "Barbie hair" wigs (at times over hair that is already blond).[10] I understand these parodic practices to be attempts to contest the legacy of white liberal feminism (much as the artists in chapter 2 sought to use the logics of private property and nationality to resignify the subject positions associated with these logics). These practices represent the artists' critical disidentification with their own cultural and racial privilege.[11] The artists I explore reflect, refract, and exaggerate tropes of 1960s and 1970s feminist art—particularly the over-earnest politics symbolized by underarm hair and "vaginal scrolls"—in order to break with them, in order to signal their refusal of an inherited feminist script. These artists instead play with these tropes, using them to signify nothing or signify differently, all in service of claiming a sense of ownership over their own representation.

My discussion of artists who have taken up this performance strategy focuses primarily on younger white artists because the cultural legacy of white liberal feminism and its resources (the symbolic cultural and political capital) are still largely concentrated among white women; the question of inheritance or legacy is less relevant to those who have historically been excluded from such intergenerational resource transfers. Even as they struggle under precarious economic conditions, the artists I discuss make work that reflects their own structural implication in systems of privilege: they are white women who have benefited from legacies of capital accumulation and racial privilege passed on through mechanisms of social reproduction. However, these white performance artists' appropriation of earlier white performance artists' works (even in the reflexive mode of self-critique) performs yet another erasure of trans feminists and feminist women of color, repeating the marginalization performed by historiographies of feminist art, which, as Uri McMillan has shown, treat "white female subjectivity . . . as an unofficial norm."[12] These younger artists' emphasis on generation also elides the significant differences between feminists from the second wave and present-day feminists, differences that go beyond issues of precarity. So while these artworks do little to directly redress the legacy of white liberal feminism's exclusions (and may therefore compound these violences), I see them as contesting the idea of legacy itself—contesting its logic of racial and cultural inheritance (which unequally creates precarity), perhaps even contesting the notion that legacy can exist, that there is something to leave, that a future exists in an increasingly dystopian world.

What is especially challenging about the works I examine is that here the critique of the host is expressed *even more* indirectly—a divergence from the more clearly delineated parasite-host incursions I have described in previous chapters. These artists challenge the host's authority not explicitly but through performances that disavow the host's originality; these challenges are mounted by their disidentification with the historical influence of the (always overdetermined and caricatural) feminist foremother, a disidentification that they perform in their creative practice. This disidentification is sometimes expressed through spectacles of aggressive overcitation (a hyperderivative aesthetic I call *parasitical homage*) and at other times through spectacles of willed historical ignorance (what I call *parasitical disavowal*). (We see both of these techniques at work in Young's performance with Arcade.) At yet other times their disidentification with the legacy of the liberal feminist host warps into a kind of reflexive self-critique, a self-parody of their own implication in the structures they find intolerable and want to challenge (what I call *manic autogenesis*).

This version of parasitism looks less like the slowly weakening resistance I have described in previous chapters and more like a mutation of this logic, a form of zombification—an endlessly reanimating and self-cannibalistic feminist aesthetics. The chapter explores what happens when the host in question is neither patriarchal nor misogynist but matriarchal and feminist—and when the parasite does not simply undermine the host but embodies and imitates it *and iterates that imitation*, thereby revising, reiterating, reproducing, and infecting it for its own ends. Later in the chapter I attend to the difficulty of reading the feminist substance of this highly ambiguous aesthetic gesture. Under what conditions can, or should, this gesture's refusal of legibility be read as feminist? What is the feminist politics of the often dizzying strategies of re-reproduction, imitation, parody, refraction, doubling, and multiplication employed by these artists? Although these parasitical strategies afford a kind of protective feminist illegibility within the contemporary art market (they prevent these artists from being too easily identified or pinned down, from losing their place at or near the table), they also serve as modes of self-making or self-generation, by which these artists negotiate their position as both inside and outside a cultural inheritance that cannot be given back even when it is refused.

PATRONIZING PRECARITY

In the late 2000s feminist performance art was undergoing a cultural revival in the United States. During this period there was a major symposium at the Museum of Modern Art called "The Feminist Future: Theory and Practice in the Visual Arts" (2007) and two marquee retrospective exhibitions were mounted: *WACK! Art and the Feminist Revolution* at Los Angeles's Museum of Contemporary Art (2007), which later traveled throughout North America, and *Global Feminisms* (2007) at the Brooklyn Museum, which was becoming a major collector of feminist art. Also in 2007 the Brooklyn Museum opened the Elizabeth A. Sackler Center for Feminist Art, now the permanent home of Judy Chicago's landmark work, *The Dinner Party* (1979), widely regarded as the first major feminist artwork.

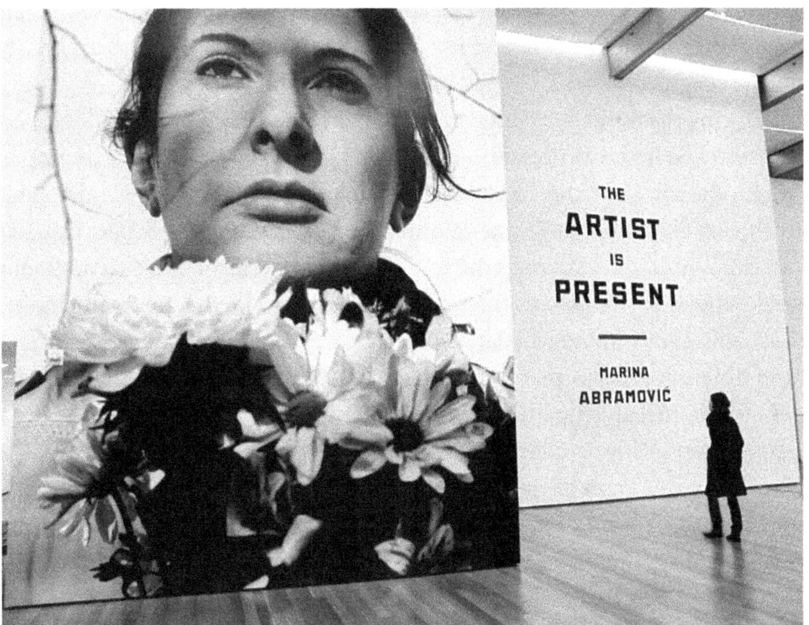

FIGURE 4.1 *Marina Abramović: The Artist Is Present*, Museum of Modern Art, 2010. Source: MoMA Talks.

These events celebrated the glory days of bygone eras while largely bracketing the status of the feminist art present. *WACK!* promised a historical survey of feminist art from 1965 to 1980, focusing heavily on U.S.-based artists, whereas *Global Feminisms* was promoted as an international survey of feminist art from 1990 to the present. The feminist artist and writer Mira Schor points out that the two timelines effectively erased from the historical archive the 1990s generation of publicly politically committed feminist artists.[13] These exhibitions thus denied an unambiguously feminist cadre of artists historical recognition, instead celebrating as the preeminent woman artist of the modern era a figure who has steadfastly renounced the label "feminist artist," Marina Abramović. At these events, Schor writes, Abramović introduced herself by saying "I have never had anything to do with feminism"; here Schor adds, "(as she does at every *feminist* art event to which she is invited)."[14] Abramović, who has received more mainstream recognition than any other woman artist in recent memory, was catapulted into the popular spotlight by her 2010 MoMA retrospective, which brought her extreme, durational body art to a wider audience (figure 4.1). The retrospective, curated by Klaus Biesenbach, comprised both "a new, original," "single solo piece" by Abramović and live "reperformances" of the Serbian artist's most recognized works, carried out by younger performers.[15]

During the retrospective's mid-March–to–late-May run, Abramović performed *The Artist Is Present*, a piece lasting over seven hundred hours, in which she sat silent and immobile in the museum atrium at a wooden table with two chairs opposite one another. In her staging of this performance Abramović literally assumes the role of host: the performance's scenography makes her a permanent fixture of the museum, while the guests (including both museum visitors who sit across from her and her equally anonymous and itinerant reperformers) come and go. Abramović has said that her aim was to channel an empathetic presence of pure receptivity, "to be fully present, concentrating on connecting with whoever came in to sit down opposite her."[16] But this empathy seems absent in her relation with the reperformers of her work. This is quite different from Chicago's germinal feminist work *Dinner Party*; this large-scale dinner table installation, made up of thirty-nine elaborate place settings representing the contributions of thirty-nine different women, was intended to symbolize a redress of women's exclusion from the proverbial table of history. In contrast, Abramović celebrates only her own arrival at what is effectively a table for one (and the various reflections of that one). The artist's reperforming stand-ins are present but elided (in an exhibition that could more accurately be called *The Artists Are Present*). The exhibition and performance drew 750,000 visitors to the museum (among them the celebrities Lou Reed, James Franco, and Björk) and many more via web feed. It garnered considerable critical attention, including a 2012 documentary directed by Matthew Akers, *The Artist Is Present*, about the making of the retrospective. It also garnered mass media coverage, further launching Abramović into the art celebrity stratosphere; she was the subject of a video game, appeared on the covers of fashion magazines, and participated in subsequent collaborations with the likes of Lady Gaga and Jay-Z. "It was [a] complete surprise," Abramović later said, "this enormous need of humans to actually have contact."[17]

Although Abramović's hospitality came with strict conditions (visitors were instructed not to touch or speak to her), I am less interested in these conditions than in the way that the framing of the exhibition, its stated goal of creating a space of mutual contemplation for facilitating deep connectivity and openness, worked to absolve Abramović of her active participation in and patronage of a new labor economy that concentrates all resources—wealth, fame, critical acclaim, originality—into her hands (and the hands of those like her) by exploiting the conditions of precarity and scarcity faced by younger feminist performance artists.

Abramović did not see herself as exploitative, as a coercive host—or at least she did not admit to it. She framed herself instead as a *generous* host, one who was there to distribute her largesse to the next generation. Her sense that she legitimately held a proprietary claim on performance art and its resources and could distribute them as she wished is condensed in her documented investment in protecting her artistic legacy. Shortly after *The Artist Is Present*, in 2011 she began a regular column called "Marina's Diary" in *Flash Art*, declaring her efforts to establish a legacy not only for her own work but for the genre of performance art itself: "For me, the education of young artists has always been part of my work. I have always wanted to give unconditional experience to the younger generation. . . . My generation of performance artists stopped performing by the end of the '70s. Only a few of us are still here. To keep performing art is so emotionally and physically demanding that it is not easy to continue for a long period of time. At the moment, all my attention goes toward *establishing a legacy* that will permit performance art to continue growing and developing."[18] (Until a few years ago Abramović often referred to herself as "the grandmother of performance art"; she recently disowned the label "grandmother" in favor of "pioneer.")[19]

For Abramović, the future of performance art lay in reperformance, a "practice of re-playing or re-doing a precedent event, artwork, or act."[20] This inherently privileges the historical and the previous over the potential creativity of new works and younger performers; in this paradigm, younger performers must stifle their own ideas to reperform the ideas of others, and the practice itself contributes to shutting these performers out of the limited art market, as its bandwidth is increasingly taken up by restaging already known pieces.[21] In 2005 Abramović reperformed a series of major performance art pieces from the 1960s and 1970s at the Guggenheim Museum; for this work, which she called *Seven Easy Pieces*, she reperformed works by Bruce Nauman, Vito Acconci, Valie Export, Gina Pane, and Joseph Beuys, as well as two of her own previous works. "Reperformance is the new concept, the new idea!" she proclaimed at a MoMA workshop about preserving and exhibiting performance art held before the opening of her retrospective. "Otherwise it [performance art] will be dead as an art form."[22] In a *New York Times* piece exploring the implications of performance art's absorption by high art institutions like MoMA, Carol Kino writes:

Ms. Abramović saw [*Seven Easy Pieces*] as a way "to take charge of the history of performance." In the 1990s, as younger artists became interested in work of the '60s and '70s, she said she noticed that some were restaging historical works themselves, often without consulting or even crediting the originator. "I realized this is happening because performance is nobody's territory," she said. "It's never been mainstream art and there's no rules." Finding this unjust, she decided to set them herself, by recreating the works in consultation with the relevant artists and estates. Better she do it now, she said, because "they will do it anyway when you're dead behind your back."[23]

By claiming as her property the historical archive of her practice via reperformance, Abramović made herself the sole benefactor of her work, in perpetuity (figure 4.2).[24] "My idea was to establish certain moral rules," she explains, describing a particularly restrictive approach to intellectual property as if it were the only way, ignoring licensing options that allow free sharing (not to mention the fact that parody and transformational works are not covered by copyright): "If someone wants to remake a performance, they must ask the artist for the rights and pay for it, just like it's done with music or literature. For me, this is the honest way to do it, even if you want to make your own version."[25] Here Abramović frames her discussion of copyright and ownership in terms of morality. Indeed she uses morality as an alibi for her installation of a financial and legal debt structure atop the (supposedly radical and revolutionary) field of performance art: she equates "moral rules" with royalty payments. She cloaks a system of contractual and financial obligation in the language of honor and fidelity, in effect demanding that younger artists pay taxes on her artistic legacy (an inheritance that, as we will see, many of them do not even want). Abramović's "one-sided" investment in legacy (as she says, she is interested in "*establishing* a legacy," not passing on a legacy that she herself inherited from others) begins and ends with her; she advocates for a future of compulsory acknowledgment and debt—a future from which she exempts herself as an artist who insists on always being present.[26]

In her campaign to stake her legacy in the *permanent* present of performance, Abramović advances a proprietary form of reproducibility—a freezing in time, a legacy of repetition, that betrays what some performance theorists have characterized as the art form's transient and immaterial ontology. For example, Richard Schechner declared in 1985, "Performance originals disappear as fast as they are made. No notation, no reconstruction, no film

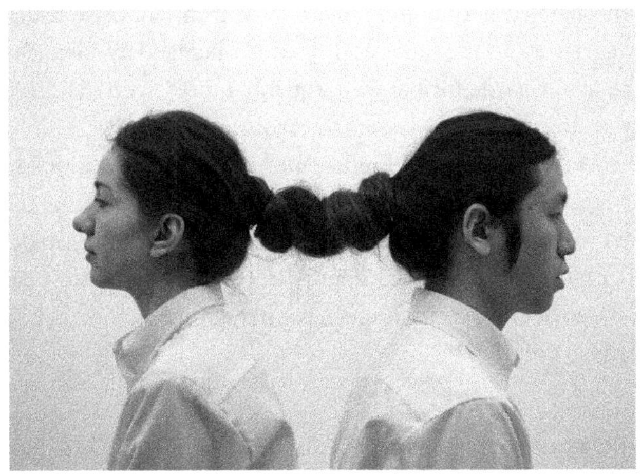

FIGURE 4.2 *Relation in Time*, reperformed by Arna Sam and Hsiao Chen. Photo by Jonathan Muzikar © The Museum of Modern Art, New York. © 2019 Marina Abramović. Courtesy of Sean Kelly Gallery / (ARS), New York.

or videotape recording can keep them. . . . One of the chief jobs challenging performance scholars is the making of a vocabulary and methodology that deal with performance in its immediacy and evanescence."[27] Peggy Phelan echoes this sentiment: "Performance's only life is in the present. Performance cannot be saved, recorded, documented, or otherwise participate in the circulation of representations of representations: once it does so, it becomes something other than performance. To the degree that performance attempts to enter the economy of reproduction, it betrays and lessens the promise of its own ontology. Performance's being . . . becomes itself through disappearance."[28] Both of these accounts define live performance as singular, noniterable, and grounded in presence (although others, like Rebecca Schneider, have countered by arguing that performance is always already mediated).[29]

Abramović has her cake and eats it too. Her discourse borrows and capitalizes on the auratic originality of presence that Schechner and Phelan ascribe to performance, while at the same time making performance a reproducible and thus ceaselessly commodifiable form. By securing originality for herself and reproducibility for others, Abramović assumes the role of host—a duplicity evident in the very architecture of *The Artist Is Present* retrospective, which in the very same moment finds the artist imparting the pure generosity of her presence on visitors in one wing of the museum while exploiting the labor power of fellow performers in another. Abramović's desire to enter the halls of the "Great Masters," Schneider observes, runs counter to performance art's historical aversion to high art institutions: "The battle of the 'rebel art' to enter the esteemed galleries of high art museums should be approached with a great measure of irony, since so much performance-based artwork in the 1960s and 1970s (influenced by a lengthy heritage of 'anti-art' avant-garde forms) was arguably more invested *at that time* in seceding from the . . . Great Masters than joining [them]."[30]

Schneider connects Abramović's desire to enter high art institutions to her interest in her legacy: "Marina Abramović herself is interested in the 'correct' transmission of 'seminal' works, including 'extremely strict instructions,' payment of copyright, and permissions to reperform—and she sees the move into venerated art museums as ensuring her ability to control history from beyond the grave."[31]

THE ECONOMICS AND ETHICS OF REPERFORMANCE

Abramović's embrace of reperformance reflected a larger shift in the art market, which in the early 1990s moved toward what Claire Bishop has called "outsourced" or "delegated performance"—a shift away from the paradigm of art as located in the artist's personal body and toward the business logic of subcontracting the performance to other bodies to maximize profits. As Bishop puts it, "Artists of the late '60s and early '70s—for example, Marina Abramović, Chris Burden, Vito Acconci, and Gina Pane—turned to their own bodies as the privileged site of artistic action. . . . Today their bodies also function art historically, as signs of an artistic practice that consciously placed itself at one remove from the market: in Western Europe and North America, performance and body art of the late '60s and early '70s frequently stood as a refusal of the portable object and the circulation of commodities."[32]

Abramović adopted this logic of outsourcing performance via reperformance, a form of bodily commodification that her original performances worked to undermine by virtue of being live; as Bishop points out, Abramović's own body no longer functions artistically but "art historically"—as part of an artistic legacy—when she turns to permanently subcontracting these performances, privatizing the live artwork, participating in the market shift toward reperformance and thereby denying a younger generation of artists a living wage. Abramović maintains her status as author of these performances, retaining the financial reward and agency of creative authorship while displacing the emotional and physical labor of performance onto younger artists. In this economy of reenactment, other, younger bodies are substituted for Abramović's to feed the machine of her artistic legacy. As one commenter (Steven Kaplan) on the online art magazine *artcritical* notes,

"The idea of substituting new, younger performers is what leads to the appearance of inequities and the charge of abuse of privilege. When Abramović herself was the performer, willingly suffering the slings and arrows for the sake of her art, the worst charge that could be leveled was masochism. But when other bodies—young, powerless, on display for the delectation of the powerful—are drafted for the sake of aggrandizing the arts institution, and for the ambitions of art plutocrats, there is obvious exploitation."[33]

Three of the reperformers of *The Artist Is Present*—Abigail Levine, Gary Lai, and Rebecca Brooks—published an open letter asserting that their initial offer from MoMA "struck many of us as untenable: $50 for a 2½ hour performance shift, no compensation for prep time or time in between shifts, and, most troublingly, no workman's compensation, which would cover us in the case of injury." "Through a first round of negotiations, we achieved a modest pay increase and a change of status to 'temporary employee,' which provided us workman's compensation and some other benefits," continue Levine, Lai, and Brooks (who note that MoMA's operating budget was $160 million in fiscal year 2008–9). "However, we were only able to approach a fair wage for our work after two fainting performers made evident the difficulty and risk of our work."[34] Pushing the burden onto young artists is especially exploitative; the financial burdens and limited professional horizons faced by working artists reflects a larger trend for younger people.[35] College-educated millennials, like many of the artists examined in this chapter, have seen the classic playbook of middle- and upper-middle-class social mobility ripped up before their eyes.[36] Education and hard work now bring not guaranteed success but guaranteed debt, with no expectation of secure work to offset it. "In order to fully recognize the scope of these changes," urges the critic Malcolm Harris, "we need to think about young people the way industry and the government already do: as investments, productive machinery, 'human capital.'"[37]

The MoMA reperformers' experience corroborates other accounts of the under-remuneration and lack of institutional support for Abramović's reperformers. The legendary dancer and feminist filmmaker Yvonne Rainer became the public spokesperson for another reperformer, this time for a gala performance at LA's Museum of Contemporary Art. According to one account, Rainer felt compelled to write to Jeffrey Deitch, the museum director, after hearing an account of the audition process from the dancer Sara Wookey.[38] Rainer's letter (which may or may not have been sent to Deitch before it was obtained and published by various media outlets) denounced the fact that, according to Wookey, in a scene calling to mind Roman Bacchanalia, performers had been asked to spend three hours with "their heads protruding through the gala's tabletops, kneeling on Lazy Susans below to slowly rotate in circles while maintaining eye contact with guests [while other] performers [were to] lay nude on tables with fake skeletons on top of them, recreating Abramović's famous *Nude With Skeleton* performance, as reperformers did at her MoMA retrospective." For this difficult, strange, and highly vulnerable work, the reperformers were to be paid $150 and to receive a one-year MOCA membership. Wookey informed Rainer, "Of course we were warned that we will not be able to leave to pee, etc. That diners may try to feed us, give us drinks, fondle us under the table, etc., but will be warned not to. Whatever happens, we are to remain in performance mode and unaffected."[39] While Rainer's letter drew attention to the treatment of younger artists, it also exacerbated the problem that it attempted to alleviate, effectively dispossessing Wookey of her own exploitation; it was Rainer's letter rather than Wookey's complaint that received attention in a social media controversy widely billed as "Rainer vs. Abramović/Deitch."[40]

The curatorial practice capitalizes on a winner-take-all contemporary art star system in which a few artists are given the majority of the resources and the majority of artists receive little to no compensation.[41] When reperformance offers younger performers low pay and few protections, it takes advantage of their economic and professional vulnerability in an era of austerity to push them into reperforming the works of famous artists rather than pursuing their own creative opportunities.[42] Exploiting what Lauren Berlant sees as the retraction of sociodemocratic promises of "the good life"—the withdrawal of promises of upward mobility, job security, and the social safety net in recent decades—these sorts of required reperformances hinder younger artists' shots at professional advancement or creative fulfillment.[43] Reperformance interrupts the "natural transmission" of opportunities and resources from avant-garde generations past to present (in other words, the transmission of resources without hope of gain—a form of legacy that is disinterested rather than interested, that does not offer the testator control or self-enrichment). Reperformance, and Abramović's use of it in particular, is both coercive and exploitative, only *posing* as hospitable—the classic position of the host who says one thing ("I'm open and receptive") and does another (privatizes resources and access, takes the money and runs).

Harris and others assert that this unprecedented political and economic climate has been unduly minimized or even dismissed by older generations, baby boomers in particular, who view it as young people "paying their dues." The journalist Michael Hobbs writes of the intergenerational conflict that attends the increasingly insecure work and life conditions faced by young people, "This is what it feels like to be young now. Not only are we screwed, but we have to listen to lectures about our laziness and our participation trophies from the people who screwed us. . . . From job security to the social safety net, all the structures that insulate us from ruin are eroding. And the opportunities leading to a middle-class life—the ones that boomers lucked into—are being lifted out of our reach. Add it all up and it's no surprise that we're the first generation in modern history to end up poorer than our parents."[44]

While intergenerational conflict (feminist or otherwise) is nothing new, I argue that under neoliberalism the structure where this conflict plays out—that of the host-parasite relation—*is* new. What can *The Artist Is Present*, as both a durational enactment and a disavowal of the absolute asymmetry of the host-guest relation, tell us about how older generations of feminists, both those in the art world and those in other fields, perceive the political struggles faced by today's emerging artists and intellectuals? Some of these powerful feminists retain an outdated idea of their own subject positions; they see themselves as marginalized, a view that has not caught up with the fact that they are now in the institutional positions of power—well-connected, professionally and financially secure—that they had at one time aspired to overturn. They have a standing seat at the table.

Indeed, the art world and the world of higher education—two somewhat politically progressive sites—reflect each other in many ways. A number of op-eds have discussed the precaritization of higher education, emphasizing the generational betrayal felt by younger scholars at the patronage model that underpins a neoliberal academy built on insecure and contingent labor conditions produced by decades of austerity and adjunctification. "Imagine if these protected and relatively privileged academic workers had the foresight, the solidarity, and the courage to stand and refuse to disown their present and future colleagues—not to mention their students—coming up behind," writes Joseph G. Ramsey.[45]

In this context, once-radical academic feminists are (like Abramović) at times perceived as hosts. In 2018 the feminist philosopher Avital Ronell, an academic star, was accused of harassment in a Title IX lawsuit filed by her former graduate advisee Nimrod Reitman. Many, many radical feminist, queer, and postcolonial thinkers, including Judith Butler, Jack Halberstam, Lisa Duggan, Gayatri Chakravorty Spivak, and Joan Wallach Scott, quickly closed ranks around Ronell. (In a blog post, Chris Kraus, whom I discussed in chapter 3 as parasiting the academic cultural critic Dick Hebdige, who served as host, issued her own startlingly aggressive and premature takedown of Reitman.)[46] Nick Mitchell has characterized the bitter debates that followed as "an archive of generational antagonism" that lays bare "a class struggle disavowed by the protocols of professionalization." "What happens when [your boss's or advisor's] understanding of what it means to be an intellectual means that they don't see themselves as your boss?" Mitchell asks.[47] Senior scholars defending Ronell and their junior academic counterparts spoke from entirely different subject positions.[48] Established scholars emphasized the ever-increasing demands of the neoliberal university and the nonhierarchical conventions of queer intimacy, effectively minimizing the power differential between the two groups; graduate students and other members of the academic precariat insisted on one simple fact: they cannot refuse their advisors' demands, no matter how outré or bizarre, without fear of compromising their livelihood and future employment.[49] For Mitchell what the senior professoriate fails fully to recognize is that the infrastructure necessary for doing radical academic work no longer exists in the same way it once did.

In Abramović's defense, the performance scholar Lydia Brawner (one of Abramović's reperformers) suggests that some of her detractors are motivated by ageism and sexism, that the critiques of the pioneering artist for exploitation are in fact alibis for the real resentment: that Abramović dares to remain in the spotlight while aging.[50] In the final analysis, the exploitative structure of *The Artist Is Present* is both *about* Abramović and not about her (much as Kraus's feminine abjection enacted in *I Love Dick* is both *about* Hebdige and not about him). Abramović is both a parasite and a host, for while she exploits others, she is herself (according to her) exploited by much larger structures of exploitation and oppression. (Abramović has pointed to what she perceives as the system's exploitation of her: for mounting *The Artist Is Present* she was paid only an honorarium of $100,000, which she said did not cover the year of work, the cost of maintaining a staff and office, and the three years it took her to physically recover from the performance.)[51]

What is at stake in *The Artist Is Present* (and, I will argue, in the parasitical homages and disavowals it elicits from younger performance artists) is *a claim to the entire present,* a claim to the right to occupy the present rather than having to cede one's place to others. For Abramović, the others are the generation of young artists who come after—and threaten to supersede—her. For the younger generation, the others are the older generation of feminist artists who came before—and threaten to exploit and overshadow—them. I invoke Berlant's use of the term *present*: an affective purchase on the contemporary that is always up for grabs, a "mediated affect" that is "under constant revision," an "extended now whose very parameters (when did 'the present' begin?) are also always there for debate."[52]

What is problematic in Abramović's approach is her desire to *own* the reperformance in perpetuity, rather than the fact of the reperformance itself. Her enthusiastic promotion of reperformance-with-permission (a reiteration rather than a reimagination of the original) seems designed to exclude younger female performance artists who wish to reinterpret iconic works on their own terms. In order to participate in the art economy, this younger generation must accept the terms established; performances of historical indebtedness have become compulsory. In Abramović's claim to the present—to being *the past, present, and future* of feminist art—she performs her coercive hospitality. The established artist invites a younger generation of performance artists to the museum, not to *be present* but to *re-present*. The competing temporal and ontological meanings of *presence* and *present* here index the contradictions of this ungenerous invitation. Abramović's *presence* represents an appeal to the past, sold over and over again, that echoes a blind spot of the high art market, which seems able to look only backward or forward, never at the present.

Younger performance artists have resisted the system's demand for reperformance, which concentrates profit in the hands of established creators. Instead of simply reperforming or strictly reenacting earlier works, some younger artists re-create or reinterpret iconic feminist artworks on their own terms. Among these artists are Lauren Barri Holstein, Emily Roysdon, and Gretchen Holmes, who have re-created Carolee Schneemann's iconic feminist performance *Interior Scroll* (1975), and Lilibeth Cuenca Rasmussen, who performed thirteen different re-creations within a three-hour span, including Shigeko Kubot's *Vagina Painting* (1965), Ana Mendieta's *Blood Signs and Body Tracks* (1974), and Janine Antoni's *Loving Care* (1992–96), as well as one of her own works.[53] These artists reinterpret these pieces for their own context. In a 2010 piece, Holmes observed that the political context of Schneemann's performance (defined by such causes as "the ERA, Equal Pay for Equal Work, education reform") was unambiguous compared to the dispersed and ambivalent feminist political climate that framed her re-creation of it. "While the original 'Interior Scroll' emerged at the confluence of Fluxus Happenings and Women's Liberation, a site primed for the radical gestures and collaborative interventions characteristic of 60s and 70s feminist art," she writes, "my recreation was submerged in a contemporary feminism overwhelmed by contradictory attitudes towards femininity, sexuality, and feminism itself."[54]

Still other younger performance artists reject the position of the protégé and instead adopt that of the parasite. In what follows I differentiate three aesthetic strategies by which younger performance artists have performed their disidentification—by appropriating, reperforming, challenging, and resignifying—with the legacy of feminist art. These young artists reimagine their broader structural positions in the art world, particularly their relation to the political and aesthetic legacies imposed by white liberal feminism. I call these strategies *parasitical homage*, *parasitical disavowal*, and *manic autogenesis*. The remainder of this chapter explicates these three strategies, particularly as they become increasingly more reflexive, turning their social critique inward on themselves, examining and highlighting their own complicity. Ultimately, parasitism here describes not simply this younger cohort of white performance artists' disidentification with their white liberal feminist forebears but the strategies by which they disidentify with the legacy of white liberal feminism more generally and the impoverished representations that it makes available to them.

PARASITICAL HOMAGE

If you choose to be a performance artist, you really drink the Kool-Aid. Your brain goes off the grid of success. Big cars, flashy jewels, home ownership. Recessions don't really matter, because your life is just one long recession.—ANYA LIFTIG, "ANXIETIES OF INFLUENCE"

In this chapter's clearest and most recognizable example of the "classic" type of parasitism, the Brooklyn-based performance artist Anya Liftig's intervention into *The Artist Is Present* imitated and literalized Abramović's refusal to cede her place to a younger generation of artists.[55] For the performance, the younger artist dressed as Abramović (in a long, dark blue dress, black braid swept over one shoulder); sitting across from Abramović, Liftig mirrored her for the entirety of March 27. Liftig refused to cede the guest chair in a timely manner, creating a kind of standoff between the two artists (figures 4.3–4.5). But her parasitical challenge only played within the bounds that the space implicitly allowed; as a fellow artist, Tatiana Berg, later told Liftig, "No one said you couldn't be dressed a certain way, no one could say you had to get up and let someone else have a turn." Liftig insisted that her performance was an expression of veneration, that she accepted the rules of the encounter in order to author something new within the frame of Abramović's unfolding artwork: "I wanted to operate within the piece as Marina had defined it to create something that was more ambiguous." She would later say that the experience gave her "*even* more respect" for Abramović's work.[56] Liftig's performance demonstratively is not original, seeming instead to be a poor copy: she mimics Abramović, doing exactly what Abramović does. Rather than elevating Liftig, the overall effect of this mirroring staged the asymmetry between the two artists. Over the course of their showdown this asymmetry can be seen in the invisible advantages accorded Abramović over Liftig, such as her ability to go to the bathroom; if Liftig had left the guest chair, she would have been replaced by the next guest. The artists' ability to meet their basic physical needs speaks to the false pretense of equality in Abramović's performance: she had an invisible system hidden within her dress and under her chair that allowed her to relieve herself without leaving the space, an infrastructural support built into the very apparatus of the museum. Liftig recalls, "I wanted to pee really badly. . . . I wanted a way in. I wanted my contacts to stop falling out of my eyes. Every time I thought about leaving the chair, I got pissed at myself. I got pissed at her. I got pissed at the museum. I just got pissed. And damn it felt GOOD." Liftig's parasitical homage is an ironic (if also partly sincere) performance of humility and flattery. (It recalls the overexaggerated reverence that Roisin Byrne performs for Hendricks and Chris Kraus for Dick.) Appearing to venerate Abramović—imitating and refracting Abramović's performance—affords Liftig the opportunity to call out the older artist's undeniable position as a host by challenging her own replaceability. The art historian Indra K. Lācis observes, "Construed as a slyly humorous, mocking gesture and as a profound homage to the older, established artist, Liftig's six-hour staring contest with Abramović zeroed in on the main concerns currently preoccupying performance art historians and critics. As Abramović's döppelganger for a day, Liftig confronted issues of authenticity, authorship and collaboration; copy and original; influence, reverence and derivation; as well as the problem of managing one's brand."[57]

Liftig titled the piece *The Anxiety of Influence* (2010), a nod to the literary critic Harold Bloom's 1973 treatise by the same name, where he famously proposes that poets are hindered in their creative process by an ambiguous relationship to the poets who came before them. Bloom argues that "the poet in a poet" may be inspired by reading another poet's work, but the poetry produced is derivative, weaker because it is unoriginal.[58] Liftig recalls her encounter with Abramović:

FIGURES 4.3–4.5 Anya Liftig, *The Anxiety of Influence*, 2010. Portrait photographs by Marco Anelli © 2010. Video still captured by MoMA's live video feed.

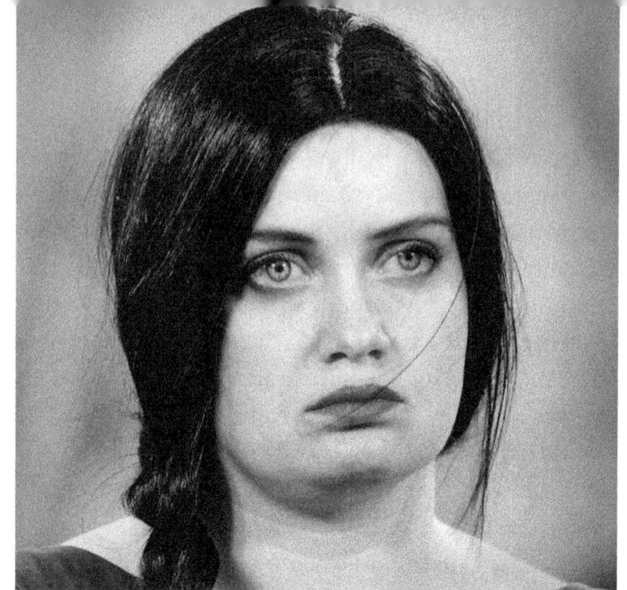

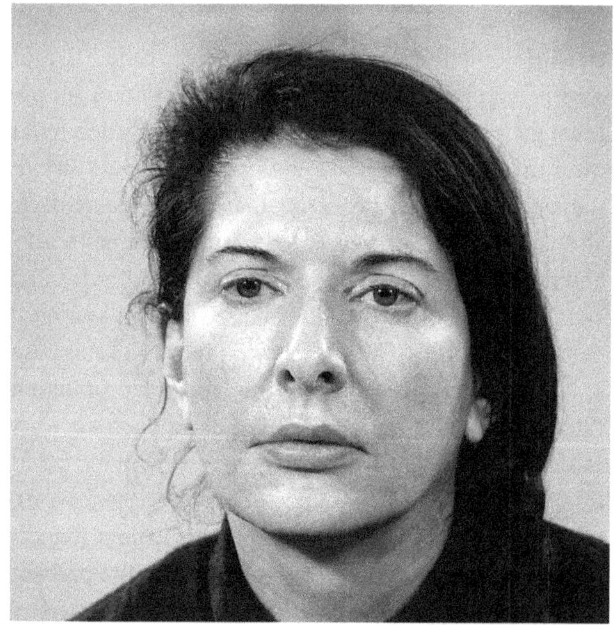

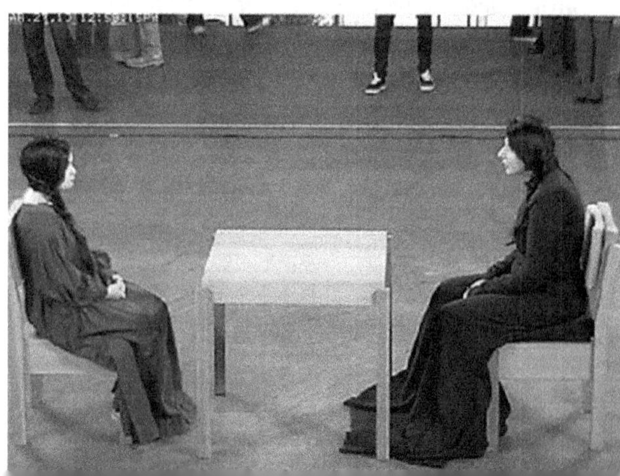

> I went through so many transformations as I sat there. Initially, I wanted some rise out of her, some acknowledgement of my gesture. Then I wanted to confess, as if I had been a bad child. Then, I felt myself get so angry that I almost started to cry. Why was she so special and why was I so small and weak? The glory of the venue wore off rather quickly. At a certain point, I felt like we were locking horns. She leaned forward and so did I. I started aping her every little movement and I kept hearing myself say, "move over bacon, here comes sausage." Then I would crack again. She's so strong. I was intimidated. She is like a mountain. She is my hero.[59]

Liftig's performance as guest makes more visible the cracks in Abramović's performance of receptivity; it shows that she is not as charitable or messianic as she seems. Liftig has said that Abramović gave her a slight smile when it was over, but that when she attempted to approach and thank her afterward, Abramović avoided her, literally watching her own back—a demonstration (like Amazon's decision to settle out of court with Ubermorgen) of the host's desire to keep its parasites at a comfortable distance.

> She kept making eye contact with me and avoiding me, almost running away. . . . Eventually I just left, but we ended up on the same escalator. I turned, and she said, "Those *eyes*. I remember those *eyes*." I was like, "Yes, Marina. I'm the girl who sat with you all day." She said, "I *know*. I *remember*." I was like, "Well, I just wanted to say thank you, it was a really great experience." She said, "Thank you. Thank you, too, thank you," and then she scurried away, walking backwards, facing me.[60]

PARASITICAL DISAVOWAL

While Liftig accepts the invitation offered by the structure of Abramović's performance in order to intervene in it, Ann Liv Young denies any anxiety of influence, even as she titles her first solo exhibition after Abramović's most famous work. *Ann Liv Young: Sherry Is Present* opened at the Louis B. James Gallery in New York City's Lower East Side in early December 2011. Spanning the holiday season, the ribald exhibition was advertised as a camp exercise in holiday overkill, Young's own version of the "Twelve Days of Christmas," with nightly events, including a lecture on coping with holiday stress, a tree-trimming session ("Trim the tree and then trim your bush," the gallery advertised), and a "holiday masturbation workshop." The exhibition allowed seemingly endless opportunities for Young's obliging self-commodification as the omnitalented Sherry, professional multitasker (couples Sherapy® for $75 per session! Sherr-aoke party!).

Young had gained a steady audience as a performance artist, regularly booking shows at festivals and experimental venues in New York City and Europe and having her work consistently puzzled over in the pages of *Artforum* and the *New York Times*, when she began in the early 2010s to perform regularly as "Sherry," her trash-talking, entrepreneurial southern alter ego, who has earned the artist more than a few enemies.[61] Empathetic, brash, and indifferent to internal contradiction, Sherry embodies the hyper-assimilated logic of evangelical capitalism. Always looking for new avenues of spiritual self-commodification, she is a therapeutic guru, a self-employed self-starter, a karaoke maestro, and a Christian radio host—all rolled into one white southern woman who is constantly taking off her pants and losing her wig. Young created Sherry when she was pregnant with her first child and could not maintain the strenuous rehearsal schedule required by her choreography-intensive performances. According to Young, Sherry was "borne [*sic*] out of [her] desire to create an economically sustainable performance model that 'always succeeds.'"[62] The Sherry shtick is thus a performance technology for a neoliberal era, a character built to weather the insecurity and inconsistency of the experimental performance and art market by being able to secure an audience without having to rely on institutional funding. The character has her own "Sherry Truck," which enables the artist to take her practice on the road, making her less reliant on traditional art institutional bookings (just as food trucks have made the restaurant industry more accessible to low-capital entrepreneurs). As one bio put it, "Sherry . . . has been branching out and breaking free of the churches and theaters of the bourgeoisie."[63]

Ann Liv Young: Sherry Is Present quite obviously borrows its title from *Marina Abramović: The Artist Is Present*. With this title (which, tellingly, is misidentified on Young's own CV as *Ann Liv Young: The Artist Is Present*) Young restages by allusion Abramović's exhibition, not in the lofted white cubes of midtown Manhattan but in the cramped quarters of Louis B. James's downtown location.[64] Upon entering the gallery, one is greeted by acrylic cases containing Sherry's fake nails and yellow pumps, exhibited alongside the artist's urine displayed in perfume bottles. The gallery's lower level has been transformed into the "Sherry Shop," a veritable garage sale of Young's performance props and castoffs (figure 4.6). "Everything is for sale!" a young woman supervising the shop booms as she greets newcomers. "*Everything* is for sale!" And she isn't kidding. Young's curatorial shakedown

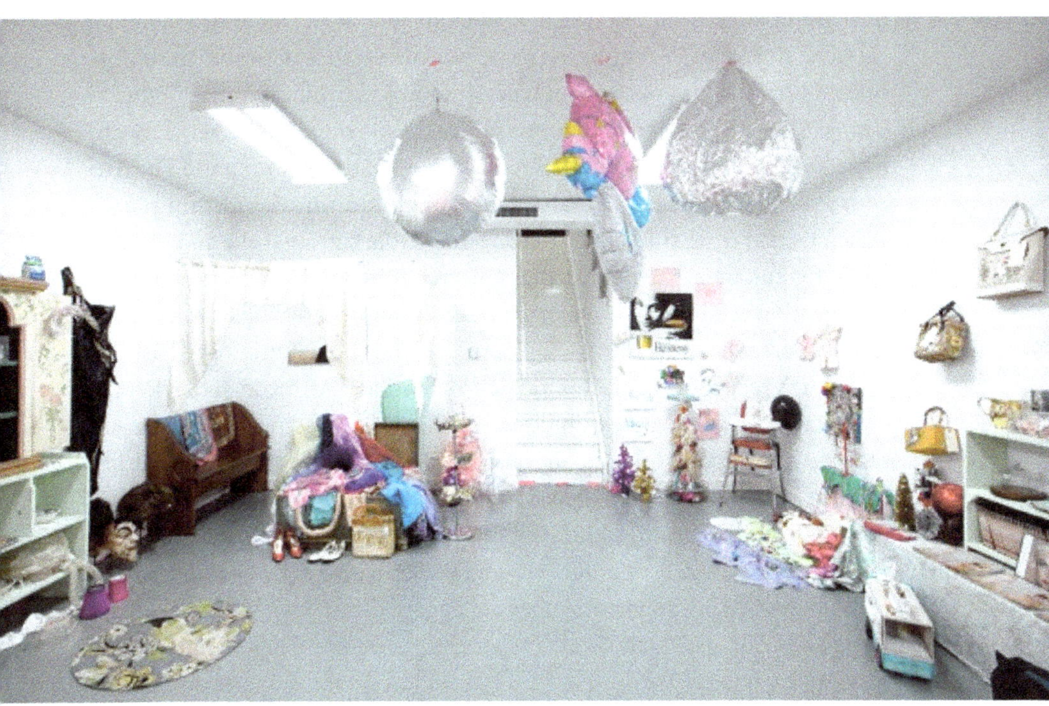

FIGURE 4.6 Installation view of *Ann Liv Young: Sherry Is Present,* Louis B. James Gallery, New York City, 2011–12. Source: Louis B. James Gallery.

knows no shame; a half-inflated unicorn balloon from an earlier performance hangs pitifully from the gallery ceiling, available for purchase.

Young's reimagining of *The Artist Is Present* as a tacky garage sale strips away the slick veneer of high art conferred by a major museum exhibition, highlighting the economic precarity of the younger generation of performance artists as they scrape together resources to support themselves and their art careers; for these artists, everything is literally for sale, as many sell possessions or work side hustles to pay rent. Young's Sherry show also lampoons the high production cost and elitist sensibility of Abramović's performance at the MoMA by inverting the dynamic, reimagining the show as a low-rent, low-class version of itself. (However, it should be noted that, while Young trades in an amateur aesthetic, she has enjoyed more support from major institutions and curators than most of her peers.) The artist's garage sale installation revels in a kitschy debunking of the idea that performance art can exist outside the vulgar economies of commodification. (The show calls to mind Martha Rosler's *Monumental Garage Sale* [1973], a work that, fittingly, Rosler herself restaged at MoMA in 2012 as *The Meta-Monumental Garage Sale*.) When Young asked me to write the wall text for the exhibition, I noted her obvious appropriation of Abramović's exhibition title: "*Ann Liv Young: Sherry is Present* lampoons the austere self-importance of the much-hyped 2010 Museum of Modern Art exhibition, *Marina Abramović: The Artist Is Present*, challenging Abramović's claim to the throne of feminist art." When I sent her what I had written, Young wrote back that she and her collaborator and then-partner Michael Guerrero did not think there should be any mention of Abramović: "sherry doesn't know or care who M A is . . . unless of course she's met her at a bible study (which i don't think she has)."[65]

Young's repurposing of Abramović's exhibition title throws into relief the contrast between the two exhibitions, highlighting differences in the present that these two artists inhabit. Sherry may not have heard of Abramović, but of course Young has. Nevertheless, in pretending to be someone who hasn't the younger artist seems to locate a certain creative freedom, a certain distance from the anxiety of influence. And yet she has something important in common with Abramović. She does not engage directly with Abramović, as Liftig does, but insists, above all, on her ability to control her own narrative.

ADOLESCENT SELF-PARODY

Before I proceed with my discussion of the third central aesthetic strategy deployed by these young artists, I must first make visible a crucial element of several of the younger artists' works I discuss in this chapter: their adolescent aesthetic. These performances exploit the already performative aesthetic of the adolescent girl as she is construed in mainstream and feminist discourse, refracting this figure into generative and ironic reflections: a chain of significations, a network of reflections that bounce off each other—the adolescent girl, the girliness of girl power, the riot grrrl, the girl with her doll, the girl *as* the doll—the adolescent girl is always multiple, overdetermined, allegorical, and caricatural. These artists mobilize the tactics of adolescent performance and adolescent refusal to exploit the impurity of these reflections, to expose them as constructed and unrealistic, reappropriating images that have been projected onto them but that they do not recognize as representative.

As a reaction to notions of generation or legacy, this aesthetic is a form of self-parody (more accurately, "self"-parody). More specifically it is an attempt to disidentify with white feminism by appearing to *overidentify* with it, following Stevphen Shukaitis's theorization of overidentification as a dissimulating form of resistance, whereby one feigns hyperbolic agreement with authority in order to sow dissent. In its over-the-top, plastic, hyper-commodified, grotesque manifestations, I understand this parody form as an attempt to try on many alternative positions in order to break out of the overdetermined molds of white femininity and white feminism. This adolescent aesthetic is essential to understanding the posture of illegibility and evasiveness—of reflection, doubling, multiplicity—cultivated by these artists, for this posture is more scattered, more referential, more illegible, and more difficult to pin down than the parasitical tactics I have previously examined in this book.

Young's aesthetic practice exemplifies this posture, characterized as it is by an unflinching embrace of all things kitsch and juvenile. Any day of the week Young's crackpot personal website might display something like the following (which appeared in the spring of 2009): "march 12th/7pm/bring your girls along and let's do a girls night. It's a girl's night out. tickets are $15 per person. we'll do facials, nails, a little cooking and some masterbation [*sic*] techniques! (of course we do not descriminate [*sic*] against men or trans.)" Young's appeal to all her "girls" satirizes third-wave feminism's slogan "girl power"; her over-the-top fervor for "girl stuff" (facials, nails, cooking, masturbation) lampoons the production and exploitation of a particularly commodified representation of white bourgeois feminism ("$15 per person"). Her comical attempt to DIY this cheaper version of commodified feminism has the effect of estranging and denaturalizing the more polished commercial version. It parodies the commodification of feminism, reflecting it back in a way that makes it appear foolish.

In Young's kitschified fairy tale online universe, careless spelling errors, cursing, unicorns, dogs, and naked exhibitionism reign. On her website one is greeted with what sounds like the voice of a demented witch screaming: "Mwahahahaaa!! Welcome to my website. I am Ann Liv Young, demon master!!!" Her homepage features collaged, scrapbook cutout images of evil trees, a fairy castle, and Young in a bikini with a young child playing beside her. Further in, one finds a selection of buttons on a background of ornamental doilies, lavender doodles, and amateur drawings done in Microsoft Windows Paint: "DVDs," "Dance company," "Performances," "Animals," "Raps," "Contact Us," and "Copy right" (a misspelling that suggests, in contrast to Abramović, an irreverent and nonsystematic relationship to copyright protocols) (figure 4.7). Almost none of the links work.[66]

This girly aesthetic that Young's website captures is particularly characteristic of Young's early career performances (2005–10), before she began performing regularly as Sherry. It is these performances that I am most

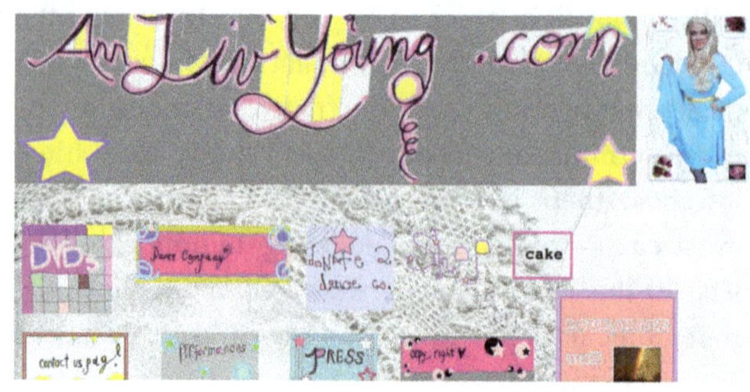

FIGURE 4.7 Ann Liv Young's personal web page, annlivyoung.com, 2011. Source: Ann Liv Young.

interested in here. After 2010 her work became more improvisational and concerned with dynamics of audience confrontation and less interested in the aesthetic of reflection, in working out her ambivalent relationship with popular culture and institutional authority, be it feminist art history or the art world. After this period Young performed primarily as Sherry, gaining a reputation for performances that border on bullying, even on violence—performances that make her clash with Penny Arcade look tame. (Although I publicly supported Young's earlier work, and while I admire her talent and conviction as a performer, I have been less willing to offer the same critical support of this later body of work in light of what I perceive to be its menacing turn.) As Sherry, she has variously performed in blackface, gyrated naked on unconsenting audience members, and interrupted and verbally abused the lesser-known artist Rebecca Patek during a piece (purportedly) about Patek's sexual assault.[67] Young's trademark "Sherapy" is an audience interaction–based performance of psychological quackery during which Sherry encourages, even intimidates audience members into sharing traumatic histories and memories. The theater historian Andrew Friedman captures the general progression of Young's Sherry shows well: "The shows centre on Sherry's efforts to question and reveal the fraudulence of others' affectations through Young's own phony persona. These encounters begin with Sherry asking audience members innocuous questions and quickly proceed towards invasive lines of inquiry, including one's relationships, sexuality, or—equally troubling—thoughts about the show itself or art in general. . . . Young's desire to forcibly engage her audiences echoes the assaultive language and methods of the antagonistic avant-garde."[68] Young's Sherapy is a manipulative instrumentalization of others' personal pain that exceeds Abramović's pretension to the healing power of presence in *The Artist Is Present*. In some cases these performances have cost Young hard-earned institutional support, recalling the threat that Kraus's reckless parasitism posed to her personal and professional hosts—namely, Sylvère and Semiotext(e). Friedman notes the self-destructiveness and lack of regard for professional consequences in Young's recent performances: "Even if such behaviours accrue symbolic capital, they can result in the loss of actual income: the stuff that pays the rent. While the link between institutions and provocation may be continual, some works *actually* and *purposefully* risk the destruction of their institutional relations."[69]

But before Sherry took over, Young's earlier works—deranged, camp fairy tale adaptations like *Melissa Is a Bitch* (modeled on *Peter Pan*), *Snow White*, and *Cinderella*—garnered the artist a loyal, if befuddled cult following. It is in these works that Young would craft and hone her persona of adolescent performance. She displays in this kitschy, consumerist early work a self-conscious aesthetic of failure, but this failure is in fact highly rehearsed. Throughout the performances Young shouts commands (onstage and off) at her performers like a drill sergeant. The bawdiness of her play with graphic (if utterly de-eroticized) nudity and foul language becomes surreal under her militaristic direction and disciplined choreographic methods. She is a perfectionist reigning over a total mess. This aesthetic of failure is in fact an adolescent refusal to internalize and comply with particular narratives: of professional art practice, with its insistence on acknowledging one's legacy; of the compulsory performance of artist, of woman, of feminist.

But Young's intentional aesthetic of failure has been consistently misread as an actual artistic failure on her part—as an attempt to fulfill these expectations that falls short. In early November 2010 she opened *Cinderella* at Brooklyn's ISSUE Project Room. After three "false starts," the performance began when Young-as-Sherry-as-Cinderella glided out on a pair of roller skates through a field of iridescent balloons. In a review of *Cinderella*, filed as a dance review, the *New York Times* critic Alastair Macaulay makes clear that he came to the show expecting to see a particular brand of avant-garde virtuosity (pegging Young, at the outset of the review, as "belong[ing] to the movement in the arts that was labeled Sensation in the 1990s") and left disappointed. He writes, "There are three things for which I was unprepared on Friday night . . . the startling ineptitude of Ms. Young's performance; the campy, cliquey way she assumed that everyone present already knew all about this show and her previous ones; and the silly consensus whereby most of her audience, giggling coyly now and then, encouraged her." Macaulay scolds Young for her general ineptitude, boring performance style, and weak diction: "[The show's] first 95 minutes demonstrated many layers of failure. Principally, Ms. Young lacks technique. In addition to the problems already cited, she had to consult notes, repeat passages to get them right and tell her audio technician to change things."[70]

The review's hostility condenses all the things that Macaulay simply doesn't get about what Young is doing as an artist: principally her fearlessness onstage, her ability as an improvisor, and her shrewdness in deploying this aesthetic of failure. For Young cannot fail, since failing is exactly what she sets out to do in the first place. Failure is success. Failure is the condition of possibility for the creation of something unpredictable and surreal. Poorly fitting prom dresses, campy animal balloons, terrible wigs, false starts, cheesy pop music—to call Young's performances "bad" is to state the obvious. (As an adolescent might say, "Duh.") Macaulay critiques the artist (and her audience) using the very aesthetic and ideological frameworks that her performance practice works against—frameworks that postulate, for instance, that art must aim toward ideals of mastery, beauty, coherence, professionalism, and resolution. In so doing, Macaulay and likeminded critics unwittingly validate the relevance of her method, providing more grist for the mill of an artist who has said of her process, "I want to regurgitate what people think of me onstage."[71] Young's practice unerringly exposes institutional orthodoxies and the hypocrisies they mask.[72] Andrew Friedman observes, "The central opponents for Young/Sherry are the values of the art world, which is 'full of people that think they have the authority to say, "This is good, this is bad. This is art, this is not. This is worth fifty thousand dollars, this is worth nothing.' . . . Most objectionable to Young is accepting an aesthetic that seemingly renders sincerity impossible."[73]

Despite Macaulay's savage pan of the show, many weird and interesting things were, in fact, happening during her performance of *Cinderella*, a performance that really began in the lobby, where a female usher badgered waiting audience members into buying candy from her for five cents. Inside the theater, Young's collaborator Michael Guerrero, whom in one interview Young comically describes as playing a "stunt double" in the show, is adorned in an even cheaper version of Young's own spectacular costume: a worse-fitting wig and even tackier cerulean Lycra leotard with what appears to be a menstrual stain down the back.[74] As the show begins, he fidgets with the tech under Young's hostile glare. Before long, Suzanne Vega's 1984 a cappella hit "Tom's Diner" plays over the speakers, while one of Young's two male backup dancers, increasingly sweating and exhausted as the song continues, resorts to keeping the rhythm by violently cracking a whip against the floor. The innocent and nostalgic quality of Vega's folk-inspired song is disrupted by the lurid spectacle of a young South Asian

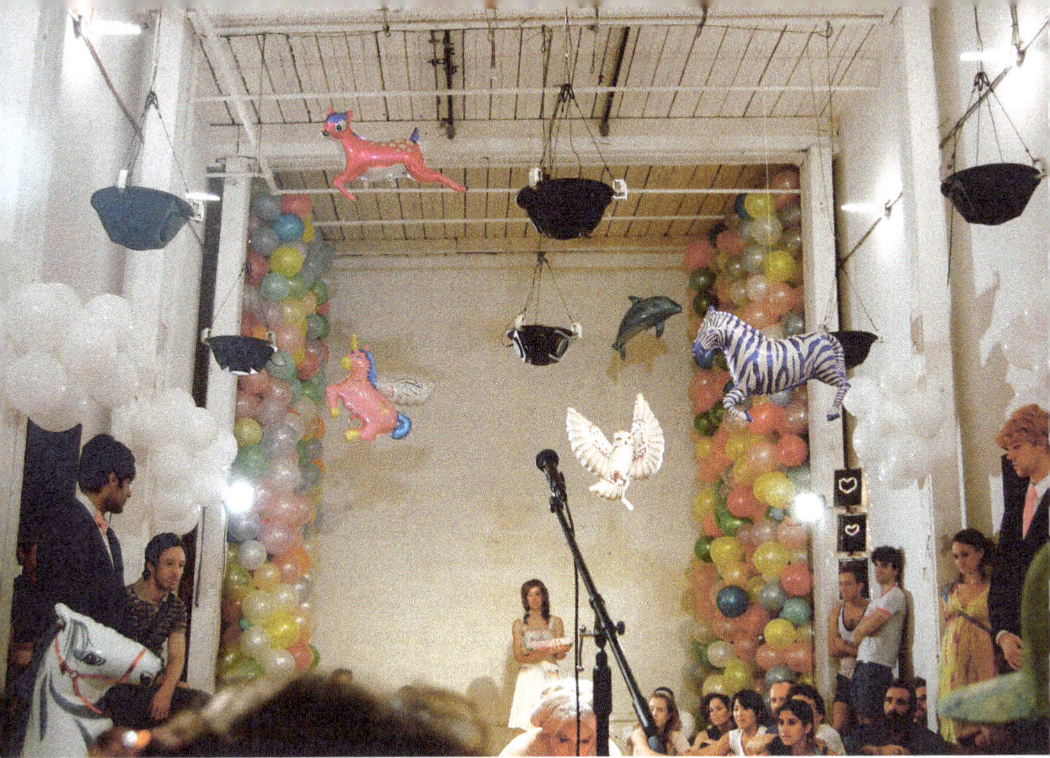

FIGURE 4.8 Ann Liv Young, *Cinderella*, ISSUE Project Room, Brooklyn, 2010. Photo by Davide Trentini.

male dancer forced to labor to its saccharine beat. Amid the trappings of a little girl's birthday party, the dancer stops when Vega stops and starts when she starts, highlighting consumer culture's complicity with racialized labor and implicating the audience in a particularly earnest portrait of whiteness (figure 4.8).

Next, Young performs her trademark hardcore karaoke, singing Whitney Houston's "I Wanna Dance with Somebody" and rapper T.I.'s "Whatever You Like" as if her life depended on it. She sings T.I.'s graphic lyrics ("Stacks on deck / Patrón on ice / And we can pop bottles all night / Baby you can have whatever you like [you like] . . . / Late night sex so wet and so tight . . . / Baby you can go wherever you like [you like]") earnestly and intensely. The soberness of her vigorously performed hip-hop minstrelsy refuses the conniving wink that might defuse the cringe effect of her aesthetic choices. Rather than rushing through particularly graphic lyrics, she enunciates them as one might declaim romantic poetry. Young's performed overidentification with the song's misogyny, which presents women as easily acquired and easily discarded materialists (a reading that the song's music video reinforces), is itself a kind of disidentification, dissonant rather than straightforwardly critical.

Young borrows the camp fairy tale from drag performers. (Esther Newton explains the typical drag scenario: "Almost every joke the camp makes elaborates . . . the stories of Snow White or Cinderella." The drag queen, explains Newton, says, "'Mirror, mirror on the wall, who's the fairyest of them all?' and the mirror [responds] [sarcastically], 'you are, girl.' . . . But usually the mirror brutally replies, 'Snow White, you ugly bitch!' ")[75] The artist defiles her fairy tale princesses, staging deconstructed versions in which her protagonists appear lost, their gowns dirty and tattered and their romances perverted. In *Snow White*, "Prince Charming" is played by a young actress who dons a nude strap-on to Aaliyah's "Are You That Somebody?" *Cinderella* concludes not with a "happily ever after" but with Young attempting to defecate on command. Despite the show's fairy tale titles, Young's work borrows more from drag subcultures than from Disney; in her narrative the white fairy tale princess, represented as the pure and unqualified ideal of white femininity, is camped, debased, and worn down.

Consider another performance artist whose work plays with an adolescent aesthetic in order to complicate not only stereotypical femininity's racial politics but also its heterosexism. Amber Hawk Swanson made *The Feminism? Project* (2006) while an MFA student at the School of the Art Institute of Chicago. The artist asked women from her home state of Iowa, including fellow sorority sisters and her own mother, to describe their relationship to feminism. In a series of short videos, Swanson performs these responses as monologues while engaged in charged or graphic sexual scenarios: having her toenails painted by her father, giving a hand job to her then-boyfriend, being spanked and penetrated by him, being fondled by a woman, and being penetrated by another woman. In the scene with her father, the artist props herself up on a ruffled bedspread in a lavender bedroom.[76] Wearing a matching pink sweatshirt and shorts, the artist poses in the foreground with a teddy bear perched behind her. In another, Swanson applies depilatory cream on her eyebrows and upper lip in the bathroom mirror as she deadpans a script with Valley-girl intonation:

> I don't really spend a lot of time thinking about feminism because I view women and men as *equals* and *that's the definition, so* . . . I do think it is represented in me. I don't ever think of myself as *inferior* to a *man*. In fact, most of the time I find myself smarter or more well-rounded. But I don't know, I mean, men and women are equal and whether the guy next to me

thinks so or not, this is *my life, so* . . . I mean I know a lot of women, and not necessarily *lesbians*, or people who are really *political*, spend a lot of their life fighting for it. I guess I just have *other things to do.*[77]

Swanson's naïve delivery of these scripts underscores the disjointedness, the lack of logical connectors, the moments of trailing off in the women's repudiation of feminism, which they often characterize as culturally outmoded ("because men and women are equals and *that's the definition*"). Feminism is a project reducible to "*lesbians*" or "people who are really *political*," and thus peripheral to the women originally interviewed, who claim that feminism constitutes more of a threat than "the guy next to [her]." Swanson calls attention to the adolescent quality of the original speaker's discourse and its suspended inarticulation ("I mean . . ."; "I guess . . ."; "*so* . . .") by ironically restaging it, by reflecting it back without comment—a deadpan technique that highlights the naïve and uninformed nature of these arguments via Swanson's mere repetition of them.

Swanson's delivery of these monologues while engaged in graphic sex acts undercuts the clichéd rhetoric and stereotypical gender performances of these sorority girls and suburban princesses. These scenes track a progression, beginning with Swanson being infantilized by her actual father in a sexualized way, moving to her being infantilized by her boyfriend (by being spanked), and ending with her having sex and orgasming with women. This trajectory suggests a feminist progression in the transition from patriarchal approval to lesbian sexual fulfillment. As the scenes get progressively gayer, the sex becomes less and less perfunctory. In the final scene Swanson's performance climaxes in an interruption of the artist's feminist script as she reaches orgasm with a female partner. As the scenes progress, Swanson, herself a former sorority girl, outs herself as the lesbian that the young woman had phobically coded as feminist. Swanson thus performs and herself embodies the disjuncture between mass culture's stereotypes of feminism and the artist's own sexual identity narrative—a narrative that presumably reveals a kind of answer to the question of contemporary feminism posed in her title.

In a subsequent project, *To Have and to Hold and to Violate* (2006–8), Swanson orders a Realdoll—the Hollywood special effects version of a blow-up sex doll—in her own likeness (figure 4.9) and makes it into her own personal voodoo doll and lover. Part coming-out project and part public experiment in sadomasochism, the Pygmalionesque project explores themes related to her until-now-latent lesbianism alongside a performance of hyper-

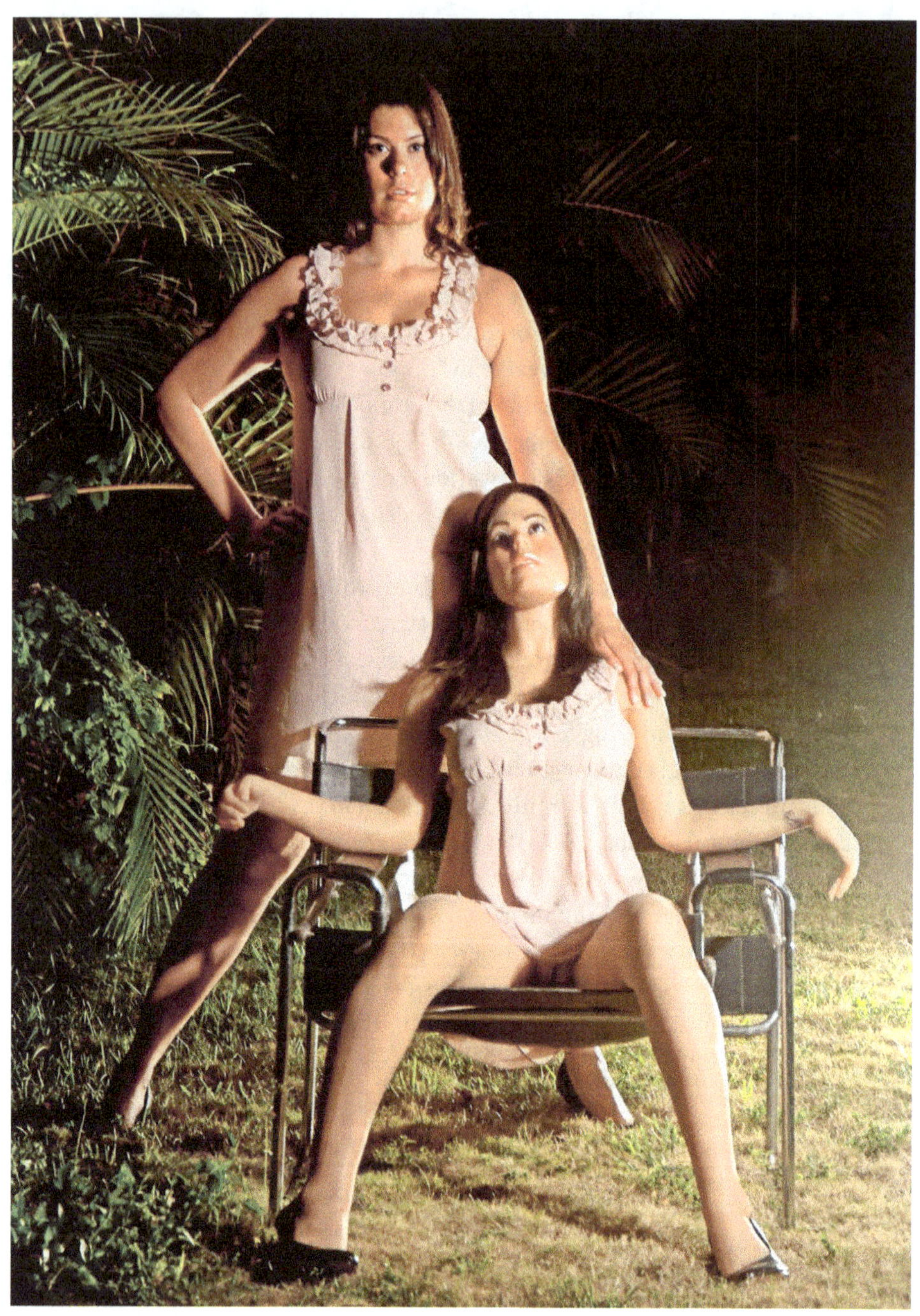

FIGURE 4.9 Amber Hawk Swanson, *To Have and to Hold and to Violate,* 2006–8. Source: Amber Hawk Swanson.

femininity, a conceptual and aesthetic juxtaposition that has become her trademark. The artist (who has the word *Bully* tattooed on her wrist) and her doll (with the word *Prey* painted on its wrist) were married in a backyard ceremony. The performance event was documented in an eleven-minute video, during which guests were invited to interact with Amber Doll for the cutting of the cake, the first dance, the tossing of the garter, and the bouquet toss. Reception guests could also pose with Amber Doll, and the portraits were later exhibited as part of the project. Swanson's work explores the aesthetic impact of her "double embodiment of femininity": as a lesbian (whose art practice explores sadomasochistic desire) and as the Realdoll, her literal double, her other self. Swanson examines this double femininity as that which would seek both to "have and to hold" itself; she offers her image as both object of self-possession (*its to-be-hadness*) and object of self-abandonment (*its to-be-heldness*).

Swanson's creation and manipulation of the doll, which is associated with a disquieting sexualized femininity, conflates two sites of femininity's commodification that typically are seen as contradictory. Amber Doll disturbingly combines and confuses the child's doll with the sex doll, with the same signifier simultaneously invoking both innocence and perversion. Swanson has said of her decision to acquire the Amber Doll, "I was looking for a receptacle for the onslaught of attention and negative feedback—a stand-in for myself. It was just the right amount of crazy to order a $12,000 doll." She continues, "The total time from the beginning of my discussions with them to eventually picking her up to be mine was nine months. Which of course cracks me up, thinking about her as my twin, my wife, and a baby of sorts."[78] The doll is a parody, but a parody of herself, in her own likeness. By making the doll symbolize women's objectification— by making herself into an object for her own objectification— Swanson produces herself as an objective correlative of femininity through which she can exorcise her own ambivalent feelings toward "herself."

Let's finally consider a last, brief example of an artist who, like Young and Swanson, foregrounds a girlish aesthetic as a feminist form of self-development. Kate Gilmore is a performance artist known for methodically constructing physical obstacles and claustrophobic environments—propelled objects, plaster walls, piles of rocks—that she must either withstand or demolish in her short performances, which she documents as videos.[79] The artist kicks, hacks, claws, and hurls her weight through these obstacles during her physically demanding performances. Her targeted actions are reminiscent of conventions established by Fluxus artists, as if she were following a simple score

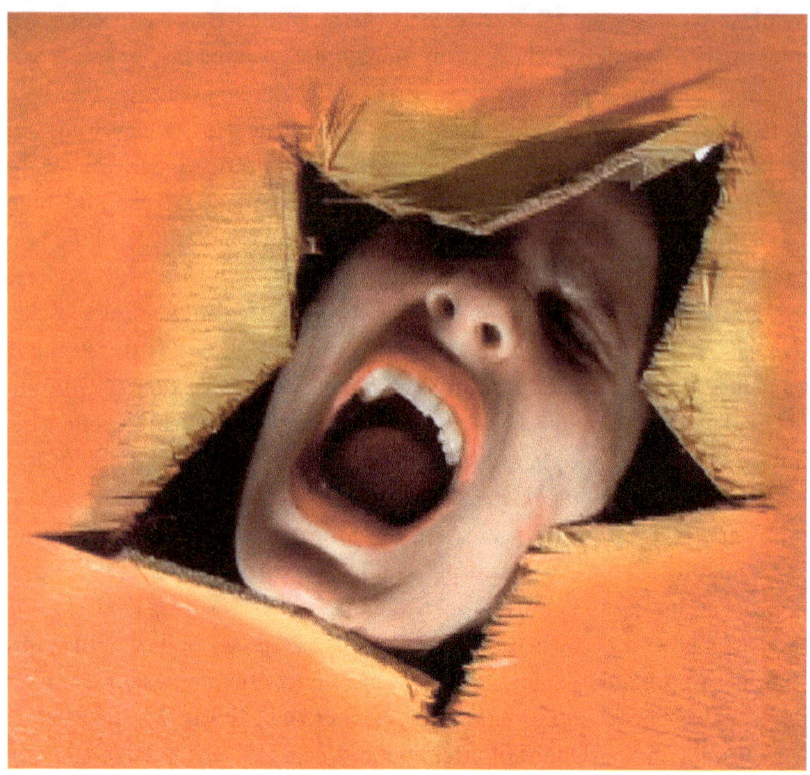

FIGURE 4.10 Kate Gilmore, *Star Bright, Star Might,* 2007. Source: Kate Gilmore.

or set of instructions for performing the work: keep smiling while things are thrown at you, break through a wall, stuff your head through a wooden cutout of a star (figure 4.10). In *Walk This Way* (2008), Gilmore performs for a still camera. Wearing a color-coordinated dress and high heels, she begins to knock down an exposed wall, hurling the weight of her body against it, battering it with her heel (figure 4.11). The vaginal-like rupture she creates reveals that the interior side of the wall is a glossy magenta, matching the silk flower in her hair. For *Standing Here* (2010), featured in the 2010 Whitney Biennial, Gilmore, in a polka-dotted dress and a ponytail, exerted the full force of her weight to puncture holes, find footing, and ultimately scale the inside of a self-designed column—an uncanny structure that echoes a vertical tunnel or an upstanding birth canal. Referencing Schneemann's iconic feminist performance *Interior Scroll*, the art critic Lyra Kilston writes of Gilmore, "The bluntness of her acts seems appropriate for the female stereotypes Gilmore parodies, yet this is *not your mother's* feminist video art:

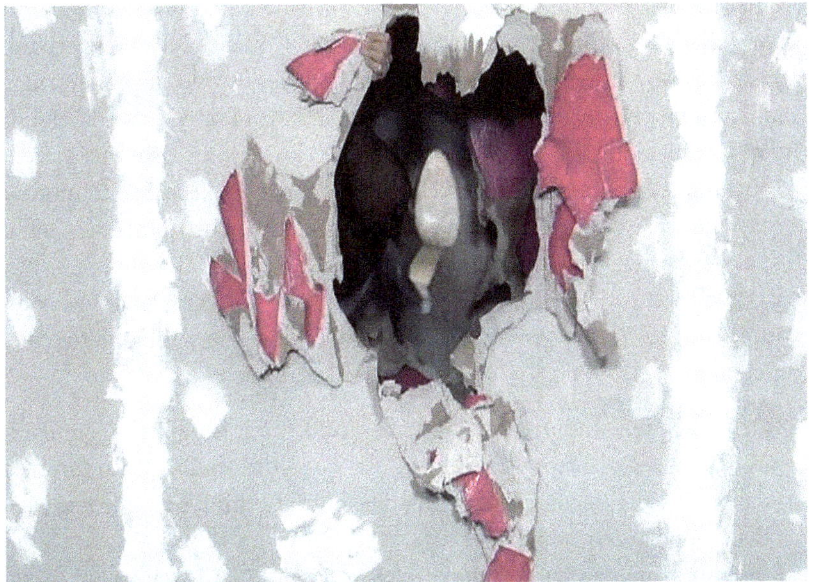

FIGURE 4.11 Kate Gilmore, *Walk This Way*, 2008. Source: Kate Gilmore.

lipstick, color-coordinated hair ribbons, and an eager-to-please smile usurp 1970s scraggly underarm hair and vaginal scrolls."[80] Often these young artists are clearly drawing on the history of feminist art. But as we will see, as they become increasingly more reflective and imitative, they also become increasingly less inclined to credit (or even admit that they know) their original sources.

NOT YOUR MOTHER'S PERFORMANCE ART

On one level, the works of Young, Swanson, and Gilmore certainly read as feminist art. They utilize the familiar tropes of abjection and shock (cringe and disgust, ingestion and expulsion, explicit nudity and sexuality) associated with feminist performance art, and they carry the affective charge associated with those tropes. But while women performance artists of the 1960s, 1970s, and 1980s engaged in arguably more sincere, explicit, and overtly politicized body art practices, the work of these contemporary artists registers a certain amount of ambivalence about what it means to explicitly and publicly avow a feminist position—which is not the same as ambivalence about in fact *being* a feminist. When asked directly in a 2007 interview about *Snow*

White, "Is this a feminist piece?," Young answered, "I don't know. I don't know what the fuck it is. I mean, some people would say it is. We're actually doing two shows in Italy this year, and one is a women's-gender yadda yadda. These people are really into the piece, which I find very interesting. It makes sense that they would be, but I don't know. I feel like this piece is so open-ended. I guess I don't really see it as a feminist piece. I see it more as a solo."[81] Here Young disarticulates her practice from the tradition of feminist art, framing it as singular and iconoclastic, as not inheriting from any particular political position or aesthetic tradition. But in my own interview with the artist, Young responded to this same question with an altogether different answer:

> Definitely. One hundred percent for sure. I think [the works] are feminist because I'm a female and I made it. The word *feminist* is so funny to me because it's become such a broad term, and I think that in some ways that's good and in some ways it's sort of confusing. I think they are feminist, but I am not trying to make feminist work.... Whatever I am thinking about at that time, whatever I'm trying to do at that time is . . . I'm not like "Women should be free." You know what I mean? For Sherry, it is like "Women should be free." But that's not my goal. My goal is to portray this character. But yeah, I think they are definitely feminist. I don't see how they couldn't be. . . . It's like *yes* and *no* mean the same thing to me. I could say "Maybe."[82]

Young reserves for her alter ego Sherry the clear statement of the (feminist-identified) belief that "women should be free," using Sherry as an alibi to say what she will not say herself. It is *Sherry* who represents a liberationist position as a caricature, and it is *Sherry* who defers revolutionary politics to the land of make-believe. By reserving the emancipatory outlook for her alter ego, Young offers a sly critique of the outmodedness of a feminist approach that could imagine such a thing as freedom to be within the realm of possibility. When she speaks for herself, she refuses to be pinned down to a particular position. Her position is illegible, and deliberately so. Like Tristan Tzara's provocation in his "Dada Manifesto" that "affirmation=negation," she engages in maneuvers of obfuscation and multiplication: *yes, no, maybe*.[83] Young, a self-described "escape artist" when it comes to explaining her practice to other people, performs ideological inconsistency and historical ignorance to avoid having to maintain a single political pose that would too easily risk becoming dogmatic or fossilized over time.[84]

In the question "Is your work feminist?" Young hears instead "Is your work original?" She explicitly rejects the idea that her work inherits feminist art traditions, that it is part of a history. By making her work and her ideas and affiliations illegible, she routes around political expectations of transparency or internal coherence that would enable her and her work to be placed within an institutional context and history. This type of illegibility, of committing to no coherent ideological position that lasts past the moment, this posture of refusal—these are the characteristics of the parasitical artists in this chapter. They are still parasites, but this insistence on incoherence, on multiplying reflections and parodies, on copying and stealing and refusing credit is what sets apart the particular artists I examine here (and this generation of artists) . Young encapsulates this contemporary parasitical sensibility when she insists on the original authorship of her work: "I guess I don't really see it as a feminist piece. I see it more as a solo." She goes on to say that she "[doesn't] really know what feminist art is"; that "to be perfectly honest" she had never heard of Marina Abramović; that she knows only "a little bit about" Annie Sprinkle; and that until "the other day," she had "never seen anything by" Karen Finley (although the two are constantly compared). It seems impossible that Young's assertions are true. Echoing many of Finley's performances, Young poured chocolate all over herself in her 2006 performance *Solo* (figures 4.12 and 4.13)—an ironic title that rejects the idea of being part of a tradition of feminist art while at the same moment clearly reflecting and referencing a famous body of work that came before.

Young doesn't shy away from referring to (even, as in the case of *Solo*, partially reperforming) these previous foundational works. Instead she refuses to cite them, refuses to be identified as inheriting their legacy. Claims Young, "What is so funny is that I am really not influenced by anybody else and I think for some people that is frustrating because I don't go see performances and I don't support my community, whatever that is supposed to mean. I think that is so silly because what is supporting community? Is there only one way to do that? By making work I am supporting my community. Yes it's feminist art."[85] Like Penny Arcade (who during their onstage confrontation called Young "a fake radical" who "lacks material" and "has no technique"), critics don't buy Young's professed ignorance of her feminist foremothers' work nor the originality of her own: "Karen Finley has been doing basically the same thing for 30 years, only better," writes Andy Horwitz, a dance and theater blogger. "For that matter Penny Arcade, Diamanda Galás and countless other women performers have explored these ideas—and presen-

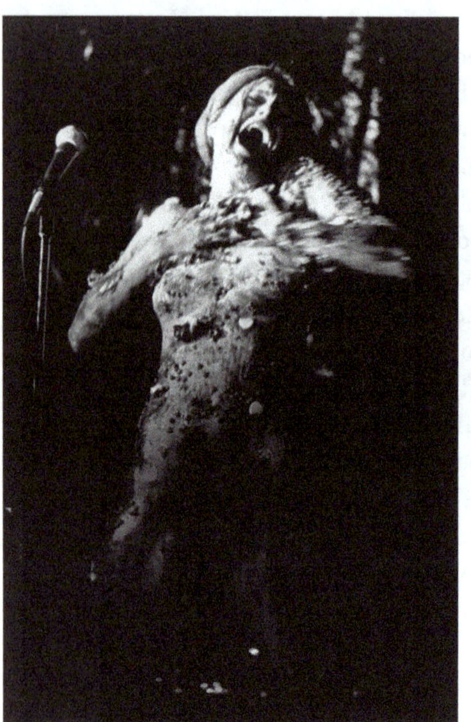

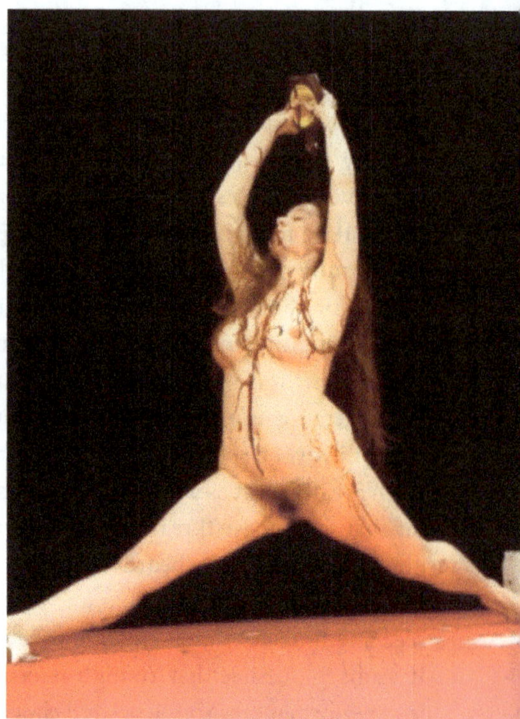

FIGURE 4.12 Karen Finley, *We Keep Our Victims Ready,* 1990. Source: Walker Art Center Archives.
FIGURE 4.13 Ann Liv Young, *Solo,* 2006. Source: Ann Liv Young.

tations of the human body—in more intelligent, capable, insightful and artful ways."[86] Similarly the *New York Times* critics Claudia La Rocco and Gia Kourlas write of Young's show *The Bagwell in Me* (2008), "There was nothing in this half-baked mess that many an artist hasn't done before, and better. Ms. Young has trumpeted her willed artistic ignorance and disdain for her peers. Let's hope for her sake that's the truth, as, just 27, she still has time to look around and learn her history. Either of these actions would enrich her compellingly raw but one-note stage presence. If only she would show less of herself and more of the world."[87]

Yet Young remains undeterred. The artist's "willed artistic ignorance" extends to her interactions with the well-known artists whose work she draws on. In 2010 Young said that she had been approached about doing a double bill with Karen Finley, an offer that she says Finley subsequently declined: "I feel like she is offended or something because she is like 'She is trying to replace me,' but I don't know anything about her. I would think that might be insulting to her. I was thinking like, should I approach her and try to get her to do this double bill with me and act as if I am a huge fan? Or should I tell her, 'I don't know anything about your work'?"[88] Finley seemed to take small revenge (whether intentionally or not), returning Young's willed ignorance; a few years later, when she and Young were co-headliners for a panel on the politics of censorship and performance at NYU in 2013, Finley persistently referred to Ann Liv throughout alternately as "Ann" and "Anna."

Young responds with a shrug of ironic indifference to those who have come before her, a reaction that is perhaps in alignment with the antiestablishment aesthetic and political values of Abramović as well as many of her feminist predecessors (although where Young answers *yes, no, maybe* to the question of her feminism, Abramović answers only *no*). Perhaps Young's reflection and rearticulation of the feminist art tradition is more faithful to its founding values than the grandes dames of feminist performance might like to admit, at least when they are on the receiving end of it. It is certainly more aligned with their radical spirit than the reverence called for by La Rocco and Kourlas. These critics' expectations betray their own misunderstanding of artists such as Schneemann and Finley, whose body art critiqued precisely the masculinist formal preoccupation with concepts such as originality and genius—the same concepts that they wish Young would internalize. While Young is sensitive to the charge of unoriginality, she lays no claim to novelty ("I'm not trying to break some boundary"), instead (like Swanson and Gilmore) employing hackneyed signifiers, generating an aesthetic of failure that troubles the overly prescriptive politics of an institutionalized feminist art whose radical politics has been sanitized. These artists take pains to avoid using these signifiers by superimposing a positive feminist meaning in the empty place where politics used to be—a refusal that is at times maddening. In this way their work shifts from an active to a passive feminist aesthetic. When Young sidesteps the logic of art historical progression (*yes, no, maybe*), perhaps she is refusing the anxiety that comes with acknowledging the influence of the feminist art "mother"—anxiety that would (though ironically) put her into deeper conversation with the previous generation of artists, the artists whose legacies she would inherit. But, like an adolescent, she refuses that potential affinity and slams the door behind her.

It ultimately does not matter whether or not Young *actually* knows her art history. (In truth, her ignorance appears to be both an over-the-top put-on and the effect of years of studied indifference.) But her adolescent performance of "willed artistic ignorance," whether conscious or not, stages a compelling tactic that can be used by others. She implicitly challenges the desirability of a patrimony-based model (a structure of legacy and inheritance) for the politics of feminist identification. This critique is itself not original, recalling prior feminist critiques such as those of Sandra M. Gilbert and Susan Gubar, who critiqued Bloom's *The Anxiety of Influence* for its treatment of poetry as an Oedipal struggle, as "intensely (even exclusively) male, and necessarily patriarchal." "Where, then, does the female poet fit in?" they ask. "Does she want to annihilate a 'forefather' or a 'foremother'? What if she can find no models, no precursors?"[89]

What if, instead of wagging a finger at Young and her peers for failing to fall into line with a larger historical schema, we read Young's claimed ignorance as a queer feminist performance of political forgetting—a "shadow feminism," a willful interruption of generational modes of transmission (following Jack Halberstam)?[90] How might her aesthetic of parasitical disavowal allow for the emergence of a different conception of history? These artists inhabit the *structure* of feminism, although their works (and their identifications) do not necessarily bear feminism's name. By saying "I think [the works] are feminist, but I am not trying to make feminist work," Young suggests that her kind of feminism exceeds the possibility of its representation, that it thwarts the consolidation of feminism with a particular set of visual and rhetorical practices. These artists activate the adolescent as a figure of overdetermination or caricature, one that works to distance their relation not to feminist politics itself but to a particular set of assumptions about feminist art. They are feminist in that they reject older structures, but this is not a gesture of empty iconoclasm; it is a means of resisting the co-option of their voices. Yet they articulate no positive alternatives to the feminist art traditions they decline to inherit.

MANIC AUTOGENESIS

Swanson's practice exemplifies the third of the shared tactics used by some of these younger feminist artists: artists who engage in what I call "manic autogenesis" reject legacy by doubling and reproducing themselves, by creating themselves outside of the tradition of feminist art. This autogenesis (origination with no external cause, or self-generation) ruptures the expected (patriarchal) forms of legacy and inheritance.[91] Their works pay homage to the simulacrum—repetition, refraction, iteration, multiplication—while at the same time suggesting a nostalgia for a lost origin through the artist's aesthetic accumulation of signs borrowed from childhood: fairy tales, sentimental pop, baby-doll dresses. The depropriative quality of this work—its quality of a certain political homelessness—signals that, for these artists, everything is borrowed. The undecidability of irony, its constitutive doubleness makes it a fitting mode for these artists' passive expression of parasitical feminism. They advance an ironic and refracted aesthetic of self-representation, reworking borrowed images of themselves to represent (or to occlude) themselves. Manic autogenesis is, at its best, a parodic disidentification with feminist art's institutionalization as I have described it here, but it can also shade into a self-serving nihilism that is muddled to the point of unintelligibility.

In their performed ignoring, forgetting, and disavowing of the figure of the foremother, and in their reluctance to accept their generational position as the daughters of liberal feminism, these artists make visible an uncanny wish to *birth themselves*. Young sees her work "more as a solo." Gilmore's work obsessively reenacts a birthing of the self through her own physical materials, pushing her face through holes, breaching barriers with the full force of her being. Swanson undertakes to produce herself as her own child, "giving birth" to Amber Doll. This desire to re-produce the self comprises both the *desire* to birth the self (bypassing the figure of the mother) and the *method* of birthing the self: by producing multiple images of themselves, these artists create themselves as political subjects. (To understand the gesture of representing the self as a source of power, one need only think of how significant the genres of autobiography and self-portraiture have been to feminism.) Yet this gesture of self-representation also seems to eat its own tail: by producing multiple representations and refractions of their selves, these artists seem also to disavow the coherence of identity. Artists like Swanson, Gilmore, and Young appear to be actively disidentifying both with feminism and with themselves, with those commercialized images of womanhood that claim to represent them in mainstream culture and with the overdetermined feminist identifications on offer to them.

Consider an example that literalizes my reading of Young's work as a performance of "self"-refraction and ideological multiplication. *37 Sherrys* (2011) is a piece that emerged out of Young's artist residency at the Amsterdam Theaterschool (School voor Nieuwe Dansontwikkeling). The performance, based on Young's character Sherry, was created by Young in collaboration with thirty-six students, all of whom performed wearing Sherry's trademark synthetic blond wig. During the performance, however, a handful of the copycat Sherrys turned on the original Sherry, in what Young would later insist was an unrehearsed ambush by four students (figure 4.14). As if to

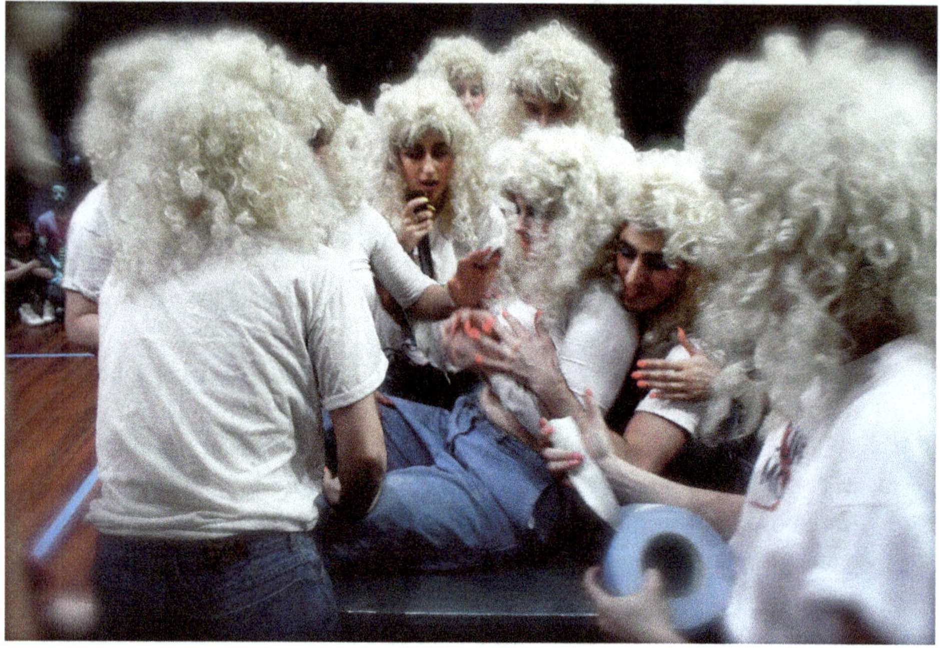

FIGURE 4.14 Ann Liv Young in collaboration with the Amsterdam Theaterschool (School voor Nieuwe Dansontwikkeling), *37 Sherrys*, 2011. Photo by Michael A. Guerrero.

demonstrate the reversibility of the parasitical tactics of homage, disavowal, and autogenesis all at once, these students hijacked Sherry, turning on their own "mother" by turning her methods against her. In a social media post, Young (as Sherry?) described the event: "I think they were saying that Sherry forces people to do things so they were gonna force me onto a table and tape me down but they didn't get that far."[92] The students put into practice the very no-holds-barred improvisational method that Young herself practices as Sherry. By turning her methods against her, the students parasitized the parasite—and in so doing they converted Young's position from that of parasite to that of host.

The artists I examine here turn the signifiers *white, liberal, feminist, bourgeois, femininity* on their heads in multiple ways. In the hands of Young, Swanson, and Gilmore these signifiers are declassed, queered, worn down, and emptied out: gowns are worn too tight or too baggy, stained and dirty, lopsided and terribly unflattering, as in Young's perfectly disturbed portrayal of a defecating *Cinderella*; in Gilmore's work, in which she is all dressed up with nowhere to go but through walls, soiling and breaking down her high heels; in the makeup caked on like a clown's by Young's alter ego Sherry. When they perform these distorted and degraded versions of the adolescent female figure, Swanson's, Gilmore's, and Young's amateurish aesthetics of failure work to caricature the commodification of third-wave feminism by dragging its girl power. They stage tactical refusals of commercialized images of feminism that they do not recognize as representative of their own feminist politics.

By performing in cheap blond Barbie wigs, Sherry and the thirty-six artists who mirrored her reflect and parody what is overprocessed or synthetic about white femininity. Young's blond wig is a gendered and racialized prosthesis, following in the tradition of Cindy Sherman's *Untitled Film Stills* or Vanessa Beecroft's durational, performance-based installations. But the wigs do not celebrate white femininity; they caricature it in the same way that, as Muñoz observes, Jack Smith's work upends its seeming "orientalizing and tropicalizing aspects," which are "imbued with a performativity that surpass[es] simple fetishization" and which "help[s] toxic images expand and become much more than quaint racisms."[93] As a tactical disidentification with whiteness, Sherry and company's blond wigs serve a purpose closer to the black drag performance artist Vaginal Davis' disidentificatory performance of white girlness (worn in pigtails with a polka dot dress), theorized by Muñoz.[94] Sherry's blond wig also echoes the racial drag of Nikki S. Lee's photo-performances of passing (*The Ohio Project*, 1999) and Kalup Linzy's lo-fi video art performances (*Conversations wit de Churen* series, 2005)—anti-identitarian works that, like Young's, insist on disassociating *identification* from *identity*.

These performances enact a double disidentification: they challenge both second and third wave feminism in their performances of self-creation. These artists' rebirthed images of themselves, far from idealized or aspirational, model a politics that does not aspire to emancipation or even redemption. In these works the self engendering described by autogenesis is a form of alienated self-parody that disavows inheritance through ironic representations of the self that are neither pure reproduction nor pure refusal.

These artists complicate representations of themselves through performance in order to renegotiate the models imposed on them by others. As performances, these works are deliberately illegible; they take an ironic stance that attaches to feminism a multiplicity of meanings (*yes, no, maybe*) that cannot be pinned down. These artists perform the adolescent for her ability to say things that authority does not completely understand, things that cannot be easily co-opted or overdetermined because they are already caricatures. These performances of alienated self-parody thus turn the parasitical model back on themselves as a gesture of feminist self-making.

COPIES WITHOUT ORIGINALS

In March 2011 a review entitled "How 1 Become 2" appeared in the online London dance magazine *Bellyflop*.[95] The unattributed post accused the London-based American performance artist Lauren Barri Holstein of plagiarizing the work of her contemporary Ann Liv Young. "This is shock value Live Art, you'll never seen [*sic*] anything like it. Oh wait, you will, because actually Ann Liv Young is the real deal," it read. "Some might argue we're talking mere inspiration or appropriation, but I don't buy that." Silly grandiosity and slapdash prose aside, the review had a point. Holstein, like Young, often performs in a blond wig; her shows borrow heavily from fairy tales and feature gratuitous nudity; she vigorously performs pop karaoke. Holstein, like Young, started out as a dancer and choreographer, also undertaking an M.A. at Trinity Laban Conservatoire of Music and Dance. Holstein—who performs as "The Famous," an alter ego she describes as "part-time sex object, part-time flailing mess, part-time feminist"—has long proven a polarizing figure on the London experimental performance circuit.[96] Her unsparing performances of grotesque hyperfemininity, which have an even more aggressive edge than Young's work in the same vein, have found her thrashing around naked while suspended in a harness; popping balloons filled with red fluid with a knife inserted, handle-side up, into her vagina; "birthing" a McDonald's Happy Meal toy; and urinating onstage while wearing a deer costume head.

Despite clear commonalities between the two artists, the anonymous reviewer failed to appreciate the rather spectacular irony of positioning an artist like Young—an avowed and shameless appropriator (whom the reviewer calls with a straight face "the real deal")—as the original of Holstein's reproductions. (When I mentioned the accusation to Young, she simply shrugged at the idea, saying she'd never heard of Holstein. "Yeah I've never even seen her before, which is strange. I don't think it looks anything like what I make.")[97] It is hard to imagine that the irony of earnestly investing in Young as an original artist is lost on Holstein, who wrote her master's thesis partly on Young.[98] In fact Holstein's work differs from Young's reliable performance of ignorance primarily in its historical fidelity and critical rigor. Holstein completed a doctorate in English and drama at Queen Mary in

2015, with a dissertation that explores what she calls the "displayed" body's access to self-determination in the works of artists such as Lynn Hershman Leeson and Hannah Wilke. While it's never clear whether Young has done her homework, Holstein most assuredly has—even if onstage it looks, at least to this reviewer, like she has copied someone else's. Audiences of Holstein's 2013 performance of *Splat!* at London's SPILL Festival of Performance saw The Famous suspended upside down and covered in ketchup, but they will likely never know about Holstein's companion piece explaining how the show's strategic deployment of "incompleteness" works against what she characterizes as "pop-feminist narratives of trauma and survival in which the affirmative female subject is defined by her victimization."[99]

Unlike Young, Holstein is unambiguous in her feminist commitments, and she enthusiastically acknowledges the influence on her work of 1960s and 1970s feminist artists such as Schneemann and Finley.[100] (In her studied reverence for feminist art history, Holstein is perhaps closer to Liftig than to Young on the continuum of generational parasitism I trace in this chapter.) For her 2011 performance *How 2 Become 1* at the Barbican's SPILL Festival of Performance in London, Holstein (who has also reimagined Yoko Ono's iconic *Cut Piece*) staged her own reenactment of Schneemann's *Interior Scroll* (figures 4.15 and 4.16). She would describe the performance as her response to the *Bellyflop* review's accusation of plagiarism, during which she proceeded to pull from her vagina "a scroll," reenacting Schneemann's gesture in the original work. But Holstein's scroll, unlike Schneemann's, does not contain a feminist diatribe against those who criticize her work for its "diaristic indulgence"; Holstein's scroll lists the names of all the people the artist claims to have "plagiarized" (figure 4.17). The list begins with "Carolee Schneemann, Karen Finley, Ann Liv Young, Hannah Wilke, Marina Abromovic [*sic*]" and eventually gets around to scholars like Judith Butler and Laura Mulvey, pop stars like the Backstreet Boys, and fictional characters like Mr. Bubble and the Easter Bunny.

Holstein's parasitism is not a performance of refusing to acknowledge her debts to a larger system of feminist influence. Rather than the ironic amnesia or simple reference without citation deployed by the other artists discussed in this chapter, Holstein's defense is one of *hyper*citationality. She might be said to overcompensate by providing *too many* acknowledgments (naming *too many* influences, a move that minimizes Young's clear influence on Holstein's practice), and she eventually abandons the sincerity of the gesture altogether when she trails off into cartoon characters, ending with Mickey Mouse and Rainbow Brite.

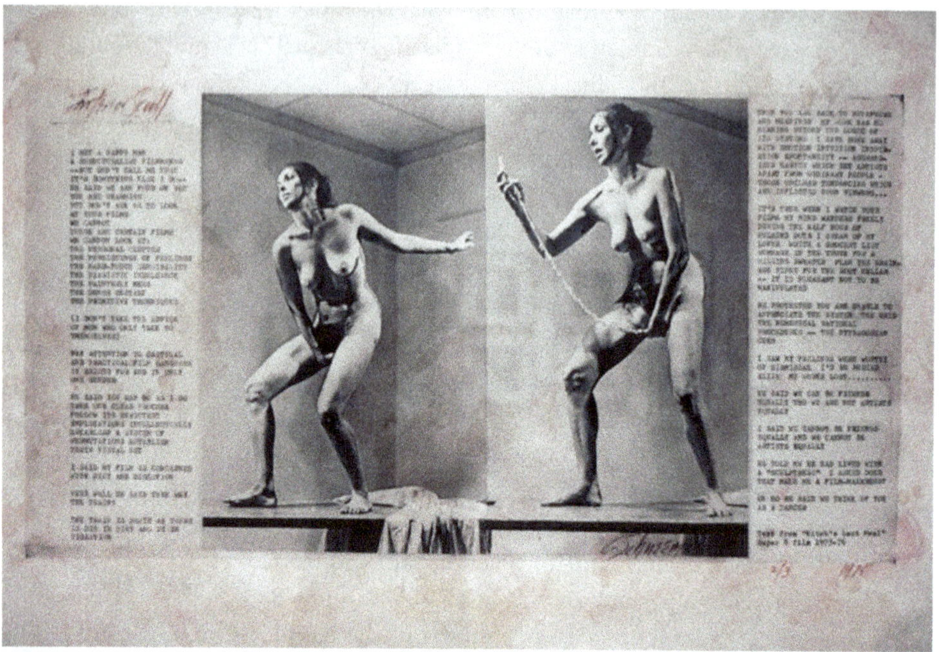

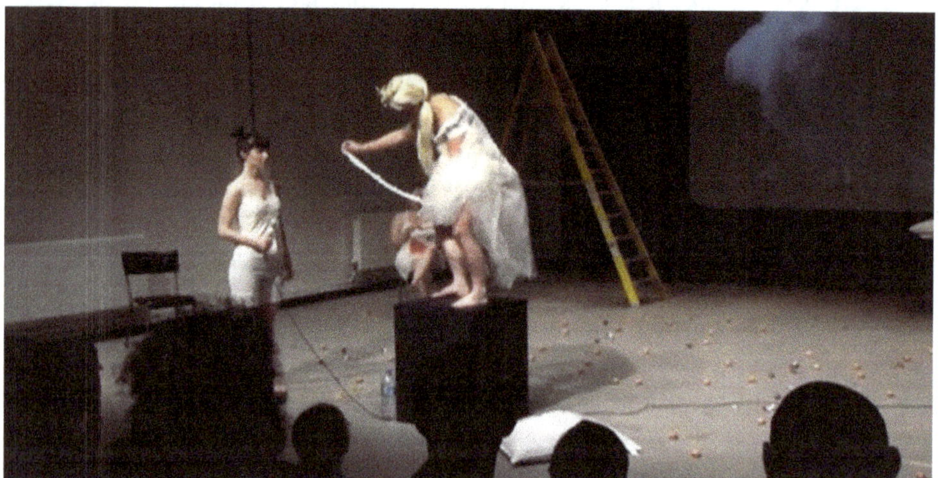

FIGURE 4.15 Carolee Schneemann, *Interior Scroll*, 1975. Source: Carolee Schneemann.
FIGURE 4.16 The Famous Lauren Barri Holstein, *How 2 Become 1*, 2011. Source: Lauren Barri Holstein.

FIGURE 4.17 Lauren Barri Holstein's interior scroll acknowledging her feminist influences. From *How 2 Become 1*, 2011. Source: Lauren Barri Holstein.

But Holstein's response to the accusation of plagiarizing a contemporary—the gesture of *reenacting a forebear*—is a curious, even defensive choice, for she is an artist for whom appropriation obviously functions as a metacitational feminist strategy rather than a symptom of creative deficiency. In a blog post she describes the intentions behind her restaging of Schneemann's iconic work: "A few weeks before my performance at the Spill Festival 2011, a 20-year-old idiot who knows absolutely nothing about the history of feminist performance wrote that I was plagiarizing another artist, presumably the only other feminist performance artist she'd ever heard of. In reality, I'm plagiarizing all of them, and lots and lots of other people."[101] Holstein posted a clip of her adaptation to Vimeo with the title "I'm a Plagiarist. Sorry, Ms. Schneemann. It's only because I love you." Unlike Young-as-Sherry, who would dismiss the accusation in a single folksy gesture, Holstein herself (not The Famous) responds with seeming sincerity (and without the armor of her persona) to the charge of plagiarism. In contrast to the strategies of parasitical homage, parasitical disavowal, and manic autogenesis I have outlined in this chapter, Holstein's performance embraces reenactment earnestly and openly (if without securing the official approval that Abramović would insist on—hence Holstein's characterization of her work as "plagiaristic"). Holstein pays in sincerity the debts she owes to the earlier generation of feminist artists, who continue to inspire and move her.

Still, the *Bellyflop* reviewer's naïve indignation at Holstein's plagiarism evidences a vestigial attachment to measuring the quality of an artwork by its originality. The reviewer, rather startlingly, refers to Holstein's work as "vintage Ann Liv Young," a stark if comic reminder of the ever-evolving nature of notions of old and new. This is yet another turn of the generational screw; Young, who herself parasitizes a more established generation of artists, including Finley and Abramović, is here positioned as the host to Holstein's parasite—suggesting there is no way to immunize oneself from parasites. As the coda explores in the work of Roisin Byrne (who is the ne plus ultra of this political and aesthetic move within feminist performance art), when parasites gain access to resources—even the smallest bit of recognition—even parasites can be parasitized in their turn. It is only a matter of time.

CODA IT'S NOT YOU, IT'S ME

ROISIN BYRNE AND THE PARASITE'S SHIFTING ETHICS AND POLITICS

The parasited one parasites the parasites. One of the first, he jumps to the last position. But the one in the last position wins this game. He has discovered the position of the philosopher.—**MICHEL SERRES, *THE PARASITE***

In this book I have advanced parasitism as a tactical mode or loophole by which certain precarious subjects (those with enough social capital to get a foot in the door) can leverage the minor advantages of appearing familiar and nonthreatening to those who hold power over them. This modality is appropriable and reversible; it can be used indiscriminately and can be turned on anyone. The parasite's comparatively minor leverage can be harnessed as a tool of solidarity and redistribution, just as it can be used in bad faith for reactionary or self-serving proprietary ends. As a remedy, it comes with unwanted side effects. Like the parasite itself, its targets are complex and contingent. With each chapter in this book, the ethical and political valences of parasitical resistance have grown murkier as the power differential between the parasite and the host has narrowed. Whereas the extreme dominance of multinational corporate leviathans or the exclusionary legacies of private property, nationality or racial belonging, and debt or inheritance represent largely unambiguous targets of critique, parasitism's ethical and political dimensions grow increasingly difficult to parse as its encounter with the host becomes more intimate, personal, and—as the host and parasite increasingly resemble one other—subjective. In what follows I return to the conceptual artist Roisin Byrne, with whose practice I opened the book, to examine what happens when the power differential between parasite and host is negligible—when it is not fully clear which is parasite and which is host.[1]

In 2011 Byrne began to flatter, steal, and contest my reading of her work as parasitical. Our correspondence would set off a yearlong chain of events wherein the artist appropriated my criticism on her practice while I appropriated her practice for my criticism. This uncanny period of creative (if not always consensual) mutualism proved strange and exhilarating. This encounter also lifted into view the inherent ethical and political indeterminacy of parasitism, as well as parasitism's tendency to conceal and displace the violence it enables (concealment that is the condition for its special form of access). I take Byrne to be a problematic exemplar of what I have explored in the second half of the book as parasitism's compromised feminist potential—a potential that is heavily reliant on a white heterosexist matrix in order to accommodate itself to hosts, which allows it to remain undetected. I argue that Byrne's body of work tests the limits of parasitism as a paradigm of resistance: Is it worth it to take advantage of the loopholes enabled by gendered mechanisms of exclusion when doing so means propping up other structures of oppression? Our exchange raises new questions about the critical and practical value of parasitical resistance, particularly its utility as a feminist analytic and mode, and also the difficulty of critiquing something with which one is entangled.

MISS APPROPRIATION

When our correspondence began, Byrne was fresh off of her appearance on the BBC4 reality TV series *Goldsmiths: But Is It Art?* (2010). The (rather unfortunately titled) documentary series showcased the young conceptual artist as one of three MFA students struggling to jump-start their careers in the shadow of the global financial crisis.[2] The show promoted itself as a glimpse into the inner workings of the university's art program, which is a hotbed for conceptual art, having produced a generation of artists that includes Gillian Wearing, Steve McQueen, and, most famously, Damien Hirst. (Hirst became notorious for his project *The Physical Impossibility of Death in the Mind of Someone Living* [1991], a tiger shark preserved in a tank of formaldehyde.) The two-part series highlighted Byrne's tactic of openly stealing the concepts of well-established male conceptual artists.[3] A single mother of a young son, living in London, Byrne characterized her controversial methods as necessary to her survival. "Being an artist and a single mum, you [become] very creative [with] what's available to you. It can be very expensive spending money on materials, paying rent and fees. I just need to think on my feet. Stealing or robbing or appropriating—that's what I do."[4]

In 2009 Byrne made *Look What You Made Me Do* (figure C.2), described in the introduction. She used her position within the university and her friendly rapport with the artist to divert Jochem Hendricks's honorarium for a visiting stint at Goldsmiths, replacing his bank information with her own and using the funds to make a copy of his most famous work, *Tax* (2000) (figure C.1). For that piece, Hendricks had purchased gold bars in the exact amount that he owed the government and claimed them as "artist's materials" on his tax return (a loophole in tax law since said to have been closed).[5]

Hendricks's work often explores loopholes in the law: for *Luxus Avatar* (2009) he made a life-size gold replica of himself and purchased luxury items (including a sports car and Hermès clothing) for this replica, writing them off on his taxes as artist's materials and exhibiting them as part of his show *Legal Crimes*. Rather than exploring legal loopholes, Byrne's work explores the unwritten laws of social mores. The implications of Hendricks's actions are explicit and straightforward: it's legal or it's not. In contrast, Byrne negotiates the realm of the implicit, identifying in the extralegal gray area of conceptual art a loophole, a certain amount of play in the system, that allows her to investigate the double standard in the critical reception of their work. While Hendricks's incursions are "clean" and masterful, hers are "dirty" and parasitical.

Recall that Hendricks attempts to police the boundaries of art, to exclude Byrne's work while offering an alibi for his own. (He suggests that her work is not "serious," characterizing *Look What You Made Me Do* as a joke.) He concludes his email to her by asking Byrne to send further justification of the merit of the piece if she wants to be treated as a peer. While Hendricks is perfectly valid in questioning the quality of her conceptualization (and, as he rightly notes, her expropriation is not at a loss to him), in so doing he misses the real trap she has laid for him: his attachment to his own originality. Byrne calls Hendricks out for being proprietary over his cultural capital—which he earned by making antiproprietary art. She shows how, when faced with the threat of her parasitism, he retreats into the very discourses of artistic mastery and intellectual property that his practice ostensibly works to subvert. Ever the transgressor, Hendricks, as I argue of Dick in chapter 3, resists being transgressed, preferring the role of mentor and pedagogue to colleague.

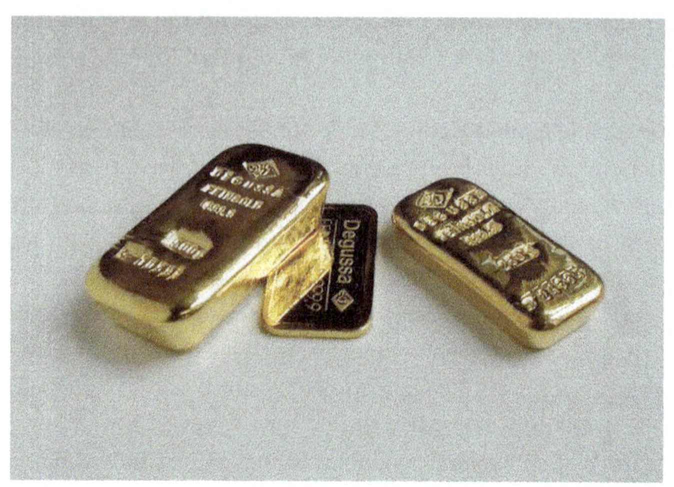

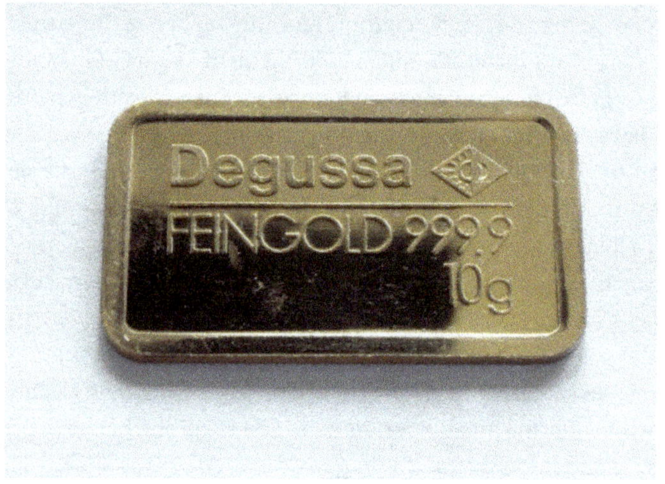

FIGURE C.1 Jochem Hendricks, *Tax,* 2000. Source: Jochem Hendricks.

FIGURE C.2 Roisin Byrne, *Look What You Made Me Do,* 2009. Source: Roisin Byrne.

13 May 2009 11:05:01

Subject: Re: Hello

Roisin,

Of course I was laughing when I read your confession. But you are aware that you are dealing with my expenses, it is not even a profit. . . . If you are able to convince me with a profound concept and content, we can talk. Up to now, I can only see a game, which is related to my work. Meaning, content are the major points.

Looking forward to your explanations.

Best wishes,
J.M.

To this missive Byrne responds with an unfazed "I was wondering how you might take the news!" Upbeat and confessional, her email is also unapologetic: *Jochem, I don't have to sell this work to you, because you've already paid for it.* "I have fallen in love with your work and you," she continues, echoing Kraus's and Calle's lovesick masquerades. "My explanation is one of simply pure unadulterated desire . . . the desire for something of yours, a piece of work, perhaps a piece of you." Though it is formulated in the language of seduction, hers is less a desire *to be with Hendricks* than *to signify like him*, to possess the authorizing power of his signature.

15 May 2009 20:24:55

Subject: Re: Hello

Dear JM,

Thanks so much for your reply. I was wondering how you might take the news! And I guess I was also secretly hoping for you to ask me to "sell" it to you so to speak as a profound concept. I'm not sure as I have to remind you that you have paid for it already. But joking aside, maybe I will give you an explanation at least and a concept at most.

My explanation is one of simply pure unadulterated desire. By this I mean that I have fallen in love with your work and you by association the artist Jochem Hendricks. The desire for something of yours, a piece of work, perhaps a piece of you. You and your bank details became the raw materials that made my work possible, they and you became the medium by which I produced a 24 Carat Gold Bar, the closest thing to owning an authentic Jochem Hendricks as I could ever hope to get to. The only thing missing now of course is your signature.

Roisin

The piece is typical of Byrne's practice. It's one of five different works for which she has engaged prominent male artists over email, using flattery to get what she wants from them. She has also stolen, copied, and forged the works of the conceptual artists Santiago Sierra, Roberto Cuoghi, Ryan Gander, and Simon Starling. In one piece Byrne professes to have tracked down one of the four female prostitutes that Sierra paid with a shot of heroin to be tattooed, in a work titled *160 cm Line Tattooed on 4 People* (2000). Byrne claims that she used laser removal to erase the prostitute's tattoo and had it tattooed on her back instead. In another pilfered piece, Byrne claims that when she placed an order for a neon sign that she intended to exhibit, she was told that she was the second artist that week to place such an order—a "stroke of luck" that's hardly believable.[6] Supposedly the other order, which read "Massage," had been placed by the British artist Ryan Gander (a story he disputes). Upon learning this, Byrne claims, she canceled her original order and instead ordered an exact replica of Gander's sign, which she exhibited as *Massage* (2009). It should be noted that Byrne's manner of exhibition provides little evidence that these actions actually took place. These conceptual artworks are "indexed" by digital photographs and aphoristic captions, presented as "documentary evidence" of otherwise unverified performances; it is this evidence that is exhibited in galleries and on the artist's personal website (roisinbyrne.co.uk).[7]

In 2009 Byrne initiated an email correspondence with Starling. Widely praised for his ambitious environmental actions and installations, Starling received the Turner Prize, arguably the world's most prestigious award for contemporary art, in 2005 for his meticulously researched and crafted *Shedboatshed (Mobile Architecture No. 2).* In this work he converted an old shed he found on the banks of the Rhine into a boat, which he paddled to Art Basel and painstakingly rebuilt into a shed, which he exhibited in the gallery. Byrne, claiming admiration for his work, posed as a fan wishing to admire

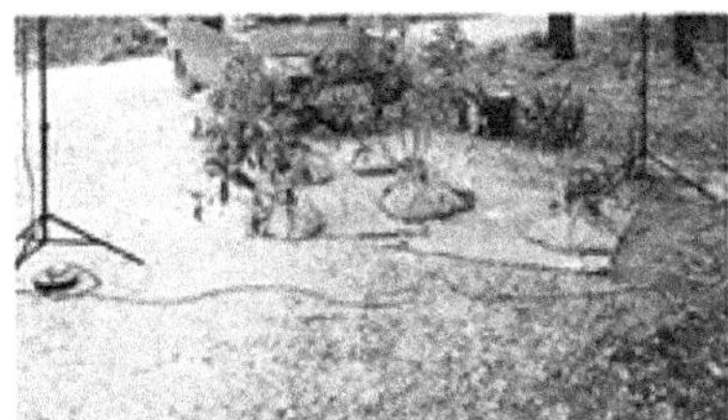

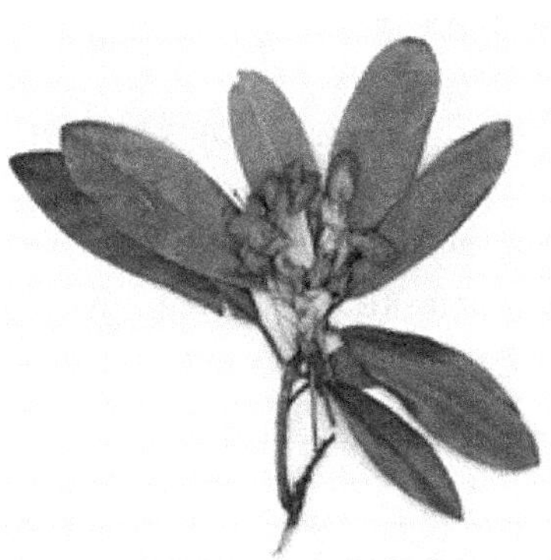

FIGURE C.3 Roisin Byrne, *You Don't Bring Me Flowers Anymore,* 2009. Source: Roisin Byrne.

one of his works in situ. "You are obviously a very busy man," she cooed. She asked him where she could find the plants he had transplanted to the Parque Los Alcornocales in Spain for his earnestly titled 1999 installation *Rescued Rhododendrons.* She then used against him the information she gained when she posed as a horticulturist, stole one of the shrubs, and smuggled it back with her on a budget airline flight. For her final student show at Goldsmiths, she exhibited their correspondence in full, hanging printouts of the emails with black electrical tape alongside the withering plant in a piece she entitled *You Don't Bring Me Flowers Anymore* (figure C.3). This is one of the least palatable examples in the book, not least because the host is consciously working to redistribute. The parasitical act is much harder to stomach when the target is not someone taking advantage of their privilege but instead someone who is trying to use it for the betterment of others. It is Byrne, in this case, who takes what is being distributed and keeps it for herself.

"It's like the residue of somebody else's, *like a Turner prizewinner's,* process," she said of the plant, observing on *Goldsmiths: But Is It Art?* that Starling had won the Turner Prize "in 2004 or something like that," performing to her colleague a kind of "willed ignorance" similar to what Young performs to her feminist art forebears. Byrne continued, "So what kind of value does that embody, and if I take it, what does that mean?"[8] When Byrne informed Starling of what she'd done, he was stunned. "I'm sad and disappointed," he wrote to her. "I understood you had a certain empathy for what I was doing as an artist." Upon receiving this email, Byrne merely shrugged: "He's a bit upset. But you can't be taking these things too seriously." Starling (like so many of the other hosts that I have described in this book) later threatened legal action but never pursued it.

IT'S NOT YOU, IT'S ME

I became interested in Byrne's work when I was in the early stages of writing about performance artists that I read as manifesting feminism's more ambivalent dimensions. I found her work to be symptomatic of the kind of interventionist practice I was beginning to theorize as parasitical.[9] The relatively scant curatorial and journalistic writing about her artistic practice had focused almost solely on questions about the ethics of stealing and forgery, but in my early writing I asked what possibilities were opened up by reading her practice as a performance that literalizes and hyperbolizes the stereotypical feminized other—one of many such performances, as the previous two chapters have shown. What if, rather than moralize about the actions of one individual woman artist, we regarded her performance as structural, as playing a position? I saw Byrne's work as being in line with the high-femme interventions of Chris Kraus, Sophie Calle, and Jill Magid, all of whom engage in practices of "tactical flirting," a phrase that Sarah Kanouse has used to describe the radical feminist dance troupe The Pink Bloque.[10] I saw Byrne's methods as having clear precedents in the work of "theft artists" such as Dennis Oppenheim, Ann Messner, and most notably the Bulgarian artist Ivan Moudov, who steals fragments from artworks exhibited in galleries and museums, re-exhibiting them with extreme attentiveness (*Fragments*, 2002–7). I saw her methods as inheriting from an earlier generation of feminist appropriation artists, namely Elaine Sturtevant and Sherrie Levine, both of whom are known for making replicas of iconic works by famous male artists. Sturtevant and Levine were at the forefront of the conceptualist critique of male authorship, debunking the masculinist myth of originality by showing that they could be just as masterful as the original authors.[11] Byrne steals and forges not to claim the works as her own but to use mimicry as her alibi; when they say "You can't do that," she answers, "Well, *you* did." Similarly Sturtevant and Levine made no attempt to pass off their copies as the original works. Instead they actively promoted their projects as *appropriations of* the male artists' works.

Byrne exhibits her works specifically as *appropriations* of work by more established hosts, and it is this that makes her work parasitical. Unlike Sturtevant and Levine, Byrne is conceptually invested not in the materiality of her re-presentation of the male artists' works but *in the social conditions* that make possible her parasitical appropriations of their work in the first place. Levine and Sturtevant emphasize their structural exclusion from the aura of mastery and prestige that is conferred on male artists like Duchamp and Warhol, whose originality lay in their *rejection* of originality as an aesthetic principle—though they did not reject originality as the basis of the system of rewards by which male artists accrue power and influence. In contrast, Byrne emphasizes *her access to that aura*, however compromised and contingent that access is.

Byrne weaponizes feminine stereotypes. She embodies the logic and tactics of parasitism: she plays herself, overidentifying with the role she is already given to play, like the younger performance artists in chapter 4. She flatters the male artist who sees her only as a schoolgirl admirer, a minor character in his story, a hanger-on to the great egos of the male avant-garde. Blandishing the host, she leverages professional flattery and flirtation to lower her target's defenses; after emailing Starling to tell him that she had taken his plant, she compares the anxiety she feels awaiting his response to "feel[ing] like the girl waiting for the fucking phone call." She takes advantage of her appearance as nonthreatening, as "like but unlike" the host; she is a white woman with a British passport and the cultural capital represented by a Goldsmiths MFA, like enough to pass undetected but not like enough to challenge the host's power or possessions. She gains the trust of prominent male artists through the lateral access enabled by her performance of heterosexual flirtation, her assumed socioeconomic connivance, and all the myriad ways that middle-class whiteness and femininity are invited into, regarded as loyal and resigned to, the fundamental structures of power. Her interventions assume the heterosexuality of the male artists she targets and the heteronormativity of their relations. Byrne's imposition of a romantic script highlights their ability to benefit from masculine heteronormative privilege, indifferent to the artists' actual sexualities or whether or not they identify with her imposed script. Her incursions play the obsequious young artist off the seasoned master, turning the intimate protocols of both chivalry and professionalism to her ends: luring the artist into unwittingly assisting in the theft or forgery of his own work.

"I'm not interested in placing it in some kind of art discourse," Byrne has said of her work. "I'm interested in a relationship to information and to ownership. The separation between you and that thing you desire is changing."[12] What Byrne calls "that thing you desire," that coveted object taken without permission, is the very cultural and commercial capital possessed by the male artists whom she targets. Reading Byrne's practice as parasitical—indeed as a self-conscious feminist performance of parasitism—opens up a number of questions: How does the actor's minoritarian status affect how we read the ethics and politics of an action? What are the grounds (moral, taste-based, or otherwise normative valuative terms) for characterizing women's drive to acquire cultural and commercial capital—awards, renown, financial success—as a parasitical imposition? What might be possible for a feminism that is unbounded by the ethical imperatives of autonomy, propriety, and sincerity in an eminently unethical system? How might parasitism free up a set of experimental feminist tactics of resistance in a moment when frontal or affirmative political actions are often rapidly suppressed?

Byrne takes without giving—a reversal of the terms by which feminized subjects are expected to give without taking. She does not attempt to redress women artists' historical marginalization by changing the structures that exclude them; instead she short-circuits exclusion by simply taking symbols of the capital she covets. She exhibits the fruits of her labor as conceptual art, a frame within which otherwise illegal or immoral acts are imbued with critical potential. Her projects—indeed all the projects examined in this book—challenge and reflect on modernist investments in originality, prompting questions about authorial intention and legitimacy, private property and zones of illegality. Byrne exploits the relatively recent recognition of appropriation as a recognized aesthetic practice, latching on to the deregulatory zeitgeist of the neoliberal art market and securing it as her host. It guarantees her claim to that which is otherwise beyond her reach.

As a part of a biweekly research group, I uploaded an early draft of my writing on Byrne onto a university-sponsored wiki—a collaborative online space for sharing files—to be shared with my fellow graduate students for workshopping. A few weeks later, on April 17, 2011, I received a Facebook friend request and then a message from Byrne. Our wiki had not been password-protected, and the artist had found my unpublished draft about her work through a Google Alert she had set for herself. In her message, Byrne praised my reading of her work; a few days later she emailed me to ask permission to "take some terms" of mine for her artist's statement for an upcoming solo exhibition in Madrid.[13]

Subject: Hello

April 17 at 6:17 am EST

Hello Anna

I thought i would drop you a line to run something by you..i hope you don't mind. I have a solo show coming up at the end of May at my gallery in Madrid and i would really like for the works to be positioned properly ..it's time!...

Anyhows, i was wondering if i could ask you whether it might be possible to take some terms you use... for my blurb for my upcoming show???

With no publication on Byrne to cite, I was faced with having my own ideas rendered unoriginal—an uneasy position. Despite her reputation as a theft artist, Byrne's record gave little indication that she neither would pose a threat to me, for I was neither male, nor affluent, nor well established. Nevertheless the request brought into conflict the difference between the academy's and the art world's appropriative protocols. As Wilson Mizner famously said, "Copying one book is plagiarism, copying many is research."[14] While academic criticism, like conceptual art, is a hypercitational genre, the scholar's accepted parasitism turns on the quotation mark and the requisite works cited; the parasitism of the conceptual artist depends for its citation on the viewer's art historical knowledge. Finding myself in the place of Hendricks and Starling, I was made aware of my own attachment to seeing my work as somehow original. After some deliberation, I responded:[15]

Subject: Re: Hello

April 19 at 5:29 pm EST

Hi Roisin,

I am honored that you are interested in my work. Would this be for a catalog essay? If so, I would be thrilled if you quoted me (I could provide you with a quote if so) and perhaps even better, I could write something about your work for it.

As a young female graduate student who is working to establish myself as a critic—just as you are as a young artist—it means a lot for my ideas to be acknowledged (and yes those are my phrasings). Perhaps we could collaborate on something here.

She wrote back:[16]

> Subject: Re: Hello
>
> April 20 at 2:53am EST
>
> Hi Anna,
>
> I am delighted I found your ideas! and i think it would be a good thing to do something together. You articulated things in my work in a way that no one else has which i am i have to say really happy about. A collaboration sounds like something i would be more than happy to do.
>
> At this stage the gallery in Madrid won't be doing a catalogue, it would just be a press blurb positioning the work, do you think you would be interested in being credited on something like this? It's small fry but . . .

"Small fry or not," I wrote back to Byrne, assuring her that I would indeed appreciate being acknowledged and providing her the information to do so. I did not hear back from her.

On May 26 I received a group Facebook invitation to her exhibition *It's Not You, It's Me* at The Goma in Madrid. The artwork being exhibited was Byrne's effort to assume the identity of the Italian artist Roberto Cuoghi, who himself was said to have assumed his ailing father's identity, undergoing a dramatic physical transformation in the process.[17] Byrne could not find out much about the project, but she decided that if Cuoghi had become his father, then she would become him.[18] She claimed to have legally changed her name to Roberto Cuoghi for that project, and under that name to have obtained a credit card, created an online persona, and exhibited work, including two "self-portraits" at the Irish Museum of Contemporary Art (IMOCA). In the body of the Facebook invitation was Byrne's artist's statement (figure C.4). Not only had she appropriated without attribution my reading of her work as parasitical; she had also lifted a passage from Nathan M. Martin's 2003 article for the Carbon Defense League, which she had most likely encountered when she came across it in my essay, where it served as the epigraph. (It is now the epigraph of this book's introduction.) Six months later, when the exhibition moved to London's Alma Enterprises, Byrne struck again, this time even more brazenly: the press release and web-

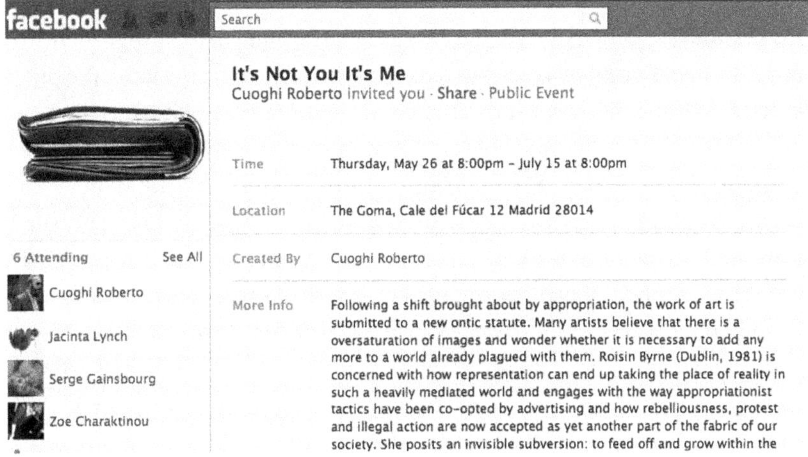

FIGURE C.4 Facebook invitation to Roisin Byrne's *It's Not You, It's Me* exhibition, 2011.

site for the show reproduced an entire paragraph of my unpublished dissertation prospectus.

By appropriating my reading of her work as feminist, Byrne short-circuited it, reclaiming from me the position of parasite. She fed on the structure of feminist reflexivity I articulated, seeking to capitalize on the attention brought her by my overstatement of her feminist politics. It seemed that the hosts to whom Byrne would play parasite had changed between her earlier projects and 2011. Perhaps her professional and economic situation had become more precarious, necessitating a tactical slippage from powerful, well-established male artist hosts to female peers. Perhaps Byrne's parasitism had never had a stable ethical dimension in the first place. In my reading of her work, carried out for my professional advancement (a form of scholarly parasitism), had I projected the feminism I found there? Had I attributed political intention where none existed?

Or perhaps the parasite's value cannot be made legible by the orthodoxies of intentionality. It is not a stable liberal moral agent. Rather, the parasite might be said to occupy a deictic structural position, as the linguistic shifters *you* and *me* of her exhibition title suggest. Michel Serres observes that to be a parasite is precisely to be a shifter: "To play the position or to play the location is to dominate the relation. . . . And that is the meaning of the prefix *para-* in the word *parasite*: it is on the side, next to, shifted;

it is not on the thing, but on its relation. It has relations, as they say, and makes a system of them."[19] Serres's crucial insight here is that identities are contingent on their place within a network of social relations. We play a given role in relation to others' given roles. Rather than ask who or what is behind the mask of the parasite (*Is Byrne bad or good? Was she always bad, or did she become bad?*), Serres proposes to ask what the mask can do. Byrne shifts; she plays the relation. And in so doing she shows that the parasite is not an ethical actor in the conventional sense. The parasite is not an identity but rather a mode of playing the system, a form of agency without a predetermined moral coherency. Since its agency unfolds in a dynamic system of play, parasitism is not an ethics of the individual but an ethics of relation. Its actions must be judged in relation to the actions of others, particularly those who set the rules of the game. The parasite's ethics are not relevant, for ethics is predicated on internal coherence. Instead, the parasite *shifts* the question, moving it away from morality (which is predicated on identity) toward *positionality*. As a paradigm of resistance, it is not about *who you are* but *where you are situated* within a set of relations. Byrne is thus not feminist in a moral sense; she is feminist only to the extent that she reveals something about the structural makeup of a shifting field of power relations.

Byrne's work shifted the focus from identity to positionality, compelling me to reassess both my position as a critic and my own latent investment in originality, which comes with my relative precarity within academia. My positions here render me what we might call a *contingent host* (someone who occupies the position of host precariously or only under certain circumstances, who doesn't have the kind of capital that a host typically does). By addressing me directly, Byrne made me consider my role within the contemporary art economy, my position in the relations between the art world and the scholarly world. These relations go both ways: scholarly validation is essential for building artists' careers, and conversely, engaging original objects of study is vital to producing hireable and tenureable scholarship.

A few months after this initial exchange, I published a short piece detailing my entanglement with Byrne.[20] As the online text was being formatted the editorial manager received an unexpected email. "The encounter you describe with Roisin in your text has . . . been slightly echoed," she wrote to me. Byrne had learned of the essay's publication before I had, again preemptively discovering the piece through her Google Alert, and she had inquired of the editor how soon it would be advertised. My essay positioned Byrne's work within the larger frame of a discussion of contemporary feminist art (and situated me as a *host*); Byrne promoted it on her Facebook and

Twitter accounts as a "monumental review" of her work (situating me as a *parasite*).

Is the critic a parasite or a host of its object of study? Is the critic-object relation truly parasitical, or is it symbiotic, mutually beneficial as it increases the cultural capital (potentially convertible to financial capital) for both parties? In his essay "The Critic as Host," J. Hillis Miller examines the critical practice of quotation and citation in these terms: "Is this [quotation] different from a citation, echo, or allusion within a poem? Is a citation an alien parasite within the body of its host, the main text, or is it the other way around, the interpretative text the parasite, which surrounds and strangles the citation which is its host? . . . Or can host and parasite live happily together, in the domicile of the same text, feeding each other or sharing the food?"[21] The parasite's opportunistic timing (it *comes after* the host in order to *come first,* to beat the host to the punch) had resurfaced—the same timing that Byrne displayed in asking to para-cite me before there was anything yet to cite. As digital technologies have enabled unprecedented forms of intimate access, proximity, and familiarity, they have dissolved traditional boundaries; Byrne seized upon the window of opportunity created by email and social media to gain immediate access to her critic, unsettling the usual safe distance between critics and their objects created by geographical distance, temporality of publication, and so on. In other words, Byrne pre-cited my work before it could be stamped as my own, as original, by the legitimation machine of academic publishing. My authority as a scholar came from observing this delay; Byrne's reputation as an artist depended on getting there first. I, in turn, scrambled to establish ownership over the ideas before she could by slapping together a website about my research.

The target of an act of parasitical appropriation is essential to the gesture's political signification. Is the target well-resourced or precarious? Does the parasite appropriate up or down? But equally essential is the question of whether the parasitical act reduces the original work's vitality or enhances it. (For Byrne, taking Starling's plant and getting his response "completed the piece," enabling her work to thrive, whereas Starling said that her use of his plant had "completely destroy[ed] the work.") For my part, Byrne's appropriation, while initially vexing, helped refine my reading of her and brought increased scholarly and public attention to my work.

By the time the encounter was picked up by several news sites in late 2011, eventually becoming the basis of a 2013 performance art piece at Brooklyn's Grace Space by the feminist performance and curatorial collective HAG, it had grown more difficult to disentangle who was the parasite and who the host.[22] In the weeks that followed the publication of my essay, I took a page from Byrne's playbook and set up my own Google Alert. A few days later I received an alert that an Austrian online fashion magazine called *Fashion-Office* had run a mobile feature about my article. Observed an art reviewer advertising Byrne's show in *Time Out London*, "I'm not sure if there is such a thing as 'parasitic art' but it's certainly a description applicable to the work of Roisin Byrne." The news forum *Big Think* featured an article by the art blogger Bob Duggan with the title "Is Parasitism the Future of Feminist Art?"—a title that stood in marked tension with my own article's stated desire to move away from a developmental or solution-based model of feminist futurity.[23] Duggan offered his own reading of my encounter with Byrne, which he framed as a review of my article—albeit in terms I no longer recognized as my own.

Byrne advertised the *Big Think* piece on her Facebook page, but her tone had changed from elation to ridicule, likely caused by the fact that Duggan focused on the critical reading over the artwork. Duggan observes that "Byrne herself may have felt [that she] more than . . . intellectually articulated [the issues of her work], at least until Fisher came along to provide the words." Byrne's responses to my work grew increasingly hostile. As hosts do, she disavowed her own tactics when she found them aimed at her. "First a thief now a feminist!" she tweeted. In a Facebook comment responding to my article, she wrote, "i can't say feminist tactics have ever much been a concern of mine." After the *Big Think* piece, she commented more aggressively: "i can't say i give a shit that i am a woman. i can say i give a massive amount of thinking time about being part of a structure that keeps you dependant on it if you let it." A Facebook friend of Byrne's chimed in, neatly summing up this coda's argument about the exchangeability of the host-parasite positions: "well for all Fisher's whining that she was used as host, she has pretty successfully parasited her way out of obscurity on the back of your work!"

But this relatively narrow view obscures how the interests of the larger forces that hosted my encounter with Roisin Byrne also shaped the way it played out. The critic's and artist's repeated exchanges of who is host and who is parasite is a dynamic that is all too easily accommodated by—even supported by—corporate digital platforms, mediums that are designed around appropriation and recontextualization. Social media's parasitical hold revealed itself as I attempted to detach myself from Byrne's lure (and vice versa). It contrived to make it difficult for me not to respond to Byrne and for Byrne not to respond to me: my Facebook News Feed fed me new material about the artist, and her Google Alert repeatedly drew her back into the fray. As the invisible substrates that made our dialogue possible, Facebook, Twitter, and Google posed as mere platforms for our exchange, but in fact they were highly interested hosts whose interests lie in users generating ever more content. In our entanglement Byrne often appeared parasitical to me in her very proximity to and obliging use of these technologies; she channels the market's appropriative force, her art both exposing and exploiting the conditions that make her practice possible. To question only the artist's morals attends to the parasite but ignores the host system; it displaces the more difficult work of questioning the corporate and institutional infrastructures.

THE CHARM OFFENSIVE

After our exchange I went back through the material available about Byrne's previous interventions with a finer comb. Where Hendricks had condescended to Byrne, Starling had responded affably to her initial emails asking for information about where the plants were located. "I remember that they grow in amongst cork trees and are mainly between the main road that runs along the coast and the the [*sic*] top of the hill," he had replied. "I would love to know if my plants are still alive but would be really surprised if you find them. I think I left a little ribbon on them." When she told him what she'd done, he (like Hendricks) did not acknowledge her act as a work of art, reframing it instead as an act of vandalism and theft. Starling insists on the moral and legal consequences of Byrne's actions and rejects their potential financial or artistic value.[24] Byrne refuses to revere the aura of Starling's original, thus reducing the plant to its value as a symbolic object of economic exchange: "I would like to keep it alive, yes. Because as an artwork, it has a value so I reckon it's more valuable alive than dead." But the plant ultimately withers and dies while on display.

Like the guest who knows that her host has to make her comfortable or risks appearing ungenerous, Byrne (like Kraus and Calle) personifies the feminine delicacy associated with her social demographic in order to play the threshold of care required by protocols of chivalry and professional etiquette. She exploits these protocols' reliance on whiteness, middle-class-ness, and femininity as moral virtues. She taunted that she had read Starling's little ribbon marking the work as a romantic embellishment intended for her: "The moment I saw them there . . . beautifully healthy and full of flowers I felt that in some way you had left them there for me . . . and in so doing you were presenting me with a token of your affection so I took one." Further taunting him, she reassures Starling that she was not harmed in the process of stealing his work: "I had to chop it up into four pieces nervous i would be seen by park security. But I wasn't, I am ok." Byrne plays the threshold of care only up to a point, taking only what she can get away with; she calibrates her risk to her situated privilege. And she does get away with it. Starling drops the charges, responding with emotion rather than legal action. Byrne is shielded from material or physical retaliation by a racial, sexual, and class logic (of white femininity as nonthreatening and nonequal) that is not mobilized innocently.[25]

Byrne is able to risk her performances of criminality, to count on art as her alibi, because of her taken-for-granted ability to resist, an ability that is not granted to all. As a white, middle-class subject, working in the context of a (comparatively) democratic society, her sense of security that she will not be arrested (to count on the police not being called, or if they are, the likelihood of her being perceived as an empathetic subject in the eyes of the state) is safeguarded by her white privilege. Similarly, her artistic *performances of stealing and forgery* are safeguarded by their institutional recognition as conceptual art, while these same actions are likely to be considered simply as *stealing and forgery* by an artist of color, a trans artist, or an artist without a European passport. This distinction rests on who has the social capital to claim the position of the performance artist and be recognized as such (as opposed to vandal, terrorist, mentally unwell person)—a question of signification prominent in the work of the black performance artists William Pope.L, Tameka Norris, Zachary Fabri, and Dread Scott, who often perform in public spaces. Byrne's assertation that she performs parasitism out of situational necessity conceals her complicity with the same system of rewards that confers greater success on her male hosts than on Byrne herself. While Byrne is indeed a lower-income single mother, she is also an educated, white, cisgender British citizen with access to the cultural capital offered by an institution like Goldsmiths.

Even as she casts Starling as an earnest, naïve Boy Scout type (as much of the art press has), Byrne proves indifferent to the political dimensions of *Rescued Rhododendrons*, which was made as a statement against British immigration policy. Starling undertook the project after learning that the rhododendrons, originally imported from the south of Spain to the north of Scotland in the eighteenth century, had come to be considered weeds (in other words, parasites) and would be uprooted and destroyed. Thwarting this plan, Starling returned the plants to their original homeland in Spain in the back of a Volvo (figures C.5 and C.6). He had originally intended

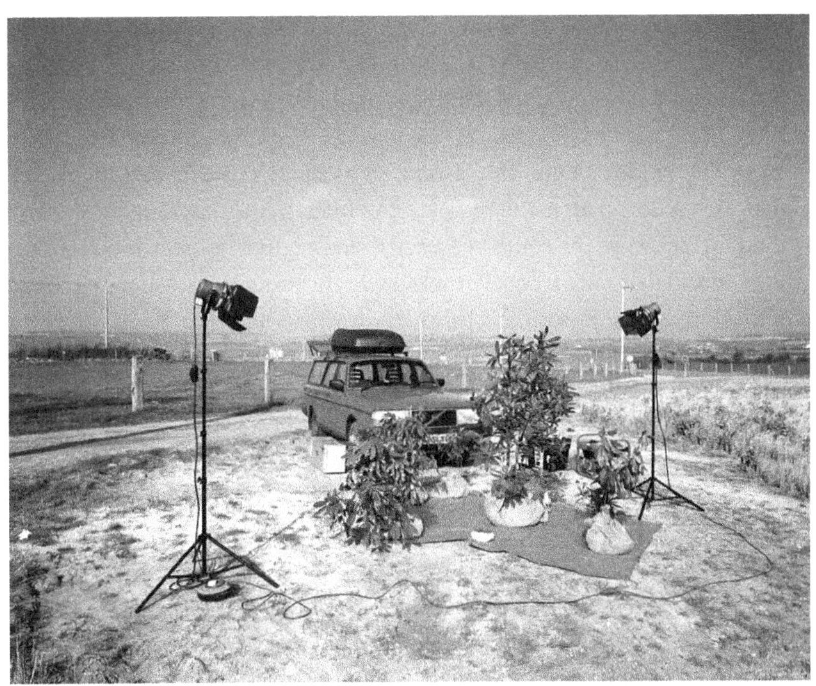

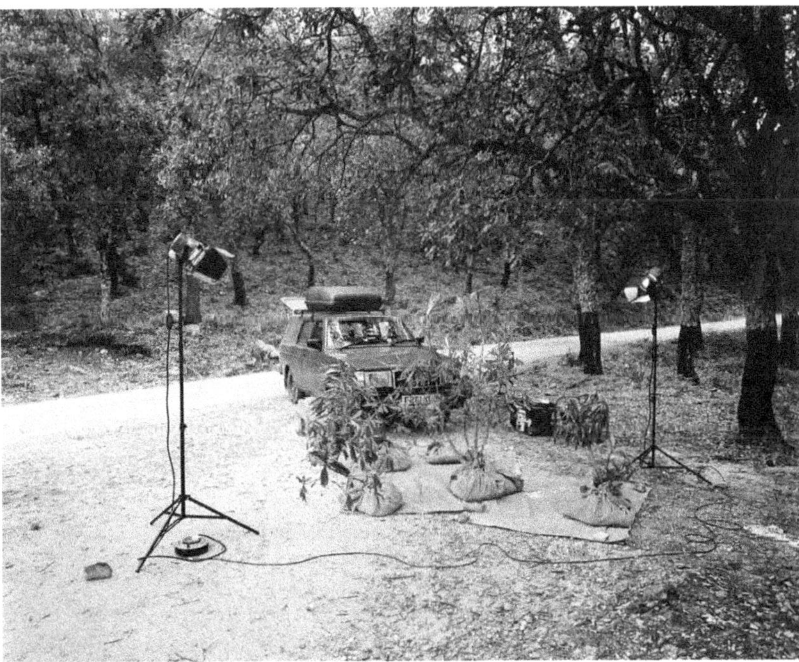

FIGURES C.5 AND C.6 Simon Starling, photographs from *Rescued Rhododendrons,* 2000. Source: Simon Starling.

to transfer them to what he saw as a sanctuary, a new homeland, a floating island of rhododendrons in the middle of the freshwater Scottish lake Loch Lomond. However, the floating sanctuary idea was scrapped when he realized that the national conservation agency Scottish National Heritage, an important funder for the "Island of Weeds" project, had *themselves* spent £5 million trying to eradicate the plants. Starling instead reintroduced the plants in the south of Spain, their original home, which is where Byrne found them. As a conceptual statement about the refugee crisis, this conclusion seems to posit, despairingly, a world in which there can be no sanctuary for refugees. This complication in the making of the work suggests that although Byrne presents Starling as a foolish, earnest idealist, he is in fact quite aware of the political contingencies of his own practice. Byrne's act of appropriation blithely disregards the larger implications of Starling's work, which is a sustained engagement with issues of labor and migration, immigration policy and national security, ethnic cleansing and genocide, all framed as social parasitism by existing structures of power.

Byrne demonstrates the danger of working against certain kinds of power and privilege while at the same time employing other kinds of power and privilege in order to do so. She channels the appropriative indifference of a free market that, in its singular focus on maximizing capital value, throws off the burden of contextual specificity. The secondary framing of the parasitical act of appropriation can divorce the original work from its context and meaning, for there is a structural displacement at work in parasitical appropriation. Capitalizing on this displacement, Byrne selects for some aspects of power in the work (e.g., gender inequity in the art world) and deselects for others (the contingencies of racial and ethnic difference, capacity and ability, sexual orientation, unexpected political solidarities, and so on). This makes certain features of difference advance and others recede, as if she plays her parasitism in order to trump his. Her work levies the same implicit feminist critique of masculine privilege against every artist (whether a "bad boy" like Hendricks or a "good boy" like Starling), indifferent to other identitarian markers beyond their status as male artists and the politics of their body of work. She turns them all into monolithic Dicks.

As a number of the artworks from the second half of this book make evident, parasitism's violence comes from its essentialization of the host as nothing but a host: it conflates very different people, turns individuals into a mere symbol of power. Byrne's disregard for complexity is emblematic of parasitism, for it treats all hosts as created equal (much as my early writing that Byrne appropriated threatened to treat all parasites as created equal, as a vector only for feminist rebellion). Byrne's critique of Hendricks is the same as her critique of Starling, Gander, Sierra, and others—presumably a critique of their masculine privilege in the art world and beyond. Byrne's flattening out of the complexities of their work proves especially violent in the case of Starling, an artist of whose work it has been said that "backstory is everything."[26] Her actions, which may circumstantially or instrumentally signify as feminist, hold Starling's work hostage to the problem of gender inequity; in other words, her conceptual reframing of Starling's work through the lens of masculine privilege drowns out the important political critiques staged by his art. Unlike Hendricks, Starling does not overplay his position. He is a redistributive host, while she is a self-serving parasite. He shows that having some cultural capital is not itself necessarily the problem.

Byrne's stereotypical portrait of Ryan Gander, whose neon sign concept she claims to have stolen, likewise proves incomplete. The fact that Gander works from a wheelchair is left out of Byrne's conceptual narrative, as is his and Starling's shared investment in appropriation as a mode of institutional critique. In this sense, Byrne, who enjoys different degrees of privilege compared to Gander (as able-bodied) and to the immigrants and refugees referenced in Starling's work (as someone with a European passport), fails to recognize her own relative status as a host. In other words, she ignores the intersectionality of identities.[27] Whatever its conceptual intentions (or lack thereof), the feminist critical value of Byrne's project, which subverts only the white female or white male paradigm, fails to model a viably intersectional parasitical resistance.

Here we might ask whether the parasite, in playing the threshold of care, can ever be fully feminist or resistant if its tactical possibility is conditioned by its performance of complacency with other forms of oppression. Feminism remains a useful space for tackling the problem of resistance's complicity with structural inequity, so long as it relinquishes its investments in purity and does not disavow its own dependencies—in other words, so long as it recognizes its own parasitism, its own complicity. Byrne's work raises the question of how we can become better, more redistributive parasites while remaining under the host's radar—while sustaining our complicit positions with our hosts.

Byrne charges Hendricks with not recirculating the capital he acquires—a practice in which her work also engages. She represents not a parasitical model of redistribution but one of unapologetic absorption and free-market individualism. One of her artworks in particular, *Old Work* (2010) (figure C.7), makes this remarkably explicit. Taking a page out of Hendricks's playbook, Byrne claims that she "illegally extracted" money from the British welfare system and used it to make a large neon sign of the word *work*, which she stipulated could only ever be exhibited turned off. What is the difference between Hendricks's parasitism of the state and Byrne's? Byrne too exploits the resistant potential of parasitism as a loophole by which the system of white supremacist heteropatriarchy might be made to accommodate its own undermining. Yet Hendricks's exploitation of the minimal generosity of the state with *Tax* may have contributed to the closure of the loophole in tax law that provided modest tax benefits for working artists; similarly, in February 2013 the Paris Court of Appeals announced the closing of Byrne's exploited loophole that had allowed what the court called "artistic parasitism." The judgment ruled that if a work of art was found to be too similar to an existing work, what was of most consequence was the fame of the first artist—a decision that effectively made it easier to steal from people who are not famous than from those who are.[28] By taking parasitism's name in vain, one might argue that Byrne overexposed it, potentially putting it on the radar of official systems and thereby closing it as a loophole for others who might employ it toward redistributive ends. And yet this decision to protect and consolidate the position of the host is hardly surprising, or the fault of the parasite. It only makes it that much harder for those who do not already have status or influence to get ahead and ultimately to survive in a system stacked against them.

What is the *work* of the parasite, the contribution of an actor that seems to take without giving back? The parasite, who must survive to disrupt, but who must be seen as nonthreatening in order to survive, is always under threat of being either eliminated from the system or put to work within the normative economy of the host. The parasite thus always operates between two or more frames; the prefix *para-* points to this duplicity, meaning at the same time both "with" (*near* or *beside*) and "against" (*counter*). It must walk a fine line between the resistant and the reactionary (and the reproductive, in the sense of potentially reproducing existing relations of power). It is this quasi-belonging, this insider-outsiderness, that allows it to leverage a certain

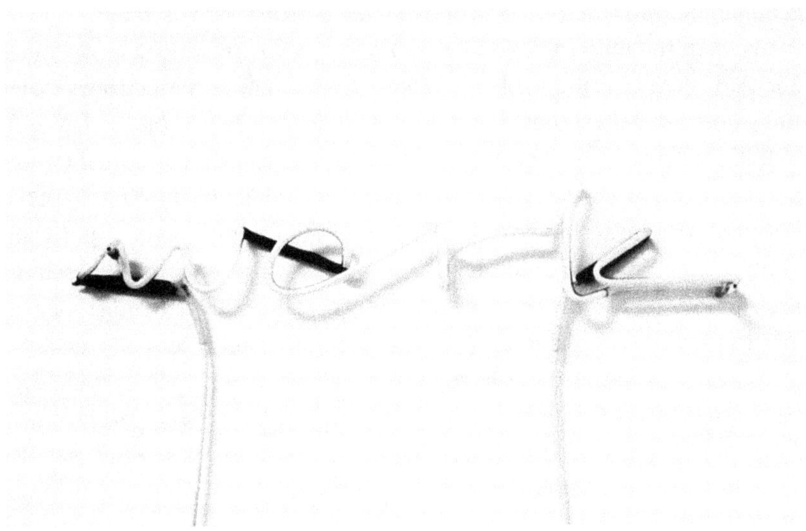

FIGURE C.7 Roisin Byrne, *Old Work,* 2010. Source: Roisin Byrne.

critical distance between itself and its host milieu, which makes it possible for it to play the position in which it finds itself. It rides this line, exploits this opening in the system, as long as it can. In its ideal, socially progressive form, the resistant parasite only *simulates* its complicity, working behind the host's back, but in some cases (as in Byrne's) the parasite plays its position opportunistically or in bad faith.

As my entanglement with Byrne illustrates, the parasite is both dangerous and generative precisely *because* there are no guarantees against its mechanisms. Byrne's performance of parasitism shows that it need not work *toward something* (a focused goal, an ethical logic); it *just works*. The parasite thus threatens the integrity of boundaries (self/other, criticism/art, a private draft/public persona). The parasite is an unstable agent not simply because it refuses to abide by the rules but because it appropriates the mechanisms of its hosts, who make the rules of the game but do not always follow them. Throughout the book we have seen artists who, perceiving themselves to be out of options, resort to using the tools of the host against it: using Google to take down Google, using private property law to unthink private property, using cultural studies to make a cultural study of Dick, using white feminist legacy reenacted to disidentify with white feminist legacy. Byrne is the ultimate version of this trend toward a politics of mirroring, reflection, mediation. If the labor of her art is showing her enmeshment in her economic-artistic milieu, the scandal of her persona is that she refuses to be better than the moral and legal economies of value in which she operates. She both stages a critique of the system in which she acts and draws material gain from her critique. Yet it is hardly adequate to respond to her with moral disgust, for her parasitism refuses the dictates of institutional morality. Her moral or ethical status cannot fully be disentangled from that of the systemic structures that host her. She models the way one can, as powerful entities often do, sit on and play the system in which one finds oneself. In such a moment, the critical safeguards we typically rely on to judge such an artist's work are compromised by our own implication in it.

My early thinking about Byrne was caught up in whether it would ever be possible to dissociate her critical potential from her opportunistic performance of capitalist mimicry. Now I think that it is precisely the inability to separate these things that gives the parasite its resistant power. Without clear boundaries (ethical, spatial and temporal, or otherwise), what separates a work from its context, and how do you know when it is over? Perhaps it is over when there is no more resistance, no more interference on the line; when the parasite has been fully absorbed into the host or when it has been expelled from the system; or when even the ultimate opportunist doesn't seem to be able to survive a transforming, brutally competitive art market. Byrne's representing gallery The Goma no longer lists her as part of their stable of artists, and I can find no sign that she is still actively producing work. Her former artist website (roisinbyrne.co.uk) is now permanently down. "You don't have permission to access," reads an error message marked "Forbidden" when I first noticed it was no longer running. In a halting irony, her website has since been bought by someone who appears to be a different Roisin Byrne, a British business guru, and is now home to Roisin Byrne's Business Boutique ("Home of the Ambitious Upstart"), though the possibility that the website might be yet another stunt by the artist, while unlikely, can't fully be ruled out.[29] *"Are you an entrepreneur struggling to get started? Did you already start a business but can't seem to get off the ground? Is your business hitting a plateau and you can't seem to grow any further?"*

I tried instead to write to Byrne to see how she's been.

I didn't hear back.

ACKNOWLEDGMENTS

It is customary in acknowledgments to observe that books are collective rather than individual undertakings. But in a book concerned with challenging the uses of intellectual property to concentrate resources, reputation, and influence, it is all the more important that I acknowledge the many interlocutors, readers, editors, advisors, teachers, students, colleagues, mentors, and support systems without which this book could not have been written.

This book was made possible by the patronage of many generous hosts. Institutional and financial support from several fellowships and grants afforded me the time and resources to write and think at pivotal moments: a Pembroke Seminar Graduate Fellowship in Brown University's Pembroke Center for Teaching and Research on Women; an Andrew W. Mellon Postdoctoral Fellowship in Cornell University's Society for the Humanities and Department of Performing and Media Arts; and two ADVANCE Faculty Summer Writing Grants at the University of Michigan.

The seeds of this book were sown by my mentors and their inspiring scholarship and teaching. It was they who helped me formulate the questions vital to both my work and my life and who provided me with the critical vocabulary and frameworks for grappling with them. I thank Wendy Hui Kyong Chun for seeing promise in these ideas early on, for guiding and supporting my professional development over the years, and for the formidable model of her work. I thank Rebecca Schneider for the special relationship we have shared and for the many doors she has opened in my thinking. Lynne Joyrich was a crucial supporter and early interlocutor for this project, and it was in conversation with her that my interest in the parasite first came to the surface. The late José Esteban Muñoz continues to be the person I write for. My personal and intellectual debt to him, and to the legacy of his scholarship, informs every page. A heartfelt thanks to my first mentor, Kristine

Stiles, who exposed my naïve undergraduate self to the transformative potential of feminist art and performance. This formative encounter instilled in me many of the questions to which this book finds me, all these years later, still searching for a way to answer.

I am grateful for the support of my colleagues in the Department of American Culture and the Digital Studies Institute at the University of Michigan. First, I thank Lisa Nakamura for warmly welcoming me into the fold, for her support each step of the way, and for the scholarly community that she makes possible. I am deeply grateful for her generous counsel, intellect, friendship, and vision. Yeidy Rivero, Jonathan Freedman, Kristin Hass, and Jon Wells offered crucial wisdom and support for navigating my first years at Michigan. I am grateful for the departmental leadership of Greg Dowd, Alex Stern, June Howard, Jesse Hoffnung-Garskof, and Anthony Mora, who have enabled my work as a scholar and teacher in so many ways. I am lucky to have colleagues like Maria Cotera, Magda Zaborowska, Evelyn Alsultany, Larry La Fountain-Stokes, Scott Larson, Melissa Borja, Nancy Khalil, Ava Purkiss, Sara Blair, Holly Hughes, Leslie Rogers, Clare Croft, Irina Aristarkhova, John Cheney-Lippold, Colin Gunckel, Stephen Berrey, Christian Sandvig, Megan Ankerson, Peggy McCracken, Melanie Yergeau, Justin Joque, Sheila Murphy, Nicole Ellison, Scott Campbell, André Brock, Sophia Brueckner, Osman Khan, Tung-Hui Hu, Adam Fure, and Ellie Abrons, whose models of criticality, mentorship, and activism enrich my days and inspire my work. My work as a scholar and as a teacher would not be possible without the supreme competence of Judy Gray, Mary Freiman, Andrew Reiter, Jenny Hong, Kate Klemm, Katia Kitchen, Abbie Dykstra, Marlene Moore, and the late Tammy Zill. I am also grateful for the nurturing community and goodwill of colleagues in the Residential College: Sueann Caulfield, Jennifer Meyers, Carl Abrego, Candice Middlebrook, Jeffrey Evans, Susan Rosegrant, Deborah Gordon-Gurfinkel, Catherine Brown, Charlie Bright, Naomi André, and Cindy Sowers.

I have benefited tremendously from the trusted community and good humor of an uncommonly supportive junior faculty cohort at UM. Deep thanks to Silvia Lindtner and Sarah Murray, dear friends and spirited fellow travelers, for helping carry me across the finish line. I am also especially grateful to Charlotte Karem Albrecht, William Calvo-Quirós, and Manan Desai for lifting me up in the hard moments.

I thank those colleagues who have read the whole manuscript and provided frank and productive feedback at key junctures: Lisa Nakamura, Steven Shaviro, Rita Raley, Tung-Hui Hu, and Irina Aristarkhova. Their questions and challenges sharpened my ideas and helped me get to the next stage in the project. Irina's thoughtful, extensive feedback on the early manuscript and Steven's support at every stage of the process bear special mention. I thank Rebecca Schneider, Faith Wilding, Mariellen Sandford, and Aliza Shvarts for generous and detailed feedback on an early version of chapter 4 and Jasbir Puar and Patricia Clough for vital feedback on an early draft of chapter 3. The chapters are better for their input.

I offer my deepest thanks to the many friends and colleagues whom I have subjected to readings of this book, who pored over various drafts and offered me valuable feedback and encouragement along the way: Annie McClanahan, Silvia Lindtner, Seb Franklin, Yeidy Rivero, Coleman Nye, Lynn Badia, Paige McGinley, Jonathan Mullins, Faith Wilding, Erika Balsom, Verity Platt, Ben Parris, and Paige Sarlin. Alex Pittman is a treasured interlocutor, sounding board, and collaborator; he has read these pages many times, and each time he has expanded and steered my thinking in crucial ways. Johanna Gosse is likewise an indispensable ally in the trenches. I also owe a special debt of gratitude to the singular Amanda Jo Goldstein, who significantly advanced this text through her repeated readings and key insights. My special thanks to Manan Desai, who graciously read and improved many drafts, kept me accountable, and most of all helped me refind my resolve during the revision process. My whip-smart writing group at UM gave me the necessary push to finish the manuscript: Hadji Bakara, Molly Lynch, Sarah Ensor, Ingrid Diran, and Antoine Traisnel enabled me, at last, to let this one fly. I especially thank Ingrid for numerous insightful gems and for extra offline engagement with the project above and beyond the call of duty of our regular meetings.

I have benefited considerably from the engaged feedback of audiences at talks and conferences, who enabled me to test and refine these ideas: the Faculty of Information at the University of Toronto, the Film and Media Studies Program at Colgate University, the Science and Literature Research Group at the Université Paris 3 Sorbonne Nouvelle, the Parsons New School of Design, the Critical Visualities Workshop at the University of Michigan, the LGBT Graduate Research Group and the Department of History of Art and Visual Studies at Cornell University, American Studies Association, Performance Studies International, Society for Cinema and Media Studies, the American Society for Theatre Research, the Association for Theatre in Higher Education, and the National Women's Studies Association, among others. I thank these audiences for their attention and engagement, and my hosts for their generous invitations, especially Pierre-Louis Patoine, Ani Maitra, Mary Simonson, the late George Pitts, and Patrick Keilty.

I also thank those individuals who sat down and chewed over these ideas with me over the years: Wendy Brown, Nicholas Ridout, Lauren Berlant, Mark Tribe, Ellen Rooney, and Stephanie Rothenberg. These conversations opened up new lines of discovery, guided me to essential reading, and helped me refine my argument. I thank Imre Szeman and Eva-Lynn Jagoe for the opportunity to further the project while taking in the majestic vistas of Banff, Alberta, as a part of a Banff Research in Culture Residency Fellowship. While I was a postdoc at Cornell, this project benefited immensely from being in community and dialogue with colleagues in the Society for the Humanities. My special thanks to Tim Murray for creating such a rigorous and generative space and for allowing me to be part of it. Thanks too to the people who enabled and enriched my time at Cornell: Brett de Bary, Cathy Caruth, Tracy McNulty, Renate Ferro, Michael Ashkin, Mary Ahl, Emily Parsons, Paula Epps-Cepero, and many others.

I thank Karen Shimakawa, Tavia Nyong'o, Barbara Browning, Nick Mirzoeff, and Michael Silverman for being important early sounding boards for this material. The formative queer fellowship of my NYU MA cohort, among them Liz Rosenfeld, Lydia Brawner, Branden Jacobs-Jenkins, Jonathan Mullins, and Alex Pittman, helped me chart a path to this work. I'm grateful to my Brown doctoral cohort and offer special thanks to members of the Speculative Critique Mellon workshop, who thoughtfully engaged this book's earliest drafts: Ani Maitra, Coleman Nye, David Bering-Porter, Matt Tierney, Eleanor Skimin, Pooja Rangan, Patrick McKelvy, Hunter Hargraves, Jen Schnepf, Andrew Starner, Lindsay Goss, and Christine Mok. The Department of Modern Culture and Media would not have been the same without Susan McNeil and Liza Hebert.

Many thanks to my brilliant collaborators in the Precarity Lab network—Lisa Nakamura, Cass Adair, Kalindi Vora, Jackie Wang, McKenzie Wark, Cindy Lin, Iván Chaar-López, Cengiz Salman, Silvia Lindtner, Irina Aristarkhova, Tung-Hui Hu, and Meryem Kamil—for showing me what feminist collaboration can do. I am grateful for the broader community of feminist and queer performance and media scholars who has engaged and supported my work and stimulated and pushed my thinking: Alex Pittman, Johanna Gosse, Katie Brewer Ball, Nijah Cunningham, Leon Hilton, Summer Kim Lee, Marissa Brostoff, Lakshmi Padmanabhan, John Andrews, Iván Ramos, Vivian Huang, Amber Musser, Genevieve Yue, Damon Young, Hentyle Yapp, Debra Levine, Yelena Gluzman, Erica Levin, Emanuela Bianchi, Ariel

Osterweis, Patrick Keilty, Scott Richmond, Danny Snelson, Tung-hui Hu, Jim Hodge, Patrick Jagoda, and Kris Cohen.

I extend deep thanks to the artists on whose work I have imposed. You have challenged, astonished, and stuck on and with me. Thank you in particular to Ann Liv Young, Amber Hawk Swanson, Lauren Barri Holstein, Kenneth Pietrobono, Roisin Byrne, Anya Liftig, and Chris Kraus for sharing your work with me, supporting my efforts, and responding to my inquiries.

I owe a special debt of gratitude to my students, from whom I have learned so much. The book has especially benefited in its final stages from the attuned engagement of the graduate students in my "Digital Aesthetics and Resistance" seminar and the Digital Studies Workshop at UM. A special thanks to Cengiz Salman, Meryem Kamil, Casidy Campbell, Yuchen Chen, Jathan Day, Sarah Hughes, Andrea Jacoby, Adrian King, Kyle Lindsey, Sam McCracken, Andrew Moos, Katie Van Zanen, Rachel Wilson, Riley Wilson, Crystal Zanders, Iván Chaar López, Jasmine Ehrhardt, Rae Moors, Abhishek Narula, Jasmine An, Kelly Wheeler, Isaiah Zeavin-Moss, Kristina Perkins, Leena Ghannam, Joseph Deleon, and Megan Rim.

I could not ask for a better editor at Duke University Press than Elizabeth Ault, who has guided me through the process with extreme competence and great care; I thank her for her early commitment to the project and for her superb notes on the manuscript, which helped me push each draft that much further. I gratefully acknowledge my two anonymous readers for their vital and deeply thoughtful engagement with the manuscript; the book is much better for the keen and constructive pressure these readers put on the book's critical and political stakes. Kate Herman, Susan Albury, Christopher Robinson, and the rest of the production and marketing staff at Duke UP have been a pleasure to work with. My thanks to Aimee Harrison for her splendid work on the cover design. I am grateful to the artist, Julie Mehretu, for permission to reprint the image (and to Kris Cohen for introducing me to her work). I thank Judith Hoover for her meticulous copyediting and Scott Smiley for his diligent work on the index. The manuscript considerably improved in the capable hands of editors Kim Greenwell and Heath Sledge.

This book benefited from the research assistance of Yeshua Tolle, who expertly provided research support in addition to preparing the bibliographic notes. I also gratefully acknowledge the skillful research assistance of Cengiz Salman and Pau Nava. Thanks to the Office of Research and the College of Literature, Science, and the Arts at the University of Michigan for generous funding that allowed both for me to print images in color and for the book to be available open access.

For reminding me that there is life beyond work, I acknowledge other cherished friends near and far: Tom McEnaney, Vivian Choi, Patty Keller, Emily Nacol, Merike Andre-Barrett, Alex Livingston, Ben Parris, Nandi Theunissen, Davide Trentini, Stephanie Bosch Santana, Chris Chalmers, Kris Trujillo, Joseph Lee, Amanda Alexander, Marc Arthur, Francesca Inglese, Jan de Wilde, Annie Lewandowski, Retika Desai, Viviana Maggioni, Mauro Resmini, Eli Friedman, Julia Chang, Andrew Moisey, Athena Kirke, Diana Allan, Curtis Brown, Ben Piekut, Tim Bewes, Thangam Ravindranathan, Marion Bacrot, Gregoire Archière, Meena Krishnamurthy, Ana Sabau, Gavin Arnall, Sara McClelland, Clare Croft, Henry Cowles, Anna Bonnell Freidin, Julia Jaffe, Alexis Conason, and Mackinzie Rogge.

Love and thanks to my parents, Gwen and Evans Fisher; my sister and brother-in-law, Kelly and Erik Severson (and nephews Jack and Carter); and my French family, Catherine and Christian Traisnel. I thank my friend-family, especially Jonathan Mullins, beloved confidante and bosom buddy, for keeping me laughing and always making me feel understood.

Most of all, I am grateful to my partner, Antoine, for his open-hearted and tireless commitment to this book, at all hours of the day and night, and to me. It is simply impossible to take the measure of his support and influence. These pages are one long conversation with him. And so now begins another.

An early version of chapter 1 appeared as "User Be Used: Leveraging the Play in the System" in *Discourse: Journal for Theoretical Studies in Media and Culture* 36, no. 3, USC and Wayne State Press (fall 2014), which was reprinted in "Traversing Technology," special double issue, edited by Patrick Keilty and Leslie Regan Shade, *S&F Online (Scholar & Feminist Online)* 13, no. 3–14, no. 1 (summer/fall 2016), and in *New Media, Old Media: A History and Theory Reader*, edited by Wendy Hui Kyong Chun and Anna Watkins Fisher (with Thomas Keenan) (New York: Routledge, 2015). An early version of chapter 3 appeared as "Manic Impositions: The Parasitical Art of Chris Kraus and Sophie Calle," in the special issue, "Viral," edited by Patricia Ticiento Clough and Jasbir Puar, *WSQ (Women's Studies Quarterly)* 40, nos. 1–2 (spring/summer 2012), and "Parasitical Politics and Epistolary Games: The Art of Chris Kraus and Sophie Calle" [Politique parasitaire et jeux épistolaires: Les jeux d'adresse de Chris Kraus et de Sophie Calle], *Le Texte étranger* 8 (October 2011). Since significantly revised, an early iteration of chapter 4, "Like a Girl's Name: The Adolescent Drag of Amber Hawk Swanson, Kate Gilmore, and Ann Liv Young," appeared in TDR *(The Drama Review)* 56, no. 1 (spring 2012). An earlier version of the coda appeared as "We Are Parasites: On the Politics of Imposition" in *Artforum* and *e-flux journal*'s *Art&Education* (July 2011).

NOTES

INTRODUCTION. TOWARD A THEORY OF PARASITICAL RESISTANCE

1. Scholars have mostly written about Ubermorgen in the context of discussions about art hacktivism and tactical art and media. See the following representative works: Arns, "Feeding the Serpent Its Own Tail"; Bernhard and Lizvlx, *UBERMORGEN.COM*; Raley, *Tactical Media*; Broeckmann, "Software Art Aesthetics"; Dieter, "Amazon Noir"; Kampf and Cox, "Using Digital Art"; Mihai, "Art Hacktivism"; Thoburn, *Anti-Book*; Vavarella, "Art, Error."

2. "All of our work is done out in the open," the group noted in a press release about the project. Ubermorgen, "Press Release," November/December 2006, www.amazon-noir.com/TEXT/PRESS_RELEASE_151106.pdf.

3. "The Hacking Monopolism Trilogy," Face to Facebook, accessed December 27, 2017, www.face-to-facebook.net/hacking-monopolism-trilogy.php.

4. A press release announcing funding for *Amazon Noir* describes the piece as "question[ing] the inconsistencies in the enforcement of copyright law" and "point[ing] out the hypocrisy of the digital copyright lobby." Amazon Noir collaborator Paolo Cirio explained in an interview, "When a common good has been given to people for free or for a cheap price, the whole of society grows. Every day we see the rampant privatization of commons [*sic*], as soon as people become more poor and ignorant. The latest movements of CC [Creative Commons], Wikipedia, P2P free networks, etc. are a much needed [*sic*] resistance in a world where the use of cultural content is ever less a right and ever more a business." Edith Ross Haus for Medienkunst, "Stipends 2006," entry "ubermorgen .com, 'Amazon Noir—The Big Book Crime,'" accessed May 16, 2018, www.edith -russ-haus.de/en/grants/grants/archive/stipends-2006.html; Cirio, Ludovico, Bernhard, and Lizvlx, "The Big Book (C)rime."

5. Thoburn, *Anti-Book*, x.

6. Pasquale, *The Black Box Society*, 89.

7. See Philip, "What Is a Technological Author?," on "good versus bad" open source as a function of a Western versus a non-Western paradigm. In his "Guerrilla Open Access Manifesto," the digital prodigy and activist Aaron Swartz challenged as hypocritical big corporations' moralistic stance against open access: "It's called stealing or piracy, as if sharing a wealth of knowledge were the moral equivalent of plundering a ship or murdering its crew. But sharing isn't

immoral—it's a moral imperative. Only those blinded by greed would refuse to let a friend make a copy."

8. In a 2004 online article for the Independent Book Publishers Association, Jonathan Kirsch, an attorney specializing in copyright and publishing law, wrote, "Amazon, of course, is such a dominant player in the book industry that many publishers, and especially independent publishers, feel compelled to participate even though they fear that it might not be in their best interest to do so. . . . Although there has been much grumbling among both authors and publishers about the Amazon programs . . . no one has gone so far as to test the legality of the programs in court." Kirsch, "Danger! Amazon's Inside the Book Programs Pose Legal Risks for Publishers," Independent Book Publishers Association, June 2004, articles.ibpa-online.org/article/danger-amazons-inside-the-book-programs-pose-legal-risks-for-publishers/.

9. The rise of an explicitly authoritarian figure like Donald Trump, however, has attested to an ascendant form of naked sovereign power in U.S. mainstream politics that does not feel the need to dissimulate its bigotry, misogyny, nepotism, and jingoism under the guise of hospitality.

10. Frank Pasquale defines a black box as "a useful metaphor . . . [that] can refer to a recording device, like the data-monitoring systems in planes, trains, and cars. Or it can mean a system whose workings are mysterious; we can observe its inputs and outputs, but we cannot tell how one becomes the other. We face these two meanings daily: tracked ever more closely by firms and government, we have no clear idea of just how far much of this information can travel, how it is used, or its consequences" (*The Black Box Society*, 3).

11. For helpful discussions of digital technologies and neoliberalism, see, among others, Chun, *Control and Freedom*; Dean, *Democracy*; Shaviro, *Post-Cinematic Affect*; Taylor, *The People's Platform*; Chun, *Updating*; G. Hall, *The Uberfication*; Srnicek, *Platform Capitalism*; Cohen, *Never Alone*.

12. The perceived inefficiencies of an earnest form of revelatory criticism find support in the resignation that has generally characterized mainstream public response to the seismic bursts of transparency that followed the Wall Street bailouts; Wikileaks, Snowden, and the Panama Papers; and a revolving door of Trump whistleblowers—suggesting ours to be a moment when the exposure of corruption or extralegality cannot be said to produce revolution or even regulation. As dismissals of the politics of revolution seem perpetually proven wrong, it is not that on-the-ground protest or the epistemology of exposure are not useful or even crucial gestures but rather that we cannot expect them alone to fix what they make manifest. Nico Baumbach, Damon R. Young, and Genevieve Yue write, "[Since 2009] we have witnessed what looked briefly like the implosion of the global financial system followed by a wave of protest movements challenging the neoliberal consensus, but business as usual has returned, indeed with a renewed sense of inexorability. Capitalism is both broken and all-pervasive. . . . The global financial system to which we are all beholden has never been more opaque in its operations, or more transparent in its effects" ("Introduction," 1).

13. As Steven Shaviro argues, "transgression no longer works as a subversive aesthetic strategy . . . Transgression is now fully incorporated into the logic of political economy. It testifies to the way that, under the regime of real subsumption, 'there is nothing, no 'naked life,' no external standpoint . . . there is no longer an 'outside' to power'" ("Accelerationist Aesthetics").

14. Since the 1990s, the practice of hiring "white-hat hackers" (many of whom are "black-hat hackers" who turned coat) to locate vulnerabilities in corporate or government software and cybersecurity systems has become more and more prevalent. Google, Facebook, Microsoft, Samsung, Uber, Tesla, Apple, and even the U.S. government all have cash-for-bugs schemes, enlisting end users as bug-hunters. "A Bug-Hunting Hacker Says He Makes $250,000 a Year in Bounty," *MIT Technology Review*, August 22, 2016, https://www.technologyreview.com/s/602224/a-bug-hunting-hacker-says-he-makes-250000-a-year-in-bounty/. See also "A Framework for a Vulnerability Disclosure Program for Online Systems (Version 1.0)," U.S. Department of Justice Cybersecurity Unit, July 2017, https://www.justice.gov/criminal-ccips/page/file/983996/download/. Accepting payments in exchange for helping fortify state and corporate power appears to stand in clear opposition to the hacktivist ethos, which Gabriella Coleman associates with "an enthusiastic commitment to antiauthoritarianism and a variety of civil liberties" that is generally concerned with checking mechanisms of state control and supporting internet freedoms ("Hacker," 160).

15. "[Artists] can easily become extensions of the museum's own self-promotional apparatus, while the artist becomes a commodity with a special purchase on 'criticality,'" writes Miwon Kwon in *One Place after Another* (47).

16. Stevphen Shukaitis observes that "in the current functioning of capitalism, the critical function of governance is to be more critical than the critics of governance itself. Functionaries in a system of power, by presenting themselves as their worst critic, thus deprive critique of its ammunition and substance, thereby turning the tables on it. This is to go beyond both the arguments put forward by Boltanski and Chiapello; that critique has been subsumed within capitalism and that, within autonomist politics, reactive forms of social resistance and insurgency still remain a driving motor of capitalist development. This hints at the possibility that strategies for the neutralisation of the energies of social insurgency are anticipated even before they emerge" ("Overidentification," 28). See also Boltanski and Chiapello, *The New Spirit*.

17. Deleuze, "Postscript." Since Deleuze, media theorists have called upon the concept of control to advance an analysis of the postdisciplinary logics of domination as the everyday experiences of exploitation have only become more discreet, internalized, and automatic—in a word, participatory. For discussions of the diagrams of power advanced by digital networks, see Galloway, *Protocol*; Chun, *Control and Freedom*; Raley, *Tactical Media*; Franklin, *Control*; Hu, *A Prehistory*; Jagoda, *Network Aesthetics*.

18. This is a quote from Byrne's description of *Look What You Made Me Do* on the artist's website, formerly roisinbyrne.co.uk.

19. When asked by an interviewer about the choice to count the grains by hand (punishing work in which the artist himself claims also to have actively participated), Hendricks responded, apparently unironically, "You have to consider that my 12 assistants received money for something which other people pay a lot of money. Anyone, for instance, who attends meditation courses, and attempts to achieve a sense of nothingness has to dig deep into their pockets for the privilege. I give them money for it!" "Interview: Conversation between Eva Linhart and Jochem Hendricks," in Hendricks, *Legal Crimes*, 29.

20. Sally Churchward, "Fighting Dogs, Theft and Avoiding Tax—Artist Jochem Hendricks Brings His Controversial Work to Southampton," *Daily Echo*, November 5, 2012, https://www.dailyecho.co.uk/leisure/news/10026459.fighting-dogs-theft-and-avoiding-tax-artist-jochem-hendricks-brings-his-controversial-work-to-southampton/.

21. This method is captured by the title of Hendricks's 2002 artist's monograph, *Legal Crimes*.

22. What is so threatening about the feminized copy, Rebecca Schneider argues, is its potential to destabilize a patriarchal order that masquerades as original and foundational. "Perhaps one result of a mimesis not properly vilified would be that the seeming first would have to acknowledge its indebtedness to the second" ("Hello Dolly," 96).

23. Ahmed, *Living a Feminist Life*, 253.

24. "The piece is a performative media-installation and thus continues the historical tradition of happenings and performance art. Provoking reactions from conventional media and business is an integral part of the project," reads the work's entry on the website announcing the funding it received from the Edith Ross Haus for media art. Edith Ross Haus for Medienkunst, "Stipends 2006."

25. Like *Amazon Noir*, *Look What You Made Me Do* translates as installation art when it is represented in a gallery space (an effect of exhibiting the piece's component parts), while it presents as conceptual art in its exhibition on the artist's website, which takes the form of a brief description and digital images that metonymically stand in for the larger work.

26. In *Living a Feminist Life*, Sara Ahmed observes that this is how white men come to embody "an institution": "White men refers also to conduct; it is not simply who is there, who is here, who is given a place at the table, but how bodies are occupied once they have arrived" (153).

27. Insofar as the artists in this book achieve a kind of solidarity with more marginalized and exploited communities in their attempts to undermine the host, it is at a remove, from a position that does not take on the challenges and risks faced by these communities and that lacks affective ties to them.

28. My use of the designation *women* refers not to a biological category but a political and historical one. I follow Silvia Federici, who has argued for the necessity of maintaining the category *woman* to confront the economic and insti-

tutional forces that produce it, its problematic positing of a universal political subject notwithstanding ("Sipping Tea").

29. Serres's *The Parasite* is credited with parasitism's arrival on the scene of contemporary art, design, and architecture in the 1980s. For discussions of parasitism as an artistic, design, and curatorial practice, see Sara Marini, "Parasitical Architecture," *Domus*, May 10, 2010, www.domusweb.it/en/architecture/2010/05/10/parasitical-architecture.html; Fitzpatrick and Brothers, "A Productive Irritant"; Jahn, *Byproduct*; Pilcher, "Parasitic Art"; Anagnost, "Parasitism." The very language of parasitism is used to signify cutting-edge art and curatorial experimentation, as the term's appearance in the names of exhibition spaces such as Ljubljana's P.A.R.A.S.I.T.E. Museum of Contemporary Art, Hong Kong's Para/Site Art Space, and the German online art magazine *Berlin-ArtParasites* attests. For figurations of the parasite in digital interventionist practice, see Martin, "Parasitic Media"; Lovink, *Dark Fiber*; Critical Art Ensemble, *Digital Resistance*; David Garcia and Geert Lovink, "The ABC of Tactical Media," January 10, 2008, *Tactical Media Files*, www.tacticalmediafiles.net/articles/3160; Raley, *Tactical Media*. See also *the parasite*, a massive Alternate Reality Game (ARG) experiment led by Patrick Jagoda at the University of Chicago: H. Coleman, "the parasite." Invocations of parasitism in the work of Michel de Certeau, such as the passive tactics of free riding (working slowly, pursuing nonwork efforts while on the clock, squatting), will be familiar to many. "The space of a tactic is the space of the other," writes de Certeau. "Thus it must play on and with a terrain imposed on it and organized by the law of a foreign power. . . . It does not have the means to keep to itself, at a distance, in a position of withdrawal, foresight, and self-collection" (*The Practice*, 37). Such "weapons of the weak" (to use James C. Scott's phrase) follow a parasitical logic in that they are improvisational, short term, and fragmentary practices of resistance available to those constrained within spaces of domination. See also Scott, *Weapons* and *Domination*.

30. Combes, *The Art of Being a Parasite*, 8–12.

31. Nixon, *Slow Violence*; Berlant, *Cruel Optimism*. I am indebted to Ingrid Diran for this insight and phrasing.

32. Muñoz, "Feeling Brown," 70.

33. Muñoz, *Disidentifications*, 11–12.

34. In *Bodies That Matter* Butler asks, "What are the possibilities of politicizing disidentification, this experience of misrecognition, this uneasy sense of standing under a sign to which one does and does not belong? . . . It may be that the affirmation of that slippage, that the failure of identification, is itself the point of departure for a more democratizing affirmation of internal difference" (219). See also Butler, *Bodies That Matter*, 121–40.

35. Harney and Moten, *The Undercommons*, 31, 26.

36. Stevphen Shukaitis, Jean Baudrillard, and others have described "overidentification" and "overacceptance" as manic maneuvers by which one pretends to take the system at its word, performs sincerity at a fevered pitch, or plays so

close to its script that the system shudders at the intensity of one's participation. For a compelling analysis of overidentification, see Shukaitis, "Overidentification." For a discussion of overacceptance, see Jean Baudrillard, "The Masses: The Implosion of the Social in the Media," trans. Marie Maclean, in *New Media, Old Media: A History and Theory Reader*, ed. Wendy Hui Kyong Chun and Anna Watkins Fisher with Thomas Keenan, 2nd ed. (New York: Routledge, 2015), 515–22.

37. Butler, "The Body," 84.

38. Lauren Berlant's influential diagnosis of aspirational political attachment as a form of "cruel optimism" powerfully conveys the high cost of political idealism in this moment.

39. Peter Gilliver, "Precarious," OED *Online*, *Word Stories* (blog), accessed February 10, 2017, http://public.oed.com/aspects-of-english/word-stories/precarious/.

40. Wang, *Carceral Capitalism*, 53.

41. See Harvey, *A Brief History*; Boltanski and Chiapello, *The New Spirit of Capitalism*; Berlant, *Cruel Optimism*; Giroux, *Neoliberalism's War on Higher Education*; W. Brown, *Undoing the Demos*; Feher, *Rated Agency*.

42. Regarding the challenge to survival, we might think, for example, of Lester A. Spence's discussion of the neoliberal transformation of the term *hustler* over the past thirty years, from a "person who tried to do as little work as possible in order to make ends meet" to "someone who consistently works" (*Knocking the Hustle*, 2). As higher numbers of black men in the United States have been expelled from the formal labor economy, their choices limited by lack of education and jobs, criminal records, and discrimination, some have turned to informal economies or shadow markets for income. In this context they are vulnerable to arrest and police brutality (as was the case for Eric Garner, who sold loose cigarettes, and Alton Sterling, who peddled CDs, both killed by police who approached them for petty street hustles).

43. Emily Badger, "It's Unconstitutional to Ban the Homeless from Sleeping Outside, the Federal Government Says," *Washington Post*, August 13, 2015, https://www.washingtonpost.com/news/wonk/wp/2015/08/13/its-unconstitutional-to-ban-the-homeless-from-sleeping-outside-the-federal-government-says/.

44. Davis, "Fortress L.A.," 104; Edward Delman, "Should It Be Illegal for Supermarkets to Waste Food?," *Atlantic*, May 29, 2015, http://www.theatlantic.com/international/archive/2015/05/law-france-supermarkets-food-waste/394481/.

45. Caroline Mortimer, "Space, Not Spikes Protest Artist Says 'Hostile Architecture' Is 'Anti-Human,'" *Independent*, July 23, 2015, http://www.independent.co.uk/arts-entertainment/art/features/space-not-spikes-protest-artist-says-hostile-architecture-is-anti-human-10409673.html. Even bourgeois customers are subject to disciplinary strictures. A sign outside of one Whole Foods Market, a grocery chain that serves an upper-middle-class customer base, informs shoppers of the expiration date on their welcome: "Warning: 3 Hour Customer Parking Only." The capitalist mandate to keep circulating reframes paying customers as trespassers.

46. John Kennedy, "How Digital Disruption Changed 8 Industries Forever," *Silicon Republic*, November 25, 2015, https://www.siliconrepublic.com/companies/digital-disruption-changed-8-industries-forever.

47. See Terranova, *Network Culture*. For discussions of how women of color built the internet and what they have done to fix it, see Nakamura, "Indigenous Circuits" and "The Unwanted Labour." For a discussion of the shift from a model of permanent to temporary ownership, from buying a product outright to temporarily licensing it, see Perzanowski and Schultz, *The End of Ownership*.

48. Gillespie, "The Politics of 'Platforms.'"

49. Drawing on feminist accounts of hospitality by Tracy McNulty and Irina Aristarkhova that extend the philosophies of Kant, Levinas, and Derrida, I understand the concept of hospitality as necessarily implying a coercive dynamic, for ownership (the privilege of having an official right of permission or possession in the face of another who does not) makes the act, in its unconditional form, structurally impossible. Given the power differential that subtends it, the hospitality relation can never be fully consensual. See McNulty, *The Hostess*; Aristarkhova, *Hospitality of the Matrix*; Derrida and Dufourmantelle, *Of Hospitality*.

50. Writes Tracy McNulty, "Hence *potis* identifies not only the master, but the master who is 'eminently himself'" (*The Hostess*, ix).

51. "Some bodies are deemed as having the right to belong," writes Nirmal Puwar, "while others are marked out as trespassers, who are, in accordance with how both spaces and bodies are imagined (politically, historically, and conceptually), circumscribed as being 'out of place'" (*Space Invaders*, 8).

52. Serres, *The Parasite*.

53. Anders M. Gullestad writes, "Again according to the OED, as a noun, 'parasite' was first used in the current scientific sense in Ephraim Chambers' *Cyclopædia* (1728), when he—under the heading 'PARASITES, or PARASITAICAL [*sic*] Plants'—defined the subject as 'in Botany, a Kind of diminutive Plants, growing on Trees, and so called from their Manner of living and feeding, which is altogether on others'" ("Parasite").

54. Arnott, "Studies," 162–63. See also Gullestad, "Parasite"; Hassl, "Der klassische Parasit" and "The Parasitic."

55. "Gift exchange forms part of what is called an 'embedded economy,'" writes Anne Carson, "that is, a sociocultural system in which the elements of economic life are embedded in noneconomic institutions like kinship, marriage, hospitality, artistic patronage and ritual friendship" (*Economy*, 11–12). Carson is particularly interested in the complicit role of court singers and poets who come to be stitched into the embedded economy by trading their art for food and shelter in Homer's *Odyssey*. "At the moment when Odysseus, in the banquet hall of Alkinoos, carves out a hot chunk of pig meat from his own portion and proffers it in gratitude to the singer Demodokos 'so that he may eat and so that I may fold him close to me,' we see the embedded economy in its ideal version," she writes (14).

56. Gullestad, "Parasite." Drawing on the work of W. Geoffrey Arnott, Gullestad notes that "over time the parasite ended up as a more or less interchangeable rival to the earlier comedic stock character of the *kolax* (the flatterer) as a name for those characters in Greek and Latin comedy looking for a free lunch, be it in a literal or metaphorical sense." See also Damon, *The Mask of the Parasite.*

57. In *How to Tell a Flatterer from a Friend*, Plutarch "acknowledges that the comic parasite, on stage, is impossible to miss, given his stereotypical traits and blatant self-abasement. But he goes on to warn of the dangers we face when parasitism and flattery become hard to detect, when the flattered takes on the standard features of civilised elite behaviour, hiding his nefarious purposes behind him: 'Whom, then, do we need to guard against? . . . He is usually sober, he is busy, and he thinks it necessary to get involved in everything, and wants to be in on all the secrets, and plays the part of friendship seriously, like a tragic actor, not a satyric or comic one'" (Jason König, "Philosophers and Parasites," in *Saints and Symposiasts*, 243–44).

58. Jonas A. Barish quotes Plato: "The painter's craft thus reduces itself to an effort of slavish mimicry. And the same holds, says Socrates, for the tragic poet, who, like the painter, is an imitator, and hence 'thrice removed from the king and from the truth'" (*The Antitheatrical Prejudice*, 6).

59. See Gullestad, "Parasite." For a brief essay on the evolving political currency of parasitism, see Samyn, "Toward an Anti-Anti-Parasitism."

60. Serres's extraordinary 1982 book, *The Parasite* (which first appeared in French in 1980), offers a framework for thinking through complex systems of power. Serres's treatise is as virtuosic as it is elliptical, and it may be for this reason that its contributions have still not fully been contended with. His elusive philosophy is concerned less with parsing the politics of the parasite, which remains largely opaque in his account, than with unearthing a lively and ambitiously intertextual theory of the parasite. Serres tracks the term's tripartite semantic resonance in the domains of anthropology, biology, and information theory, noting that the French sense of *parasite* means "noise" or "static" (a semantic dimension lost in English). But what the figure yields is ultimately a study of systems.

61. Serres, *The Parasite*, 191, 202.

62. Serres, *The Parasite*, 202.

63. Writes Muñoz: "At times, resistance needs to be pronounced and direct; on other occasions, queers of color and other minority subjects need to follow a conformist path if they hope to survive a hostile public sphere" (*Disidentifications*, 5).

64. Serres, *The Parasite*, 217.

65. Stanford Open Policing Project, "Findings," 2019, https://openpolicing.stanford.edu/findings/. See also: NYCLU, "Stop-and-Frisk Data," 2019, https://www.nyclu.org/en/Stop-and-Frisk-data.

66. It is helpful to bring a sense of the scale of the host system into this discussion, as Nathan M. Martin does in "Parasitic Media." Martin contends that in larger systems, larger tolerances are given for error; in smaller systems, the stan-

dard deviation is already so small (and the monitoring so direct) that it is difficult for a parasite to remain invisible and still be able to function properly. He writes, "An example would be the amount of theft by employees that occur[s] at a small business where the owner is a visible source of monitoring being much lower in most cases than a large corporation where the owner is not present and possibly not known. Retail thefts, like employee thefts, increase with the size of a business. Corporations such as Wal-Mart factor the losses they will see due to theft into their financial planning and cost analysis. Usually if the amount of theft grows relative to the size of the corporation, the level of standard deviation will not increase and no alarm will go off that will force the host to change its behavior." Martin (for the Carbon Defense League), "Parasitic Media."

67. See Hartman, *Scenes of Subjection*; Bhabha, *The Location of Culture*; Scott, *Weapons of the Weak* and *Domination and the Arts of Resistance*.

68. For Riviere, the masquerade of womanliness is "worn as a mask, both to hide the possession of masculinity and to avert the reprisals expected if she was found to possess it" ("Womanliness," 306).

69. Hartman, *Scenes of Subjection*, 8.

70. See Pederson, "Autopoiesis."

71. "This project does not present itself as a solution," explains Rakowitz. "It is not a proposal for affordable housing. Its point of departure is to present a symbolic strategy of survival for homeless existence within the city, amplifying the problematic relationship between those who have homes and those who do not have homes." Quoted in Mike Hanlon, "The paraSITE—An Inflatable Shelter for the Homeless that Runs Off Expelled HVAC Air," *New Atlas*, August 19, 2005, http://newatlas.com/go/4455/.

72. "What does it mean when the tools of a racist patriarchy are used to examine the fruits of that same patriarchy?" asks Lorde. "*It means that only the most narrow perimeters of change are possible and allowable. . . . For the master's tools will never dismantle the master's house.* They may allow us temporarily to beat him at his own game, but they will never enable us to bring about genuine change. And this fact is only threatening to those women who still define the master's house as their only source of support" ("The Master's Tools," 110–11, emphasis mine).

73. See Ouellette, "'Take Responsibility."

74. See Sara Ahmed on the "desire for resistance" as a way of suturing over discussions of racism too quickly, so as to will them to go away ("A Phenomenology," 165). For discussions of the queer, black, and feminist of color politics of refusal and escape, see Hartman, *Scenes of Subjection*; Camp, *Closer to Freedom*; Brooks, *Bodies in Dissent*; Mengesha and Padmanabhan, "Introduction," 1–8; Brewer Ball, "The Only Way Out"; Moten, "Taste Dissonance"; Keeling, *Queer Times*; Campt, "The Visual Frequency."

75. The OED shows that *complice* derives from the Latin *complicō*, which according to the *Oxford Latin Dictionary* means "fold up, bend, tie up, involve, wind, roll, curl up, double up." The entries on both *complice* and *complicity* also

make reference to declensions of *complector*—that is, "embrace, encircle, surround, include, grasp, seize, involve, welcome, take in."

76. The etymology of *complicity* reveals two definitions. The first and most common is that of a moral or legal judgment of indirect culpability ("the being an accomplice"); the second, which is more value-neutral, speaks merely to the fact of being embedded in a given structure, to be folded in or subject to two or more realities that are never fully commensurable (Joseph and Rubin, "Promising Complicities," 436–37).

77. For a critique of the racial and gender politics of interventionist tactics, specifically of the prankster, see Kanouse, "Cooing Over the Golden Phallus."

78. Jagoda, *Network Aesthetics*, 221.

79. See Cheney-Lippold, *We Are Data*.

80. Brunton and Nissenbaum, *Obfuscation*, 55.

81. This issue is illustrated by the term *Anthropocene*, which indiscriminately lumps together every human being under the homogenizing banner *anthropos*. "As the Anthropocene proclaims the language of species life—anthropos—through a universalist geologic commons, it neatly erases histories of racism that were incubated through the regulatory structures of geologic relations," writes Kathryn Yusoff (*A Billion Black Anthropocenes*, 2). Feminist critique has questioned the "we" that subtends this category. Claire Colebrook, for instance, writes, "The Anthropocene has tended to erase the problem of scale. . . . The policy implications of the Anthropocene have tended to suspend the typically feminist questions of this 'we' that we seek to maintain and has instead led to the return to supposed species solidarity. . . . How is it that geological readability (of a specific scale) has become that which defines the human?" ("We Have Always Been Post-Anthropocene," 11). On feminism's special purchase for the historical situation of extreme enmeshment that is the Anthropocene, see Grusin, *Anthropocene Feminism*.

82. Haraway, *Staying with the Trouble*, 1; Tsing, *The Mushroom at the End of the World*, 25; Jagoda, *Network Aesthetics*, 225. In the face of this sense of political impasse, Jagoda proposes "ambivalence" as a strategy of resistance. Forgoing the gratification of oppositional or escapist political models, ambivalence "is not a variety of opting out. If anything, it suggests a process of opting in completely. Going all in, however, need not be reduced to naïve complicity or the hyperbolic extremism of strategies such as accelerationism. . . . Ambivalence[, rather,] is a process of slowing down and learning to inhabit a compromised environment."

83. Shotwell, *Against Purity*, 204.

84. This book investigates not utopian or pessimistic narratives of resistance imagined as escaping or irreducible to economic or semiotic formalization but the pragmatic and temporal conditions of resistance immanent to the system. In this it follows Eugenie Brinkema's critique of affect theory's tendency to see excessive affects as inherently salvific, subversive, or resistive. Brinkema, *The Form*.

85. "These projects are not oriented toward the grand, sweeping revolutionary

event," writes Rita Raley, "rather, they engage in a micropolitics of disruption, intervention, and education." Tactical media "are more interested in repurposing, modifying, and disrupting than they are in remaining invisible" (*Tactical Media*, 1, 14).

86. Sedgwick, "Paranoid Reading."

INTERLUDE. THRESHOLDS OF ACCOMMODATION

1. Explains Ellison's narrator, "I learned in time though that it is possible to carry on a fight against them without their realizing it. For instance, I have been carrying on a fight with Monopolated Light & Power for some time now. I use their service and pay them nothing at all, and they don't know it. Oh, they suspect their power is being drained off, but they don't know where. All they know is that according to the master meter back there in their power station a hell of a lot of free current is disappearing somewhere into the jungle of Harlem. Several years ago (before I discovered the advantages of being invisible) I went through the routine process of buying service and paying their outrageous rates. . . . That was based upon the fallacious assumption that I, like other men, was visible. Now, aware of my invisibility, I live rent-free in a building rented strictly to whites, in a section of the basement that was shut off and forgotten during the nineteenth century" (*Invisible Man*, 5–6).

2. Spillers, "Peter's Pans," 5.

3. Ellison, *Invisible Man*, 14. See Malik Gaines's discussion of Spillers on Ellison's *Invisible Man* in his theorization of Nina Simone's transfiguration of alienated marginality into a radical position of black subjectivity (*Black Performance*, 39–40). For more recent discussions of the retooling of tropes of darkness and opacity in black radical practice, see also Moten, *Black and Blur*; Keeling, *Queer Times*; Nyong'o, *Afro-Fabulations*; and Musser, *Sensual Excess*.

4. Harney and Moten, *The Undercommons*, 26.

5. Browne, *Dark Matters*. For discussions of "infrastructural whiteness" and state biometric capture systems' disproportionate failure to read women, people of color, and people with disabilities, see Pugliese, "The Biometrics of Infrastructural Whiteness," in *Biometrics*; and Magnet, *When Biometrics Fail*.

6. McGlotten observes that for black and brown subjects, for whom the threat of surveillance is often most severe, performative tactics of evasion are often least available. "Techniques of refusal, such as anonymous massification vis-à-vis masks, are unevenly available. There are some for whom flight may not be possible and/or for whom it may be forced. For example, becoming clandestine or deserting are not really options for populations already subject to spatialized forms of control." The predominantly black and Latino neighborhoods in which the New York Police program Stop-and-Frisk almost entirely operates, McGlotten writes, are "contexts in which people yearn to escape police harassment and violence but where efforts to evade surveillance or to contest it only result in heightened forms of scrutiny" ("Black Data," 273).

7. In 2018, in only the span of several weeks, there were at least a half-dozen incidents widely reported in the mainstream U.S. press when a white person has called the police about a black person for merely existing in certain spaces, including a Starbucks, a Nordstrom Rack, a Yale University dorm, an LA Fitness, a convenience store, an Airbnb, and a golf course. At the same time, in direct contrast, news of Marilyn Hartman, a white woman in her mid-sixties who was arrested after successfully bypassing multiple checkpoints and airport security, boarding planes and successfully stowing away without a ticket or passport, has made headlines. Ray Sanchez, "She Claimed a 9-Year-Old Boy Groped Her. Then She Apologized," *CNN*, October 13, 2018, https://www.cnn.com/2018/10/13/us/new-york-woman-calls-police-black-boy/index.html; Christina Caron, "No Passport or Ticket: How a Woman Evaded Airport Security and Flew to London," *New York Times*, January 22, 2018, https://www.nytimes.com/2018/01/22/us/stowaway-ohare-plane.html. Such events have been memeified on Twitter via the hashtag #LivingWhileBlack. Using data collected from approximately 90,000 tweets that engage with or directly use the hashtag, data scholar Apryl Williams argues that black activist memes constitute a form of resistance to the colonization of space, online and offline, under white supremacy (see Williams, "Black Memes Matter").

8. McNulty, *The Hostess*, viii.

9. The parasite's figuration as an outsider recalls the logic of supplementarity as theorized in Derrida's *Of Grammatology*. The supplement is presented "as exterior, foreign to the 'essential' nature of that to which it is added or in which it is substituted." Yet, as Derrida shows, the supplement is in fact no less essential than the supposedly complete and self-sufficient entity to which it is purportedly attached. See Culler, *On Deconstruction*, 103.

10. Esposito argues that in Nazi propaganda parasitism ceases to be a metaphor of exclusion and becomes literalized: "Certainly the characterization of the Jews as parasites is part of the secular history of anti-Semitism. Nonetheless, such a definition acquires a different valence in the Nazi vocabulary. . . . What to a certain point remained a weighty analogy now actually took form: the Jews didn't *resemble* parasites; they didn't behave *as* bacteria—they *were* bacteria who were to be treated as such" (*Bíos*, 116–17, emphasis in the original).

11. Schlossberg, "Introduction," 2.

12. Lee, *The Exquisite Corpse of Asian America*, 126.

13. McNulty, *The Hostess*, x.

14. Hartman, *Scenes of Subjection*, 89.

15. On the institutional politics of diversity, inclusion, and erasure, see Melamed, *Represent and Destroy*; Ahmed, *On Being Included*; Ferguson, *The Reorder*; Harney and Moten, *The Undercommons*; Hong, *Death beyond Disavowal*; Nash, *Black Feminism*. For the trope of the model minority or racial and ethnic minority endowed with honorary whiteness, see Tuan, *Forever Foreigners or Honorary Whites?*; Kim, "Critical Thoughts."

16. Here we can think of the performance studies scholar Richard Schechner's foundational claim that, in the act of performing, the performer is "not me" and

yet "not not me," or Gregory Bateson's influential articulation of the metacommunicative "as if" double register of play. Theorists of performance and play alike have described the concepts as the "staging of a paradox," by which one's actions during play signal the message "I am hereby placing myself on a different register of existence which nevertheless stands in for its suspended analogue" (Massumi, *What Animals Teach Us about Politics*, 4; Schechner, *Between Theater and Anthropology*, 112). See also Schechner, *Performance Studies*, 92–93.

17. See Michel Feher's public talk, "The Neoliberal Condition."

18. White women are structurally complicit with a system of care in which white men accrue status and power by assigning themselves the role of white women's protectors and defenders, against (and counter to) those nonwhite subjects to whom by the same logic they deny care, justice, and citizenship. Insofar as those who are accommodated under the signs of femininity and whiteness are the beneficiaries (whether they like it or not) of white patriarchal structures of care, both femininity and whiteness function parasitically. For discussions of white women's complicity with white supremacy, see McIntosh, "White Privilege"; Frankenberg, *White Women*; Jones-Rogers, *They Were Her Property*.

19. Wiltz, "Persecuting Black Men," 162. For a discussion of the racial politics of innocence, see Bernstein, *Racial Innocence*.

20. Wilderson, *Red, White, and Black*, 45.

CHAPTER ONE. USER BE USED

1. Olivia LaVecchia and Stacy Mitchell, "Amazon's Stranglehold: How the Company's Tightening Grip Is Stifling Competition, Eroding Jobs, and Threatening Communities," Institute for Local Self-Reliance, November 2016, https://ilsr.org/wp-content/uploads/2016/11/ILSR_AmazonReport_final.pdf, 7.

2. Chun, *Control and Freedom*.

3. Russell, *Open Standards and the Digital Age*, 1–2.

4. Nathan Schneider, "The Meaning of Words," in Scholz and Schneider, *Ours to Hack and to Own*, 14.

5. These are the terms with which Astra Taylor sets up her argument on her book jacket and publicity materials for *The People's Platform*.

6. Taylor, *The People's Platform*, 22.

7. Gillespie, "Politics of Platforms."

8. Srnicek, *Platform Capitalism*, 47.

9. Digital platforms, Gillespie asserts, enjoy an inordinate degree of legal protection as the result of a safe harbor carved out in Section 230 of U.S. telecommunication law. This cover is aptly captured by a common phrase included in their terms and services agreements, stating that they have "the right but not the responsibility" to remove user content ("The Myth of the Neutral Platform," 31; see also 24–44).

10. Walmart increasingly functions like a platform. The company has pioneered a supply chain management model called "vendor-managed inventory,"

which offloads the responsibility of maintaining its inventory onto its suppliers. Some vendors may use the data to stock the shelves in a store, but the exchange remains relatively traditional: Walmart buys a certain quantity of an item and it is responsible for selling that item and for any loss of revenue; the vendor just determines the quantity. However, this can look more like transactions similar to the digital platforms Airbnb and Uber: Walmart does not buy any of the vendor's product but allows them to place the items on its shelves and pays only for the items that sell. The vendor, in this case, remains responsible for the unsold items, and Walmart does not lose any money on these items. I'm grateful to Cengiz Salman for bringing this to my attention.

11. Srnicek, *Platform Capitalism*, 27.

12. Srnicek, "The Long Downturn," in *Platform Capitalism*, 9–35; G. Hall, "The Sharing Economy," in *The Uberfication of the University*, 1–6.

13. G. Hall, *The Uberification of the University*, 4, emphasis in the original.

14. Vaidhyanathan, *The Googlization of Everything*, 1.

15. Vaidhyanathan captures the dynamic by which users are given a false sense of agency: "Our blind faith in Google has allowed the company to claim that it gives users substantial control over how their actions and preferences are collected and used. Google pulls this off by telling the truth: at any time, we may opt out of the system that Google uses to perfect its search engine and its revenue generation. But as long as control over our personal information and profiles is granted at the pleasure of Google and similar companies, such choices mean very little. There is simply no consistency, reciprocity, or accountability in the system. We must constantly monitor fast-changing 'privacy policies.' We must be willing to walk away from a valuable service if its practices cause us concern" (*The Googlization of Everything*, 83–84, emphasis mine).

16. Vaidhyanathan, *The Googlization*, 88–89.

17. Horkheimer and Adorno, *Dialectic of Enlightenment*, 96.

18. Chun, *Control and Freedom*, 28.

19. Hafner and Lyon, *Where Wizards Stay Up Late*, 71.

20. Hafner and Lyon, *Where Wizards Stay Up Late*, 72–73.

21. "A host computer, or simply 'host,' is the ultimate consumer of communication services," reads a blueprint of an early ARPAnet RFC protocol entitled "Requirements for Internet Hosts," which defines the internet as a system of hosts. Galloway, *Protocol*, 38.

22. Though it stands to reason that early protocol could equally be said to be dependent on users to make up the network, a mutuality effaced by the idea that one is host first.

23. Galloway, *Protocol*, 7, 243.

24. J. Brown, *Ethical Programs*, 1.

25. Galloway, *Protocol*, 29.

26. Galloway, *Protocol*, 11.

27. Galloway, *Protocol*, 7.

28. Galloway, *Protocol*, 7–8.

29. Chomsky, "The Death of American Universities," emphasis mine.

30. Scott Keyes, "Walmart Holding Canned Food Drive for Its Own Underpaid Employees," *ThinkProgress*, November 18, 2013, thinkprogress.org/economy/2013/11/18/2960371/walmart-food-drive/.

31. Allison Kilkenny, "Ohio Walmart Holds Food Drive for Its Own Employees," *Nation*, November 18, 2013, https://www.thenation.com/article/ohio-walmart-holds-food-drive-its-own-employees/.

32. Adam Peck, "McDonald's Advice to Underpaid Employees: Sell Your Christmas Presents for Cash," *ThinkProgress*, November 19, 2013, thinkprogress.org/economy/2013/11/19/2970651/mcdonalds-advice-underpaid-employees-sell-christmas-presents-cash/.

33. Clare O'Connor, "'I Have to Choose between Food and Rent': Meet the McDonald's Workers Fighting for Fair Wages," *Forbes*, July 22, 2013, https://www.forbes.com/sites/clareoconnor/2013/07/22/i-have-to-choose-between-food-and-rent-meet-the-mcdonalds-workers-fighting-for-fair-wages/#51a2e1156639.

34. Laura Shin, "Will the McDonald's Employee Budget Help Get the Minimum Wage Raised?," *Forbes*, July 18, 2013, https://www.forbes.com/sites/laurashin/2013/07/18/will-the-mcdonalds-employee-budget-help-get-the-minimum-wage-raised/#bb9d5e964b9, and "Why McDonald's Employee Budget Has Everyone Up in Arms," *Forbes*, July 18, 2013, https://www.forbes.com/sites/laurashin/2013/07/18/why-mcdonalds-employee-budget-has-everyone-up-in-arms/#17d9f7965216.

35. Visa, Practical Money Skills, "About," accessed November 20, 2017, www.practicalmoneyskills.com/about.

36. Visa, Practical Money Skills, "Track Your Spending," http://www.practicalmoneyskills.com:80/mcdconnect/spending/spending.php (link inactive and article currently unavailable), and Practical Money Skills, "Budget Journal," accessed September 24, 2018, http://www.practicalmoneyskills.com:80/mcdonalds/documents/McD_Journal2.pdf (link inactive; accessed through Wayback Machine Internet Archive).

37. Writes David Graeber, "Debt is a very specific thing. It first requires a relationship between two people who do not consider each other fundamentally different sorts of being, who are at least potential equals, who *are* equals in ways that are really important, and who are not currently in a state of equality—but for whom there is some way to set matters straight" (*Debt*, 120).

38. Visa, Practical Money Skills, "Pay Card," accessed November 21, 2017, http://www.practicalmoneyskills.com:80/mcdonalds/paycard/index.php (link inactive; accessed through Wayback Machine Internet Archive). In a class action lawsuit filed in 2013, one employee contended that a northeastern Pennsylvania franchise's requirement that she accept payment via a JP Morgan Chase Payroll Card was in violation of the Wage Payment and Collection Act. "If you don't activate the card, there is no way for us to pay you," her manager allegedly told her. Dan Packel, "Pa. McDonald's Hit with Class Action over Debit Card Wages," *Law360*, June 18, 2013, https://www.law360.com/articles/450950/pa-mcdonald-s-hit-with-class-action-over-debit-card-wages.

39. One consumer finance website noted that while the fees McDonald's employees pay for using the cards are "not publicly available," a similar card "shows charges of 75 cents to check the balance statement and $1.75 for withdrawals, along with a $5-per-month inactivity fee." Chris Cumming, "McDonald's Budget Backlash Hits Visa Payroll Cards," *American Banker*, July 19, 2013, https://www.americanbanker.com/news/mcdonalds-budget-backlash-hits-visa-payroll-cards.

40. Both Visa and McDonald's budget (originally available at the URL www.practicalmoneyskills.com/mcdonalds/index.php) and payroll page (www.practicalmoneyskills.com/mcdonalds/paycard/index.php) now redirect to http://www.practicalmoneyskills.com/errors/.

41. "McResources 'Help' Line," YouTube, October 24, 2013, posted by Fight for 15, https://www.youtube.com/watch?v=olUsgn-Ubho.

42. McDonald's pulled the McResource Line website but chose not to close the phone line, likely a strategic calculation based on the different stakes of accountability attending the two mediums (i.e., the immediacy and publicness of the internet vs. the unfolding temporality and relative privacy associated with the telephone).

43. The original URL for McDonald's statement now redirects to an error message that reads "The page cannot be found." See the original webpage via the Wayback Machine Internet Archive, accessed November 17, 2017.

44. Management of the McResource phone support service is outsourced to Nutur Health, Inc., which advertises the service as a "work-life" help line for employees who want to, as the slogan goes, "Get a little lovin' support" by consulting with "caring professionals" about "life's issues and questions." In a website highlighting the McResource Line, C. Edwards Group, Inc. (an operating company for McDonald's restaurants in western North Carolina) describes the McResource Line in the following way: "Exclusively for McDonald's employees, we CAN provide help FOR many of life's issues and questions." McResource graphic, 2015, accessed November 17, 2017, https://www.cedwardsgroup.com/team/2015-06-04-13-10-36/mcresource-line.html.

45. Lisa Gitelman, "New Media </Body>," in *Always Already New*, 126.

46. As of November 2013, the URL for the "Digging Out of Holiday Debt" was https://mcdonalds.mynurturlife.com/Articles/Item/af026109-6b5e-e211-a253-782bcb32e6a1. The McResource line homepage URL was http://mcdonalds.mynurturlife.com.

47. De Kosnik, *Rogue Archives*, 48.

48. While the Wayback Machine ostensibly promises to record everything that has ever appeared online, Abigail De Kosnik challenges the idea that it "successfully preserves digital culture memory in an automated fashion," because when a page's ownership is turned over, its history is retroactively scrubbed. "The Wayback Machine, though it sometimes proves very useful for the recovery of 'dead' websites, also adheres to policies that cause sites to be erased from its index. . . . rendering it an untrustworthy archive that will likely become more

unreliable as time goes on, as more domain names expire." De Kosnik, *Rogue Archives*, 50.

49. Gitelman, "New Media </Body>," 131, 132.

50. In a *Forbes* puff piece on the error messages linked to Amazon, the tech journalist Zara Stone writes, "It's a cool way to handle customer dissatisfaction, and also promotes Amazon culture as extremely cool, making the company look like an awesome place to work." "The Clever Reason behind Amazon's Puppy Filled Error 404 Pages," *Forbes*, May 2, 2017, https://www.forbes.com/sites/zarastone/2017/05/02/amazons-404-error-pages-are-pup-licious/#bba978182904. See also Day One Staff, "How Much Does Amazon Love Dogs? Just Ask One of the 6,000 Pups That 'Work' Here," *Amazon Blog*, January 25, 2018, https://blog.aboutamazon.com/working-at-amazon/how-much-does-amazon-love-dogs-just-ask-one-of-the-6-000-pups-that-work-here.

51. Ngai, *Our Aesthetic Categories*, 22.

52. Ouellette, "Citizen Brand," 59, 61.

53. Milton Friedman, "The Social Responsibility of Business Is to Increase Its Profits," *New York Times*, September 13, 1970, 32, cited in Ouellette, "Citizen Brand," 62.

54. Vogel, *The Market for Virtue*, quoted in Ouellette, "Citizen Brand," 62, emphasis mine.

55. Ouellette argues that to decry corporate responsibility as an evil ploy is to miss the fact that it is internal to a larger structure of consumer-market relations, wherein consumers want to feel good about the products they buy.

56. According to a 2013 report by the progressive coalition Americans for Tax Fairness, Walmart's low-wage workers received an estimated $6.2 billion in public assistance. Walmart itself has claimed that its employees make up 18 percent of the food stamp market, accounting for $13.5 billion of the $76 billion of total food stamp sales in 2013. Clare O'Connor, "Report: Walmart Workers Cost Taxpayers $6.2 Billion in Public Assistance," *Forbes*, April 15, 2014, https://www.forbes.com/sites/clareoconnor/2014/04/15/report-walmart-workers-cost-taxpayers-6-2-billion-in-public-assistance/#7913f82e720b. U.S. taxpayers are said to contribute $7 billion a year in annual public assistance to fast-food workers and their families, according to a report by the economist Sylvia Allegretto and others, drawing on publicly available data by UC Berkeley and the University of Illinois at Urbana-Champaign. A second study based on this study found that McDonald's workers received the most public assistance of all of these, at $1.2 billion per year from 2007 to 2011. Susan Berfield, "Fast-Food Wages Come with a $7 Billion Side of Public Assistance," *Bloomberg Businessweek*, October 16, 2013, https://www.bloomberg.com/news/articles/2013-10-15/fast-food-wages-come-with-a-7-billion-side-of-public-assistance.

57. The words *parasite* and *host* intertwine in their etymology, both containing the other's reciprocal, antithetical meaning in it. The Latin *hostis* designates both host and guest, just as *para* indexes, as J. Hillis Miller observes, "the boundary line, threshold, or margin, and at the same time beyond it . . . at once a per-

meable membrane connecting inside and outside [and] confusing them" ("The Critic as Host," 441). Derrida wrote extensively of hospitality's deconstructive logic as a concept that always contains itself within its other: "Hospitality . . . presupposes waiting, the horizon of awaiting and the preparation of welcoming. . . . On the other hand, the opposite is also nevertheless true. . . . To be hospitable is to *let oneself be overtaken*" ("Hostipitality," 361).

58. David McNally, "The Commodity Status of Labour: The Secret of Commodified Life," in *Not for Sale: Decommodifying Public Life*, ed. Gordon Laxer and Dennis Soron (Peterborough, Canada: Broadview Press, 2006), 44.

59. Jon Keegan, "Blue Feed, Red Feed: See Liberal Facebook and Conservative Facebook, Side by Side," *Wall Street Journal*, last updated August 19, 2019, graphics.wsj.com/blue-feed-red-feed/.

60. Eva Feder Kittay and Ellen K. Feder, introduction to *The Subject of Care*, 4. See Fraser and Gordon, "A Genealogy of *Dependency*."

61. Alleging that some are cheating the system is a divisive ploy that politicians use in election years. Figuring prominently in fundraising speeches, the populist myth of mass dependency was leveraged in repeated sound bites during the 2012 U.S. presidential election by Paul Ryan, who stated that "more Americans are 'Takers' than 'Makers'" while campaigning for his plan to replace Medicare with a voucher system, and Mitt Romney's so-called gaffe in being secretly recorded at a $50k-a-plate private fundraiser confiding to donors that half of Americans are "dependent on government," believe they're "victims," and are "entitled to healthcare, to food, to housing, to you name it." *Welfare queen* was introduced by Reagan during his 1976 presidential campaign stump speeches. With the ascent of right-wing extremism in the United States with the election of Trump in 2016 (as well as in European mainstream politics), the white supremacist logic implicit in this rhetoric was made explicit when the white nationalist Richard Spencer claimed in a 2016 speech at an Alt Right conference at D.C.'s Ronald Reagan Building, "We build. We produce. We go upward. And we recognize the central lie of American race relations. We don't exploit other groups. We don't gain anything from their presence. They need us and not the other way around." "'Hail Trump!' Richard Spencer Speech Excerpts," YouTube, November 21, 2016, posted by *Atlantic*, https://www.youtube.com/watch?v=106-bi3jlxk.

62. Josh Levin, "The Welfare Queen," *Slate*, December 19, 2013, http://www.slate.com/articles/news_and_politics/history/2013/12/linda_taylor_welfare_queen_ronald_reagan_made_her_a_notorious_american_villain.html. For more on the transformation of social parasitism in U.S. political discourse, see Gustafson, *Cheating Welfare*.

63. The neoconservative rhetoric of parasitism works by isolating individual actors for denigration. In *Where We Stand: Class Matters*, bell hooks writes, "Many greedy upper- and middle-class citizens share with their wealthy counterparts a hatred and disdain for the poor that is so intense it borders on pathological hysteria. It has served their class interests to perpetuate the notion that the poor are mere parasites and predators. And, of course, their greed has set up

a situation where many people must act in a parasitic manner in order to meet basic needs—the need for food, clothing, and shelter" (45).

64. David A. Graham, "'Insult to Homicide': Cleveland Sues Tamir Rice's Family for Ambulance Fees," *Nation*, February 11, 2016, http://www.theatlantic.com/national/archive/2016/02/cleveland-tamir-rice-bill/462354/.

65. As the journalist David A. Graham notes, despite the city's apology to the Rice family, the logic of this claim follows the city's victim-blaming discourse in the aftermath of Rice's death: "Yet this is not even the first moment the city has done such a thing. In March, [Mayor Frank] Jackson apologized for language that Cleveland had used in a brief that blamed Rice for causing his own death by 'failure . . . to exercise due care to avoid injury.'" Graham, "'Insult to Homicide'"; Kashmira Gander, "University 'Charges Students Hundreds of Dollars' to Clean Up Mattresses from Emma Sulkowicz Anti–Sexual Assault Solidarity Protest," *Independent*, November 13, 2014, www.independent.co.uk/news/world/americas/university-charges-students-hundreds-of-dollars-to-clean-up-mattresses-from-emma-sulkowicz-anti-9859916.html; Ben Mathis-Lilley, "Flint Sends Overdue Notices to Residents Who Aren't Paying for Their Water, Which Is Poison," *Slate*, January 13, 2016, http://www.slate.com/blogs/the_slatest/2016/01/13/flint_sends_overdue_notices_for_water_payments.html.

66. Wang, *Carceral Capitalism*, 16–17, 18.

67. Quoted in Daniel Denvir, "Criminalizing the Hustle: Policing Poor People's Survival Strategies from Eric Garner to Alton Sterling," *Salon*, July 8, 2016, www.salon.com/2016/07/08/criminalizing_the_hustle_policing_poor_peoples_survival_strategies_from_erin_garner_to_alton_sterling/. See also Spence, *Knocking the Hustle*.

68. Puar, "Regimes of Surveillance."

69. "User Unfriendly" was the name of Ubermorgen's first gallery exhibition.

70. Trebor Scholz, "How Platform Cooperativism Can Unleash the Network," in Scholz and Schneider, *Ours to Hack and to Own*, 20–26.

71. Robin Hood Cooperative has received scholarly attention in the fields of Marxist theory and media theory. Representative works include Berardi and Virtanen, "From Arbitrary Power"; Piironen and Virtanen, "Democratizing the Power of Finance"; Terranova, "About the Robin Hood Asset Management Cooperative"; Virtanen, Nelms, and Maurer, "Is It Art?"; Virtanen, "Robin Hood Collective."

72. Quoted in Terranova, "About."

73. Bill Maurer makes this observation in Virtanen, Nelms, and Maurer, "Is It Art?"

74. Virtanen, Nelms, and Maurer, "Is It Art?"

75. The group did not respond to an email I sent requesting more information about what projects they support and what percentage of their total profits is apportioned to those projects.

76. Terranova, "About the Robin Hood Asset Management Cooperative."

77. Terranova, "About the Robin Hood Asset Management Cooperative."

78. Brett Scott, "The Activist Hedge Fund," *Heretic's Guide to Global Finance:*

Hacking the Future of Money, October 2, 2016, suitpossum.blogspot.com/2016/10/the-activist-hedge-fund.html.

79. The Detroit Community Technology Project (detroitcommunitytech.org), based in highly segregated and predominantly Latino and African American neighborhoods in Detroit, runs a web access network for locals to decide how they will use their local area connections and monitor equitable bandwidth usage among themselves. Cooperation Jackson (cooperationjackson.org), a project based in Jackson, Mississippi, aims to build a regenerative economy by growing and selling food, running a construction coop, and offering cooperative housing. The grassroots movement works in collaboration with a global network of cooperatives to resist the acceleration of technological development and automation that has turned the Black working class into a disposable population. Precarity Lab, *Technoprecarious.*

80. Hans Bernhard and Lizvlx with Alessandro Ludovico and Paolo Cirio, "Hack the Google self.referentialism: Google Will Eat Itself," press release, December 18, 2005, www.gwei.org/pages/press/press/Press_Releases/pressrelease_art_12122005.html.

81. The original Practical Money Skills page linked to http://www.practicalmoneyskills.com:80/mcdonalds/resources/resources.php (no longer active).

82. Lori Andrews, "Facebook Is Using You," *New York Times*, February 4, 2012, www.nytimes.com/2012/02/05/opinion/sunday/facebook-is-using-you.html?pagewanted=all.

CHAPTER TWO. AN OPENING IN THE STRUCTURE

1. See Inda's "Foreign Bodies." My thanks to William Calvo-Quirós for bringing this work to my attention. See also Rosello's *Postcolonial Hospitality* for a treatment of this question in the context of France and its former colonies in North and sub-Saharan Africa.

2. Josh Levin, "The Welfare Queen," *Slate*, December 19, 2013, http://www.slate.com/articles/news_and_politics/history/2013/12/linda_taylor_welfare_queen_ronald_reagan_made_her_a_notorious_american_villain.html. For more on the transformation of social parasitism in U.S. political discourse, see Gustafson, *Cheating Welfare*.

3. The Department of Homeland Security website's "About" section reads, "The Department of Homeland Security has a vital mission: to secure the nation from the many threats we face. This requires the dedication of more than 240,000 employees in jobs that range from aviation and border security to emergency response, from cybersecurity analyst to chemical facility inspector. Our duties are wide-ranging, and our goal is clear—keeping America safe." "About DHS," Department of Homeland Security, accessed August 21, 2018, https://www.dhs.gov/about-dhs.

4. "[It creates] a warm first impression, and first impressions are important," Undersecretary for Public Diplomacy and Public Affairs and former Bush advi-

sor Karen Hughes has said of the video. Karen Hughes, "Disney Video Launch 'Welcome—Portraits of America,'" *DipNote: U.S. Department of State Official Blog*, October 26, 2007, accessed through Wayback Machine Internet Archive; Condoleezza Rice and Michael Chertoff, "Rice-Chertoff Joint Vision: Secure Borders and Open Doors in the Information Age," U.S. Department of State Archive, January 17, 2006, https://2001-2009.state.gov/r/pa/prs/ps/2006/59242.htm; *Welcome: Portraits of America*, YouTube, posted by U.S. Embassy Kuala Lumpur, September 26, 2011, https://www.youtube.com/watch?v=UmFlS2SNt_M; Walt Disney Corporation, "2008 Corporate Social Responsibility Report," accessed September 25, 2018, accessed through Wayback Machine Internet Archive.

5. Magnet, *When Biometrics Fail*, 5.

6. Chun, *Control and Freedom*, vii.

7. Scott McCartney, "Shopping for a Rolling Pin, Scissors or a Bat? This Auction Is for You," *Wall Street Journal*, July 16, 2012, www.wsj.com/articles/SB10001424052702304373804577521210993059828.

8. Mike Brunker, "How TSA's Big 'Bet' to Sell Travelers on PreCheck Program Fell Short," *NBC News*, May 21, 2016, www.nbcnews.com/news/us-news/how-tsa-s-big-bet-sell-travelers-precheck-program-fell-n577631.

9. Lisa Lerer, "What's Next in Airport Security? Advertising," *Forbes*, January 10, 2007, www.forbes.com/2007/01/10/securitypoint-rolodex-advertising-tech-security_cx_ll_0110tsa.html.

10. "The program is a good example of a public-private partnership that saves taxpayer dollars," a TSA spokesman said, claiming that the program came "at no cost to taxpayers" (a refrain invoked in descriptions of the Disney–Department of Homeland Security partnership as well). Bob Greene, "The Airport Ads You Can't Miss," CNN, January 16, 2011, www.cnn.com/2011/OPINION/01/16/greene.air.security.ads/. See also Thomas Frank, "TSA Allows Ads in Bins across U.S.," *ABC News*, November 4, 2008, https://abcnews.go.com/Travel/story?id=6175777.

11. See Seth Freed Wessler, "Call Centers: Returning to Mexico but Sounding 'American,'" *Aljazeera America*, March 16, 2014, america.aljazeera.com/features/2014/3/mexico-s-call-centers.html. See also Glass and Wessler, "520."

12. Neal Colgrass, "Many Call Center Workers Are Deported Mexicans," *Newser*, August 22, 2014, www.newser.com/story/192834/many-call-center-workers-are-deported-mexicans.html.

13. Ana Gonzalez-Barrera and Jens Manuel Krogstad, "U.S. Deportations of Immigrants Reach Record High in 2013," *Pew Research Center*, October 2, 2014, http://www.pewresearch.org/fact-tank/2014/10/02/u-s-deportations-of-immigrants-reach-record-high-in-2013/; Walter A. Ewing, "The Growth of the U.S. Deportation Machine," *American Immigration Council*, March 1, 2014, https://www.americanimmigrationcouncil.org/research/growth-us-deportation-machine. According to figures from the first year of the Trump administration, despite Trump's pledging to make deportations a signature of his presidency, Immigration and Customs Enforcement (ICE) has deported fewer immigrants during the period than under Obama. However, the reasons may be more bureau-

cratic than representative of will. Anti-immigrant sentiment is at a high, with arrests showing significant spikes of "non-criminal immigration violators," suggesting that ICE no longer follows the same pattern. "ICE has taken the gloves off, and they are going after whoever they want and for whatever reason," observes Ray Ybarra Maldonado, an immigration attorney in Phoenix. "It's a free-for-all now." Quoted in Nick Miroff, "Deportations Fall under President Trump Despite Increase in Arrests by ICE," *Chicago Tribune*, September 28, 2017, https://www.chicagotribune.com/nation-world/ct-trump-deportations-20170928-story.html.

14. "U.S. Government Partners with Disney to Welcome International Visitors," *BusinessWire*, October 22, 2007, https://www.businesswire.com/news/home/20071022006072/en/U.S.-Government-Partners-Disney-International-Visitors.

15. Fiskesjö, *The Thanksgiving.*

16. Sesé, "La Creadora." Representative scholarly work in contemporary art criticism on Güell (mostly published in Spanish) includes the following: Finkelpearl, "Education Art"; Garbayo-Maeztu, "Maternidad"; Mekdjian, "Urban Artivism"; Pardo and Ferruz, "Dispositives of Precariousness"; Queiroz, "Excavating, Walking, Working"; Rovira, "There Was Earth in Them."

17. See Max Andrews, "Critics' Guide: Barcelona," *Frieze*, June 30, 2016, https://frieze.com/article/critics-guide-barcelona.

18. See Güell, *Apátrida por voluntad propia*.

19. This appears as a handwritten annotation, presumably a clarification from Güell to her attorney, on the attorney's report. Advocada: Illustre collegi d'advocats de Barcelona, "Legal Report on the Status of Stateless," February 27, 2015, http://www.nuriaguell.net/projects/38/legal_report_1_eng.pdf.

20. Hannah Arendt explores the question of "the right to have rights" in "The Perplexities of the Rights of Man," in *The Origins of Totalitarianism*, 369–84.

21. Güell, *Apátrida*, emphasis mine.

22. Autonomic acquisition "refer[s] to acquisition by natural descent, by birth on Spanish territory or by adoption," as provided for in Articles 17.1 and 19.1 (Advocada, "Legal Report," 6).

23. Kenneth Pietrobono, email to author, June 25, 2019.

24. Kenneth Pietrobono, email to author, June 25, 2019.

25. Spivak, *Outside in the Teaching Machine*, 44.

26. In his 1977 study of red tape, Herbert Kaufman writes, "When people rail against red tape, they mean that they are subjected to too many constraints, that many of the constraints seem pointless, and that agencies seem to take forever to act." *Red Tape*, 1, quoted in Bozeman, "A Theory of Government 'Red Tape,'" 274–75.

27. Bozeman, "A Theory of Government 'Red Tape,'" 273–76.

28. Pasquale, *The Black Box Society*, 2, 3.

29. See Field, "A Taxonomy for Tax Loopholes," 553 (emphasis mine).

30. Butler, *Gender Trouble*, 93.

31. The meaning of the loophole is bound to the conditions of one's subjugation to the law and its enforcement. In *Incidents in the Life of a Slave Girl, Writ-*

ten by Herself, Harriet Jacobs/Linda Brent tells of the seven years she spent hiding from her enslaver in her "loophole of retreat," the cramped garret in the roof of her grandmother's home. Jacobs/Brent's loophole speaks to the form of escape opened up not by access to an outside but by locating a blind spot within that is not detected by the surveillance of those who would seek her capture. The loophole of retreat is, Simone Browne asserts, "a space of debilitating freedom," at once a prison and a refuge (*Dark Matters*, 171, 22).

32. The Spanish version of the winning letter is available on Güell's website, along with the other entries ("Epistolario," accessed July 17, 2017, http://www.nuriaguell.net/projects/10/Epistolario.pdf).

33. "Humanitarian Aid," YouTube, December 27, 2013, posted by Núria Güell, https://youtu.be/ovofou8wnBs.

34. The Spanish version of her artist's statement is on her website: "Los principales recursos que utiliza son el coqueteo con los poderes establecidos, la complicidad con diferentes aliados y el uso de los privilegios que tienen las instituciones artísticas con las que trabaja, así como los que le son otorgados socialmente por su condición de española y europea" ("Statement," accessed July 17, 2017, http://www.nuriaguell.net/).

35. Barish, *The Antitheatrical Prejudice*, 42.

36. Yordanis Martinez, "Ayuda Humanitaria," Soundcloud, 2012, https://soundcloud.com/ayuda-humanitaria/tracks; "Núria Güell," Immigrant Movement International, accessed June 15, 2019, http://immigrant-movement.us/wordpress/nuria-guell/.

37. Unless otherwise attributed, all quotes by Pietrobono are from my interview with the artist, July 10, 2017, via Skype.

38. Pietrobono explains, "An original idea if I recall was to take the plot I worked with, calculate the percentage of their property it was and then invoice that percentage of their overall property tax into the project (to me basically). I do recall there being a long discussion over this idea of extracting a kind of 'livelihood' from property of others (which is designed to exclude and force others to labor for sustenance). So a hack essentially. There was a long dialogue with the lawyer who informed me that in Vermont there is actually a minimum plot size under the law (again, would need to do work to cite) and that the space I was planning to dig was much smaller than that minimum so actually being able to survey that spot and register it in any way would not have been possible (from what I understand)." Kenneth Pietrobono, email to author, June 25, 2019.

39. Kenneth Pietrobono, email to author, June 25, 2019.

40. Van Haaften-Schick, "Art," 32.

41. This essential paradox of ownership, which Derrida termed the "aporia of hospitality," is built into hospitality, an ethical ideal that for Derrida is coextensive with Western religious and philosophical thought. See Derrida and Dufourmantelle, *Of Hospitality*.

42. Irina Aristarkhova writes, "How can one give away what one owns if one wants to continue to be hospitable, to give away?" (*Hospitality of the Matrix*, 36).

43. Kenneth Pietrobono, email to author, July 6, 2019.

44. Pietrobono has begun to receive serious critical attention in contemporary art history and performance studies. Representative scholarly attention to his work is Chambers-Letson and Pietrobono, "North American Field Guide"; van Haaften-Schick, "Art after Property."

45. Chambers-Letson, "North American Field Guide," 14.

46. Elena Sheppard, "Artist Interview: Kenneth Pietrobono Searches for Answers to the Big Questions of the Millennial Generation," *Hype*, September 19, 2012, https://mic.com/articles/15058/artist-interview-kenneth-pietrobono-searches-for-answers-to-the-big-questions-of-the-millennial-generation#.rt1aRBJ6e.

47. In 2016 Pietrobono began to make the T-shirts available for purchase on his website as part of a new phase of the project *Terms and Conditions (On Wanting)*. The artist makes no profit, selling the shirts for $45 each, the price he pays to make them. As of July 2019 he had sold only two, both to the artist Jenny Holzer ("Self-Work" and "Self-Interest").

48. The Stream Festival reflects a bustling contemporary art corridor between New York City and southern Vermont. With themes that include meditations on helplessness and reconsiderations of the term *Anthropocene*, it has featured works by Harun Farocki and Andrea Fraser.

49. Kenneth Pietrobono, email to author, June 12, 2019.

50. Karl Marx, "The Historical Tendency of Capitalist Accumulation," in *Capital*, 927–28.

51. Saidiya V. Hartman, "The Burdened Individuality of Freedom," in *Scenes of Subjection*, 115–16.

52. Kenneth Pietrobono, "The Opposite of Property: Sample Text—In Progress," 2017, kennethpietrobono.com/artwork/4196516-The-Opposite-of-Property-Sample-Text-In-Progress.html.

53. Occupy Museums is the work of a group of artists committed to making art and cultural institutions accountable for economic and social injustice. For more on the group, see their website, http://www.occupymuseums.org/.

54. This idea is explicated in the contribution by Güell's collaborator Qmunty, "The Mandrake Mechanism," in Güell, *How to Expropriate*, 5–14.

55. Enric Duran, "Manual: Step by Step," in Güell, *How to Expropriate*, 15–30; Lucio Urtubia, "I Don't Believe in Nothing, but I Believe in Everything," in Güell, *How to Expropriate*, 53–62.

56. Marie Trigona, "Lucio, the Good Bandit: Reflections of an Anarchist," *Upside Down World*, July 22, 2008, upsidedownworld.org/archives/argentina/lucio-the-good-bandit-reflections-of-an-anarchist/.

57. Duran announced his actions in an online article titled "I Have 'Robbed' 492,000 Euros from Those Who Rob Us the Most, in order to Denounce Them and Build Alternatives for Society" (English translation) and an online video that was also published in the free magazine *Crisis*, in Catalan, with 200,000

printed copies distributed by volunteers throughout Catalonia. The English translation of the article is available on Duran's website, accessed July 1, 2019, http://enricduran.cat/en/i-have-robbed-492000-euros-whom-most-rob-us-order-denounce-them-and-build-some-alternatives-society-0/. The video was accessed July 1, 2019 at http://okupemlesones.blip.tv/file/1280692/ (link inactive; not accessible via the Wayback Machine Internet Archive).

58. Duran, "I Have 'Robbed.'"

59. N. Schneider, *Everything for Everyone*, 116–17; see 115–32. See also Enric Duran, "FairCoop," in Scholz and Schneider, *Ours to Hackand to Own*, 82.

60. Feher, "Self-Appreciation; or, The Aspirations of Human Capital," 22; see 21–41.

61. Feher, "Self-Appreciation," 21.

62. Duran, "I Have 'Robbed.'" See also Strike Debt, "The Debt Resisters' Operations Manual," strikedebt.org.

63. Foucault, *Discipline and Punish*, 292.

CHAPTER THREE. HANGERS-ON

1. "As it transpired, she was 20 years early. Her first novel was so far ahead of its time that only now does its star seem to be approaching its apex, two decades after it was first published." Elle Hunt, "Chris Kraus: *I Love Dick* Was Written 'in a Delirium,'" *Guardian*, May 29, 2017, https://www.theguardian.com/books/2017/may/30/chris-kraus-i-love-dick-was-written-in-a-delirium. See also Elaine Blair, "Chris Kraus, Female Antihero," *New Yorker*, November 21, 2016, https://www.newyorker.com/magazine/2016/11/21/chris-kraus-female-antihero.

2. Kraus, *I Love Dick* (2006), 263.

3. Rimanelli, "I Love Dick," S7.

4. Dick, described in the book as "an English cultural critic who's recently relocated . . . to Los Angeles," was identified as Dick Hebdige (who at the time had recently accepted a position at CalArts) in a 1997 article in *New York Magazine*. The piece included an interview with Hebdige, his only known public statements about the book. Nic Zembla, "See Dick Sue," *New York Magazine*, November 17, 1997, 20.

5. Kraus, *I Love Dick* (1997), 143. Unless otherwise noted, all citations are to the 1997 edition.

6. Scholars of the epistolary genre note that the personal or "familiar" letter was first thought of as a literary form in the sixteenth century, with male commentators saying that the genre seemed "particularly suited to the female voice." Cherewatuk and Wiethaus, introduction to *Dear Sister*, 1.

7. Tracey Emin's "drawings of naked women on their hands and knees" depict what Jennifer Doyle describes as "ordinary, exhilarating, and humiliating aspects of living in a sexual body" ("narratives of abuse, unwanted pregnancy, sexual conquest, and humiliation"). Doyle has written extensively about the "inti-

macy of Emin's work—its materialization of [the artist's supposed] physical and emotional availability [to the viewer]," which Doyle has characterized as mobilizing the address of the love letter (*Sex Objects*, xxvii, 107, 114).

8. Butler, "Collected and Fractured," 441–42.

9. Rimanelli, "I Love Dick," S7.

10. Gumport, "Female Trouble," ellipsis and emendation in the original.

11. Angela McRobbie, "Settling Accounts with Subcultures: A Feminist Critique," in *Feminism*, 25.

12. S. Hall, "Cultural Studies and Its Theoretical Legacies," 282.

13. See Brunsdon, "A Thief"; Probyn, "A Feminist Love Letter."

14. S. Hall, "Cultural Studies," 282–83. My thanks to Kim Greenwell for pointing me to this passage.

15. Kraus's decision to single out Dick Hebdige for condemnation is comparable (if also different in significant ways) to various women's decisions to publicly expose famous men for their mistreatment of women, which have drawn bitter and widespread debate from all corners of the internet in the wake of the Me Too movement. In a blog post entitled "Not That Bad" responding to a January 2018 anonymous op-ed that publicly named the actor Aziz Ansari as at worst a sexual assault offender and at best a callous lover, Katie Anthony writes, "As a woman, I am supposed to take what's given to me, to shrink my pain, ignore my bad feelings about what just happened, and generally be FINE WITH EVERYTHING!" Katie Anthony, "Not That Bad," KatyKatiKate.com, January 15, 2018, https://www.katykatikate.com/the-blog//2018/01/not-that-bad_15.html?rq=Not%20That%20Bad.

16. Beauvoir, *The Second Sex* (1993), 695.

17. Shelden, *Young Titan*, 175–77.

18. Musser, *Sensational Flesh*, 59, 77.

19. "When *I Love Dick* was published in 1997," writes Kraus in "The New Universal," "mid-way through the first iteration of Native Agents, it was more ridiculed than praised: 'a book not so much written as secreted' (*Artforum*); 'a stream of fawning love letters so intrusive they amount to epistolary stalking' (*New York Magazine*), etcetera. What people reacted against most strongly was the idea that the 'privacy' of the recipient—who remained unnamed in the book—would be violated."

20. See Fisher, "Parasitical Politics" and "Manic Impositions."

21. Kraus herself has attributed the new reception to a "huge shift among younger women in the last half-decade" as they have championed feminist representations, abetted by internet culture's transformation of notions like privacy and professionalism, that are more confessional, amateur, and performative in character (Kraus, "The New Universal").

22. Marketed as a "cerebral comedy-drama," the show stars Kevin Bacon as Dick and Kathryn Hahn as Chris. LA and New York's poststructural academic and art worlds are displaced onto the bohemian Marfa, Texas, art scene. Created by Jill Soloway and Sarah Gubbins, it was canceled in January 2018 after one season.

23. Browning, "I'm Trying to Reach You." I thank her for sharing the text with me.

24. Kraus, *I Love Dick*, 11.

25. Kraus, *I Love Dick* (2006), 172.

26. Browning, "The Performative Novel," 49.

27. Schechner, *Between Theater and Anthropology*, 112.

28. Kraus, *I Love Dick*, 217.

29. R. Schneider, *The Explicit Body in Performance*, 2, 114–17.

30. Barbara Browning writes, "But one could also posit that the way was paved for such 'oversharing' storytelling strategies in the world of performance—and specifically in the work of performance artists who rose to prominence in the '80s. Before the advent of the blog, in live performance venues, monologists like Spalding Gray and Karen Finley were already radically shifting our notions of appropriateness in terms of both self-exposure and narrative technique. (And it's worth pointing out that before she achieved notoriety as a writer, Chris Kraus was herself a part of that scene: Eileen Myles recalls Kraus staging a 'quasi-strip-theory performance' at the Poetry Project in those heady days, and another in which Kraus and her then-lover narrated from offstage the slow collapse of their relationship)" ("The Performative Novel," 49).

31. Kraus, *I Love Dick*, 16–17, 23, 98.

32. Derrida, *The Post Card*, 9.

33. Kraus, *I Love Dick*, 17, 26, 273.

34. See Rubin, "The Traffic in Women."

35. Amelia Gentleman, "The Worse the Break-up, the Better the Art," *Guardian*, December 13, 2004, https://www.theguardian.com/artanddesign/2004/dec/13/art.art.

36. Calle, *Take Care of Yourself*, n.p.

37. Calle, *Take Care of Yourself*, n.p.

38. In the book version of *Take Care of Yourself*, the breakup email is signed *G*. Calle has said that in order to protect his identity, she replaced the name with an *X* when she circulated the letter to her readers.

39. I thank Clara Lipfert for sharing with me her insights into this online feminist culture (email, January 6, 2014). Calloway's debut novel *what purpose did I serve in your life* (2013) distinctly parallels *I Love Dick* (Jesella, "What Purpose").

40. Irigaray, *Elemental Passions*, 27.

41. "This man isn't spared. But *Prenez soin de vous* [*Take Care of Yourself*] replies to the email rather than the man. The book, incidentally, ends with these words: 'This was about a letter. Not a man'" (Calle and Desplechin, "*Take Care of Yourself*, Venice and Writing," 132).

42. Kraus, *I Love Dick* (2006), 267.

43. Calle, "He Loves Me Not."

44. This is not the only one of Calle's works that begins with the artist making a copy of a man's book. For what was to become *Double Game/The Gotham Handbook*, Calle xeroxed pages from Paul Auster's novel *Leviathan*, in which the author based his character Maria on Calle. Calle then used a red pen to highlight

those passages that relate to her work and to annotate points where Auster's fiction departed from her practice.

45. Bois, "Character Study."

46. Bois, "Character Study," 129.

47. Bois, "Character Study," 129.

48. O'Neill-Butler, "The Savage Detective."

49. Stuart Jeffries, "Sophie Calle: Stalker, Stripper, Sleeper, Spy," *Guardian*, September 23, 2009, https://www.theguardian.com/artanddesign/2009/sep/23/sophie-calle.

50. Bois, "Character Study," 130.

51. Quoted in O'Neill-Butler, "The Savage Detective."

52. Barthes, *A Lover's Discourse*, 31.

53. Rimanelli, "I Love Dick," S7. In 1997 *New York Magazine* reported that Kraus responded to Hebdige's threat to sue her by "dropping the character's last name and placing him at a different school" (Zembla, "See Dick Sue," 20). "I would love to make a project about being sued," Calle has said, adding that she has almost been sued on two separate occasions (public interview).

54. Gumport, "Female Trouble."

55. Hunt, "Chris Kraus."

56. Zembla, "See Dick Sue," 20.

57. Deleuze and Guattari, *Kafka*, 9, 29.

58. Walter Benjamin describes Kafka's literary fathers not as hosts but as "giant parasites": "Uncleanness is so much the attribute of officials that one could almost regard them as enormous parasites. This, of course, does not refer to the economic context, but to the forces of reason and humanity from which this clan makes a living. In the same way the fathers in Kafka's strange families batten on their sons, lying on top of them like giant parasites. They not only prey upon their strength, but gnaw away at the sons' right to exist. The fathers punish, but they are at the same time the accusers. The sin of which they accuse their sons seems to be a kind of original sin" ("Franz Kafka: On the Tenth Anniversary of His Death," trans. Harry Zohn, in *Illuminations*, 114).

59. Deleuze and Guattari, *Kafka*, 9, 10.

60. Singer, *The Manor*, vii, 85.

61. *Oxford English Dictionary Online*, s.v. "parasite," June 2005.

62. As I discuss in the interlude, this gendering of the parasite is in marked distinction to the figural imagery that often accompanies racialized and ethnicized invocations of the parasite, that of "welfare queens" and "illegal aliens" as represented by visual metaphors of infestation and references to swarms of insects and animals (e.g., vermin, mites, fleas).

63. Miller, "The Critic," 440.

64. William Shakespeare, *The Comedy of Errors*, in *The Norton Shakespeare*, vol. 1, 2.2.175–81.

65. Wollstonecraft, *A Vindication of the Rights of Woman*, 90.

66. Schreiner, *Woman and Labour*, 82.

67. Rosa Luxemburg, "Women's Suffrage and Class Struggle," trans. Rosmarie Waldrop, in *Selected Political Writings*, 219–20, cited in MacKinnon, *Toward a Feminist Theory of the State*, 9.

68. Beauvoir, *The Second Sex* (1993), 724.

69. Steinem, "What It Would Be Like If Women Win"; Greer, *The Female Eunuch*, 22, 330. Greer, resuscitating the metaphor for a different cultural moment, famously declared war on "feminine parasites" in her book *The Female Eunuch*, suggesting that such women should not be included in the feminist sisterhood.

70. "A parasite sucking out the living strength of another organism . . . The [housewife's] labor does not even tend toward the creation of anything durable," writes Beauvoir. "Woman's work within the home . . . is not directly useful to society. . . . It produces nothing. . . . [The housewife] is subordinate, secondary, parasitic. . . . It is for their common welfare that the situation must be altered by prohibiting marriage as a 'career' for woman" (*The Second Sex* [1993], 724).

71. Lorde, "The Master's Tools Will Never Dismantle the Master's House," 111.

72. Firestone, "The Dialectic of Sex," 25.

73. This quote appears in the introduction to Solanas's play. Valerie Solanas, *Up Your Ass*, Andy Warhol Museum Archives, Pittsburgh.

74. In her feminist separatist writing, Marilyn Frye writes, "There is an idea floating around in both feminist and anti-feminist literature to the effect that females and males generally live in a relation of parasitism, a parasitism of the male on the female . . . that it is, generally speaking, the strength, energy, inspiration, and nurturance of women that keeps men going, and not the strength, aggression, spirituality, and hunting of men that keeps women going. . . . One can and should distinguish between a partial and contingent material dependence created by a certain sort of money economy and class structure, and the nearly ubiquitous spiritual, emotional, and material dependence of males on females" ("Some Reflections on Separatism and Power," 93).

75. Lucy Delap writes of Schreiner's views, "Both internal effort and external intervention [were] needed to overcome parasitism, but 'the will' was seen as the most fundamental site of reform, since 'the ultimate effect of parasitism is always a paralysis of the will'" (*The Feminist Avant-Garde*, 37).

76. Beauvoir, *The Second Sex* (2011), 653; (1993), 724: "Women are 'clinging,' they are dead weight, and they suffer for it; the point is that their situation is like that of a parasite sucking out the living strength of another organism. Let them be provided with living strength of their own, let them have the means to attack the world and wrest from it their own subsistence, and their dependence will be abolished."

77. In the context of the Egyptian women's piety movement, Mahmood asks, "Does the category of resistance impose a teleology of progressive politics on the analytics of power—a teleology that makes it hard for us to see and understand forms of being and action that are not necessarily encapsulated by the narrative of subversion and reinscription of norms?" (*Politics of Piety*, 9). See Spivak, "Can the Subaltern Speak?"; Zerilli, *Feminism*.

78. Power, *One-Dimensional*, 3.

79. Ronell, "Avital Ronell," 127.

80. W. Brown, *States of Injury*, 67, 68.

81. Beauvoir, *Second Sex* (2011), 522.

82. Musser, *Sensational Flesh*, 66, 64, 82, 60.

83. Berlant, *Cruel Optimism*, 24.

84. Ronell, *The Telephone Book*, 5.

85. Chris Kraus, "Dialing: Back: Darkness," *Theory Illuminati*, August 19, 2018, https://theoryilluminati.com/texts-and-contexts/f/dialing-back-darkness (link inactive).

86. Kraus further stated that "Reitman—or any Ph.D. student at NYU—is hardly an innocent," noting too that "Avital's style of pedagogy was no secret, and he sought her out." Kraus, "Dialing."

87. Nick Mitchell writes of another widely circulated defense of Ronell penned by the NYU professor Lisa Duggan, "It was as if nearly everything 'structural' about power consisted in that which makes the professor vulnerable rather than in what makes the professor possible. The queer professor, in other words, gets to claim suffering the negative consequences of neoliberalism without risking being a neoliberal herself." Mitchell, "Summertime Selves."

88. Kraus, *I Love Dick*, 153–54.

89. Calle has said that she tries "to find a natural end" to her projects (public interview).

90. Hunt, "Chris Kraus."

91. Glass, "95."

92. Kraus, *I Love Dick*, 11.

93. See Fisher, "Parasitical Politics."

94. Chris Kraus, email to author, May 20, 2011.

95. Chris Kraus, email to author, May 26, 2011.

96. Gumport, "Female Trouble." François Cusset explains that the magazine and books series, which Lotringer established in 1983, played "a pathbreaking role in the early diffusion of French theory": "The small, black, inexpensive paperbacks published by Semiotext(e)'s Foreign Agents imprint introduced a generation of American students to a number of French authors, among them Paul Virilio, Jean-François Lyotard, and Jean Baudrillard. (The first title in the series—an excerpt adapted from Baudrillard's *Simulacra and Simulation*—sold more than 20,000 copies.) Lotringer imagined these complex but unacademic volumes as how-to books: what they taught you was 'how to think with your own mind . . . how to eroticize thinking, make it a pleasure of the senses.' It was, he declared, "philosophy for the boudoir" (quoted in Gumport, "Female Trouble").

97. Brunsdon, "A Thief," 276.

98. The choice of Native Agent as the name for a series is worth remarking on. It conveys an attempt to make women writers like Ann Rower, Eileen Myles, and Barbara Barg *at home within* Semiotext(e).

99. Sylvère Lotringer and Chris Kraus, foreword to Sacher-Masoch, *Venus in Furs*, 6, 7.

100. Stewart, *Sublime Surrender*, 87, 66–67.

101. Mara Goldwyn, "Chris Kraus on Confessionals in Art and Feminism," *Sleek*, November 23, 2012, https://www.sleek-mag.com/article/art-world-confessional.

102. Miller, "The Critic as Host," 441.

CHAPTER FOUR. A SEAT AT THE TABLE

1. Ann Liv Young has received scholarly attention in the fields of contemporary experimental dance studies, performance studies, and theater studies. See the following representative scholarly works: Conlan, "She's Magnificent"; Fisher, "Like a Girl's Name"; Friedman, "Festivals"; Miranda, "Staring at the (Clitoral) Sun"; Miranda, "'What Do Women Want?'"; Thomas, "Viewing the Pornographic Theatre."

2. Frank DiGiacomo, "Hipster Warfare Breaks Out during Performance Artist Ann Liv Young's Show at Delancey Lounge," *New York Daily News*, January 12, 2011, http://www.nydailynews.com/entertainment/gossip/hipster-warfare-breaks-performance-artist-ann-liv-young-show-delancey-lounge-article-1.153676.

3. Young has said her approach is informed by a preference for popular culture over art history, craft over fashion, observing social dynamics over the history of choreography and theater. She explains in an interview, "I wasn't interested in any sort of choreographers at all. I wasn't influenced by that. I never even took a dance history class. . . . I think I'm more influenced by like social dynamics . . . then I am like, 'Oh I love this visual artist.'" Interview with author, March, 6, 2010, Brooklyn, New York.

4. DiGiacomo, "Hipster Warfare."

5. It is difficult to distinguish between "performance art" and "feminist art" given the strong feminist tradition in 1960s, 1970s, and 1980s U.S. and European performance art. For this reason, I treat them, in certain contexts, as interchangeable.

6. Despite continued coverage of her performances in high-profile outlets like the *New York Times*, Arcade has not received this kind of high art and scholarly canonization.

7. Ridout and Schneider, "Precarity and Performance," 6.

8. For influential writing on 1960s, 1970s, 1980s, and 1990s Euro-American feminist art and performance, see Broude and Garrard, *The Power of Feminist Art*; Nochlin, "Why Have There Been No Great Women Artists?"; Parker and Pollock, *Framing Feminism*; Jones, *Body Art*; O'Dell, *Contract*; Goldberg, *Performance*; R. Schneider, *The Explicit Body*; Phelan, *Live Art*.

9. Astrid Henry's 2004 study, *Not My Mother's Sister*, describes a tendency, particularly popular in the 1990s, to articulate feminism by drawing generational

lines to argue that an overemphasis on metaphors of generational rebellion has come at the expense of political action.

10. I thank Joseph Roach for pointing out to me Ann Liv Young's use of the blond wig in her performances.

11. Performances that more overtly parody and critique white liberal feminism include Lee Minora's *White Feminist* (2018) and Young Jean Lee's *Untitled Feminist Show* (2011), neither of which is analyzed here.

12. McMillan, *Embodied Avatars*, 3, 228.

13. Mira Schor, "Generation 2.5," in *A Decade of Negative Thinking*, 48. See also Mira Schor, "'I Am Not Now nor Have I Ever Been . . . ,'" *Brooklyn Rail*, February 6, 2008, http://brooklynrail.org/2008/02/artseen/i-am-not-now-nor-have-i-ever-been.

14. Schor, "Generation 2.5," 65, parentheses in original.

15. "Marina Abramović: The Artist Is Present," MoMA, New York City, March 14–May 31, 2010, accessed July 9, 2018, https://www.moma.org/calendar/exhibitions/964.

16. Emma Brockes, "Performance Artist Marina Abramović: 'I Was Ready to Die,'" *Guardian*, May 12, 2014, https://www.theguardian.com/artanddesign/2014/may/12/marina-abramovic-ready-to-die-serpentine-gallery-512-hours.

17. "The Artist Is Present," MoMA Learning, 2010, accessed July 9, 2018, https://www.moma.org/learn/moma_learning/marina-abramovic-marina-abramovic-the-artist-is-present-2010.

18. In the post Abramović goes on to describe her efforts to raise millions of dollars to fund plans for her Marina Abramović Institute for the Preservation of Performance Art in Hudson, New York. These plans were scrapped after she was not able to meet the $31 million target. Marina Abramović, "Marina's Diary," January 23, 2016, https://flash---art.com/article/marinas-diary-3/ (emphasis mine).

19. "Grandmother of Performance Art: Yoko Ono or Marina Abramović?," *Moving Image Arts London*, September 20, 2016, https://mialondonblog.wordpress.com/2016/09/20/grandmother-of-performance-art-yoko-ono-or-marina-abramovic/.

20. R. Schneider, *Performing Remains*, 2.

21. Reperformance is, naturally, an appealing strategy for a neoliberal art market that has sought innovative ways of making performance—previously conceived as an ephemeral commodity resistant to archive and sale—reproducible, and thus financially marketable, long after the originator has ceased performing the work.

22. Carol Kino, "A Rebel Form Gains Favor. Fights Ensue." *New York Times*, March 14, 2010, http://www.nytimes.com/2010/03/14/arts/design/14performance.html, quoted in R. Schneider, *Performing Remains*, 4.

23. Kino, "A Rebel Form," quoted in R. Schneider, *Performing Remains*, 4.

24. These reperformers included Maria José Arjona, Brittany Bailey, John Bonafede, Lydia Brawner, Rachel Brennecke (aka Bon Jane), Rebecca Brooks,

Isabella Bruno, Alfredo Ferran Calle, Hsiao Chen, Rebecca Davis, Angela Freiberger, Kennis Hawkins, Michael Helland, Igor Josifov, Elana Katz, Cynthia Koppe, Heather Kravas, Gary Lai, Abigail Levine, Jacqueline Lounsbury, Isabelle Lumpkin, Elke Luyten, Alexander Lyle, Justine Lynch, Tom McCauley, Nick Morgan, Andrew Ondrejcak, Juri Onuki, Tony Orrico, Will Rawls, Matthew Rogers, George Emilio Sanchez, Ama Saru, Jill Sigman, Maria S. H. M., David Thomson, Layard Thompson, Amelia Uzategui Bonilla, Deborah Wing-Sproul, Yozmit, and Jeramy Zimmerman.

25. Quoted in R. Schneider, *Performing Remains*, 6.

26. While Abramović may be the most influential and visible of a veteran generation of performance artists, her proprietary approach to legacy is not representative of other artists of the same generation. The feminist artist Faith Wilding, for one, represents a striking countermodel in her open-access approach to reperformance and reputation for teaching and mentoring younger artists. Amelia Jones writes, "Wilding has released any copyright and the script for [her] piece. . . . She encourages anyone to reperform the work at any time without permission" ("LOST BODIES," 142).

27. Schechner, *Between Theater and Anthropology*, 50.

28. Phelan, *Unmarked*, 146.

29. R. Schneider, *Performing Remains*.

30. R. Schneider, *Performing Remains*, 4.

31. R. Schneider, *Performing Remains*, 4.

32. Bishop, "Outsourcing Authenticity?," 111, 119.

33. See comments section on David Cohen, "Who Will Rein Her In? Marina Abramović versus Yvonne Rainer," *artcritical*, November 12, 2011, http://www.artcritical.com/2011/11/12/abramovic-rainer/.

34. Abigail Levine, Gary Lai, and Rebecca Brooks, "Three Reperformers from 'Marina Abramović: The Artist Is Present' Respond to the MOCA Gala Performances," *Performance Club*, November 28, 2011, http://theperformanceclub.org/2011/11/three-reperformers-from-marina-abramovic-the-artist-is-present-respond-to-the-moca-gala-performances/.

35. These economic and social transformations disproportionately affect young racial and ethnic minorities, despite the fact that discussions of generational precarity tend to emphasize the generalization of insecurity and poverty to middle-class, college-educated whites, intellectual workers, and the creative class.

36. The artists discussed in this chapter, born in the late 1970s and early 1980s, represent the outermost edge of the millennial generation.

37. Harris, *Kids These Days*, 5.

38. Julia Halperin, "Yvonne Rainer Denounces Marina Abramović's Planned MOCA Gala Performance as 'Grotesque,'" *Artinfo*, November 11, 2011, http://mx.blouinartinfo.com/news/story/750038/yvonne-rainer-denounces-marina-abramovics-planned-moca-gala-performance-as-grotesque (link inactive).

39. Halperin, "Yvonne Rainer Denounces."

40. For Sara Wookey's own open letter about the incident and her reasons for refusing to participate in the MOCA performance, see "The 1%: Marina Abramović and Jeffrey Deitch," *(Un)Occupy | Decolonize | Liberate*, November 23, 2011, https://occupyduniya.wordpress.com/2011/11/23/abramovic-deitch/.

41. As of 2012 the National Endowment for the Arts dedicated less than 2 percent of its already limited budget to grants for individual artists; state arts agencies dedicated only 3 percent of their grant money to individual artists; and the bulk of philanthropy in the arts went to only 2 percent of the nation's arts institutions, which are among those with the largest budgets. Alexis Clements, "New Data Reveals Artists Aren't Getting' Paid," *Hyperallergic*, April 10, 2012, https://hyperallergic.com/50226/new-data-reveals-artists-arent-gettin-paid/. In this context the activist and advocacy organization W.A.G.E. (Working Artists and the Greater Economy), founded in 2008, has sought to regulate the payment of artist fees by the nonprofit arts organizations and institutions that subcontract artistic labor in a contemporary art economy "where the unpaid labor of artists supports a more than $60 billion-dollar [*sic*] industry." In a landmark survey of working contemporary artists conducted by the group in 2010 (the same year as *The Artist Is Present*), W.A.G.E. found that the majority of respondents (58.4 percent) had received no payment, compensation, or reimbursement for exhibiting or presenting their work in New York City. Forty-three percent of these respondents were between thirty-one and forty years old. "2010 W.A.G.E. Survey," W.A.G.E., accessed July 22, 2019, https://wageforwork.com/work/2010-w-a-g-e-survey#top.

42. Analysis of the Census Bureau's American Community Survey by BFAMFAPhD, a collective "concerned with the impact of debt, rent, and precarity on the lives of creative people," found that the median income of people with art degrees who made their living as artists in New York City in 2012 was $25,000. This economic and social inequity is further reflected in who has opportunity and resources to pursue a career in the arts; the population of working artists in New York City is 224 percent whiter than the population of the city as a whole. Clements, "What Are the Chances?"

43. Berlant, *Cruel Optimism*.

44. Millennials carry at least 300 percent more student loan debt than their parents did (according to the College Board) and are half as likely to own a home as their counterparts in 1975 (U.S. Census, young adults twenty-four to thirty-five). One in every five millennials lives in poverty (U.S. Census, young adults eighteen to thirty-four). These statistics are cited in Michael Hobbes, "FML: Why Millennials Are Facing the Scariest Financial Future of Any Generation since the Great Depression," *HuffPost*, accessed July 22, 2019, https://highline.huffington-post.com/articles/en/poor-millennials-print/.

45. Joseph G. Ramsey, "The Invisible Faculty," *Chronicle of Higher Education*, January 2, 2019, https://www.chronicle.com/article/The-Invisible-Faculty/245399.

46. Chris Kraus, "Dialing: Back: Darkness," *Theory Illuminati*, August 19,

2018, https://theoryilluminati.com/texts-and-contexts/f/dialing-back-darkness (link inactive).

47. Mitchell, "Summertime Selves."

48. Trans graduate student Andrea Long Chu, who previously served as a teaching assistant for Ronell, made this observation: "i think it's safe to assume that avital really has been persecuted: certainly no woman in the academy, especially coming up when she did, escapes the relentless misogyny of the university. but what seems to have happened (and this is just my own opinion) is that now, even when she does have status and power and celebrity, she still thinks of herself as a vulnerable grad student in need of care and protection, ie, she thinks she still is the person reitman is saying *he* is." Quoted in Masha Gessen, "An N.Y.U. Sexual-Harassment Case Has Spurred a Necessary Conversation about #MeToo," *New Yorker,* August 25, 2018, https://www.newyorker.com/news/our-columnists/an-nyu-sexual-harassment-case-has-spurred-a-necessary-conversation-about-metoo.

49. "The pressure to comply with an advisor's wishes or else drop out are rising in a neoliberal academy that intentionally creates more cheap labor than it can employ," writes Nefertiti Takla in "Reitman vs. Ronell: Rethinking the Role of Gender and Patriarchy in Sexual Harassment Cases," *Feminist Interventions*, September 2, 2018, feministinterventions.com/2018/09/02/reitmanvsronell.

50. Brawner, "The Artist Is Present," 214.

51. Andrew Goldman, "The Devil in Marina Abramovic," *New York Times*, June 13, 2012, https://www.nytimes.com/2012/06/17/magazine/the-devil-in-marina-abramovic.html; Hannah Ghorashi, "'. . . But We Can't Pay You': Performance Art and Money's Knotty Relationship," *Artnews*, October 29, 2015, www.artnews.com/2015/10/29/but-we-cant-pay-you-performance-art-and-moneys-knotty-relationship/.

52. Berlant, *Cruel Optimism*, 4.

53. See Rebecca Schneider's treatment of "feminist remimesis" as a troubling of the masculine imperatives of originality and authorship and in particular, her discussion of Roysdon and Holstein's reenactments of *Interior Scroll* ("Remembering").

54. Gretchen Holmes, "Re-Examining Feminist Performance," *Chicago Art Magazine*, August 12, 2010, chicagoartmagazine.com/2010/08/re-examining-feminist-performance/.

55. The epigraph quotes Anya Liftig, "Anxieties of Influence: Performance Art, Celebrity, and the Self," *Other Journal,* May 19, 2011, https://theotherjournal.com/2011/05/19/anxieties-of-influence-performance-art-celebrity-and-the-self/.

56. Tatiana Berg, "The Anxiety of Influence," BOMB *Magazine*, March 29, 2010, https://bombmagazine.org/articles/the-anxiety-of-influence/, emphasis in original.

57. Lācis, "Fame," 99.

58. The piece's title is perhaps also a cheeky nod to her own intellectual inheritance, as Liftig is herself an alum of Yale, where Bloom held a distinguished professorship. See Gilbert and Gubar, *The Madwoman*, 47.

59. Anya Liftig, "The Anxiety of Influence," *Homemade Libations*, March 28, 2010, http://homemadelibations.blogspot.com/2010/03/anxiety-of-influence.html.

60. Liftig, "The Anxiety of Influence."

61. In February 2010, during Brooklyn Is Burning at the PS 1 Contemporary Art Center (now MoMA PS1), Young was abruptly shut down when PS 1's director Klaus Biesenbach ordered the power cut in a windowless room. Young, performing as her alter ego Sherry, had confronted the performer who went on just before her, Georgia Sagri, and, according to the account in the *New York Times*, had "embarked on a blunt, profane monologue accompanied by masturbation, urination and an attack on Ms. Sagri's work." Sagri and friends responded by threatening Young in return and, according to witnesses, had to be restrained. Claudia La Rocco, "Provocative Artist Fights for Return to P.S. 1," *New York Times*, August 11, 2010, http://www.nytimes.com/2010/08/12/arts/design/12young.html.

62. "Ann Liv Young 'Sherry Is Present,'" *NY Art Beat*, accessed March 2, 2017, http://www.nyartbeat.com/event/2011/E805. See also Friedman, "Festivals," 123.

63. "Ann Liv Young (US)," bio, Steirischer Herbst Festival, accessed February 16, 2017, http://editions.steirischerherbst.at/2013/_mod/_calendar/biography.inc.php?lang=en&kid=2035 (link inactive).

64. Ann Liv Young's Louis B. James solo exhibition is incorrectly identified on her online CV as *Ann Liv Young: The Artist Is Present* instead of *Ann Liv Young: Sherry Is Present*. Young, "Resume," accessed June 24, 2019, on Wayback Machine Internet Archive.

65. Ann Liv Young, email to author, November 30, 2011.

66. Young claims the website's inaccessibility is an aesthetic choice: "People actually say 'I can't find where the button is,' but it would be really easy for me to make a little button that says 'Click here'" (interview with author).

67. For a discussion of this disruption and the knotty ethical and political questions it raises in the context of the avant-garde performance tradition, see Andrew Friedman's excellent piece, "Festivals: Conventional Disruption, or, Why Ann Liv Young Ruined Rebecca Patek's Show."

68. Friedman, "Festivals," 123–24.

69. Friedman, "Festivals," 117.

70. Alastair Macaulay, "This Time the Trouble Isn't Wicked Stepsisters," *New York Times*, September 5, 2010, http://www.nytimes.com/2010/09/06/arts/dance/06cinderella.html?_r=2&ref=alastair_macaulay. By comparing Young to one of the Young British Artists, such as Tracey Emin or Damien Hirst, and then chastising her for failing to measure up, Macaulay insists that Young be, in spite of all, commercially appealing.

71. Conlan, "She's Magnificent," 31.

72. In September 2010 David Velasco wrote in *Artforum*, "Sherry is, after all, not as mad as she appears: she dramatizes the capriciousness of power, but when confronted with authority, she seizes the occasion to expose its 'twisted' logic, making authority reflexive, getting it to turn in on itself" ("Drama Queen," 148).

73. Friedman, "Festivals," 124.

74. Gia Kourlas, "Ann Liv Young Poops on Command in *Cinderella*," *Time Out New York*, August 23, 2010, https://www.timeout.com/newyork/art/ann-liv-young-poops-on-command-in-cinderella.

75. Newton, *Mother Camp*, 56. The artist Carrie Mae Weems restages this scene in a photograph from her series *Ain't Jokin'* (1987–88). The scene highlights the psychic violence of the fairy tale's idealization of white femininity to black girls. Rather than Newton's drag queen, in Weems's photograph a young black woman stands before a mirror with the caption "Looking into the mirror, the black woman asked, 'Mirror, mirror on the wall, who's the finest of them all?' The mirror says, 'Snow White, you black bitch, and don't you forget it!!!'"

76. This scene cites the opening credits of Stanley Kubrick's film adaptation of Vladimir Nabokov's *Lolita*, where the viewer first sees Lolita (played by Sue Lyon), lying down while Humbert Humbert (played by James Mason) paints her toenails.

77. Amber Hawk Swanson, "Not a Feminist Way of Thinking, Daddy's Little Girl," *Feminism? Project*, 2005–6, artist's video.

78. Kelly McClure, "When Amber Met Amber," *Chicago Reader*, August 2, 2007, http://www.chicagoreader.com/chicago/artist-amber-hawk-swanson-look-alike-sex-doll-realdoll/Content?oid=4258953.

79. Claudia La Rocco, "Dance Review: Oh, Mirror, Mirror, on the Wall, Who's the Naughtiest of Them All," *New York Times*, March 17, 2007, http://www.nytimes.com/2007/03/17/arts/dance/17youn.html.

80. Kilston, "Introducing," 32.

81. Gia Kourlas, "Dance Review: Pure as the Driven Snow?," *Time Out New York*, March 8–14, 2007, archived at http://guiadosteatros.blogspot.com/2008/04/snow-white-na-zdb.html.

82. Interview with author.

83. Tzara, "Dada Manifesto," 7.

84. Young explained her response when asked what her profession is: "I'm always like, 'I'm sorry I don't really know what I do.' . . . If it is somebody who I don't want to understand what I do and for instance, if it is somebody who doesn't know what a choreographer is, I usually use the word *choreographer*. . . . And if it is someone who would know what a choreographer is, I usually say *performance artist*. It's evasion. I am an escape artist." Interview with author, March 6, 2010, Brooklyn, New York.

85. Interview with author, March 6, 2010.

86. DiGiacomo, "Hipster Warfare"; Horwitz quoted in La Rocco, "Provocative Artist Fights for Return."

87. Claudia La Rocco and Gia Kourlas, "Dance Review: The Bagwell in Me," *New York Times*, October 3, 2008, http://www.nytimes.com/2008/10/04/arts/dance/04roun.html.

88. Interview with author, March 6, 2010.

89. Gilbert and Gubar, *Madwoman in the Attic*, 47.

90. Halberstam, *The Queer Art of Failure*, 161.

91. See *Oxford English Dictionary Online*, s.v. "autogenesis," June 2011, accessed February 25, 2017.

92. Comment on Facebook page, February 19, 2011, accessed February 25, 2017.

93. Muñoz, *Disidentifications*, x.

94. Muñoz, "The White to Be Angry," in *Disidentifications*, 93–103.

95. Apri Cot, "How 1 Become 2," *Bellyflop Magazine*, March 13, 2011, accessed on Wayback Machine Internet Archive.

96. Holstein, "The Cyclical Pleasures," in Kartsaki, *On Repetition*, 120; see also Fisher and Holstein, "Part-time Feminist."

97. Ann Liv Young, interview with author, September 9, 2013, New York City.

98. Lauren Barri Holstein's thesis, "How (Not) to Be a Woman: The Performative Politics of Ambiguity in Gender and Signification," was submitted toward the fulfillment of the artist's master's in dance theater (The Body in Performance) at Laban in October 2010.

99. The essay, attributed both to Holstein and her alter ego, is exemplary of the ambiguity between the two that the artist maintains. See Holstein, "*Splat!*"

100. In "The Complete History of Feminism," a performative manifesto published in *Feminist Times*, Holstein (writing as The Famous) mocks public and popular media sentiment that would suggest that feminism is irrelevant or unnecessary today: "In the 'new millennium,' everyone decided feminism wasn't really necessary anymore, seeing that women weren't being raped anymore; they were being paid something . . . and were being represented in the media, not as boobilicious incentives to buy things, but as well-rounded sex objects who've chosen sex object as career. Go women!" Lauren Barri Holstein, "The Complete History of Feminism, According to the Famous Lauren Barri Holstein," *Feminist Times*, October 13, 2013, accessed on Wayback Machine Internet Archive.

101. Lauren Barri Holstein, "Interior Scroll," *The Famous*, May 3, 2012, http://laurenbarri.blogspot.com/2012/03/interior-scroll.html.

CODA. IT'S NOT YOU, IT'S ME

1. Roisin Byrne has received modest scholarly attention in the fields of contemporary art criticism and curatorial studies: Benson, "Acts"; Fisher, "We Are Parasites"; Kushnir, "When Curating."

2. *Goldsmiths: But Is It Art?*, episodes 1 and 2, directed by Victoria Silver, aired April 12 and 19, 2010, on BBC. Thanks to Andrew Lison for bringing the show to my attention.

3. Jonathan Jones, "The Artist Who Steals for a Living," *Guardian*, April 14, 2010, https://www.theguardian.com/artanddesign/2010/apr/14/roisin-byrne.

4. Louise Jury, "Goldsmiths Star's Shoplifting in the Name of Art," *London Evening Standard*, April 13, 2010, http://www.standard.co.uk/news/goldsmiths-stars-shoplifting-in-the-name-of-art-6458439.html.

5. Nathalie Levi, "'Bad Artists Copy, Good Artists Steal.' [1], What's Yours Is Mine, Roisin Byrne and Duncan Wooldridge at Tenderpixel," *Nathalie Levi's Blog*, October 15, 2010, https://nathalielevi.wordpress.com/2010/10/15/bad-artists-copy-good-artists-steal-1-what's-yours-is-mine-roisin-byrne-duncan-wooldridge-at-tenderpixel/.

6. The neon sign that she claims to have originally ordered before pursuing Gander's "Massage" concept instead was to read "Work will set you free." The reference to the dictum *Arbeit macht frei* hung over the entrances of many Nazi concentration camps, most famously Auschwitz, is an obvious provocation. If this is true, her reproduction of the phrase out of context performs, under the banner of irony, a self-serving display of historical indifference.

7. Evidence of the work remains largely virtual, circulating via coverage in the mainstream art press and contemporary art blogosphere in addition to the odd gallery exhibition.

8. *Goldsmiths: But Is It Art?*, episode 1.

9. Beauvoir, *The Second Sex* (2011), 653.

10. Kanouse, "Cooing."

11. Sturtevant accomplished this by painstakingly mastering each work's respective medium, whereas Levine utilized various media to reproduce the works, most famously rephotographing Walker Evans's iconic photographs. (Sturtevant, who hated the word *copy*, added subtle changes to her versions and called them "replications"; Levine called her exhibition *After Walker Evans*.) By marking both the virtual equivalence of the quality and manifest content of the original and copied works and yet the nonequivalence of their reception, Sturtevant and Levine highlighted (and found a way to profit from, as conceptual artists) the secondary treatment of women's work within the art market.

12. Jones, "The Artist."

13. The emails reproduced here are excerpted.

14. Quoted in Randall, *Pragmatic Plagiarism*, viii.

15. Anna Watkins Fisher, Facebook message to Roisin Byrne, April 19, 2011.

16. Roisin Byrne, Facebook message to author, April 20, 2011.

17. Cerizza, "Roberto Cuoghi."

18. MacGlip, "Interview."

19. Serres, *The Parasite*, 38.

20. See Fisher, "We Are Parasites."

21. Miller, "The Critic," 439.

22. On April 30, 2013, the self-described "post post feminist" performance and curatorial collective HAG, comprising Clara Lipfert and Jasmin Risk, performed a show at Grace Space in Bushwick called *PARASITE*. Their performance trolled J. P. Marin, who was in the audience, about what they perceived to be a patronizing review he had written about my article about my encounter with Byrne, "We Are Parasites: On the Politics of Imposition." The performance mocks Marin's "mansplaining" of feminist art by playing a recording of his review while naked and surrounded by makeup and sex toys, so as to represent "feminist art" in

its most cliché form. The duo said that they played a recording of his review to highlight the way the review represented a male critic's appropriation of feminist art, their denial of a voice about their own relationship to feminist theory and practice by a male-centric discourse. "Having no words of our own, that is, speaking his review out loud, we wished to render literal the feeling of being talked at, talked over." Clara Lipfert, emails to author, October 28, 2013, and January 6, 2014. For more about the performance see HAG, "Parasite." For more about HAG, see their Tumblr page, hagcollective.tumblr.com. For Marin's review of the performance about his review (and the full text of his original review), ee J. P. Marin, "Self-Described Feminist Appropriative Performance," *childproof tv*, May 17, 2013, http://www.childproof.tv/popular-dialectics/2013/05/17/self-described-feminist-appropriative-performance/.

23. Bob Duggan, "Is Parasitism the Future of Feminist Art?," *Big Think*, July 18, 2011, http://bigthink.com/Picture-This/is-parasitism-the-future-of-feminist-art.

24. His assistant responded by telling Byrne that the plant now had no value, since she was prohibited from selling it as a work of Starling's. Starling himself added, "Even if this is the right rhododendron . . . the plant in itself has no real value—it perhaps had some value were [*sic*] it was but certainly not now."

25. In *The Bluest Eye*, observes Robin Bernstein, Toni Morrison depicts the dichotomizing of racial innocence along the axis of femininity: "an imagining of white girls as tender, innocently doll-like, and deserving protection, and black girls as disqualified from all those qualities" (*Racial Innocence*, 29).

26. The *Guardian* art critic Adrian Searle has contended, "Back-story is everything in Simon Starling's work." Quoted in Stuart Jeffries, "'I Got a Lovely Poem from a Lady in St. Albans about Sheds,'" *Guardian*, December 7, 2005, https://www.theguardian.com/artanddesign/2005/dec/07/art.turnerprize2005.

27. Patricia Hill Collins and Sirma Bilge write, "Intersectionality is a way of understanding and analyzing the complexity of the world, in people, and in human experiences. The events and conditions of social and political life and the self can seldom be understood as shaped by one factor. They are generally shaped by many factors in diverse and mutually influencing ways. When it comes to social inequality, people's lives and the organization of power in a given society are better understood as being shaped not by a single axis of social division, be it race or gender or class, but by many axes that work together and influence each other" (*Intersectionality*, 2).

28. François Herpe, "La notion de 'parasitisme artistique': Une arme contre les contrefacteurs astucieux," *Eurojuris France*, June 21, 2013, https://www.eurojuris.fr/articles/la-notion-de-parasitisme-artistique-une-arme-contre-les-contrefacteurs-astucieux-1208.htm.

29. This Roisin Byrne's entrepreneurial enthusiasm and story of personal rebirth is so cliché and overstated that the website has the air of a fake.

BIBLIOGRAPHY

Ahmed, Sara. *Living a Feminist Life*. Durham, NC: Duke University Press, 2017.

Ahmed, Sara. *On Being Included: Racism and Diversity in Institutional Life*. Durham, NC: Duke University Press, 2012.

Ahmed, Sara. "A Phenomenology of Whiteness." *Feminist Theory* 8, no. 2 (August 2007): 149–68.

Anagnost, Adrian. "Parasitism and Contemporary Art." In *Beyond Critique: Contemporary Art in Theory, Practice, and Instruction*, edited by Pamela Fraser and Roger Rothman, 79–96. New York: Bloomsbury Academic, 2017.

Arendt, Hannah. *The Origins of Totalitarianism*. New York: Schocken Books, 2004.

Aristarkhova, Irina. *Hospitality of the Matrix: Philosophy, Biomedicine, and Culture*. New York: Columbia University Press, 2012.

Arnott, W. Geoffrey. "Studies in Comedy, I: Alexis and the Parasite's Name." *Greek, Roman and Byzantine Studies* 9, no. 2 (1968): 161–68.

Arns, Inke. "Feeding the Serpent Its Own Tail: Counterforces to Tactile Enclosure in the Age of Transparency." In *Throughout: Art and Culture Emerging with Ubiquitous Computing*, edited by Ulrik Ekman, 385–98. Cambridge, MA: MIT Press, 2013.

Barish, Jonas A. *The Antitheatrical Prejudice*. Berkeley: University of California Press, 1981.

Barthes, Roland. *A Lover's Discourse: Fragments*. Translated by Richard Howard. New York: Hill and Wang, 1978.

Baumbach, Nico, Damon R. Young, and Genevieve Yue. "Introduction: For a Political Critique of Culture." *Social Text* 34, no. 2 (June 2016): 1–20.

Beauchamp, Toby. *Going Stealth: Transgender Politics and U.S. Surveillance Practices*. Durham, NC: Duke University Press, 2019.

Beauvoir, Simone de. *The Second Sex*. [1949]. Edited and translated by H. M. Parshley. New York: Knopf, 1993.

Beauvoir, Simone de. *The Second Sex*. [1949]. Translated by Constance Borde and Sheila Malovany-Chevallier. New York: Vintage, 2011.

Benjamin, Walter. *Illuminations: Essays and Reflections*. Edited by Hannah Arendt. Translated by Harry Zohn. New York: Schocken Books, 1968.

Benson, Ciarán. "Acts Not Tracts! Why a Complete Psychology of Art and Identity Must Be Neuro-cultural." In *Art and Identity: Essays on the Aesthetic Creation of Mind*, edited by Tone Roald and Johannes Lang, 39–66. Amsterdam: Rodopi, 2013.

Berardi, Franco, and Akseli Virtanen. "From Arbitrary Power to Morphogenesis." *Future Art Base*, September 29, 2013. Accessed June 26, 2019. http://www.futureartbase.org/2013/09/29/from-arbitrary-power-to-morphogenesis/.

Berlant, Lauren. *Cruel Optimism*. Durham, NC: Duke University Press, 2011.

Bernhard, Hans, and Lizvlx. *UBERMORGEN.COM: Media Hacking vs. Conceptual Art*. Edited by Alessandro Ludovico. Basel: Christoph Merian Verlag, 2009.

Bernstein, Robin. *Racial Innocence: Performing American Childhood from Slavery to Civil Rights*. New York: New York University Press, 2011.

Bhabha, Homi. *The Location of Culture*. New York: Routledge, 1994.

Bishop, Claire. "Outsourcing Authenticity? Delegated Performance in Contemporary Art." In *Double Agent*, edited by Claire Bishop and Silvia Tramontana, 110–25. London: Institute of Contemporary Arts, 2009.

Blair, Elaine. "Chris Kraus, Female Antihero." *New Yorker*, November 21, 2016. https://www.newyorker.com/magazine/2016/11/21/chris-kraus-female-antihero.

Blas, Zach. "Informatic Opacity." In "Tectonic Disobedience." Special issue, edited by Marc Herbst. *Journal of Aesthetics and Protest* 9 (summer 2014). http://www.joaap.org/issue9/zachblas.htm.

Bloom, Harold. *The Anxiety of Influence: A Theory of Poetry*. New York: Oxford University Press, 1973.

Bois, Yve-Alain. "Character Study: Sophie Calle." *Artforum International* 38, no. 8 (April 2000): 126–31.

Boltanski, Luc, and Eve Chiapello. *The New Spirit of Capitalism*. Translated by Gregory C. Elliott. London: Verso, 2007.

Bozeman, Barry. "A Theory of Government 'Red Tape.'" *Journal of Public Administration Research and Theory* 3, no. 3 (July 1993): 273–303.

Brawner, Lydia. "The Artist Is Present: Performing the Icon." *Women and Performance: a journal of feminist theory* 23, no. 2 (2013): 212–25.

Brewer Ball, Katherine. "The Only Way Out Is In: The Black and Queer Performance of Escape." Unpublished manuscript, 2020.

Brinkema, Eugenie. *The Form of the Affects*. Durham, NC: Duke University Press, 2014.

Broeckmann, Andreas. "Software Art Aesthetics." In "Monodisperso." Special issue, edited by Fernando José Pereira and Miguel Leal. *Mono* 1 (June 2007): 158–67.

Brooks, Daphne. *Bodies in Dissent: Spectacular Performances of Race and Freedom, 1850–1910*. Durham, NC: Duke University Press, 2006.

Broude, Norma, and Mary D. Garrard, eds. *The Power of Feminist Art: The*

American Movement of the 1970s, History and Impact. New York: H. N. Abrams, 1994.
Brown, James J., Jr. *Ethical Programs: Hospitality and the Rhetorics of Software*. Ann Arbor: University of Michigan Press, 2015.
Brown, Wendy. *States of Injury: Power and Freedom in Late Modernity*. Princeton, NJ: Princeton University Press, 1995.
Brown, Wendy. *Undoing the Demos: Neoliberalism's Stealth Revolution*. Brooklyn, NY: Zone Books, 2015.
Browne, Simone. *Dark Matters: On the Surveillance of Blackness*. Durham, NC: Duke University Press, 2015.
Browning, Barbara. "I'm Trying to Reach You." Paper presented at Performance Studies International 19 conference, Stanford University, June 29, 2013.
Browning, Barbara. "The Performative Novel." TDR *(The Drama Review)* 62, no. 2 (summer 2018): 43–58.
Brunsdon, Charlotte. "A Thief in the Night: Stories of Feminism in the 1970s at CCCS." In *Stuart Hall: Critical Dialogues in Cultural Studies*, edited by David Morley and Kuan-Hsing Chen, 276–86. London: Routledge, 1996.
Brunton, Finn, and Helen Nissenbaum. *Obfuscation: A User's Guide for Privacy and Protest*. Cambridge, MA: MIT Press, 2016.
Butler, Judith. *Bodies That Matter: On the Discursive Limits of "Sex."* New York: Routledge, 1993.
Butler, Judith. "The Body You Want: Liz Kotz Interviews Judith Butler." *Artforum* 31, no. 3 (November 1992): 82–89.
Butler, Judith. "Collected and Fractured: Response to *Identities*." In *Identities*, edited by Kwame Anthony Appiah and Henry Louis Gates Jr., 439–47. Chicago: University of Chicago Press, 1995.
Butler, Judith. *Gender Trouble: Feminism and the Subversion of Identity*. New York: Routledge, 1990.
Calle, Sophie. "He Loves Me Not." Interview by Angelique Chrisafis. *Guardian*, June 16, 2007. https://www.theguardian.com/world/2007/jun/16/artnews.art.
Calle, Sophie. *Take Care of Yourself*. Translated by Charles Renwarden. Arles: Actes Sud, 2007.
Calle, Sophie. Public interview at Art, Technology, and Culture Colloquium, University of California, Berkeley, March 28, 2011.
Calle, Sophie, and Marie Desplechin. "*Take Care of Yourself*, Venice and Writing." In *Sophie Calle: And So Forth*. New York: Prestel, 2016.
Camp, Stephanie M. H. *Closer to Freedom: Enslaved Women and Everyday Resistance in the Plantation South*. Chapel Hill: University of North Carolina Press, 2004.
Campt, Tina M. "The Visual Frequency of Black Life: Love, Labor, and the Practice of Refusal," *Social Text* 37, no. 3 (September 2019): 25–46.
Carson, Anne. *Economy of the Unlost: Reading Simonides of Keos with Paul Celan*. Princeton, NJ: Princeton University Press, 1999.

Cerizza, Luca. "Roberto Cuoghi." *Frieze Magazine* 116 (June–August 2008). Accessed February 25, 2017. https://frieze.com/article/roberto-cuoghi.

Chambers-Letson, Josh Takano, with images by Kenneth Pietrobono. "North American Field Guide: Kenneth Pietrobono's Queer Landscape of US Empire." *Women and Performance* 21, no. 1 (March 2011): 13–32.

Cheney-Lippold, John. *We Are Data: Algorithms and the Making of Our Digital Selves.* New York: New York University Press, 2017.

Cherewatuk, Karen, and Ulrike Wiethaus, eds. *Dear Sister: Medieval Women and the Epistolary Genre.* Philadelphia: University of Pennsylvania Press, 1993.

Chomsky, Noam. "The Death of American Universities." *Jacobin*, March 3, 2014. Accessed August 28, 2014. www.jacobinmag.com/2014/03/the-death-of-american-universities.

Chun, Wendy Hui Kyong. *Control and Freedom: Power and Paranoia in the Age of Fiber Optics.* Cambridge, MA: MIT Press, 2006.

Chun, Wendy Hui Kyong. *Updating to Remain the Same: Habitual New Media.* Cambridge, MA: MIT Press, 2016.

Cirio, Paolo, Alessandro Ludovico, Hans Bernhard, and Lizvlx. "The Big Book (C)rime: Interview with the 'Amazon Noir' Crew." By Franz Thalmair. *CONT3XT.NET*, November 2006. Accessed September 22, 2018. http://www.amazon-noir.com/TEXT/CONTEXT_INTERVIEW/interview_amazon_noir.pdf.

Clements, Alexis. "What Are the Chances? Success in the Arts in the 21st Century." *Los Angeles Review of Books*, November 17, 2016. Accessed July 22, 2019. https://lareviewofbooks.org/article/chances-success-arts-21st-century/.

Cohen, Kris. *Never Alone, Except for Now: Art, Networks, Populations.* Durham, NC: Duke University Press, 2017.

Colebrook, Claire. *Irony.* New York: Routledge, 2004.

Colebrook, Claire. "We Have Always Been Post-Anthropocene: The Anthropocene Counterfactual." In *Anthropocene Feminism*, edited by Richard Grusin, 1–20. Minneapolis: University of Minnesota Press, 2017.

Coleman, Gabriella. "Hacker." In *Digital Keywords: A Vocabulary of Information Society and Culture*, edited by Benjamin Peters, 158–72. Princeton, NJ: Princeton University Press, 2016.

Coleman, Heidi. "the parasite: An Alternative Reality Game for Orientation," Interview with Patrick Jagoda. *HowlRound*. January 7, 2018. Accessed January 18, 2018. https://howlround.com/parasite.

Collins, Patricia Hill, and Sirma Bilge. *Intersectionality.* Cambridge: Polity Press, 2016.

Combes, Claude. *The Art of Being a Parasite.* Translated by Daniel Simberloff. Chicago: University of Chicago Press, 2005.

Conlan, Anna. "She's Magnificent, She's Nuts." Interview with Ann Liv Young. *Dance Theatre Journal* 23, no. 2 (2009): 31–36.

Critical Art Ensemble. *Digital Resistance: Explorations in Tactical Media*. New York: Autonomedia, 2001.

Culler, Jonathan. *On Deconstruction: Theory and Criticism after Structuralism*. Ithaca, NY: Cornell University Press, 1982.

Damon, Cynthia. *The Mask of the Parasite: A Pathology of Roman Patronage*. Ann Arbor: University of Michigan Press, 1997.

Davis, Mike. "Fortress L.A." In *Common Ground? Readings and Reflections on Public Space*, edited by Anthony M. Orum and Zachary P. Neal, 100–109. New York: Routledge, 2010.

Dean, Jodi. *Democracy and Other Neoliberal Fantasies*. Durham, NC: Duke University Press, 2009.

de Certeau, Michel. *The Practice of Everyday Life*. Translated by Steven Rendall. Berkeley: University of California Press, 1988.

De Kosnik, Abigail. *Rogue Archives: Digital Cultural Memory and Media Fandom*. Cambridge, MA: MIT Press, 2016.

Delap, Lucy. *The Feminist Avant-Garde: Transatlantic Encounters of the Early Twentieth Century*. Cambridge: Cambridge University Press, 2007.

Deleuze, Gilles. "Postscript on the Societies of Control." *October* 59 (winter 1992): 3–7.

Deleuze, Gilles, and Félix Guattari. *Kafka: Toward a Minor Literature*. Translated by Dana Polan. Minneapolis: University of Minnesota Press, 1986.

Derrida, Jacques. "Hostipitality." In *Acts of Religion*, edited and translated by Gil Anidjar, 356–420. New York: Routledge, 2002.

Derrida, Jacques. *The Post Card: From Socrates to Freud and Beyond*. Translated by Alan Bass. Chicago: University of Chicago Press, 1987.

Derrida, Jacques, and Anne Dufourmantelle. *Of Hospitality: Anne Dufourmantelle Invites Jacques Derrida to Respond*. Translated by Rachel Bowlby. Stanford, CA: Stanford University Press, 2000.

Dieter, Michael. "Amazon Noir: Piracy, Distribution, Control." *M/C Journal* 10, no. 5 (October 2007). Accessed February 22, 2018. http://journal.media-culture.org.au/0710/07-dieter.php.

Doyle, Jennifer. *Sex Objects: Art and the Dialectics of Desire*. Minneapolis: University of Minnesota Press, 2006.

Ellison, Ralph. *Invisible Man*. 2nd edition. New York: Vintage International, 1995.

Esposito, Roberto. *Bíos: Biopolitics and Philosophy*. Translated by Timothy Campbell. Minneapolis: University of Minnesota Press, 2008.

Federici, Silvia. "Sipping Tea with Silvia Federici." Interview by Hanna Hurr. In "The Control Issue." Special issue, *Mask*, August 2016. http://www.maskmagazine.com/the-control-issue/struggle/interview-silvia-federici.

Feher, Michel. "The Neoliberal Condition and Its Predecessors: Redemption, Fulfillment, Appreciation." Lecture at Goldsmiths, University of London, Department of Visual Cultures, November 20, 2013. Accessed August 1, 2015. https://vimeo.com/80882516.

Feher, Michel. *Rated Agency: Investee Politics in a Speculative Age*. Brooklyn, NY: Zone Books, 2018.

Feher, Michel. "Self-Appreciation; or, The Aspirations of Human Capital." Translated by Ivan Ascher. *Public Culture* 21, no. 1 (winter 2009): 21–41.

Ferguson, Roderick. *The Reorder of Things: The University and Its Pedagogies of Minority Difference*. Minneapolis: University of Minnesota Press, 2012.

Field, Heather M. "A Taxonomy for Tax Loopholes." *Houston Law Review* 55, no. 3 (spring 2018): 545–607.

Finkelpearl, Tom. "Education Art: Cátedra Arte de Conducta." Interview with Tania Bruguera. In *What We Made: Conversations on Art and Social Cooperation*, 179–203. Durham, NC: Duke University Press, 2013.

Firestone, Shulamith. "The Dialectic of Sex." In *The Second Wave: A Reader in Feminist Theory*, edited by Linda Nicholson, 19–26. Routledge: New York, 1997.

Fisher, Anna Watkins. "Like a Girl's Name: The Adolescent Drag of Amber Hawk Swanson, Kate Gilmore, and Ann Liv Young." *TDR: The Drama Review* 56, no. 1 (spring 2012): 48–76.

Fisher, Anna Watkins. "Manic Impositions: The Parasitical Art of Chris Kraus and Sophie Calle." In "Viral," edited by Patricia Clough and Jasbir Puar. Special issue, *Women's Studies Quarterly* 40, nos. 1–2 (spring/summer 2012): 223–35.

Fisher, Anna Watkins. "Parasitical Politics and Epistolary Games: The Art of Chris Kraus and Sophie Calle." *Le Texte étranger*, no. 8 (October 2011). http://dela.univ-paris8.fr/etranger/pages/8/fisher.html.

Fisher, Anna Watkins. "We Are Parasites: On the Politics of Imposition." *Art and Education*, June 28, 2011. http://www.annawatkinsfisher.com/uploads/2/1/6/7/21677368/fisher_art_education.pdf.

Fisher, Anna Watkins, and Lauren Barri Holstein. "Part-time Feminist: Lauren Barri Holstein in Conversation with Anna Watkins Fisher." *Moving Image Review and Art Journal* 4, nos. 1–2 (spring 2016): 216–28.

Fiskesjö, Magnus. *The Thanksgiving Turkey Pardon, the Death of Teddy's Bear, and the Sovereign Exception of Guantánamo*. Chicago: Prickly Paradigm Press, 2003.

Fitzpatrick, Chris, and Post Brothers. "A Productive Irritant: Parasitical Inhabitations in Contemporary Art." *Filip* 15 (fall 2011).

Foucault, Michel. *Discipline and Punish: The Birth of the Prison*. Translated by Alan Sheridan. New York: Vintage Books, 1995.

Frankenberg, Ruth. *White Women, Race Matters: The Social Construction of Whiteness*. Minneapolis: University of Minnesota Press, 1993.

Franklin, Seb. *Control: Digitality as Cultural Logic*. Cambridge, MA: MIT Press, 2015.

Fraser, Nancy, and Linda Gordon. "A Genealogy of *Dependency*: Tracing a Keyword of the U.S. Welfare State." *Signs* 19, no. 2 (winter 1994): 309–36.

Friedman, Andrew. "Festivals: Conventional Disruption, or, Why Ann Liv

Young Ruined Rebecca Patek's Show." In *Postdramatic Theatre and Form*, edited by Michael Shane Boyle, Matt Cornish, and Brandon Wolff, 115–30. London: Methuen Drama, 2019.

Frye, Marilyn. "Some Reflections on Separatism and Power." In *The Lesbian and Gay Studies Reader*, edited by Henry Abelove, Michèle Aina Barale, and David M. Halperin, 91–98. New York: Routledge, 1993.

Gaines, Malik. *Black Performance on the Outskirts of the Left: A History of the Impossible*. New York: New York University Press, 2017.

Galloway, Alexander. *Protocol: How Control Exists after Decentralization*. Cambridge, MA: MIT Press, 2004.

Garbayo-Maeztu, Maite. "Maternidad, arte y precariedad: Estrategias desde la vulnerabilidad." *Arte y políticas de identidad* 19 (December 2018): 67–82.

Gilbert, Sandra M., and Susan Gubar. *The Madwoman in the Attic: The Woman Writer and the Nineteenth-Century Literary Imagination*. 2nd edition. New Haven, CT: Yale University Press, 2000.

Gillespie, Tarleton. *Custodians of the Internet: Platforms, Content Moderation, and the Hidden Decisions That Shape Social Media*. New Haven, CT: Yale University Press, 2018.

Gillespie, Tarleton. "The Politics of 'Platforms.'" *New Media and Society* 12, no. 3 (May 2010): 347–64.

Giroux, Henry. *Neoliberalism's War on Higher Education*. Chicago: Haymarket Books, 2014.

Gitelman, Lisa. *Always Already New: Media, History and the Data of Culture*. Cambridge, MA: MIT Press, 2014.

Glass, Ira. "95: Monogamy." *This American Life*. Radio program. March 6, 1998. https://www.thisamericanlife.org/radio-archives/episode/95/monogamy.

Glass, Ira, and Seth Freed Wessler. "520: No Place Like Home." *This American Life*. Radio program. March 14, 2014. https://www.thisamericanlife.org/radio-archives/episode/520/no-place-like-home.

Goldberg, Roselee. *Performance: Live Art since the 60s*. London: Thames and Hudson, 2004.

Goldsmiths: But Is It Art? Directed by Victoria Silver. Aired April 12 and 19, 2010, on BBC.

Graeber, David. *Debt: The First 5,000 Years*. Brooklyn, NY: Melville House, 2012.

Greenblatt, Stephen, Walter Cohen, Suzanne Gossett, Jean E. Howard, Katharine Eisman Maus, and Gordon McMullan, eds. *The Norton Shakespeare*. 2 vols. 3rd edition. New York: W. W. Norton, 2016.

Greer, Germaine. *The Female Eunuch*. London: MacGibbon and Kee, 1970.

Grusin, Richard. "Introduction. Anthropocene Feminism: An Experiment in Collaborative Theorizing." In *Anthropocene Feminism*, edited by Richard Grusin. Minneapolis: University of Minnesota Press, 2017: viii–ix.

Güell, Núria. *Apátrida por voluntad propia*. 2015–16. Accessed August 1, 2017. http://www.nuriaguell.net/projects/38.html.

Güell, Núria. *How to Expropriate Money from the Banks: Displaced Legal Appli-*

cation #1: Fractional Reserve. Text by Qmunty, Enric Duran, Simona Sarau, Col·lectiu Crisis, and Lucio Urtubia. 2013. Accessed December 12, 2017. www.nuriaguell.net/projects/12/How%20to%20expropriate%20money%20from%20the%20banks_nuria%20guell.pdf.

Gullestad, Anders M. "Parasite." *Political Concepts: A Critical Lexicon* 1 (2012). Accessed January 15, 2017. http://www.politicalconcepts.org/issue1/2012-parasite/.

Gumport, Elizabeth. "Female Trouble." *n+1* 13 (winter 2012). Accessed February 12, 2017. https://nplusonemag.com/issue-13/reviews/female-trouble/.

Gustafson, Kaaryn S. *Cheating Welfare: Public Assistance and the Criminalization of Poverty*. New York: New York University Press, 2011.

Hafner, Katie, and Matthew Lyon. *Where Wizards Stay Up Late: The Origins of the Internet*. New York: Simon and Schuster, 1996.

HAG / Jasmin Risk and Clara Lipfert. "Parasite." In *Emergency Index: An Annual Document of Performance Practice*, vol. 3, edited by Yelena Gluzman and Sophia Cleary. Brooklyn, NY: Ugly Duckling Presse, 2013. Accessed June 23, 2019. https://emergencyindex.com/volume/2013#2013-176-177.

Halberstam, Judith [Jack]. *The Queer Art of Failure*. Durham, NC: Duke University Press, 2011.

Hall, Gary. *The Uberfication of the University*. Minneapolis: University of Minnesota Press, 2016.

Hall, Stuart. "Cultural Studies and Its Theoretical Legacies." In *Cultural Studies*, edited by Lawrence Grossberg, Cary Nelson, and Paula A. Treichler, 277–94. New York: Routledge, 1992.

Haraway, Donna J. *Staying with the Trouble: Making Kin in the Chthulucene*. Durham, NC: Duke University Press, 2016.

Harney, Stefano, and Fred Moten. *The Undercommons: Fugitive Planning and Black Study*. Wivenhoe, UK: Minor Compositions, 2013.

Harris, Malcolm. *Kids These Days: Human Capital and the Making of Millennials*. New York: Little, Brown, 2017.

Hartman, Saidiya V. *Scenes of Subjection: Terror, Slavery, and Self-Making in the Nineteenth Century*. New York: Oxford University Press, 1997.

Harvey, David. *A Brief History of Neoliberalism*. Oxford: Oxford University Press, 2005.

Hassl, Andreas. "Der klassische Parasit: Vom würdigen Gesellschafter der Götter zum servilen Hofnarren." Supplement, *Wiener Klinische Wochenschrift* 117, no. S4 (2005): 2–5.

Hassl, Andreas. "The Parasitic." Accessed January 15, 2017. https://homepage.univie.ac.at/andreas.hassl/parasit/parasitike.shtml.

Hendricks, Jochem. *Legal Crimes*. Freiburg: Modo Verlag, 2002.

Henry, Astrid. *Not My Mother's Sister: Generational Conflict and Third-Wave Feminism*. Bloomington: Indiana University Press, 2004.

Holstein, Lauren Barri. "The Cyclical Pleasures and Deaths of Symbolization: *How to Become a Cupcake/The Famous' Adaptation of Frankenstein*." In

On Repetition: Writing, Performance, Art, edited by Eirini Kartsaki, 117–31. Chicago: Intellect and University of Chicago Press, 2016.
Holstein, Lauren Barri/The Famous. "*Splat!* Death, Mess, Failure and 'Blue-Balling.'" *Performance Research* 19, no. 2 (2014): 98–102.
Hong, Grace Kyungwon. *Death beyond Disvowal: The Impossible Politics of Difference*. Minneapolis: University of Minnesota Press, 2015.
hooks, bell. *Where We Stand: Class Matters*. New York: Routledge, 2000.
Horkheimer, Max, and Theodor W. Adorno. *Dialectic of Enlightenment: Philosophical Fragments*. Edited by Gunzelin Schmid Noerr. Translated by Edmund Jephcott. Stanford, CA: Stanford University Press, 2002.
Hu, Tung-Hui. *A Prehistory of the Cloud*. Cambridge, MA: MIT Press, 2016.
Inda, Jonathan Xavier. "Foreign Bodies: Migrants, Parasites, and the Pathological Nation." *Discourse* 22, no. 3 (fall 2000): 46–62.
Irigaray, Luce. *Elemental Passions*. [1982]. Translated by Joanne Collie and Judith Still. New York: Routledge, 1992.
Jacobs, Harriet A. "The Loophole of Retreat." In *Incidents in the Life of a Slave Girl, Written by Herself*, 114–17. Cambridge, MA: Harvard University Press, 1987.
Jagoda, Patrick. *Network Aesthetics*. Chicago: University of Chicago Press, 2016.
Jahn, Marisa, ed. *Byproduct: On the Excess of Embedded Art Practices*. Toronto: YYZ Books, 2010.
Jesella, Kara. "What Purpose Did I Serve in Your Life." Paper presented at Performance Studies International 19 conference, Stanford University, June 29, 2013.
Jones, Amelia. *Body Art/Performing the Subject*. Minneapolis: University of Minnesota Press, 1998.
Jones, Amelia. "LOST BODIES: Early 1970s Los Angeles Performance Art in Art History." In *Live Art in LA: Performance in Southern California, 1970–1983*, edited by Peggy Phelan, 115–84. New York: Routledge, 2012.
Jones-Rogers, Stephanie E. *They Were Her Property: White Women as Slave Owners in the American South*. New Haven, CT: Yale University Press, 2019.
Joseph, Miranda, and David Rubin. "Promising Complicities: On the Sex, Race and Globalization Project." In *A Companion to Lesbian, Gay, Bisexual, Transgender, and Queer Studies*, edited by George E. Haggerty and Molly McGarry, 430–51. Malden, MA: Blackwell, 2015.
Kampf, Constance E., and Geoff Cox. "Using Digital Art to Make the Tension between Capital and Commons Transparent: Innovation in Shaping Knowledge of Internet Business Practices as a Form of Cultural Knowledge." In *Proceedings of the Cultural Attitudes towards Technology and Communication Conference, Aarhus, Denmark*, edited by Michele Strano, Herbert Hrachovec, Fay Sudweeks, and Charles Ess, 16–24. Perth: Murdoch University, 2012.
Kanouse, Sarah. "Cooing Over the Golden Phallus." *Journal of Aesthetics and Protest* 4 (February 2005). https://joaap.org/4/kanouse.html.

Kaufman, Herbert. *Red Tape: Its Origins, Uses, and Abuses*. Washington, DC: Brookings Institution Press, 2015.

Keeling, Kara. *Queer Times, Black Futures*. New York: New York University Press, 2019.

Kilston, Lyra. "Introducing Kate Gilmore." *Modern Painters* 21, no. 1 (March 2009): 32–33.

Kim, Nadia Y. "Critical Thoughts on Asian American Assimilation in the Whitening Literature." *Social Forces* 86, no. 2 (December 2007): 561–74.

Kittay, Eva Feder, and Ellen K. Feder, eds. *The Subject of Care: Feminist Perspectives on Dependency*. Lanham, MD: Rowman and Littlefield, 2002.

König, Jason. *Saints and Symposiasts: The Literature of Food and the Symposium in Greco-Roman and Early Christian Culture*. Cambridge: Cambridge University Press, 2012.

Kraus, Chris. *I Love Dick*. New York: Semiotext(e), 1997.

Kraus, Chris. *I Love Dick*. Los Angeles: Semiotext(e), 2006.

Kraus, Chris. "The New Universal." *Sydney Review of Books*, October 17, 2014. Accessed October 23, 2017. https://sydneyreviewofbooks.com/new-universal/.

Kushnir, Alana. "When Curating Meets Piracy: Rehashing the History of Unauthorized Exhibition-Making." *Journal of Curatorial Studies* 1, no. 3 (December 2012): 295–313.

Kwon, Miwon. *One Place after Another: Site-Specific Art and Locational Identity*. Cambridge, MA: MIT Press, 2002.

Lācis, Indra K. "Fame, Celebrity and Performance: Marina Abramovic—Contemporary Art Star," PhD diss., Case Western Reserve University, 2014.

Lee, Rachel C. *The Exquisite Corpse of Asian America: Biopolitics, Biosociality, and Posthuman Ecologies*. New York: New York University Press, 2014.

Lorde, Audre. "The Master's Tools Will Never Dismantle the Master's House." In *Sister Outsider: Essays and Speeches*, 110–13. Berkeley: Crossing Press, 2007.

Lovink, Geert. *Dark Fiber: Tracking Internet Culture*. Cambridge, MA: MIT Press, 2002.

Ludovico, Alessandro, and Paolo Cirio. "The Hacking Monopolism Trilogy." In *Proceedings of the 19th International Symposium on Electronic Art, ISEA 2013*, edited by Kathy Cleland, Laura Fisher, and Ross Harley, 316–18. Sydney: Sydney University Press, 2013.

Luxemburg, Rosa. *Selected Political Writings*. Edited by Dick Howard. New York: Monthly Review Press, 1971.

MacGlip, Ali. "Interview with Roisin Byrne." *Artvehicle* 60. Accessed January 12, 2012. http://www.artvehicle.com/interview/27.

MacKinnon, Catharine. *Toward a Feminist Theory of the State*. Cambridge, MA: Harvard University Press, 1991.

Mahmood, Saba. *Politics of Piety: The Islamic Revival and the Feminist Subject*. Princeton, NJ: Princeton University Press, 2005.

Magnet, Shoshana Amielle. *When Biometrics Fail: Gender, Race, and the Technology of Identity*. Durham, NC: Duke University Press, 2011.

Martin, Nathan M. (for the Carbon Defense League). "Parasitic Media: Creating Invisible Slicing Parasites and Other Forms of Tactical Augmentation." *intelligent agent* 3, no. 1 (winter/spring 2003). Accessed January 15, 2017. http://www.intelligentagent.com/archive/Vol3_No1_polisci_martin.html.

Martin, Nathan M. (for the Carbon Defense League). "Parasitic Media: Invisibility and Other Forms of Tactical Augmentation." *subsol* (September 2002). http://subsol.c3.hu/subsol_2/contributors3/martintext.html.

Marx, Karl. *Capital*. Vol. 1. Translated by Ben Fowkes. New York: Penguin Books, 1990.

Massumi, Brian. *What Animals Teach Us about Politics*. Durham, NC: Duke University Press, 2014.

McGlotten, Shaka. "Black Data." In *No Tea, No Shade: New Writings in Black Queer Studies*, edited by E. Patrick Johnson, 263–86. Durham, NC: Duke University Press, 2016.

McIntosh, Peggy. "White Privilege: Unpacking the Invisible Knapsack." *Peace and Freedom Magazine* (July/August 1989): 10–12.

McMillan, Uri. *Embodied Avatars: Genealogies of Black Feminist Art and Performance*. New York: New York University Press, 2015.

McNulty, Tracy. *The Hostess: Hospitality, Femininity, and the Expropriation of Identity*. Minneapolis: University of Minnesota Press, 2007.

McRobbie, Angela. *Feminism and Youth Culture: From "Jackie" to "Just Seventeen."* London: Macmillan, 1991.

Mekdjian, Sarah. "Urban Artivism and Migrations: Disrupting Spatial and Political Segregation of Migrants in European Cities." *Cities* 77 (July 2018): 39–48.

Melamed, Jodi. *Represent and Destroy: Rationalizing Violence in the New Racial Capitalism*. Minneapolis: University of Minnesota Press, 2011.

Mengesha, Lilian G., and Lakshmi Padmanabhan. "Introduction to *Performing Refusal/Refusing to Perform*." *Women and Performance* 29, no. 1 (February 2019): 1–8.

Miller, J. Hillis. "The Critic as Host." *Critical Inquiry* 3, no. 3 (spring 1977): 439–47.

Mihai, Laura. "Art Hacktivism as a Form of Market Resistance." *Journal of Promotional Communications* 3, no. 1 (2015): 174–99.

Miranda, Krista. "Staring at the (Clitoral) Sun: Arousing Abjection in Ann Liv Young's *The Bagwell in Me*." *Women and Performance* 21, no. 2 (July 2011): 235–48.

Miranda, Krista. "'What Do Women Want, My God, What Do They Want?' Mimesis, Fantasy, and Female Sexuality in Ann Liv Young's *Michael*." In *The Oxford Handbook of Dance and Theater*, edited by Nadine George-Graves, 646–65. New York: Oxford University Press, 2015.

Mitchell, Nick. "Summertime Selves (On Professionalization)." *The New Inquiry*, October 4, 2019. Accessed October 10, 2019. https://thenewinquiry.com/summertime-selves-on-professionalization/.

Moten, Fred. "Taste Dissonance Flavor Escape (Preface to a Solo by Miles Davis)." In *Black and Blur: Consent Not to Be a Single Being*. Durham, NC: Duke University Press, 2017: 66–85.

Muñoz, José Esteban. *Disidentifications: Queers of Color and the Performance of Politics*. Minneapolis: University of Minnesota Press, 1999.

Muñoz, José Esteban. "Feeling Brown: Ethnicity and Affect in Ricardo Bracho's *The Sweetest Hangover (and Other STDs)*." *Theatre Journal* 52, no. 1 (March 2000): 67–79.

Musser, Amber Jamilla. *Sensational Flesh: Race, Power, and Masochism*. New York: New York University Press, 2014.

Musser, Amber Jamilla. *Sensual Excess: Queer Femininity and Brown Jouissance*. New York: New York University Press, 2018.

Nakamura, Lisa. "Indigenous Circuits: Navajo Women and the Racialization of Early Electronic Manufacture." *American Quarterly* 66, no. 4 (December 2014): 919–41.

Nakamura, Lisa. "The Unwanted Labour of Social Media: Women of Colour Call Out Culture as Venture Community Management." *New Formations: A Journal of Culture/Theory/Politics* 86 (2015): 106–12.

Nash, Jennifer. *Black Feminism Reimagined: After Intersectionality*. Durham, NC: Duke University Press, 2019.

Newton, Esther. *Mother Camp: Female Impersonators in America*. Chicago: University of Chicago Press, 1979.

Ngai, Sianne. *Our Aesthetic Categories: Zany, Cute, Interesting*. Cambridge, MA: Harvard University Press, 2012.

Nixon, Rob. *Slow Violence and the Environmentalism of the Poor*. Cambridge, MA: Harvard University Press, 2011.

Nochlin, Linda. "Why Have There Been No Great Women Artists?" In *Art and Sexual Politics: Women's Liberation, Women Artists, and Art History*, edited by Thomas B. Hess and Elizabeth C. Baker, 1–39. New York: Macmillan, 1973.

Nyong'o, Tavia. *Afro-Fabulations: The Queer Drama of Black Life*. New York: New York University Press, 2018.

O'Dell, Kathy. *Contract with the Skin*. Minneapolis: University of Minnesota Press, 1998.

Oliver, Valerie Cassel, ed. *Radical Presence: Black Performance in Contemporary Art*. Houston, TX: Contemporary Arts Museum Houston, 2013.

O'Neill-Butler, Lauren. "The Savage Detective: On Sophie Calle's 'Address Book.'" *Los Angeles Review of Books*, October 25, 2012. Accessed February 12, 2017. https://lareviewofbooks.org/article/the-savage-detective-on-sophie-calles-address-book/.

Ouellette, Laurie. "Citizen Brand: ABC and the Do Good Turn in US Television."

In *Commodity Activism: Cultural Resistance in Neoliberal Times*, edited by Roopali Mukherji and Sarah Banet-Weiser, 57–75. New York: New York University Press, 2012.

Ouellette, Laurie. "'Take Responsibility for Yourself': *Judge Judy* and the Neoliberal Citizen." In *Reality TV: Remaking Television Culture*, edited by Susan Murray and Laurie Ouellette, 223–42. 2nd edition. New York: New York University Press, 2009.

Pardo, Beatriz Cavia, and Arturo Cancio Ferruz. "Dispositives of Precariousness: On Núria Güell's Work/Dispositivos de precariedad: acerca del trabajo de Núria Güell." CROMA 6, no. 11 (January–June 2018): 20–27.

Parker, Rozsika, and Griselda Pollock, eds. *Framing Feminism: Art and the Women's Movement, 1970–85*. New York: Routledge and Kegan Paul, 1987.

Pasquale, Frank. *The Black Box Society: The Secret Algorithms That Control Money and Information*. Cambridge, MA: Harvard University Press, 2015.

Pederson, Claudia Costa. "Autopoiesis in Contemporary Bio-Arts in Mexico and Colombia." *Review: Literature and Arts of the Americas* 48, no. 1 (2015): 22–30.

Perzanowski, Aaron, and Jason Schultz. *The End of Ownership: Personal Property in the Digital Economy*. Cambridge, MA: MIT Press, 2016.

Phelan, Peggy. *Live Art in LA: Performance in Southern California, 1970–1983*. New York: Routledge, 2012.

Phelan, Peggy. *Unmarked: The Politics of Performance*. New York: Routledge, 1993.

Philip, Kavita. "What Is a Technological Author? The Pirate Function and Intellectual Property." *Postcolonial Studies* 8, no. 2 (2005): 199–218.

Piironen, Pekka, and Akseli Virtanen. "Democratizing the Power of Finance: A Discussion about Robin Hood Asset Management Cooperative with Founder Akseli Virtanen." In *MoneyLab Reader: An Intervention in Digital Economy*, edited by Geert Lovink, Nathaniel Tkacz, and Patricia de Vries, 92–103. Amsterdam: Institute of Network Cultures, 2015.

Pilcher, Jeremy. "Parasitic Art." Paper presented at Transmission: Hospitality conference at Sheffield Hallam University, July 1–3, 2010.

Power, Nina. *One-Dimensional Woman*. Winchester, UK: Zero Books, 2009.

Precarity Lab. *Technoprecarious*. London: Goldsmiths Press, 2020.

Probyn, Elspeth. "A Feminist Love Letter to Stuart Hall; Or What Feminist Cultural Studies Needs to Remember." *Cultural Studies Review* 22, no. 1 (March 2016): 294–301.

Puar, Jasbir. "Regimes of Surveillance." *Cosmologics* (winter 2014). Accessed December 5, 2014.

Pugliese, Joseph. "The Biometrics of Infrastructural Whiteness." In *Biometrics: Bodies, Technologies, Biopolitics*. New York: Routledge, 2010.

Puwar, Nirmal. *Space Invaders: Race, Gender, and Bodies Out of Place*. New York: Berg, 2004.

Qmunty. "The Mandrake Mechanism." In Núria Güell, *How to Expropriate Money from the Banks: Displaced Legal Application #1: Fractional Reserve.* Text by Qmunty, Enric Duran, Simona Sarau, Col·lectiu Crisis, and Lucio Urtubia. 2013. www.nuriaguell.net/projects/12/How%20to%20expropriate%20money%20from%20the%20banks_nuria%20guell.pdf, 5–14.

Queiroz, João Paulo. "Excavating, Walking, Working: Towards a Revision of Contemporary Art Practices/Escavar, caminhar, trabalhar: Para uma revisao da praxis da arte contemporanea." *CROMA* 6, no. 11 (January–June 2018): 12–17.

Rahmani, Aviva. "Using Art to Stop a Pipeline." Interview by Jillian Steinhauer. *Hyperallergic*, September 9, 2015. Accessed February 4, 2017. http://hyperallergic.com/235429/using-art-to-stop-a-pipeline/.

Raley, Rita. *Tactical Media*. Minneapolis: University of Minnesota Press, 2009.

Randall, Marilyn. *Pragmatic Plagiarism: Authorship, Profit, and Power.* Toronto: University of Toronto Press, 2001.

Ridout, Nicholas, and Rebecca Schneider. "Precarity and Performance: An Introduction." *TDR: The Drama Review* 56, no. 4 (winter 2012): 5–9.

Rimanelli, David. "I Love Dick." *Artforum International* 36, no. 7 (March 1998): S7.

Riviere, Joan. "Womanliness as a Masquerade." *International Journal of Psychoanalysis* 10 (1929): 303–13.

Ronell, Avital. "Avital Ronell." Interview by Andrea Juno. *Angry Women* 13 (1991): 127–53.

Ronell, Avital. *The Telephone Book: Technology, Schizophrenia, Electric Speech.* Lincoln: University of Nebraska Press, 1991.

Rosello, Mireille. *Postcolonial Hospitality: The Immigrant as Guest.* Stanford, CA: Stanford University Press, 2002.

Rovira, Jordi Morell I. "There Was Earth in Them: The Digging in Works of Santiago Sierra, Núria Güell and Regina José Galindo/Hi havia terra en ells: El cavar en obres de Santiago Sierra, Núria Güell i Regina José Galindo." *CROMA* 6, no. 11 (January–June 2018): 40–47.

Rubin, Gayle. "The Traffic in Women: Notes on the 'Political Economy' of Sex." In *Toward an Anthropology of Women*, edited by Rayna R. Reiter, 157–210. New York: Monthly Review Press, 1975.

Russell, Andrew L. *Open Standards and the Digital Age: History, Ideology, and Networks.* New York: Cambridge University Press, 2014.

Sacher-Masoch, Leopold von. *Venus in Furs and Selected Letters.* New York: Blast Books, 1989.

Samyn, Jeanette. "Anti-Anti-Parasitism." *New Inquiry*, September 18, 2012. Accessed January 15, 2017. http://thenewinquiry.com/essays/anti-anti-parasitism/.

Schechner, Richard. *Between Theater and Anthropology.* Philadelphia: University of Pennsylvania Press, 1985.

Schechner, Richard. *Performance Studies: An Introduction*. New York: Routledge, 2002.
Schlossberg, Linda. "Introduction: Rites of Passing." In *Passing: Identity and Interpretation in Sexuality, Race, and Religion*, edited by Maria Carla Sanchez and Linda Schlossberg, 1–12. New York: New York University Press, 2001.
Schneider, Nathan. *Everything for Everyone: The Radical Tradition That Is Shaping the Next Economy*. New York: W. W. Norton, 2018.
Schneider, Rebecca. *The Explicit Body in Performance*. New York: Routledge, 1997.
Schneider, Rebecca. "Hello Dolly Well Hello Dolly: The Double and Its Theatre." In *Psychoanalysis and Performance*, edited by Patrick Campbell and Adrian Kear, 94–114. London: Routledge, 2001.
Schneider, Rebecca. *Performing Remains: Theatricality, Civil War, Performance Art, Reenactment*. New York: Routledge, 2011.
Schneider, Rebecca. "Remembering Feminist Remimesis: A Riddle in Three Parts." *TDR: The Drama Review* 58, no. 2 (2014): 14–32.
Scholz, Trebor, and Nathan Schneider, eds. *Ours to Hack and to Own: The Rise of Platform Cooperativism. A New Vision for the Future of Work and a Fairer Internet*. New York: OR Books, 2017.
Schor, Mira. *A Decade of Negative Thinking: Essays on Art, Politics, and Everyday Life*. Durham, NC: Duke University Press, 2009.
Schreiner, Olive. *Woman and Labour*. London: T. F. Unwin, 1911.
Scott, James C. *Domination and the Arts of Resistance: Hidden Transcripts*. New Haven, CT: Yale University Press, 1990.
Scott, James C. *Weapons of the Weak: Everyday Forms of Peasant Resistance*. New Haven, CT: Yale University Press, 1985.
Sedgwick, Eve Kosofsky. *Touching Feeling: Affect, Pedagogy, Performativity*, 123–54. Durham, NC: Duke University Press, 2003.
Serres, Michel. *The Parasite*. Translated by Lawrence R. Schehr. Minneapolis: University of Minnesota Press, 2007.
Sesé, Teresa. "La Creadora (175): Núria Güell." *La Vanguardia* (December 2, 2013), 35.
Shaviro, Steven. "Accelerationist Aesthetics: Necessary Inefficiency in Times of Real Subsumption." *e-flux*, no. 46 (2013). www.e-flux.com/journal/accelerationist-aesthetics-necessary-inefficiency-in-times-of-real-subsumption.
Shaviro, Steven. *Post-Cinematic Affect*. Winchester, UK: Zero Books, 2010.
Shelden, Michael. *Young Titan: The Making of Winston Churchill*. New York: Simon and Schuster Paperbacks, 2014.
Shotwell, Alexis. *Against Purity: Living Ethically in Compromised Times*. Minneapolis: University of Minnesota Press, 2016.
Shukaitis, Stevphen. "Overidentification and/or Bust?" *Variant* 37–38 (spring/summer 2010): 26–29.

Singer, Isaac Bashevis. *The Manor and the Estate*. Translated by Joseph Singer, Elaine Gottlieb, and Herman Eichenthal. Madison: University of Wisconsin Press, 2004.

Spence, Lester K. *Knocking the Hustle: Against the Neoliberal Turn in Black Politics*. Brooklyn, NY: Punctum Books, 2015.

Spillers, Hortense J. "Peter's Pans: Eating in the Diaspora." In *Black, White, and in Color: Essays on American Literature and Culture*, 1–64. Chicago: University of Chicago Press, 2003.

Spivak, Gayatri Chakravorty. "Can the Subaltern Speak?" In *Marxism and the Interpretation of Culture*, edited by Cary Nelson and Larry Grossberg, 271–316. Urbana: University of Illinois Press, 1988.

Spivak, Gayatri Chakravorty. *Outside in the Teaching Machine*. New York: Routledge, 1993.

Srnicek, Nick. *Platform Capitalism*. Cambridge: Polity, 2017.

Steinem, Gloria. "What It Would Be Like If Women Win." *Time*, August 31, 1970, 22–23.

Stewart, Suzanne R. *Sublime Surrender: Male Masochism at the Fin-de-siècle*. Ithaca, NY: Cornell University Press, 1998.

Swanson, Amber Hawk. "Not a Feminist Way of Thinking, Daddy's Little Girl." *The Feminism? Project*. 2005–6. Artist's video.

Swartz, Aaron. "Guerrilla Open Access Manifesto." July 2008. Accessed October 12, 2016. https://archive.org/stream/GuerillaOpenAccessManifesto/Goamjuly2008_djvu.txt.

Taylor, Astra. *The People's Platform: Taking Back Power and Culture in the Digital Age*. New York: Metropolitan Books, 2014.

Terranova, Tiziana. "About the Robin Hood Asset Management Cooperative." *springerin* 3 (summer 2015). Accessed June 26, 2019. https://www.springerin.at/en/2015/3/umverteilung-a-la-robin-hood/.

Terranova, Tiziana. *Network Culture: Politics for the Information Age*. London: Pluto Press, 2004.

Thoburn, Nicholas. *Anti-Book: On the Art and Politics of Radical Publishing*. Minneapolis: University of Minnesota Press, 2016.

Thomas, Aaron C. "Viewing the Pornographic Theatre: Explicit Voyeurism, Artaud and Ann Liv Young's *Cinderella*." In *Theatre as Voyeurism: The Pleasures of Watching*, edited by George Rodosthenous, 166–84. New York: Palgrave Macmillan, 2015.

Tsing, Anna Lowenhaupt. *The Mushroom at the End of the World: On the Possibility of Life in Capitalist Ruins*. Princeton, NJ: Princeton University Press, 2015.

Tuan, Mia. *Forever Foreigners or Honorary Whites? The Asian Ethnic Experience Today*. New Brunswick, NJ: Rutgers University Press, 1999.

Tzara, Tristan. "Dada Manifesto 1918." In *Seven Dada Manifestos and Lampisteries*. Translated by Barbara Wright. Richmond, UK: Oneworld Classics, 2011.

van Haaften-Schick, Lauren. "Art after Property." *C Magazine* 133 (spring 2017). Accessed June 26, 2019. https://cmagazine.com/issues/133/art-after-property.

Vaidhyanathan, Siva. *The Googlization of Everything (And Why We Should Worry)*. Updated ed. Berkeley: University of California Press, 2012.

Vavarella, Emilio. "Art, Error, and the Interstices of Power." *CITAR Journal* 7, no. 2 (December 2015): 7–17.

Velasco, David. "Drama Queen: David Velasco on Ann Liv Young." *Artforum International* 49, no. 1 (September 2010): 145–48.

Virtanen, Akseli. "Robin Hood Collective." In *Ours to Hack and to Own: The Rise of Platform Cooperativism, A New Vision for the Future of Work and a Fairer Internet*, edited by Trebor Scholz and Nathan Schneider, 89. New York: OR Books, 2017.

Virtanen, Akseli, Taylor C. Nelms, and Bill Maurer. "Is It Art? Is it a Hoax? Hedging Precarity and Protecting the Commonfare: An Interview with Akseli Virtanen." *Journal of Cultural Economy Online*, February 8, 2016. www.journalofculturaleconomy.org/is-it-art-is-it-a-hoax-hedging-precarity-and-protecting-the-commonfare-an-interview-with-akseli-virtanen/.

Vogel, David. *The Market for Virtue: The Potential and Limits of Corporate Social Responsibility*. Washington, DC: Brookings Institution Press, 2005.

Wang, Jackie. *Carceral Capitalism*. South Pasadena, CA: Semiotext(e), 2018.

Wilderson, Frank B. *Red, White, and Black: Cinema and the Structure of U.S. Antagonisms*. Durham, NC: Duke University Press, 2010.

Williams, Apryl. "Black Memes Matter: Reading #LivingWhileBlack Memes as Activism." Talk at University of Michigan, Department of Communication and Media and Digital Studies Institute, January 29, 2020.

Wiltz, Meredith Clark. "Persecuting Black Men and Gendering Jury Service." In *Interconnections: Gender and Race in American History*, edited by Carol Faulkner and Alison M. Parker, 161–84. Rochester, NY: University of Rochester Press, 2012.

Wollstonecraft, Mary. *A Vindication of the Rights of Men; with A Vindication of the Rights of Woman, and Hints*. Edited by Sylvana Tomaselli. Cambridge: Cambridge University Press, 1995.

Yusoff, Kathryn. *A Billion Black Anthropocenes or None*. Minneapolis: University of Minnesota Press, 2019.

Zerilli, Linda M. G. *Feminism and the Abyss of Freedom*. Chicago: University of Chicago Press, 2005.

INDEX

Page numbers with *f* following indicate figures.

www.ingramcontent.com/pod-product-compliance
Lightning Source LLC
LaVergne TN
LVHW020506100826
845148LV00003B/709

* 9 7 8 1 4 7 8 0 0 9 7 0 2 *